The Franco-Prussian War

The German Conquest of France in 1870–1871

GEOFFREY WAWRO

Naval War College

CAMBRIDGE
UNIVERSITY PRESS

CAMBRIDGE UNIVERSITY PRESS
Cambridge, New York, Melbourne, Madrid, Cape Town, Singapore, São Paulo

Cambridge University Press
40 West 20th Street, New York, NY 10011-4211, USA

www.cambridge.org
Information on this title: www.cambridge.org/9780521584364

First published 2003
First paperback edition 2005

Printed in the United States of America

A catalog record for this book is available from the British Library.

Library of Congress Cataloging in Publication Data
Wawro, Geoffrey.
The Franco-Prussian War : the German conquest of France
in 1870–1871 / Geoffrey Wawro.
p. cm.
Includes bibliographical references and index.
ISBN 0-521-58436-1
1. Franco-Prussian War, 1870–1871. 2. France – History – Second Empire, 1852–1870.
3. Germany – History, Military – 19th century. I. Title
DC293.W38 2003
943.08′2 – dc21 2002041685

ISBN-13 978-0-521-58436-4 hardback
ISBN-10 0-521-58436-1 hardback

ISBN-13 978-0-521-61743-7 paperback
ISBN-10 0-521-61743-x paperback

"The Franco–Prussian War of 1870–1871 started the modern Hundred Years' War that did not end until 1945. Professor Geoffrey Wawro's book is the most comprehensive treatment of the subject. Thoughtful and well written, it is a major contribution to an understanding of history."
— Dr. Henry A. Kissinger

"Geoffrey Wawro has followed his exemplary history of the Austro-Prussian War of 1866 with a splendidly vigorous account of the Franco–German War that followed it four years later. He writes the best kind of military history, vividly evoking the epoch-making – and, as he reminds us, largely unexpected – French debacle in readable and often stirring prose. Those who thought Michael Howard had written the last word on the subject will relish Wawro's intimate and painstakingly acquired knowledge of the decisive battles that secured Bismarck's most dazzling victory."
— Niall Ferguson, New York University and Oxford University, author of *The Pity of War* (2000), *The House of Rothschild* (1998), and *Empire* (2003)

"As the author of a history of the Franco-Prussian War that has held the field for some forty years, I was deeply apprehensive when I learned that Dr. Wawro was at work on another. I had good cause to be. His work is magnificent. The research is both wide and deep, the operational analysis masterly, and there is not a dull page in the book. Dr. Wawro has established himself as one of the leading military historians of his generation."
— Sir Michael Howard, Emeritus Professor of Modern History at Oxford and Yale

"Geoffrey Wawro has brought us an engrossing, authoritative, superbly researched history, with a glittering cast of characters starting with Bismarck and Napoleon III. The book demonstrates the importance of the Franco-Prussian War to our modern world and will make readers feel as if they are watching the conflict unfold."
— Michael Beschloss, author of *The Conquerors: Roosevelt, Truman, and the Destruction of Hitler's Germany, 1941–1945* (2002)

"Wawro combines extensive archival research with perceptive critical insight to provide fresh perspectives on a subject dominated for almost a half-century by the work of Michael Howard. *The Franco-Prussian War* invites and withstands comparison with Howard's classic volume."
— Dennis Showalter, Professor of History, Colorado College

"A lively narrative history, based on an abundance of new research."
— MacGregor Knox, The London School of Economics

ALSO BY GEOFFREY WAWRO

The Austro-Prussian War

Warfare and Society in Europe, 1792–1914

For Winslow and Matías

Contents

Abbreviations

ACM	Archives Centrales de la Marine (Vincennes)
BKA	Bayerisches Kriegsarchiv (Munich)
CIS	Congressional Information Service (Washington, DC)
HHSA	Haus-Hof-und Staatsarchiv (Vienna)
NA	National Archives (Washington, DC)
ÖMZ	Österreichische Militärische Zeitschrift
PRO	Public Record Office (London)
SHAT	Service Historique de l'Armée de Terre (Vincennes)
SKA	Sächsiches Kriegsarchiv (Dresden)
ZS	Zeitgeschichtliche Sammlung (Dresden)

Illustrations

Acknowledgments

This book is dedicated to my sons, who almost magically took on the qualities of the French and the Prussians as I delved deeper into the material. Five-year-old Winslow became the incandescent Frenchman, swerving from side-splitting hilarity to academic introspection to *furia francese*. Three-year-old Matías, with his defiant chin, wide eyes, and white-blond shock of hair, metamorphosed into the valiant Prussian. In their regular scraps, Winslow bowls his brother over with superior weight and *élan*; Matías unfailingly clambers back with defiance, endurance, and pluck. Like the beleaguered German troops of Coulmiers or Beaune-la-Rolande, he refuses to yield. These adorable boys – and Cecilia, their hard-working, loving mother – have made my life happier and more interesting, and this book is for them.

The deep archival research and battlefield tours needed for this book would have been impossible without research fellowships. "War is a deep hole that needs constant filling" is an old Swiss proverb that applies equally to the study of war. The *Deutscher Akademischer Austausch-Dienst* (DAAD) very generously provided me with a Faculty Study Visit Grant, which paid for three or four months of work in German archives. And the DAAD grants seemed even more generous because they were issued in cash. One found one's way to a German city – Munich, Dresden, or Berlin – and then tracked down the bursar in some grim postwar university building. Hundreds of *Deutschmarks* were counted into your hand by a disbelieving clerk. You left feeling more like a buccaneer than a professor, with wads of fifty and hundred-mark notes stuffed in every pocket. For those fleeting moments of sheer avaricious delight, I am also grateful.

Thanks are also due to Oakland University and the U.S. Naval War College. Oakland awarded me a handsome Faculty Research Fellowship for a second summer of research in Germany, Austria, England, and France, which included a mad dash in a rented Citroën to see every battlefield between Sedan and Froeschwiller. The U.S. Naval War College gave me time off to work in

European archives and dash around the Loire battlefields in a Peugeot. The Austrian Cultural Institute in New York kindly permitted me to defer my dissertation prize several years so that I could spend it in Vienna on coffee houses, *Heurige*, the Austria versus Latvia World Cup qualifier, and research for this book. When the money ran out, I lodged with friends, who were always hospitable: Marc Bataillon, Jean Guellec, and Stéphane Audoin-Rouzeau in Paris, Lothar Höbelt in Vienna, and David and Caroline Noble in London. Thanks also to my patient, efficient editor, Frank Smith, and to the colleagues who have supported my work in so many ways. Rick Atkinson, Michael Beschloss, Arden Bucholz, Alberto Coll, Niall Ferguson, Michael Howard, Henry Kissinger, and Dennis Showalter have all offered advice and encouragement. The book has been much improved by Professor Holger Herwig's careful reading. Holger made a number of important suggestions and corrections, and deflected me from one or two *faux-pas*, like the regiment of Bavarian infantry that I had marching down a road singing Lutheran hymns.

In all of my books I feel a great responsibility to the thousands of young men killed or maimed in battle, remembered briefly by their grieving families, and then forgotten in our rush toward the future. This book may serve as a memorial to their brave efforts. I thought of such men on my way back to Paris from Metz, when I read the following words on the wall of the mausoleum at Verdun: "*Der Krieg, mein Lieber, das ist unsere Jugend, die hier vergessen in der Erde ruht*" – "War is our youth, my friend, lying forgotten here in the ground."

Newport, Rhode Island
2003

Introduction

There were two Prussias in 1870. One was described by Theodor Fontane in *Rambles through the Brandenburg March*, a rambling four-volume travel book that depicted a savage Prussia still emerging from its swamps and forests. "Do not expect the comforts of the Grand Tour," Fontane chuckled in the first volume, but "poverty, squalor and...no modern culture." Trains were still a luxury in this industrializing kingdom of coal and iron; they plied only between the big cities and towns. For travel between Prussian villages, hired traps were needed, but they were invariably driven by resentful provincials, who would drive you round in circles, in and out of woods and streams, and end up charging you more for a short ride between neighboring hamlets than you would pay on the railway for the five-hour trip from Berlin to Dresden.[1] Prussia in 1870 was still a "virginal wilderness," a land of bogs and pines that ran right up to the gates of Berlin itself. It was a rough country with rough manners. The Viennese – always condescending where the Prussians were concerned – derided their northern cousins as having "two legs rooted in the Bible, two in the soil." The Prussians could be knuckle-dragging, evangelical philistines, a conclusion that even a great patriot like Theodor Fontane was at pains to avoid.

The other Prussia was described by Karl Marx in the 1860s. Berlin, with its splendid Baroque palaces and Le Nôtre gardens, was a graceful, expanding city. On its edges blazed *Feuerland* – "fire land" – the busy forges and machine works of Oranienburg and Moabit. Marx gaped at the economic growth, pronounced Prussia "a mighty center of German engineering," and was stunned by the changes wrought in his birthplace: the western provinces of Rhineland and Westphalia. Sleepy and bucolic in Marx's youth, the Prussian Rhineland

---

1   Theodor Fontane, *Wanderungen durch die Mark Brandenburg*, 4 vols., orig. 1859–82, Berlin, 1998, vol. 1, pp. 12–13.

now belched smoke and fumes from coal-fired factories. Marx compared the region favorably with Lancashire and Yorkshire, the rich, smoggy heart of the English industrial revolution. Prussia now had great cities – Berlin, Königsberg, Breslau, Dortmund, Düsseldorf, and Cologne – and was producing more coal and steel in a year than France, Russia, or Austria. Moreover, with 5,000 miles of track, it had a more extensive railway network than any of its three great neighbors, an advantage that would only increase in the next decade.[2] The Prussian population was also determinedly growing, in absolute and relative terms. In 1866, Prussia had 19 million inhabitants; this was more than half the French population of 35 million and the Austrian population of 33 million. With its young, productive population and its galloping industries and railways, Berlin naturally assumed leadership of the German *Zollverein* or customs union, which, from its inception in 1834, tore down tariff barriers between the thirty-nine states of the German Confederation, stimulated trade and consumption, and magnified Prussia's leading role. Berlin's involvement with the other German states was cause for concern. Excluding the Germans of Austria, the combined population of the small and medium states of the German Confederation – countries like Bavaria, Saxony, Hanover, and Hamburg – was 20 million. If Prussia ever unified them, the new state would be the most powerful in Europe.

Yet wealth and power always sat uneasily with Prussia. On the verge of real greatness in the 1860s, Prussia was held back by its ancient élites. Ever since the Teutonic Knights had driven the Slavs from the eastern edge of the Holy Roman Empire – the borderland that eventually became Prussia – the kingdom had been dominated by descendants of the knights, semi-feudal noble landowners called *Junkers*. Although the Hohenzollern kings had shorn the Junkers of most of their political power in the seventeenth and eighteenth centuries, they had compensated them in a number of troublesome ways. Junkers acquired vast landed estates at good prices, retained local administrative authority, and also dominated the Prussian court, army, and civil service, holding most of the key ministries and offices. In return, they swore loyalty to Prussia's Hohenzollern kings, who never tested the veiled threat of a Junker in 1808: "If Your Royal Highness robs me and my children of our rights, on what, pray tell, do your own rights rely?" Attempts by Prussia's "new men" of the industrial age – manufacturers, merchants, and professionals – to force their way into this cozy marriage of throne and aristocracy were consistently rebuffed.[3] The Prussian king could keep his own counsel, veto parliamentary initiatives whenever he liked, and apportion voting rights according to wealth and social class, assuring the reactionary Junkers a prominent role until 1918.

2   John Breuilly, "Revolution to Unification," in Mary Fulbrook, ed. *German History since 1800*, London, 1997, p. 126. H. W. Koch, *A History of Prussia*, New York, 1978, pp. 241–2.
3   James J. Sheehan, *German History 1770–1866*, Oxford, 1989, pp. 302–3, 440.

Nor was the Prussian kingdom in one piece, territorially or spiritually. Physically it was broken into two halves, the eastern heartland of Brandenburg-Prussia and the western provinces of Westphalia and the Rhineland. Foreign states – Hanover, Hessia, Baden, and several smaller ones – nested in the gap between the two halves as did a great deal of cultural misunderstanding. In 1863, a Prussian infantry officer from the east joined his regiment in Aachen in the west for the first time. Although Aachen and the surrounding *Rheingau* had been a part of Prussia since 1815, the young man was astonished by the depth of anti-Prussian feeling there. Locals considered Prussia a foreign country, and called it *Stinkpreusse* – "Putrid Prussia." Fathers with sons in military service lamented that their boys were "serving with the Prussians," as if they had been abducted by a foreign power. Prussian officials were called *Polakien* ("Polacks") or *Hinterpommern* ("Pomeranian hicks"). They were taken for savages, not educated men from the schools and universities of Bonn, Göttingen, Berlin, or Rostock.[4] The resentment felt by these Rhenish townsmen and peasants was itself a reflection of Prussian weakness. In 1860, *The Times* of London had written: "How [Prussia] became a great power history tells us, why she remains so, nobody can tell."[5] It was an ungainly state riven by geography, culture, class, and history.

France in the 1860s formed a glittering contrast to Prussia. The so-called capital of Europe, Paris was the stately *métropole* of a united, fiercely nationalistic nation with colonies in Africa, the Caribbean, and Indochina. With twice the inhabitants of Berlin, Paris had a population of 1.8 million and shimmered with architectural treasures and a rich history that reached back a thousand years. Whereas Prussia appeared rough and haphazardly formed – Voltaire had snidely called it a "kingdom of border strips" – everything about France bespoke elegance and solidity. With its natural frontiers on the sea, Vosges, Alps, and Pyrenées and its 800 years as a unified state, France had cultivated a uniquely rich culture founded on food, wine, temperate weather, fashion, music, and language. But this cultural supremacy – now anchored in the 20,000 cafés of Paris and the trend-setting *grands magasins* – had always been the case, hence the ambition of every German tourist (and soldier) to "live like a god in France." What gave France the appearance of *strategic* mastery in the 1860s, what made France "the umpire of Europe," was the ambitious regime of Louis-Napoleon Bonaparte, Emperor Napoleon III.

Born in 1808, Louis-Napoleon had suffered the fate of every Bonaparte after Waterloo. Forbidden by the restored Bourbons to live in France, where he or his siblings might attempt a Napoleonic restoration, he had wandered from Switzerland to Germany to Italy and finally to England. He was a romantic, excitable young man, and finally discovered his true calling as a conspirator in Italy.

---

4   G. von Bismarck, *Kriegserlebnisse 1866 und 1870–71*, Dessau, 1907, p. 4.
5   Koch, p. 250.

The Italian peninsula in the 1820s had been divided between a half dozen small states, from the Kingdom of the Two Sicilies in the south to Piedmont in the north. The social and political atmosphere was precisely that described by Stendhal – a contemporary of Louis-Napoleon's – in the *Charterhouse of Parma*: rigid, humorless, and reactionary. Weak branches of ancient dynasties like the Bourbons (in Naples) and the Habsburgs (in Florence, Modena, and Parma) defended their thrones with great cruelty, flinging anyone suspected of liberal agitation into jails or galley slavery. The situation was aggravated by the presence in Italy of the Austrian Empire, whose territorial reward for helping quash the French Revolution (and Louis-Napoleon's famous uncle) had been the Italian provinces of Lombardy and Venetia. For Louis-Napoleon, the opportunity to revenge himself upon the very states and dynasties that had crushed France and dictated peace in 1815 was irresistible. He joined the *Carbonari*, a secret society dedicated to the national unification of Italy, and distinguished himself as an intriguer. Nearly arrested in 1830, he fled to England, posting through Paris on the tenth anniversary of his uncle's death on St. Helena. Although Louis-Napoleon still had no legal right to reside in France, he paused in Paris to admire the strength of the Napoleonic legend. Fifteen years after Napoleon I's exile and ten years after his death, ordinary people still laid wreaths at his monuments and cried "*Vive l'Empereur!*"

With sentiments like these alive in France, the government arrested Louis-Napoleon and hustled him out of the country. He lived in London until 1836, when he returned to France in an ill-advised imitation of his uncle's "Hundred Days," the return from Elba in 1815. Louis-Napoleon marched up to the gates of Strasbourg with a small entourage and demanded that the garrison there join him to "restore the Empire" and oust the "illegitimate" government of King Louis-Philippe d'Orléans, who had become king in 1830 and earned the eternal hatred of the Bonapartes by confiscating all of their assets in France. Military discipline prevailed at Strasbourg; Bonaparte was arrested, and sent back into exile, this time to the United States. In 1840, he hazarded another *coup* with fifty men. Debarking at Boulogne, they took the train to Lille and (in a reprise of Strasbourg) demanded that local troops join them in a march on Paris to depose Louis-Philippe and restore the Empire; again Bonaparte was arrested, this time sentenced to "perpetual confinement" in the fortress of Ham. On hearing the verdict, Louis-Napoleon presciently joked that "in France, nothing is perpetual."[6]

He was right; in 1846, Louis-Napoleon disguised himself in the blue overalls of a construction worker named Badinguet and strolled out the gates of Ham to freedom. Karl Marx, for one, never forgave the lapse of vigilance, and referred to Louis-Napoleon ever after as "Little Badinguet." On the lam, a

---

6   D. W. Brogan, *The French Nation*, London, 1957, p. 62.

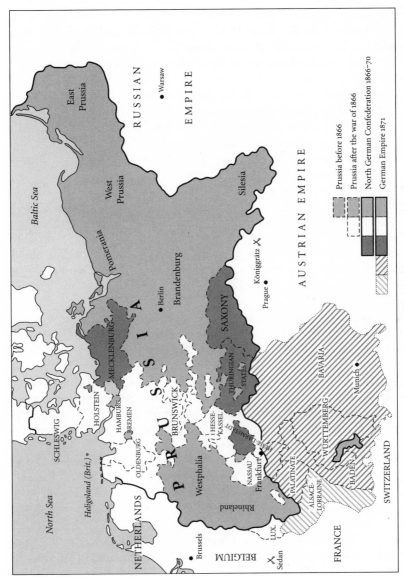

Map 1. Germany in the 1860s

failure at everything he turned his hand to, Louis-Napoleon seemed a failure. Still, he remained the Bonaparte family's "pretender," the ranking heir to the imperial throne abdicated by his uncle in 1815, and he nursed a powerful ambition that finally found an outlet in 1848 when France was rocked by revolution.

The French revolution of 1848, a radical attempt to bury monarchy and create a "social and democratic republic," shattered on the essential conservatism of France. Although urban workers – like the destitutes sketched in Victor Hugo's *Les Misérables* – wanted a socialist state, the French bourgeoisie and peasantry supported capitalism and private property, which afforded the bourgeois a high standard of living and the peasant dignity and land ownership. Observing that peasants comprised nearly 80 percent of the French population, Louis-Napoleon – free to return to France at last thanks to the first reforms of the revolutionary year – immediately made himself the candidate of the peasant voter, was elected to the new parliament, and backed the French army's strike against the radical cities in June 1848. The bloody "June Days" – 3,000 working-class insurgents were killed or wounded – left a conservative, middle-class republic in place of the radical one proclaimed in February.

One radical reform retained by the more conservative republic was manhood suffrage; realizing that few peasants recognized the names of any of the candidates running for the presidency of the new French Republic, Louis-Napoleon put himself forward and ran an American-style campaign, whistle-stopping across France and pitching himself as a reliable strongman, the true heir of his famous uncle, who had made the name Bonaparte synonomous with order, fiscal conservatism, and national pride. These were popular prescriptions in rural France, and Bonaparte won by a landslide in December 1848, receiving 74 percent of the votes cast.[7]

For Louis-Napoleon Bonaparte, this rapid, unexpected ascent to the presidency must have been stunning. Written off in his thirties, he was President of France in his forties. As chief executive, he displayed remarkable political skill. He attracted conservatives with prudent fiscal, monetary, and trade policies, and strong support for the army and the Roman Catholic church. The erstwhile *Carbonaro*, who had spent his youth plotting against the pope, now warmly embraced the Vicar of Christ. When Mazzini and Garibaldi, the most famous *Carbonari* of all, drove Pope Pius IX from Rome in 1848 and established a Roman Republic – the dream of the French president's youth – Louis-Napoleon reversed himself and dispatched French troops to crush the republic and restore the pontiff. This was less an act of piety than a bid for conservative support, and it succeeded. Priests all over France endorsed *Pouléon*

7   Roger Price, *Napoleon III and the Second Empire*, London, 1997, p. 15.

in church and in the cafés. (French peasant males were far more likely to be in the second place than the first.) Catholic support deepened when President Bonaparte gave back the parochial schools and universities that the church had lost in the revolution.[8] Conservatives were also pleased with the president's choice of wife, Countess Eugénie de Montijo, a beautiful, deeply religious Spanish reactionary, who would have been more at home in the sixteenth than the nineteenth century.

But what distinguished Louis-Napoleon from other nineteenth-century conservatives, what made him quintessentially a Bonaparte – supple, obliging, and almost breathtakingly unprincipled – was his simultaneous approach to the radical left. Although he reeled in the right with solid economic policies, patriotism, and "moral education," he reached out to the left with progressive social policies: investing heavily in road and railway construction and other public works to soak up France's pool of unemployed. Indeed the president had polled thousands of working class votes in the 1848 elections because of his book *L'extinction du pauperisme* – written in the Ham prison – that had promised just the sort of Bonapartist "war on poverty" that Louis-Napoleon ultimately delivered. In 1851, Bonaparte approached the end of his presidential term with strong popularity. The middle-class and peasants revered him, and even the urban poor had come to appreciate his public works. Unfortunately, the constitution of the Second Republic forbade a second term and many in France feared chaos in the 1852 elections.

The most likely candidate of the right was General Louis Cavaignac, who had killed, wounded, arrested, or exiled 20,000 workers in June 1848. The man of the left was Louis Blanc, a communist. Thus, assuring themselves that they were conspiring against the republic only to save it from itself, Louis-Napoleon and his advisors prepared a *coup d'état*. Generals loyal to the republic were transferred to Algeria; generals loyal to Louis-Napoleon were brought to Paris. Unreliable prefects and police chiefs were replaced with reliable ones. By December 1851, all was in place, including large garrisons of dependable troops in Paris, Lyon, and the other big cities. Louis-Napoleon struck in the night of 2 December, a date carefully chosen to evoke memories of his uncle's glorious victory at Austerlitz forty-six years earlier. After all the preparations, the coup provoked only sporadic acts of resistance, which Bonaparte dramatically flourished as sure "evidence of the social war which would have broken out in 1852" had he not intervened.[9] Louis-Napoleon reseated himself in power as "prince-president," minted new coins and banknotes bearing his image, and, one year later, went all the way, dissolving the republic and proclaiming himself Napoleon III, Emperor of the French.

8 Price, p. 16.
9 Price, p. 22. James F. McMillan, *Napoleon III*, London, 1991, pp. 45–51.

There were many similiarites between the Second Empire of Napoleon III and the First Empire of his uncle, which had lasted from 1804–14 and for 100 days in 1815. Both empires sprang from military coups in peacetime and solved grave internal political problems. Napoleon I had struck to preempt radicals at either end of the political spectrum: "white terrorists" on the right (the unapologetic adherents of the fallen Bourbons) and "red terrorists" on the left (the "neo-Jacobin" admirers of Robespierre, Marat, and St. Just). In his time, Napoleon III struck to preempt similar threats, from Legitimists (diehard Bourbonists) and Orleanists (partisans of the exiled Louis-Philippe) on the right, who wanted further to constrict voting rights that Louis-Napoleon had already constricted in 1850, and from *démoc-socs* (democratic socialists) on the left, who wanted to sweep away the "prince-president" and his wealthy backers and create a worker's state. Historically, the Bonapartes rejected extremists of any persuasion. They were free agents, bound neither to right nor left. Descended from a minor Corsican family, the Bonapartes were the consummate new men, who took their support where they could find it. They "stood above the parties" in France because they had to, hence their innate suppleness and willingness to please, which was generally interpreted as a lack of principle.

As Emperor of the French in the 1850s and 1860s, Napoleon III presided over a great economic expansion. Consumption of agricultural and industrial products increased across the board as Europe shrugged off a long recession. Louis-Napoleon primed the pump, scrapping tariffs and other taxes and founding new savings banks to soak up rural savings and channel the deposits into the French economy. Under Napoleon III, the French railway network quintupled from 2,000 miles of track in 1851 to 10,600 miles in 1870.[10] The emperor's most lasting act, and the one that aesthetically made Paris the "capital of Europe," was Louis-Napoleon's decision to demolish whole quarters of Paris and rebuild them in the grand neo-Renaissance style that came to be identified with the Second Empire. Medieval warrens were split open with broad new boulevards flanked by palatial mansions, office buildings, and department stores. This reconstruction of Paris and the other cities and towns of France cost 5 billion francs, which was an astonishing sum equal to $15 billion today.

The renovated capital fit the new emperor's grand vision of France. The nation had never really recovered from the defeat and humiliation of 1815. Territory had been lost to the Dutch, Germans, and Piedmontese. France had been relegated to a subordinate political position in Europe, beneath the world's richest power, Great Britain, and the so-called gendarmes of the Continent: Russia and Austria. Though the intervening governments of the Bourbon

10 Price, pp. 26–7.

Restoration (1815–30) and the July Monarchy (1830–48) had attempted to restore France's prestige and influence, they had largely failed; the Bourbons had acquired Algiers, but nothing more. In 1830, Louis-Philippe had actually besieged Antwerp to drive out the Dutch but then balked when offered the former French-speaking borderland lost in 1815. Faced with British opposition, he had characteristically backed down. The new state of Belgium was the result, a permanent, rather embarrassing reminder of France's waning power. Louis-Napoleon was determined to change all of this. Indeed, one reason people had voted for him in the elections of 1848 and the plebiscites of 1851 and 1852 affirming the "authoritarian presidency" and the empire was his commitment to *la grande France*, that is a France that would again dictate to the rest of Europe.

No doubt many voters had deluded themselves that the name Napoleon alone would accomplish this, but not Louis-Napoleon. The position of France had radically changed since the time of his uncle. Whereas the France of Napoleon I had easily overshadowed the rest of Europe in population, military might, and pre-industrial economic resources, the balance had shifted to the detriment of Napoleon III's France. Now France, with its population of 35 million, was a thoroughly average great power. Still more worrisome was the slow industrialization of France, a nation of artisans and small shopkeepers, who jealously defended their incomes against the encroachments of the machine age and the department store. Although this latter quality preserved the charming atmosphere of the French town and village, with cobblers hammering away at their benches and blacksmiths stoking their fires, it retarded France's economic growth, and put fewer resources in the hands of the new emperor. What, then, could the emperor possibly do to restore French prestige and leadership? That which he had always done well: plotting and intrigue. Rather than confront Britain and the gendarmes directly, he would reduce their power by indirect means: limited wars, conspiracies, and diplomacy.

For this, Louis-Napoleon had a strategy. He had spent his many years of exile and prison extracting what he called *idées napoléoniennes* – Napoleonic ideas – from the wreckage of his uncle's failed empire. The essence of the ideas was this: to restore French power, a new Napoleon needed to finish the work begun by the first Napoleon, namely destroy or weaken the repressive, multinational empires of Austria and Russia and encourage the formation of liberal new nation-states in their place that would rally around France. Healthy Polish, German, Czech, and Italian nation-states would be cut from the "corpses" of Austria and Russia, and would place themselves at the side of France from a combination of gratitude and admiration. The emperor's ultimate aim was nothing less than a "United States of Europe," whose capital would be the grandly rebuilt Paris. The strategy was audacious, but not as far-fetched as it seemed at first blush. It was based on Louis-Napoleon's penetrating critique of his uncle, who, in the new emperor's eyes, had *betrayed* the Napoleonic promise by first liberating and then enslaving the peoples of Europe. Promises of a liberalizing "Napoleonic project" for Europe had been dropped after the great victories at Austerlitz (1805), Jena (1806), and Friedland (1807), which had left Napoleon I master of the Continent. Thereafter the First Empire had slipped into corruption and war-mongering, earning the hatred of almost everyone in Europe by the end. Napoleon III vowed to improve on that record; he would free the peoples of Europe and leave them free, so long as they accepted French leadership.

The chief barrier to this daring "Napoleonic idea" – besides its paradoxical premise – was the "Congress system" of 1815, which committed the five great powers (Britain, Russia, Austria, Prussia, and France) to confer and put down any attempted changes to the borders or governments established at the Congress of Vienna. Thus, when liberal Italian nationalists attempted to overthrow the governments of Piedmont and the Two Sicilies in 1821, the powers met and authorized the Austrians to send troops to Turin and Naples to crush the revolts. Similarly, when liberal Spanish officers imprisoned their king and demanded a constitution in 1822, the powers invited the French to invade Spain with 100,000 troops to restore the Bourbons and root out the "liberal plot." The last gasp of the Congress system was in 1848–49, when the Russian, Austrian, and Prussian armies had joined to crush the liberal revolutions, the Russians marching an entire army into Austria to topple a short-lived Hungarian republic. Needless to say, a conventional statesman would have quailed before this conservative phalanx, but not Louis-Napoleon. He was notoriously unconventional – "his mind is as full of schemes as a warren is full of rabbits," Britain's Lord Palmerston once complained – and seized every opportunity to undermine the conservative powers.

The first opportunity presented itself in 1853, when Tsar Nicholas I declared war on the Ottoman Empire, which was an ill-advised declaration that provoked counter-mobilizations by the British and the Austrians who both announced their opposition to Russian control of the Balkans and the eastern Mediterranean. To Louis-Napoleon, the conflict was a godsend; it split the gendarmes and drove Britain into his arms. An Austro-Franco-British alliance was swiftly concluded and an expeditionary force dispatched to the Crimean peninsula, which was the easiest part of Russia to attack from the sea. (No one in London, Paris, or Vienna wanted to *march* to Moscow as Napoleon I had unwisely attempted in 1812.) The resulting Crimean War sputtered inconclusively for three years. The political acrimony between the allies and Russia increased in inverse proportion to the results on the battlefield, where the two sides wallowed in muddy trench lines around the great fortress and naval base of Sebastopol. In 1856, the coalition finally defeated the Russians – Nicholas I having fortuitously died, making way for a more flexible successor – and wrestled them back to their pre-war frontiers. This was a satisfactory result for the Austrians and British. For the French, it was marvelous. It exhausted the Russians – who later sold Alaska to the Americans to cover their war debts – and dealt a fatal blow to the Congress system. When the treaty ending the war was signed (in Paris, of course), Tsar Alexander II angrily turned the statuette that he kept of his Austrian cousin Franz Joseph to face the wall. In future crises, it was a safe bet that Russia would not send troops to aid the Emperor of Austria.

The "Sphinx on the Seine," as European pundits now called Louis-Napoleon, shortly cooked up another crisis. With Russia thrown back and the Congress system in tatters, he turned his attention to Austria. The Austrian Empire, the second biggest country in Europe after Russia, was the chief obstacle to Napoleon III's plan to found a Paris-centered "United States of Europe." A multinational empire, Austria sprawled across East Central Europe and united a dozen nations under the Habsburg scepter: Germans, Italians, Czechs, Slovaks, Hungarians, Slovenes, Croats, Serbs, Rumanians, Poles, and Ukrainians. Napoleon III viewed this polyglot empire as dimly as had his uncle, who had twice nearly destroyed it, at Austerlitz in 1805 and at Wagram in 1809. And yet both times Napoleon I had pulled back from the brink, detaching pieces of the Austrian Empire, but leaving its heartland intact. Napoleon III, who had definite plans for the peoples of Austria, wanted to finish the job.

His first opportunity came in 1858, when Count Camillo Cavour – prime minister of Piedmont – requested French armed assistance in the struggle for Italian unification, which had sputtered on and off since 1815. The request, tendered at a secret meeting between Cavour and Louis-Napoleon at the spa of Plombières, presented the French emperor with a golden opportunity to strike a blow at Austria without incurring the charge of aggression. At Plombières, he and Cavour conspired to provoke the Austrians into declaring war on Piedmont, which would permit France to join the war under the pretext of "defending" Piedmont. Still, Louis-Napoleon hesitated; French Catholics expected him to defend the temporal power of the pope, yet Italian nationalists like Cavour and Garibaldi were committed to the annexation of Papal Rome to a united Italy. Ultimately Louis-Napoleon resolved the dilemma in his usual style by advancing on both fronts. He loaned an army of 300,000 men to Cavour for the war with Austria and privately assured Pope Pius IX that France would never permit a Piedmontese annexation of Rome.

At the battles of Magenta and Solferino in June 1859, France and Piedmont won the war and laid claim to Austria's richest Italian province – Lombardy – that Louis-Napoleon then ceded to Piedmont in exchange for Nice and Savoy, two Piedmontese provinces coveted by France. This Franco-Austrian War of 1859 was meant to be the start of the new French order in Europe. Napoleon III not only expanded the territory of France and improved its frontiers; in his dealings with Cavour, he insisted that Piedmont not expand beyond Lombardy and, eventually, Venetia, the lush plain between Milan and Venice.

To maintain primacy and control in Italy and assure the subservience of Piedmont, Napoleon III planned to cut the rest of Italy into French-sponsored satellite states. The pope would remain in Rome and Lazio, and continue to bless the Bonapartes. Tuscany, Modena, and Parma would be formed into a Kingdom of Central Italy and given to Napoleon III's cousin Jerôme (who had married the King of Piedmont's daughter), and Naples and the south – the former Kingdom of the Two Siciles, which Garibaldi and an army of volunteers invaded in 1860–61 – would be detached and given to Lucien Murat, a descendant of Joachim Murat, the popular Napoleonic marshal who had ruled southern Italy during the First Empire.

What these Bonapartist plans for Italy in the 1860s proved more than anything else was the hollowness of Louis-Napoleon's *idees napoléoniennes*. Napoleon III's patronage came with as high a price as Napoleon I's. To evade it, Cavour moved quickly after Solferino to take as much of Italy under Piedmontese control as he could. In 1860, the Piedmontese army occupied Lombardy, Venetia, Tuscany, Modena, Parma, Romagna, Naples, and Sicily. The following year King Vittorio Emanuele II of Piedmont proclaimed himself "King of Italy." A new great power was born that united all of Italy except Rome, which – ironically – kept its French garrison. The raw speed of these Piedmontese annexations and the popular enthusiasm that they generated everywhere except the south prevented Napoleon III from intervening. He had sold the war of 1859 to a skeptical French public with the promise that he was "liberating" the Italians from Austrian rule, a gift of French civilization. How could he now reasonably fight a war with Piedmont to stop Turin from "liberating" the *rest* of Italy? The French emperor, therefore, made the best of the flawed outcome. He sponsored parades, carnivals, and illuminations all over France to celebrate Italian unification, which he belatedly trumpeted as a French achievement. Meanwhile, Louis-Napoleon searched for another pawn, someone who would join more sincerely than Cavour in the French-directed reconstruction of Europe. In 1862, he felt certain that he had found just such a client in the newly appointed Prussian minister president, Count Otto von Bismarck.

Bismarck, born to middling Prussian nobility on April Fool's Day 1815, was a shrewd man, every inch as creative, daring, and supple as Cavour. He took a realistic view of diplomacy and politics, which he called "the capacity to choose in each fleeting moment of a situation that which is ...most opportune."[11] This, in a nutshell, was *Realpolitik*; a perfect example of it was Bismarck's controversial decision to seek – or appear to seek – a French alliance in the 1850s when he was Prussian ambassador in Paris. Although the Germans had viewed the French with loathing since the Napoleonic

11   Otto Pflanze, *Bismarck and the Development of Germany*, 3 vols., Princeton, 1990, vol. 1, p. 82.

Wars – when Bonaparte had subjugated and plundered the German states to facilitate his wars of expansion – Bismarck saw opportunity in Napoleon III. His meetings with Louis-Napoleon in 1855 and 1857 satisfied Bismarck that the rather dilettantish Napoleon III was not the mortal threat that his uncle had been. Moreover, Bismarck instinctively grasped that Louis-Napoleon's avowal of the "national principle" and his hostility toward Russia and Austria – the "prisons of the nations" – were policies that Prussia could exploit. Just as Cavour had pretended to be Louis-Napoleon's pawn in Italy, Bismarck could play the same game in Germany. In June 1862, he dined at the Tuileries with Napoleon III and patiently heard the emperor's arguments that Prussia would best solve its internal problems by embracing a "German national policy" underwritten and directed by France. The project was similar to the one offered Cavour in 1858. The "border rectifications" sought by Napoleon III – as yet unspoken, but understood to be the Saar region and the Palatinate – were the German equivalents of Nice and Savoy; their annexation would push France up to the Rhine and make Prussia vulnerable ever after to a French invasion.[12]

Bismarck's genius as a statesman was never more apparent than in the dangerous 1860s. Alternately pressed by the Austrians to accept Habsburg leadership in Germany and by the French to break with the Austrians and reorganize the German states in league with Paris, Bismarck deftly juggled the two powers. In 1864, he fought a war with Denmark to improve Prussia's frontiers and take Schleswig, and shrewdly used an Austrian alliance to keep Napoleon III – who wanted the Danes, not the Prussians, to have *Slesvig* – at arm's length. In October 1865, Bismarck met secretly with Napoleon III at Biarritz and plotted a war with Austria. Though the meeting was much vaguer than Plombières in 1858, Bismarck left it confident that the French emperor approved of an Austro-Prussian war, and would not resist Prussian expansion in northern Germany afterward. Napoleon III seemed genuinely to believe that Prussia, more than any other German state, embodied "German nationalism, reform and progress," the judgment of one of his advisors in 1860.[13] Furthermore, it appeared in 1865 that Louis-Napoleon might agree to anything that would shatter the Austro-Prussian entente displayed in the Danish War; this old alliance of the two German great powers "hemmed France in" and solidified borders in Germany and elsewhere that the French emperor was determined to change.[14] Of course, with Bismarck as with Cavour, Napoleon III

12 Lothar Gall, *Bismarck*, 2 vols., London, 1986, vol. 1, pp. 178–9, 263. Pflanze, vol. 1, pp. 96, 161, 301–2.
13 Dietrich Radewahn, "Französische Aussenpolitik vor dem Krieg von 1870," in Eberhard Kolb, *Europa vor dem Krieg von 1870*, Munich, 1987, p. 38. Allan Mitchell, *Bismarck and the French Nation 1848–1890*, New York, 1971, pp. 33–4.
14 Heinrich Friedjung, *The Struggle for Supremacy in Germany 1859–1866*, orig. 1897, London, 1935, pp. 113–14.

demanded something in return for French "benevolence." At Biarritz, he mentioned Belgium, the Saar, and the Palatinate, but Bismarck was shrewd enough not to commit himself in advance.

His rear secure, Bismarck engineered a war with Austria in 1866. He demanded that the Austrians agree to major reforms of the German Confederation and give Prussia control of the north German states. When the Austrians refused, Bismarck threatened to dissolve the Confederation's "diet of princes" and replace it with a popularly elected "national parliament," which would unify the Germans by common consent. This was pure Bismarck; a conservative man with a deep fondness for Prussia and its authoritarian institutions, he had no intention of convening a national parliament. The proposal was a bluff, cleverly worded to infuriate Vienna and win friends in Paris. Accompanied by the demand that the Austrians give or sell Prussia Holstein – Vienna's share of the spoils in the Danish War – Bismarck's "national parliament" project was the greatest gamble of his career. Although he had been the king's chief minister since 1862, he was still mistrusted by virtually everyone in Prussia. The Junkers recoiled at the mere mention of a national parliament, and considered war with Austria – Prussia's oldest ally – an act of heresy. Prussian liberals hated Bismarck; There was no other word for it. He had alienated them in his very first speech to the Prussian *Landtag*, arguing that German unity would be achieved not by "majority votes and parliamentary resolutions," but by "iron and blood." He had then compounded the sin in the early 1860s by going behind parliament's back – garnishing tax receipts and privatizing state assets – to procure funds for a great army expansion that had been vetoed by the liberal *Landtag*.

Disliked by virtually everyone but the king, Bismarck staked his career on the Austro-Prussian War. If he could beat the Austrians and take the north German states for Prussia, physically joining the eastern and western halves of the kingdom, he would silence his critics. Bismarck saw clearly that the only thing Prussian liberals wanted more than his removal was a unified Germany centered on Berlin; he might yet give them one. What Prussian Junkers seemed to want was the assurance that German unity would not come at the expense of feudal power and privileges. Bismarck could allay that fear simply by stitching the authoritarian Prussian system on to a united Germany, which would more accurately be called an enlarged Prussia. He therefore forged ahead in 1866, concluding a secret treaty with the Italians in March and provoking a war with Austria in June.

Although military experts predicted an Austrian victory, the Prussians launched a crushing offensive. Grouped in three armies, 250,000 Prussian troops slid unopposed through Saxony and Silesia and into the rich Habsburg province of Bohemia, where they pummeled outlying corps of Austrian General Ludwig von Benedek's 260,000-man North Army. At the battles of Trautenau and Vysokov on 27 June, the Prussian Second Army punched its way through the Sudeten Mountains and, attacking in aggressive rifle platoons, killed or wounded 10,700 Austrians. At Skalice the next day, the Prussians debouched onto the flat marching country beyond the mountains and inflicted 6,000 more Austrian casualties (against just 1,300 of their own, the usual 5:1 ratio.) At the battles of Münchengrätz and Jicin on 28–29 June, the Prussian First and Elbe Armies broke in from the other end of Bohemia, trampling the Saxon Army and the Austrian I Corps and pursuing as far as Königgrätz on the Elbe, where General Benedek wearily turned at bay with the 240,000 Austro-Saxon troops that were left to him in the wake of the first devastating battles. Attacked on two fronts – by the Prussians in Bohemia and by 200,000 Italian troops in Venetia struggling to complete national unification – the Austrian army sagged under the pressure. That last week of June 1866 was the moment when Napoleon III finally awakened to the threat posed by Prussia. But was he in time?

Causes of the Franco-Prussian War

On 3 July 1866, even as Emperor Napoleon III made plans to dispatch an envoy to Prussian royal headquarters to urge restraint, a quarter of a million Prussian troops under the command of General Helmuth von Moltke smashed the Austrian army at the battle of Königgrätz. In just three weeks of fighting, Moltke had invaded the Austrian province of Bohemia, encircled Prague, and punched the Habsburg army into a loop of the Elbe river between the Austrian fortress of Königgrätz and the little village of Sadova. There Moltke nearly annihilated the Austrians, killing, wounding, or capturing 44,000 of them and putting the rest – 196,000 largely disbanded stragglers – to panic-stricken flight.

Königgrätz was a turning-point in history. Prussia's fifty-one-year-old prime minister – Count Otto von Bismarck – watched the battle at Moltke's side and offered the Austrians terms, when the extent of their defeat was fully comprehended in Vienna and elsewhere. In exchange for an armistice, Emperor Franz Joseph of Austria duly surrendered the authority his Habsburg dynasty had exercised in Germany since the sixteenth century, first through the Holy Roman Empire, then through the German Confederation, and gave the Prussians a free hand. Bismarck was quick to exploit it. In the weeks after Königgrätz, he abolished the thirty-nine-state German Confederation established in 1815 and annexed most of its northern members: Schleswig, Holstein, Hanover, Hessia-Kassel, Nassau, and Frankfurt-am-Main. He packed the rest of Germany's northern states – Saxony, Hessia-Darmstadt, Mecklenburg, the Thuringian duchies, and the free cities of Hamburg, Lübeck, and Bremen – into a North German Confederation that, with Berlin controlling its foreign and military affairs and most of its internal ones as well, was essentially Prussian territory. Königgrätz and its aftermath were proof that great battles can swing history one way or the other. In a matter of days, Prussia climbed from the lower rungs of great power ("Prussia unaided would not keep the Rhine or the Vistula for a month," *The Times* of London had scoffed just six years earlier) to the top, gaining 7 million subjects and 1,300 square miles of territory. Tired of sharing Germany with Austria, of "plowing the same disputed acre," Bismarck now controlled most of it, and was poised to take the rest.[1]

France gaped in astonishment. Almost overnight a rather small and manageable neighbor had become an industrial and military colossus. "Germany," an innocuous land of thinkers, artists, and poets, of dreamy landscapes and romantic oafs like Balzac's Schmucke, stood on the brink of real unification under a tough, no-nonsense military regime. Napoleon III's cabinet – stunned by the outcome at Königgrätz – demanded that the French emperor take immediate counter-measures. "Grandeur is relative," the emperor's privy counselor warned. "A country's power can be diminished by the mere fact of *new* forces accumulating around it."[2] Eugène Rouher, the French minister of state, was more direct: "Smash Prussia and take the Rhine," he urged the emperor. By "the Rhine" Rouher meant Prussia's western cities: Cologne, Düsseldorf, and the Westphalian *Ruhrgebiet* around Essen, Dortmund, and Bochum.[3] These were the industrial mainsprings of Prussia. Berlin could not exist as a great power without them. Even Napoleon III's liberal opposition in the empire's *Corps Législatif* or legislative body, always averse to military adventures, joined the clamor for war. As the war in Germany wound down, a usually moderate Adolphe Thiers insisted that "the way to save France is to declare war on Prussia *immediately*."[4] And yet Napoleon III did not declare war; instead, he tried to bluff Bismarck. A month after Königgrätz, while the Prussian army was still tied down pacifying Austria, the French emperor demanded Prussian support for the "borders of 1814," that is, the great square of German territory on the left bank of the Rhine annexed by France during the French Revolutionary Wars and returned to the German states after Waterloo. Karlsruhe, Mannheim, Koblenz, and Luxembourg were the corners of the square. Bismarck, who could not even consider the French demand without losing the support of millions of Germans, rejected it, running the risk of a two-front war with Austria and France. Luckily for Bismarck, Napoleon III did not press the demand.[5] The *surprise de Sadova* had caught him unprepared. Because he had expected the big Austrian and Prussian armies to trade

1   David Wetzel, *A Duel of Giants*, Madison, 2001, p. 15.
2   *Papiers et Correspondance de la Famille Impériale*, 10 vols., Paris, 1870, vols. 1, 3, and 4, *passim*. vol. 8, lxii, Paris, 20 July 1866, M. Magne to Napoleon III.
3   Vienna, Haus-Hof-und Staatsarchiv (HHSA), IB, Karton 364, BM 1866, 35, Vienna, 27 Aug. 1866, Belcredi to Mensdorff. Vienna, Kriegsarchiv (KA), AFA 1866, Karton 2267, 7–219, Paris, 4 July 1866, Belcredi to FZM Benedek.
4   KA, AFA 1866, Karton 2272, 13–13, 13 July and 15 August 1866, Belcredi to FZM Benedek.
5   London, Public Record Office (PRO), FO 64, 690, Berlin, 11 August 1870, Loftus to Granville. Lothar Gall, *Bismarck*, 2 vols., orig. 1980, London, 1986, vol. 1, p. 304.

blows through the summer, fall, and winter, and into 1867, he had procured no
supplies for an 1866 campaign and had left his combat troops scattered across
the globe: 63,000 in Algeria, 28,000 in Mexico, 8,000 in Rome, and 2,000 in
Indochina. Infantry companies in France had been drawn down to less than
half their usual strength, netting Louis-Napoleon scarcely 100,000 war-ready
troops after Königgrätz.[6] Prussia's army, flush with victory, was three times
larger.

Louis-Napoleon's frustration in 1866 was palpable, and oozed like an
inkspot through the months and years after Königgrätz. Before the battle, the
French emperor had boasted in a speech at Auxerre that he would use the
Austro-Prussian War to enlarge France and wring concessions from the two
German powers.[7] In the event, he was left with nothing under the severely
critical gaze of his citizenry. Though Louis-Napoleon made the best of a
bad situation, demanding and receiving Bismarck's assent to nominal independence for Saxony, Bavaria, Württemberg, Baden, and Hessia-Darmstadt,
this was a small victory, and one without flavor for a French public that
wanted territory and a French army that wanted revenge. To appease these
powerful groups, Napoleon III tried to acquire the German fortress town of
Luxembourg in 1867; it might have served as partial, face-saving payment for
France's "benevolence" in 1866. Yet Bismarck refused even the partial payment. He interfered, involved the British, who feared that a French step into
Luxembourg might carry them into Belgium, and finally agreed only to detach the duchy from Holland and neutralize it.[8] Napoleonic efforts to buy
the place were rebuffed. Here was yet another humiliation. Adolphe Thiers,
one of Louis-Napoleon's more persistent critics, rose again in the legislative
body to twist the knife: "When a hunter is ashamed of returning from the
chase with an empty bag, he goes to the butcher, buys a rabbit, and stuffs it
into his bag, letting the ears hang out. *Voilà le Luxembourg!*"[9]

Partly to distract attention from these embarrassments, Napoleon III
hosted the 1867 World's Fair, an occasion for the industrial powers to display
their wares, and for France to shine. Unfortunately, the fair's French name –
Exposition – provided yet more comic material for the fifty-nine-year-old emperor's detractors: "Who deserves the largest medal at the Exposition," went

6   *Papiers et Correspondance de la Famille Impériale*, vol. 1, pp. 6–8, Strasbourg, December
    1866, General Ducrot to General Trochu. "Zur Heeres-Reorganisierung," *Österreichische
    Militärische Zeitschrift* (ÖMZ) 2 (1867), p. 132. "Aus dem Lager von Châlons," *ÖMZ* 3
    (1868), pp. 75–6. General Jean-Baptiste Montaudon, *Souvenirs Militaires*, 2 vols., Paris,
    1898–1900, vol. 2, p. 20.
7   Otto Pflanze, *Bismarck and the Development of Germany*, 3 vols., Princeton, 1990, vol. 1,
    pp. 300–1.
8   W.E. Mosse, *The European Powers and the German Question, 1848–71*, Cambridge, UK,
    1958, pp. 260–70.
9   Ferdinand Gregorovius, *The Roman Journals, 1852–74*, London, 1907, p. 275.

one joke. Answer: *"Napoléon, parce-qu'il a exposé la France."*[10] Indeed, in the late 1860s, it was almost impossible to overestimate the dangers to which France had been exposed by German unification under Prussia. Whereas Prussia had counted just one-third the inhabitants of France in 1820 and less than half in 1860, the Austro-Prussian War and the annexations nearly evened the score, giving the North German Confederation a population of 30 million to France's 38 million and – thanks to the Prussian use of universal conscription – an army one-third larger than France's. With the annexations and amalgamations of 1866, the Prussian army grew from 70 infantry regiments to 105, from ten corps to seventeen. The smaller German states delivered entire armies into Prussian hands: Hessia-Darmstadt's three infantry regiments became the Prussian 81st, 82nd, and 83rd. The Hanoverians supplied four additional regiments; the Saxons supplied nine more. By 1867, most of these forces had been seamlessly integrated with Prussian uniforms, drill, armament, and even officers. Baden, although technically an independent country, took a Prussian general as its war minister, another as its general staff chief, and a third as its divisional commandant.[11] Germany's galloping industries only compounded the threat; in 1867, Prussian and Saxon coal mines were outproducing French mines three-to-one, and German railway construction was easily keeping pace with an all-out French effort that had yielded 10,000 miles of track by 1866.[12] These were alarming indicators that threatened a total eclipse of French power.

Faced with these various threats, Louis-Napoleon dug in his heels in the months after Königgrätz. Unable to stop Bismarck's spread across northern Germany, he vowed that the Prussians would not have the south as well: Bavaria, Württemberg, and Baden. These states contained an additional 8 million Germans, 200,000 well-trained troops, and substantial resources; they would also give the Prussians a flanking position on the French frontier.[13] This was unthinkable, as the French empress made plain to the Prussian ambassador after Königgrätz: "The energy and speed of your movements have [made it clear] that with a nation like yours as a neighbor, we are in danger of finding you in Paris one day unannounced. I will go to sleep French and wake up Prussian."[14] Indeed if based in the Prussian Rhineland *and* the German south, the Prussians would be able to invade France swiftly on a broad front

---

10 Gregorovius, p. 275.
11 "Die süddeutschen Heere," ÖMZ 2 (1869), p. 161. C. Betz, *Aus den erlebnissen und Erinnerungen eines alten Offiziers*, Karlsruhe, 1894, pp. 134–5.
12 Wilhelm Deist, "Preconditions to Waging War," in Stig Förster and Jörg Nagler, eds., *On the Road to Total War*, Cambridge, 1997, p. 320. Roger Price, *Napoleon III and the Second Empire*, London, 1997, p. 26.
13 Vincennes, *Service Historique de l'Armée de Terre* (SHAT), Lb1, "Renseignements Militaires."
14 Wolfgang Schivelbusch, *The Culture of Defeat*, orig. 2001, New York, 2003, p. 122.

from Alsace-Lorraine to Luxembourg. They had used just exactly this sort of broad, concentric invasion to encircle and rout the Austrians in Bohemia in 1866. Geography still limited their options in a war with the French, but not if they annexed Baden, the Bavarian Palatinate, and Württemberg. With these strategic considerations in mind, Louis-Napoleon warned the British foreign minister in 1868: "I can only guarantee the peace of Europe so long as Bismarck respects the present state of affairs. If he draws the South German states into the North German Confederation, our guns will go off of themselves."[15]

The image of France on a hair-trigger was certainly apt, for the emperor's finger lay heavy on the trigger by the late 1860s. Louis-Napoleon was a troubled man, who, as the popularly elected president of France in 1851, had overthrown the French Republic and crowned himself Napoleon III, Emperor of the French. At first the Napoleonic *coup* had been welcomed. President Bonaparte shrewdly exploiting his famous uncle's legacy: "The name Napoleon itself is a program: order, religion, popular welfare, and national dignity." And Louis-Napoleon had diligently implemented the program, curbing socialism, mending fences with the Catholic church, creating jobs through liberal economic policies, and restoring national dignity in the Crimean War (1854–56) and the Franco-Austrian War (1859), the former clearing the Balkans of Russian influence, the latter freeing northern Italy from Austrian control. Unfortunately, that Napoleonic *coup* of 1851, launched in the name of "order" and "popular welfare" when memories of the bloody revolution of 1848 were still fresh in people's minds, seemed ancient history to many Frenchmen by the late 1860s. They had known only peace and prosperity in the meantime, and although peasants who comprised 70 percent of the French population still revered the emperor, it was difficult to know whether this was for anything deeper than Bonaparte's subsidies to the villages and his determination to keep agricultural prices up through free trade with France's industrial neighbors. Where the real political battles were fought, in the French press, cities, and legislature, Louis-Napoleon's "authoritarian empire" was resented. The best indication of this was the eroding loyalty of even the French middle-class, who years earlier had applauded the imperial restoration of 1852 – a year after the *coup* – as a bulwark against the "red revolution." By the 1860s, a French *bourgeois* was as likely to be a republican or an Orléanist (the better-bred dynasty deposed in 1848) as a Bonapartist. Among French artisans and workers there were hardly any Bonapartists; to them, Louis-Napoleon would always be "the Man of 2 December" (the date of the *coup*), the usurper who had strangled the Second Republic in its infancy and exiled its fiercest advocates to Algeria and Devil's Island.[16]

15 Koppel Pinson, *Modern Germany*, 2nd edition, Prospect Heights, 1989, p. 142.
16 James F. McMillan, *Napoleon III*, London, 1991, pp. 46–8.

Against this stormy political backdrop, it was easy to see why the *surprise de Sadova* and Napoleon III's failure to extort real concessions from the Prussians caused such consternation in Paris. By 1866, the Second Empire had come to depend almost entirely on diplomatic and military victories – "national dignity" – for its popularity. Prussia's victory at Königgrätz and the subsequent annexations were treated as insults to France, which had long controlled German affairs: Richelieu dictating the borders of the Holy Roman Empire in 1648, Louis XIV annexing Alsace and other bits of western Germany in the 1690s, and Napoleon I liquidating the Holy Roman Empire in 1806 and creating a French-run "Confederation of the Rhine." The insult was all the more galling because Louis-Napoleon had long regarded Bismarck as a malleable protégé, naively recruiting Prussia for a French-run "United States of Europe" when Bismarck was Prussian ambassador to Paris in the late 1850s and again when he became Prussian foreign minister in 1862.[17]

Bismarck had cunningly played the part of protégé for a time – weighing French offers of German territory in exchange for Prussian participation in an anti-English alliance – but did this primarily to discourage French intervention in an Austro-Prussian conflict.[18] Once Austria was beaten in 1866, Bismarck joltingly reversed course, ignoring Napoleon III's wishes and even needling the French emperor in the hope that he too might be induced to declare war on Prussia. In Bismarck's view, the political and cultural obstacles separating Germany's Protestant north and Catholic south might take years, even decades, to overcome, but a French invasion, a *Napoleonic* invasion no less, would smash them down in an instant. Francophobia lingering from the Napoleonic Wars – when the French had taxed and looted the German states and forced 250,000 Germans into French military service – would set the machinery of the North German Confederation in motion and put the armies of the German south at Bismarck's disposal.

"Great crises provide the weather for Prussia's growth," was a Bismarck maxim.[19] What he meant was that Prussia needed occasional European dustups to obscure the threat of German unification from the other powers and divert attention from Prussia's creeping borders. When Prussia had fought Austria in 1866, the contest had seemed so even that none of the other powers had bothered to take a side, permitting Prussia to isolate Austria, beat it to the ground, and dissolve the German Confederation. The same calculation might apply in a Franco-Prussian war. France *seemed* so powerful, and had foolishly publicized its desire for Belgium, Luxembourg, and the Rhineland

17 Dietrich Radewahn, "Französische Aussenpolitik vor dem Krieg von 1870," in Kolb, ed., *Europa vor dem Krieg von 1870*, Munich, 1987, pp. 35, 38, 42. A. Plessis, *The Rise and Fall of the Second Empire 1852–71*, orig. 1979, Cambridge, 1985, p. 142.
18 PRO, FO 425, 96, #274 and #347, Berlin, 30 July and 9 Aug. 1870, Loftus to Granville.
19 Pflanze, vol. 1, p. 89.

after Königgrätz. In the crucial years after 1866, these territorial ambitions made France appear more threatening than Prussia. Bismarck understood this; indeed he discreetly stoked France's appetite for territory after Königgrätz to make Napoleon III seem menacing to the other powers. It was a clever move; rather than facilitate a French victory in a war with Prussia, the other powers would probably sit on the sidelines again, "providing the weather for Prussia's growth." As for the lesser German states, Bismarck bet that once allied with Berlin in a "patriotic war," they would not revert to their separate governments. It was a safe bet; most of the states taken in 1866 had willingly voted themselves out of existence. Such was the emotive power of German nationalism.

Therefore, the Franco-Prussian War arose from Napoleon III's need to teach the Prussians a lesson and Bismarck's overlapping need to foment a war with the French in order to complete the process of German unification. The Franco-German War that broke out in 1870 might as easily have come in 1867, 1868, or 1869, because France and Prussia went to the brink of war in each of those years and only reluctantly backed down. Bismarck wanted to buy more time for the spread of the German national idea and Louis-Napoleon wanted to complete vital army reforms. A French general, Louis Jarras, recalled the French war minister telling him repeatedly in the late 1860s that France and Prussia were not at peace; they were merely enjoying an armistice, a respite from war, that might abruptly be broken by either party.[20] The annual Franco-Prussian crises after 1866 revealed the fragility of that "armistice," but also Count Bismarck's extraordinary skill as a statesman.

In desperate need of a foreign policy success to salve national pride after Königgrätz, Napoleon III attempted in 1867 to purchase Luxembourg, an ancient duchy of the Holy Roman Empire that had been given to the Netherlands in 1815 on the condition that its defenses be looked after by Prussia and the now defunct German Confederation. When France first demanded Prussian support for the sale and annexation in the weeks after Königgrätz, Bismarck vaguely gave it, giving himself time to hammer together the North German Confederation and conclude mutual defense treaties with the south German states. When France pressed the demand for Luxembourg in March 1867, Bismarck roughly changed course, refusing to help the French at all and inciting German politicians and journalists to whip up national feeling and denounce this French grab at "an old German land." Bismarck displayed all of his legendary dexterity in the crisis. He stalled the French through the winter of 1866–67 – when he was busy allying with the south German states – and rebuffed them at the very moment that the alliances were signed and negotiations for the North German *Reichstag* or parliament were nearing a vote. Just as Bismarck had calculated, French bluster combined with the

---

20 General Louis Jarras, *Souvenirs*, Paris, 1892, pp. 30–2.

obvious importance of Luxembourg – it defended German territory on the left bank of the Rhine – served to drive even the most reluctant German states into Prussia's arms.[21] The Bavarians promised 60,000 troops for a war with France in 1867, and one German deputy after another rose in the new Reichstag to salute Bismarck's "strong policy" toward Napoleon III. Throughout the crisis, forlorn French agents stood around the main *Platz* in Luxembourg waving placards and shouting *"Vive la France! Vive Napoléon!"* By May, they had drifted away; Luxembourg became a neutral state by international agreement. Eleven mines were bored into its southern bastion and exploded, leaving the picturesque ruin that remains to this day. Paris was tense. Freshly returned from Mexico, Marshal Achille Bazaine was briefed on events in Europe by General Charles Frossard, who told Bazaine that war with the Prussians "would almost certainly come in 1867."[22] Although careful not to push the French into a corner, Bismarck had nevertheless upheld "German honor" and successfully burned off much anti-Prussian feeling in Germany.[23]

Eighteen sixty-eight brought a second Franco-German crisis, this too partly concocted by Bismarck to goad the French and spur German unification. Bismarck had negotiated his defense treaties with the south German states secretly and unilaterally. He had never consulted the French, a condition that Louis-Napoleon had insisted upon in 1866. In 1868, Bismarck tightened Berlin's ties to the German south by establishing an all-German *Zollparlament* or "customs parliament." Because Napoleon III had forbidden a Prussian union with south Germany during the 1866 armistice negotiations, the Customs Parliament was interpreted in Paris as yet another challenge to French authority. The emperor responded to the provocation by prolonging the French army's summer maneuvers a week and warning Bismarck that absorption of any of the three south German states – Bavaria, Württemberg, or Baden – would be treated in Paris as a *casus belli*. Dining with his officers at Châlons in September 1868, Napoleon III raised a glass of Rhine wine, pointed to the east, and said: "Gentlemen, I hope that you yourselves will shortly be harvesting this wine."[24] As in the Luxembourg affair, this French saber-rattling was all that Bismarck could have hoped for. When a nervous Reichstag deputy compared the brooding French army to "an avalanche that the least disturbance can plunge into the chasm," Bismarck theatrically replied that "an appeal to *fear* never finds an echo in German hearts." His words were greeted with thunderous applause. Deputies from all over Germany rallied to Bismarck, as did international opinion. Writing in 1870, an English journalist

---

21 "Die militärische Bedeutung Luxemburgs," *ÖMZ* 2 (1867), pp. 108–15. Michael Howard, *The Franco-Prussian War*, orig. 1961, London, 1981, pp. 41–2.

22 F. A. Bazaine, *Episodes de la Guerre de 1870 et les Blocus de Metz*, Madrid, 1883, p. ii.

23 Dresden, Sächsisches Kriegsarchiv (SKA), Militärbevollmächtiger 4474, Berlin, 2 and 6 May 1867, Col. von Brandenstein to War Minister. Pflanze, vol. 1, pp. 375–81.

24 HHSA, IB, Karton 5, BM 1868, 831, Paris 9 Sept. 1868, Agent E.

expressed the bemusement of most Europeans at Louis-Napoleon's curious support for the south German states: "One is astonished at the infatuation of the Empire – the Empire that professed itself the champion of nationalities everywhere – in allying itself to effete courts and staking success on exploded hereditary traditions."[25]

War did not explode in the spring of 1869. This was partly because Napoleon III needed more time to prepare his army and partly because Bismarck, although advancing on the national question, still doubted the loyalty of the south German states.[26] Although Bavaria and Württemberg had joined the *Zollparlament* and signed military pacts with Prussia, their wary governments regarded these steps as the end of the matter, not the beginning. They would trade with Prussia and join in the defense of Germany, but insisted upon political independence. As the prime minister in Stuttgart put it: "Württemberg wants to remain Württemberg as long as it has the power."[27] If independent, the southern kingdoms would enjoy the option of joining a Prussian war with France, or not; they liked that degree of flexibility. General Moltke, who was trying to construct an all-German army that could be relied upon in *any* contingency, clearly did not. Visiting Baden in 1868, the Prussian general staff chief vented his frustration: "These people must be made to understand that their future is in *our* hands, and that we are in a position to do them much good, or much harm."[28] Bismarck was more diplomatic; rather than clash with the south Germans, he pinned his plans for German unification "on the direction and swiftness with which *public opinion* develops in southern Germany." He was not a democrat, but recognized that he must create popular pressure for unification that would push the foot-dragging southern governments into the grasp of Berlin. Over and over, he returned to a thought he had first expressed ten years earlier: "There is but one ally for Prussia: the German people."[29] Though the princes, soldiers, and bureaucrats of south Germany had a vested interest in remaining outside of Prussia, millions of south German citizens wanted a nation-state, which was something only Prussia could deliver.[30]

Whereas Bismarck sought ways to break the crust of south German politics and reach down to the German masses, Napoleon III found himself confronted with the opposite problem: a tumultuously democratic France that seemed intent on weakening his throne or voting it out of existence.

25 Alexander Innes Shand, *On the Trail of the War*, New York, 1871, p. 35. Pflanze, vol. 1, pp. 396–7.
26 HHSA, IB, Karton 15, BM 1869, 1503, Paris, 26 Nov. 1869, Eduard Simon to Beust.
27 Allan Mitchell, *Bismarck and the French Nation 1848–1890*, New York, 1971, pp. 47–9. Pflanze, vol. 1, p. 391.
28 *Papiers et Correspondance de la Famille Impériale*, vol. 8, pp. 225–6. Strasbourg, 28 October 1868, General Ducrot to General Frossard.
29 Pflanze, vol. 1, pp. 140, 392.
30 PRO, FO 425, 96, #258, Darmstadt, 22 July 1870, Morier to Granville.

Conservatives thought him too liberal; liberals thought him too conservative. Most agreed that he had done too little to arrest the Prussian threat. Widely read pundits like Hippolyte Taine and Lucien Prévost-Paradol warned of French decline, and eclipse by Prussia, Russia, and America. "France languishes in its ruins, with neither honor nor power."[31] Gradually this internal crisis in France became a chief cause of the Franco-Prussian War, for Napoleon III, under constant attack in the press, streets, and legislature by 1869–70, began consciously manipulating foreign policy – the hope of "a good war" (*une bonne guerre*) with the Prussians – to restore public faith in the Second Empire.

Faith was dwindling fast, for the Second Empire was sagging by the late 1860s. Now in his sixties, Napoleon III was stooped, fat, tired, and chronically ill. Once spry and full of ideas, he was now dull and listless, frequently drugged to alleviate the pain of his gout, gallstones, and hemorrhoids, or away from Paris altogether, taking the spa waters at Vichy, Plombières, or Biarritz. Urgent political problems were a constant annoyance to the flagging emperor. Most urgent of all was the very constitution of France; after twenty years of peace and prosperity, many of the French deplored Napoleon III's constitution of 1852, which concentrated all political and administrative power in the emperor's hands. Calls for reform were all the louder because of the emperor's physical deterioration and the lack of a responsible cabinet to govern in his place.

Like his uncle, Napoleon III had surrounded himself with dubious ministers over the years; the men were chosen far more for their loyalty to the Bonapartes than the national interest. Corruption and nepotism flourished. A few examples suggest the extent of it: Each year Louis-Napoleon paid his family 1 million francs ($3 million today) from the national treasury; even a minor cousin or nephew could command 100,000 francs ($300,000) annually. And those were just the official salaries. To augment them, the emperor kept a 27 million franc ($65 million) civil list and reserved 2 million francs ($6 million) annually for "secret funds" that were never audited. More secret funds were dredged up in the colonies; Marshal Patrice MacMahon – Governor-General of Algeria in the 1860s – took 45 million francs ($135 million) a year out of the colony, five times the actual tax liability of the region. Little of this money was ever accounted for.[32] The emperor paid his English mistress, Miss Harriet Howard, a salary of 700,000 francs ($2.1 million). Because history suggested that few French regimes lasted more than twenty years, the emperor kept a constant £1 million ($75 million) on deposit in London at Baring Brothers. Even a devout Bonapartist would have had difficulty characterizing these transactions as anything other than embezzlement, and they paid for luxuries

31 Schivelbusch, pp. 119–20.
32 "Notizen: Frankreich," *ÖMZ* 3 (1868), pp. 77–8.

large and small. In 1856, the emperor spent 900,000 francs ($2.7 million) to baptize his son. In 1858, he sent Pierre de Failly, a favorite general, chocolates valued at 1,300 francs ($4,000).[33]

By the late 1860s, Louis-Napoleon's Second Empire was sinking into a morass of impropriety. The Prussian military attaché's account of the Carnival ball in February 1870 offered a glimpse of it: Napoleon III, "fat, affable, but fragile," moving ponderously among his guests, speaking slowly as if stricken, drunken officers reeling around the ballroom, prostitutes dancing the can-can, everyone collapsing in a wrack of champagne bottles at dawn.[34] Ministers and diplomats who approached the French Emperor found him languid, his left arm withered and useless, his eyes glazed over with pain and opiates.[35] The fatigue, drugs, and peccadillos were all the more alarming because they accompanied a string of foreign policy fiascos. In 1863, the emperor had tried and failed to reconstitute an independent Poland. In 1866, he had failed to wrest territory from the Prussians after Königgrätz. In 1867, he had failed to annex Belgium and Luxembourg, and military reverses half a world away had forced him to pull French troops out of Mexico, where he had squandered 360 million francs ($1.1 billion) trying to establish a French satellite state in Central America.[36] Only the French peasants, who did not generally read, let alone read newspapers, would have retained much faith in Napoleon III's government. Nor was the forty-four-year-old French empress reassuring. Eugénie de Montijo, a Spanish-born ultra-conservative, was even more despised than her husband by the liberal élites and the working class, who, after 1866, impatiently demanded a free press, responsible ministers, the right of parliament to legislate, the removal of authoritarian prefects, and the direct election of mayors. They also wanted an end to "plebiscitary democracy," the emperor's constitutional power to put questions directly to the French people and then assert a mandate. Urban liberals loathed this system; they called it "ruralocracy," and scored the emperor for manipulating the *appel à la nation* to get landslide votes of confidence from the peasants that permitted him to defy the better-informed legislative body at will. French peasants genuinely liked *Pouléon*, as they called the emperor, but also shrewdly recognized that his grants to their villages often flowed in direct proportion to the enthusiasm that they registered in plebiscites.[37]

Although the French country was manageable, the same could not be said of the cities. Urbanization had created a rootless class of workers in industrial centers like Paris, Lyon, and St. Etienne. These were dangerous men; most

33 *Papiers et Correspondance de la Famille Impériale*, Paris, 1870, vols. 1, 3, and 4, *passim*.
34 Alfred von Waldersee, *Denkwürdigkeiten*, 3 vols., Berlin, 1922, vol. 1, p. 55.
35 Wetzel, p. 22.
36 Montaudon, vol. 2, p. 27.
37 Price, p. 53. McMillan, p. 62.

were young, impressionable ex-peasants, who worked twelve-hour days in wretched conditions and passed their evenings listening to radical orators.[38] Such men demanded much more than reform; they wanted revolution and a "red republic." This social crisis peaked in 1869, when Napoleon III, having failed to push important military and education bills through an increasingly sullen legislative body, called new elections. He expected these elections to follow the pattern of previous ones. Loyal mayors and prefects would screen out opposition candidates and arrange a Bonapartist majority before votes were even cast. Unfortunately, the emperor's unpopularity by the late 1860s was such that the old tricks no longer served. One hundred and twenty opposition newspapers sprouted in the months before the May elections. Attempts to block republican candidates buckled and broke under local opposition. Although most candidates were still officially sanctioned, many mayors and prefects wondered if the regime were not doomed. Concerned about their futures, they looked the other way when moderate republicans put their names down. In the cities, angry crowds placed revolutionary socialists on the ballot. Thus, the voting in the spring of 1869 proved an overwhelming defeat for the Second Empire. Three out of four Parisian voters chose opposition candidates or abstained, which was a sign of revolutionary sentiment. Rioters set fires in the French capital for three days in June and danced around the flames singing the *Marseillaise* – the banned anthem of the republic – and shouting *"Vive la République!"* Results nationally were nearly as dismal. Government-sponsored candidates lost 1 million votes to opposition liberals and republicans, who increased their seats in the legislative body to 74 of 292. Without ballot-stuffing and gerrymandering, the balance of power would have tipped far more alarmingly to the left. More than half of the ballots cast indicated opposition to Louis-Napoleon's government. These were stunning achievements given the manifold ways in which the emperor and his prefects could manipulate returns.[39]

The so-called Liberal Empire of 1869–70 flowed from those disastrous spring elections. At first, the French emperor pretended to ignore the results, but a strike wave, more embarrassing defeats in by-elections, and a scandal involving a Bonaparte forced his hand. In January 1870, Napoleon III's cousin, Prince Pierre-Napoleon Bonaparte, shot and killed a republican journalist who had arrived on his doorstep for an impromptu interview. The slain reporter's funeral became the focal point of violent anti-imperial demonstrations. In Paris, crowds smashed windows, overturned buses, lit bonfires, and began building barricades in traditional French revolutionary style. This time they were defeated by the city-planning of Napoleon III and his chief prefect,

---

38 PRO, FO 27, 1786, Paris 20 Dec. 1869, Edw. Malet to Lord Lyons, "Report on the industrial and artisan classes in France."
39 Plessis, pp. 164–5. McMillan, pp. 125–7. Price, pp. 42–4.

Baron Georges Haussmann, who had rebuilt Paris in the 1860s to create open spaces and facilitate the work of a counter-revolution. Still, the level of violence was impressive, and on the worst night, when the bonfires approached the emperor's own Tuileries palace, Napoleon III astonished his guards by appearing fully uniformed and ringed by his adjutants at 2 A.M. He was preparing to ride out to crush the revolution.[40]

Ultimately, drastic measures were not needed. Instead, Napoleon III tried conciliation; he relaxed police powers, softened the press law, sacked a dozen reactionary prefects, and chose an outspoken liberal reformer, forty-four-year-old Emile Ollivier, as his new chief minister. Although technically a republican, Ollivier was ambitious enough to put aside his principles in pursuit of power. Napoleon III liked that about him; the emperor felt certain that, once alienated from his base, Ollivier would be easily controlled. Ollivier, a vain man, was no less certain that he would control the emperor and his shady ministers. He formed a government in January 1870, announced his intention to "save the dynasty," and issued a revised constitution in April. In the new constitution, the legislative body was finally given the right to initiate and amend legislation and question the emperor's ministers.[41] These were important steps, and the emperor, determined to fortify his new position as "head of state," moved in May to secure public backing for the new constitution in a plebiscite, which was the first since 1852.

Ollivier – despised by conservatives and now isolated from his old republican colleagues – was no threat to Louis-Napoleon. Ollivier drew his legislative support entirely from official candidates elected in 1869; these men were more loyal to the emperor than the chief minister. If Napoleon III could convince the French people to vote massively for the Liberal Empire, he could then proceed ruthlessly against the republican left with the argument that they were subverting the people's will as expressed in the plebiscite. This was the beauty of "ruralocracy." Behind Ollivier lurked the emperor's reactionary inner circle: Empress Eugénie, Jean Persigny, Georges Haussmann, Eugène Rouher, Franceschini Pietri, and the marshals, who waited with varying degrees of impatience for the emperor to lead a "second coup," like the one that had inaugurated the Second Empire twenty years earlier. Though tired and indifferent to his own prospects, Napoleon III was desperate to put the empire on a solid footing for his fourteen-year-old son and heir, Prince Louis, affectionately known as *Lou-Lou*. To get the massive "yes" vote needed, the emperor worded the 1870 plebiscite cleverly; voters were asked not to endorse him, only his "liberal changes."[42] Few could disagree with that proposition,

40 HHSA, PA IX, 95, Paris, 11 January 1870, Metternich to Beust. Waldersee, vol. 1, p. 56.
41 McMillan, pp. 128–34. Wetzel, pp. 27–9.
42 HHSA, PA IX, 95, Paris, 24 April 1870, Metternich to Beust. IB, Karton 15, BM 1869, Paris, 8 Aug. 1869, Agent Bergeron to Metternich.

and the plebisicite passed with 7.3 million "yes" votes against 1.5 million *nons*. In his postplebiscite *discours*, the emperor showed his teeth: France was embarked on a "progressive march" into the future; "dissidents [would] be *forced* to respect the national will." And yet for all of its apparent success, the plebiscite had revealed deep wells of discontent: 1.5 million had voted "no;" 2 million had abstained. The French army, given the vote for the first time to pad the emperor's majority, had disappointed: 20 percent of the troops had voted "no." Twenty-five of the emperor's own palace guards had voted "no." Reporting these results to Berlin, the Prussian military attaché in Paris confided that they had "ruined" the plebiscite for the emperor, and confirmed him in the view that the best way to "distract the army" from demoralizing political questions was to use it in battle.[43]

The relevance of these French internal convulsions to the Franco-Prussian War should be clear. By early 1870, Napoleon III had come to view war with the Prussians as a possible way out of his domestic-political embarrassments. In the first place, war with Prussia was the *only* issue on which all parties in France might agree. In March, Prince Richard Metternich, the Austrian ambassador in Paris and a close personal friend of the Bonapartes, noted this probability in a letter to his foreign minister. "All three parties – republicans (Gambetta), absolutists (Rouher), and moderates (Thiers) – now accept war as an all but accomplished fact."[44] Republicans and moderates wanted to punish Bismarck, who seemed determined to humiliate France. French "absolutists," worried by the pace of liberalization under Ollivier, thought a victory over Prussia would strengthen the monarchy and facilitate a restoration of the authoritarian institutions of the 1850s. They had already tensioned the cable for a backlash in the plebiscite; one of the "liberal changes" French voters had unwittingly endorsed was a Senate decree making the plebiscitary emperor, not the legislative body, the "true bearer of political responsibility" in France.[45]

Jean Persigny, one of the authors of that decree, told an Austrian agent in February 1870 that a second *coup d'état* was definitely in the cards. French politics were utterly gridlocked. Violent rallies, calls for female suffrage, and attacks in the press had forced Ollivier to ban public meetings as well as several opposition newspapers, just weeks after freeing them from government control. The emperor did not dare dissolve parliament and call new elections, his customary tactic, for fear that this time elections would backfire and "strengthen the agitators." Ollivier did not dare hold a confidence vote because he would almost certainly lose it.[46] Rumors of a military coup to

---

43 Waldersee, vol. 1, p. 68.
44 HHSA, PA IX, 96, Paris, 20 March 1870, Metternich to Beust.
45 Gall, vol. 1, p. 353.
46 HHSA, IB, Karton 18, BM 1870, 38, Paris 4 and 18 Feb. 1870, "Vertrauerliches Schreiben des Eduard Simon über französisches Zustände."

break the deadlock were confirmed by an Austrian agent in the Tuileries in February 1870: Napoleon III – "cold, plastic, imperturbable" – was merely awaiting the right moment to "shift from the defensive to the offensive." He would dump Ollivier and clamp down; the justification would be the same as in 1851: "Popular sovereignty" would survive through the plebiscites. The "quarrelsome" legislative body would be shut until "social peace" had been restored. But what would be the "right moment" for such a daring act? Clearly there would be no better occasion than a military victory over Prussia. War with Prussia was the one cause shared by all of the French; indeed Major Alfred von Waldersee, the Prussian military attaché in Paris in 1870, marveled at the obsession. In March, Waldersee reported that "Sadova features in every parliamentary speech."[47] Right, left, and center, peasant and bourgeois, man and woman, they all wanted a war with Prussia; people called it a *guerre faite*, an "inevitable war." *This* was the exit Napoleon III had been seeking; victory in a "revenge war" might vindicate the emperor's semi-absolutism and silence his republican opposition in a storm of national pride.[48]

Grim as the French situation was, Germany's internal affairs were little better. Wrangles with the Prussian legislature and the various German governments absorbed most of Bismarck's energy in 1869–70. By year's end, the fifty-four-year-old chancellor was played out, retreating frequently to his Pomeranian estate for long leaves. "Trees mean more to me than humans," he muttered in frustration.[49] Prussian conservatives blocked his efforts to subject Prussia – the heart of the North German Confederation – to new German laws and taxes. While Prussian liberals tried to reduce the size of the army, the Prussian army tried to exceed its budget; everywhere Bismarck, in his new role of *Bundeskanzler*, federal chancellor, stood in the middle, appeasing, vetoing, and fretting.[50] A new force, socialism, bloomed in the factory towns, where working-class organizers railed against the monarchy and the "wars of annexation."[51] Rows over taxes split the member states of the North German Confederation. Hessia-Darmstadt went so far as to make inquires in Paris as to the possibility of French military protection against Prussia.[52] Meanwhile, south German politicians continued to put distance between themselves and Berlin. To the Bavarians, the Prussians were hardly Germans at all; they were a queer tribe of eastern martinets. *Lieber französisch als preussisch* – "better French than Prussian" – was a fairly common south German electoral slogan at the time.

47 Waldersee, vol. 1, pp. 57–8.
48 HHSA, PA IX, 96, Paris, 29 Jan. 1870, Metternich to Beust. IB, Karton 15, BM 1869, Paris, 8 Aug. 1869, Agent Bergeron to Metternich.
49 Fritz Stern, *Gold and Iron*, New York, 1977, p. 101.
50 SKA, MBV, 4474, Berlin, 27 July 1867, Col. Brandenstein to General Fabrice.
51 Friedrich Freudenthal, *Von Stade bis Gravelotte*, Bremen, 1898, p. 53.
52 HHSA, IB, Karton 5, BM 1868, Berlin, 24 April 1868, Agent-Bericht. PRO, FO 425, 96, 258, Darmstadt, 22 July 1870, Morier to Granville.

In February 1870, Bavarian elections ousted the pro-Prussian government that had served (with the aid of covert Prussian pay-offs and subsidies) since 1867 and returned the devoutly Catholic, pro-independence, pro-French "Patriot Party" to power. For Berlin, maneuvering to complete German unification, searching, in Bismarck's phrase, "after the talisman that will produce German unity in a trice," the change of line in Munich was a disastrous development. The Wittelsbachs of Bavaria, Europe's most ancient dynasty, suddenly looked more distant than ever.[53] The situation was further muddied by the restless activity of "national liberals" all over Germany; these erstwhile opponents of Bismarck, who had rallied to him after 1866 because of his progress on the national question, rejected the chancellor's "cautious haste" formula for unification (*Eile mit Weile*), demanding immediate German union instead, a jarring step that would have broken the tenuous links forged between Prussia and the south German princes since Königgrätz.[54]

Overall, Bismarck's predicament in 1870 was nearly as grave as Louis-Napoleon's. To deceive the French and mollify the smaller German states, he had lumbered himself with three parliaments after 1866: the Prussian *Landtag*, the North German *Reichstag*, and the German *Zollparlament*. Each had its checks and balances, making it increasingly difficult for Bismarck to force his Great Prussian program on the smaller German states. As for the German people, they were bewildered by the overlapping parliaments and bored by the continual elections and by-elections. Although the fire of national feeling still flickered – fanned by Italy's successful unification in the 1860s – Britain's consul in Danzig observed discouragement and "stagnation" in Germany, and worried that Bismarck might try to shake things up through a war with "Louis," the derisive German nickname for Napoleon III.[55] In Paris, an increasingly anxious "Louis" found rare solace in Bismarck's troubles. In a meeting at St. Cloud in 1869, he told his impatient generals: "France has money and soldiers. Prussia will shortly have neither the one nor the other. Remain calm; everything comes to those who wait." Apprised that Prussian liberals were advocating European disarmament, Louis-Napoleon scoffed at the idea: "France will not disarm; she is fully armed; her arsenals are full, her reserves trained." In February 1869, Marshal Adolphe Niel advised the emperor's Council of Ministers that "war with Prussia is inevitable and imminent. We are armed as never before."[56] Napoleon III wanted a war to put his government back on course, but so did Bismarck. Confronted with so many

53 Wetzel, pp. 66–7, 70–1.
54 Anon., *Deutschland um Neujahr 1870*, Berlin, 1870, pp. 11–19. G. von Bismarck, *Kriegserlebnisse 1866 und 1870-71*, Dessau, 1907, pp. 4, 75–6.
55 PRO, FO 64, 651, Danzig, 21 Dec. 1868, W. White to E. Hammond.
56 "Stand der Rüstungen in Frankreich," *ÖMZ* 3 (1869), p. 92. "Le Désarmement de la France," *ÖMZ* 1 (1869), p. 379. HHSA, IB, Karton 5, BM 1868, 831, Paris 9 Sept. 1868, Agent E. IB, Karton 11, BM 1869, 75, Vienna, 14 Feb. 1869, Hoffman to Metternich.

obstacles to unification, the German chancellor viewed war as the battering ram that would put them aside.

Three successive crises in 1870 finally triggered the Franco-Prussian War that had been brewing since 1866. The first crisis concerned the *Kaiser-Titel*, the hope expressed by Bismarck and nationalists all across Germany that King Wilhelm I of Prussia would accept the title of German *Kaiser* or Emperor from the North German Confederation. The king seemed willing; opening the North German Reichstag in February 1870, Wilhelm I called for "national union" and a "common German fatherland."[57] Such words were dynamite in the ears of Napoleon III. A united Germany would tower over France. Thus, the same French emperor who had staked his career on the "national principle" and the need for a "United States of Europe" now rather embarrassingly began to make statements of Metternichian conservatism. "No more violations," Napoleon III warned Bismarck in February 1870. "If Prussia moves again, France will strike."[58]

The second Franco-Prussian crisis centered on a railway through Switzerland, which Bismarck financed in the expectation that it would anger Napoleon III. When mere Prussian involvement in the project failed to excite the French, Bismarck gave a sensational speech in which he alluded to Prussia's "strategic interest" in a railway and tunnel through Switzerland's St. Gotthard Pass. Not wanting to appear the aggressor, Bismarck was deliberately vague as to the nature of the Prussian interest, but his meaning was quickly divined in Paris. In 1866, Bismarck had allied with Italy to beat the Austrians. Now, Italy having drifted out of the French orbit because of Napoleon III's annexation of Nice and Savoy in 1860 and his stubborn defense of Papal Rome, Bismarck was hinting at the existence of a Prusso-Italian alliance aimed at France, one that would be greatly facilitated by a rail link through Switzerland. As intended, the speech ignited the French legislature where angry deputies insisted that the emperor draw the line with Bismarck.[59]

What struck an increasingly despondent Napoleon III about these crises was the lack of initiative exercised by France. Ever since the Luxembourg affair of 1867, Bismarck had confidently set the pace, concluding alliances with the south German states, convening a Reichstag and customs parliament, proffering the "Kaiser title," and driving a wedge between Italy and France, which was particularly irksome since France had fought a costly war with Austria in 1859 to help create a united Italy. Louis-Napoleon had done nothing to arrest this steady Prussian advance; by 1870, the emperor's official foreign policy – *paix au dehors*, "peace to the outside world" – seemed foolish and

57 HHSA, PA III, 101, Berlin, 12 and 14 Feb. and 28 April 1870, Wimpffen to Beust.
58 Pflanze, vol. 1, pp. 431–4. HHSA, PA IX, 96, Paris, 4 and 18 Feb. 1870, Metternich to Beust.
59 HHSA, IB, Karton 18, BM 1870, 38, Paris 10 June 1870, Eduard Simon to Beust. PA IX, 96, Paris, 18 Feb. 1870, Metternich to Beust.

self-deluding. His foreign minister, Napoleon Daru, was a dove committed to disarmament. Partly under his influence, the French army, which had put itself on a war footing in 1869, began shedding troops and equipment in 1870.[60] Clearly France needed a more forceful foreign policy; it also needed a more forceful foreign minister, a man who would put Bismarck in his place and stop the slide. In May 1870, Napoleon III thought that he had found just such a man: Duke Antoine Agénor de Gramont. Son of ancient French aristocrats of the Loire valley, who had briefly followed the autocratic Charles X into exile in 1830, Gramont had been Napoleon III's ambassador in Vienna since 1861. Critical of Daru's appeasement, he considered himself more than a match for Prussia – "*je serais Bismarck français*" – and vowed to manufacture a war from almost *any* pretext to humble Berlin and smash the treaties of 1866. Gramont's hand was strengthened by the uncritical support of Ollivier, who fully agreed that "the next rebuff [from Prussia] must mean war" – *un échec c'est la guerre.*[61] Both men also saw political gain in a patriotic war: By June 1870, Ollivier's new government was already tottering. Unable to push legislation through parliament, Ollivier had lost the confidence even of the emperor, who now considered throwing over Ollivier for Ernest Picard, an opposition liberal better liked by his colleagues. Ollivier burned with frustration. It was rumored that he "would do *anything* to remain minister."[62] The events of July 1870 would confirm the rumor.

July was always a quiet month in Europe. Armies furloughed conscripts, officers took leaves, and kings and civil servants departed for their summer holidays. July 1870 proved no exception; without a political cloud on the horizon, Bismarck left Berlin for a restorative vacation at Varzin, the 20,000-acre Pomeranian estate given to him by the Prussian parliament after Königgrätz. In Paris, Napoleon III began moving his court from the Tuileries to St. Cloud, where the summer heat was less oppressive. On 5 July, the same day Bismarck departed for Varzin, American ambassador Elihu Washburne left Paris to take the waters at Karlsbad. "Never did the peace of Europe seem better assured," Washburne scribbled in his diary.[63] That same morning, Prussia's ambassador, Baron Karl von Werther, made a routine stop at the Quai d'Orsay to announce his own summer leave. Werther was greeted not by an undersecretary, but by the French foreign minister himself, trembling with anger. Prussia, Gramont stormed, was guilty of "intolerable malice and recklessness" in the affair of the Spanish throne. Werther stared blankly back at Gramont. He had no idea what Gramont was talking about; this latest crisis, which the French press's

60 McMillan, p. 153. HHSA, IB, Karton 15, BM 1869, 1503, Paris, 26 Nov. 1869, Eduard Simon.
61 Wetzel, pp. 30, 33–4.
62 HHSA, IB, Karton 18, BM 1870, 38, Paris, 27 May 1870, Eduard Simon to Dept. II.
63 Washington, DC, National Archives (NA), Congressional Information Service (CIS), U.S. Serial Set, 1789, E. B. Washburne, "The Franco-German War and Insurrection of the Commune."

morning editions were calling *"l'affaire hispano-prussienne,"* had been a secret Bismarck operation. The Prussian minister president had been quietly
stoking it for months. Though Bismarck had initially ascribed the Spanish
crown question no more importance than the St. Gotthard tunnel project or
the "Kaiser title" – it was just one more thorn in Napoleon III's side – it rather
surprisingly became the trigger for the Franco-Prussian War.

The Spanish *Cortes* or parliament had been seeking a new royal house since
deposing the Bourbons in 1868. In September 1869, bidding for the support
of Prussia, a Spanish agent approached Prince Leopold von Hohenzollern-
Sigmaringen and offered him the throne. From the Spanish perspective, there
was much to commend Leopold; besides being the Prussian king's nephew, he
was a Roman Catholic married to a Portuguese infanta and descended from
an adopted daughter of Napoleon Bonaparte. In short, he seemed a versatile,
prestigious candidate. Unfortunately, neither Leopold nor the senior Hohenzollern, King Wilhelm I of Prussia, expressed much interest in the project. The
Spanish monarchy was shaky, and if Leopold were chased from the throne
as Queen Isabella had been in 1868, it would only embarrass the Prussians
and involve them in unwanted adventures. There the matter would have ended
had Bismarck not seized hold of it. Working patiently for the war with France
that might unite the German states, Bismarck saw in the unfolding Spanish
crown question another useful provocation. If he could slip Leopold on to
the Spanish throne before Napoleon III could react, the emperor would be
deeply compromised. France would be flanked by Hohenzollern monarchies
in Germany and Spain with nothing to show for it. Nor would there be
any talk of territorial compensations for France – "no points of attack," as
Bismarck put it – because Leopold would cross the Pyrenees at the invitation
of the Spanish parliament.[64]

In short, the Hohenzollern candidature was the perfect trap in which to
snare Napoleon III.[65] To spring it, Bismarck wrote Leopold's father in May
1870 and pressed him to accept the throne for his son on patriotic grounds.
Three weeks later, Leopold accepted the Spanish offer. Two weeks after that,
on 2 July, Marshal Juan Prim informed the French ambassador in Madrid of
Spain's choice. The news wended its way to the capitals and summer palaces
of Europe. No one was more surprised than the Prussian king, who was
taking a cure at the lovely Hessian spa of Bad Ems. "I owe this mess to Bismarck," Wilhelm growled when the crisis broke. "He has cooked it up like so
many others."[66] Of course this latest "mess" in a Catholic kingdom bordering

64 Howard, pp. 48–57.
65 Lawrence D. Steefel, *Bismarck, the Hohenzollern Candidacy, and the Origins of the Franco-
    German War of 1870*, Cambridge, MA, 1962, pp. 244–46.
66 Waldersee, vol. 1, p. 74.

France was far more combustible than any that had preceded it. Though most Frenchmen were dozing through a hot July, Gramont and Ollivier excitedly convened the legislative body and sounded the alarm. Bismarck and King Wilhelm had committed themselves; if they backed down now they would lose face. If they forged ahead, Gramont might have the war he had been appointed to foment.

Gramont drew much of his support from Empress Eugénie, a Spaniard by birth, who particularly resented Bismarck's meddling in Madrid. Although Napoleon III was enfeebled by a gout attack that coincided with the Spanish affair, she focused him on the Prussian threat, boasting at the peak of the crisis: "*c'est ma guerre*" – "it's my war."[67] Adolphe Thiers, who found the emperor torn "in the vacillating manner peculiar to his character," declared that the real push for war in 1870 came from Empress Eugénie, Gramont, Ollivier, and the military, "the generals in the hope of becoming marshals and the marshals because they desired to be dukes and princes." Eugénie pushed because she loathed Bismarck and Prussia, and worried that "France was losing her place among the nations, and must win it back, or die."[68] On 6 July, Gramont tightened the screw, appearing in the legislative body to read an inflammatory speech. The next day he instructed Count Vincent Benedetti, the French ambassador to Prussia, who had followed the Prussian court to Bad Ems, to insist that King Wilhelm compel his nephew Leopold to renounce the Spanish crown. Though a proud man, Wilhelm wobbled. Without Bismarck, who was still at Varzin, Wilhelm deferred to the senior foreign ministry official in his entourage, Baron von Werther, who had just come down from Paris. A softer man than Bismarck, Werther counseled peace, and even sent a special envoy to persuade Leopold's father to renounce the throne on behalf of his son, who, like everyone else in Europe, was on holiday.[69]

In Paris, Gramont and his journalists intensified their attacks on Bismarck. Major Alfred von Waldersee, the Prussian military attaché, reported "unnatural excitement" in the French capital on 9 July. Newspapers spoke of "Prussian perfidy," troops drilled in the public gardens, and staff officers galloped through the streets with urgent orders from the war ministry to the suburban forts and armories. At the Gare du Nord, where Waldersee watched the comings and goings, he met the Russian military attaché, who told him: "it is war; believe me; it is no longer avoidable."[70] For Gramont, the crisis was ripening perfectly until Leopold's father quite unexpectedly and

67 Edw. A Crane, ed., *The Memoirs of Dr. Thomas W. Evans*, 2 vols., London, 1905, vol. 1, p. 203.
68 PRO, FO 425, 97, London, 13 Sept. 1870, Granville to Lyons. Wetzel, pp. 22–3.
69 HHSA, PA III, 101, Berlin, 13 July 1870, Münch to Beust. Pflanze, vol. 1, p. 465. Wetzel, pp. 116–18.
70 Waldersee, vol. 1, pp. 75–6, 79.

inconveniently withdrew his son's candidacy on 12 July. Pressured by Wilhelm and Werther and unable to speak with his son, who was hiking in the Alps, the prince abruptly renounced. Of course the only statesman more disappointed than Gramont was Bismarck. Leopold's withdrawal, announced as Bismarck belatedly rattled along the rails from Varzin to Berlin, seemed to remove the threat of the war that the North German chancellor desperately wanted.

Luckily for Bismarck, Gramont wanted war at least as much as the German Chancellor. Given the military balance at the time, this was foolhardy, but Gramont was quite foolish. In the life-or-death crisis of 1870, he took for granted alliances that he had never bothered to conclude. Gramont assumed that Austria-Hungary and Denmark would join France in a "revenge war" against Prussia. The Austrians, he reasoned, would want to "erase the memories of 1866," and the Danes would want to retake Schleswig which they had lost to the Prussians in 1864. He assumed that the Italians would ally with France to show their gratitude for France's military support against Austria at Magenta and Solferino in 1859 (and that the Austrians would permit an Italian army to march through their territory to reach Germany). He assumed that the Russians would remain neutral in the war to prevent – or at least not facilitate – the creation of a mighty German state. Such assumptions, if brought to life by French diplomacy, would have been the basis of sturdy French alliances, but Gramont, a languid aristocrat, never nailed them down. Instead, he merely presumed that the Austrians and Danes would spontaneously join a Franco-Prussian war, that Italy would come along sooner or later, and that Russia would not budge.[71]

Wrapping himself in these comfortable delusions, Gramont rekindled the sputtering crisis on 12 July, instructing Benedetti that mere renunciation by Prince Leopold alone was no longer sufficient. King Wilhelm I would have to sign and publish a document linking himself with the renunciation and pledging that Prussia would never again offer candidates for the Spanish throne. Denied a war, Gramont sought at the very least to humiliate the Prussians. The next morning, still unaware of Gramont's machinations, King Wilhelm spotted Benedetti in the garden of his hotel and strolled over to congratulate the French ambassador on a peaceful end to the crisis. It was there on the *Brunnenpromenade*, the fateful "interview at Ems," that Benedetti conveyed Gramont's extra demands. Wilhelm was appalled. He listened in silence to the French ambassador, coldly tipped his hat, and walked away, informing his entourage to cancel an audience with Benedetti later that day. Even without Bismarck at his side, Wilhelm now understood that Napoleon III was after

71   Eberhard Kolb, *Der Weg aus dem Krieg*, Munich, 1989, pp. 58–64, 77–82.

something more than security; he sought to humble Prussia in the eyes of Europe.

By now Bismarck had reached Berlin. Downcast by the news of Leopold's withdrawal, he recovered his usual bounce when he read the telegram from Bad Ems describing Wilhelm's frosty interview with Benedetti in the *Kurgarten*. Though Bismarck, who was dining with Moltke and Roon when the telegram arrived, could have recommended war to punish the French for their rude treatment of the Prussian king, he was determined to make the French declare war on Prussia, so as to trigger the south German alliances and ensure the neutrality of the other great powers. All that was needed, he assured Roon and Moltke, was a "red rag to taunt the Gallic bull." The "Ems dispatch," written by one of Werther's foreign ministry colleagues, would have to serve. Bismarck took it up, struck out the diplomatic language, and passed the rewritten version to Moltke, who nodded approvingly: "Now the telegram has a different ring…[not] a parley, but a response to a challenge."[72] Whereas the original dispatch spoke of Wilhelm putting off the audience with Benedetti because confirmation had been received of Prince Leopold's withdrawal, Bismarck's rewritten version had the king gruffly canceling the audience without explanation.[73] No one at the table was in any doubt as to the likely impact of this bombshell on what Bismarck called "Gallic overweening and touchiness." Moltke glanced ecstatically at the ceiling, struck his breast, and said: "If I may but live to lead our armies in such a war, the devil may come afterward and fetch away my old carcass." Roon, who had worried that the throne question might be peacefully resolved, exploded with delight: "God still and will not let us perish in disgrace!" Bismarck promptly cabled this version of the Ems dispatch to the Prussian embassies abroad and the German newspapers, which splashed the rebuff over their front pages before news of it even reached Paris. This was a further breach of diplomatic protocol intended to humiliate Gramont.[74] Because the French were seeking nothing less than "satisfaction" in the increasingly abstract dispute, Bismarck's insolent wording alone would be interpreted as a *casus belli*. Still, Napoleon III would have to make the first move and play the part of the "Gallic bull." Here was another facet of Bismarck's genius: He deftly reversed the attempted French humiliation of Prussia, putting unbearable pressure on the French to attack. The British ambassador in Paris worriedly noted this in a conversation with Gramont on 12 July: "I pointed out [to Gramont] that the Prussian renunciation wholly changed the position of France. If a war took place now, all

72 Otto Prince von Bismarck, *Bismarck: the man and the statesman*, 2 vols., London, 1898, vol. 2, pp. 99–100. Wetzel, pp. 140–51.
73 Howard, pp. 53–5. Pflanze, vol. 1, pp. 466–9.
74 PRO, FO 425, 170, Paris, 14 July 1870, Lyons to Granville.

Europe would say that it was the fault of France, that France rushed in from pride and resentment."[75]

On 14 July, Napoleon III ordered the French army to call its reserves. As word of the mobilization order spread, crowds formed in the streets of Paris shouting "*à Berlin! à bas Guillaume! à bas Bismarck!*" – "On to Berlin! Down with Wilhelm! Down with Bismarck!"[76] With war fever mounting, the stage was set for a dramatic appearance by Ollivier in the legislative body. The chief minister was in high spirits; he planned to enter the silent, expectant chamber, cry "*vive l'Empereur*" in the grand style of the First Empire, and lay out the reasons for a war with Prussia. What actually transpired revealed just how far Ollivier and Gramont had drifted from sensible opinion in their rush to war. Though many Frenchmen – prodded by the official press – were letting their emotions run riot in the Spanish crisis, many others grasped that the withdrawal of Prince Leopold had concluded the affair. As Ollivier excitedly strode to the rostrum, he was outflanked by Laroche-Joubert, a republican deputy, who arrived there first, leaned his elbows on the lectern, and requested in a bored monotone that the minutes of the last legislative session be brought out and corrected: "The record," he began, "says that I said that you need 2,500 mules to pull 1,000 tons; in fact, I said 500 tons, with 2,500 mules, you could...."

Everyone gaped in astonishment; no one more than Ollivier, whose world-historical moment was ruined by the impertinent filibuster, which rolled on and on, Laroche speaking of roads and canal locks, angry government deputies shouting "*assez! assez!*" – "enough! enough!" At length Ollivier wrested the rostrum from the republicans. To shouts of "*vive la France! vive l'Empereur! Bravo! Bravo!*" Ollivier described King Wilhelm's gruff treatment of Benedetti and requested an immediate grant of 50 million francs ($150 million) to pay for a punitive war. Ollivier's call for war credits was feverishly acclaimed in the wash of emotion. Every man in the legislative body rose except the sixteen "irreconciliable republicans," who had fillibustered the chief minister earlier and now remained stubbornly seated around their party leader, Léon Gambetta. Before war had even been declared, cracks were opening in the French nation.

The situation was painful for Ollivier; he was a former friend and ally of the very politicians who were now defying him. He was a former adversary of the eighty diehard Bonapartists or "mamelukes" on the far right, who now rather embarrassingly rallied to Ollivier, demanding that Gambetta and the others stand and show respect for the emperor and the army. Gambetta and the sixteen remained seated, one of them shouting: "we would be the first to stand for a *national* war in defense of our homeland. We will not

75 PRO, FO 425, 738, Paris, 12 July 1870, Lyons to Granville.
76 Waldersee, vol. 1, pp. 77–80.

stand for an aggressive, *dynastic* war!" To Ollivier's chagrin, this logic quickly spread to the center benches, where moderate liberals, willing to work with the emperor if he liberalized and avoided adventures, listened carefully to the fencing between the republicans and the mamelukes. Finally old Adolphe Thiers, France's liberal doyen, rose to speak: "No one desires reparation for the events of 1866 more than me, but *this* occasion is detestably badly chosen!" Things now looked bad indeed for Ollivier. Opinion was shifting hard against the mamelukes. The Marquis de Piré – a typical reactionary plucked from a safe rural constituency – wheeled on Thiers and spat: "You are the trumpet of Anti-Patriotism and Disaster! *Allez à Koblenz!*" The last, an odd slur from a marquis, was a reference to 1792, when many aristocrats had fled revolutionary France for Koblenz and there entered Prussian service. Thiers plowed ahead, quite reasonably declaring that he *would* vote war credits if only Ollivier would show the house the diplomatic dispatches on which he proposed to base a declaration of war. Ollivier refused, citing "diplomatic conventions." He insisted that the legislative body accept his word that "Prussia had caused the war" and "made it necessary."

At this moment, Jules Favre, another leading republican, leaped to his feet. Favre compared the present crisis to Napoleon III's "Mexican adventure" of the 1860s, when the legislative body had been repeatedly assured that great expenditures and troop movements were necessary. "This is another Mexico; you tell us one thing, and we are deceived." When Ollivier, dropping his earlier scruples about "diplomatic conventions," circulated an edited summary of the dispatches to and from Bad Ems, Léon Gambetta, the republican leader, brushed it aside: "You are dissembling, hoodwinking us with extracts and allusions." Throwing "diplomatic conventions" to the wind, Ollivier then read Benedetti's actual telegrams from Ems. The effect was merely to reinforce the impression that this was a fabricated crisis. Emmanuel Arago, another republican, blasted Ollivier: "The civilized world will condemn you when this comes to light," he warned the chief minister. "Indeed if you make war on this basis it is because you want war *at any price.*" By now Ollivier was frantic; what good was he to the emperor if he could not even persuade the legislative body to support a patriotic war? Wheeling on the republicans, he made a last, rather pathetic appeal to their national pride. Explaining that Wilhelm I had deliberately, theatrically insulted Benedetti to appease the "feudal party" in Berlin – old conservatives upset by Leopold's renunciation – Ollivier asserted that such "pieces of theater" – *coups de théatre* – could not be reconciled with the dignity of France. Given the thinness of *this* pretext, his next words, which have etched themselves in history, were horribly chosen: "Yes, yes, from this day forward, my ministers and I face a great responsibility. We accept it *with a light heart.*" Those words, "with a light heart" – *avec le coeur léger* – were met with thunderous ovations from the right, shock and outrage from the left, which could not conceive of a bloody war with another great power being launched lightly or needlessly. "The blood of the nations will bleed from your light heart," a republican deputy yelled. Ollivier winced, clumsily attempted to defend his words, and then yielded the floor to the war minister: "Our cause is just, and we now confide it to the French army."[77]

77 *Journal Officiel de l'Empire Français*, 16 July 1870. Theodore Zeldin, *Emile Ollivier*, Oxford, 1963, pp. 174–80. Steefel, pp. 206–16.

2

The Armies in 1870

Marshal Edmond Leboeuf, France's war minister in 1870, would himself have winced at the task set him by Gramont and Ollivier. In 1870, the fully mobilized Prussian army would number more than a million men. Against this armed horde, the French would be lucky to amass 400,000 troops. The reason for the disparity was the differing mode of recruitment in Prussia and France. Whereas the Prussians relied on universal conscription – raking every ablebodied twenty-year-old into the army for three years, then releasing him into the reserves for four additional years and the *Landwehr* or national guard for five more – the French preferred long-service, professional soldiering, employing no reserves and recruiting fewer men but keeping them longer with a seven year hitch and bonuses for reenlistment. The two systems could not have been more different. Fifty percent of the French army in 1870 had served seven to twenty-one years on active duty.[1]

The Prussians were greenhorns by comparison. Indeed with its short, compulsory service, the Prussian army was essentially a training school for the reserves, ratcheting a relatively small peacetime strength of 300,000 up to 1.2 million with the call-up of 400,000 reservists and 500,000 *Landwehr*.[2] The chief defect of the Prussian system was its relative amateurism; the officers and NCOs were the only career soldiers in the army, which made it difficult to build an expert reserve and train new formations. The defect was all the more glaring after 1866, when the territories annexed in the aftermath of the Austro-Prussian War – Hanover, Nassau, Kassel, Schleswig-Holstein, Thuringia, Brunswick, and Mecklenburg – were assigned new "Prussian"

---

1   Vienna, Haus-Hof-und Staatsarchiv (HHSA), Politisches Archiv (PA) IX, 96, Paris, 16 August 1870, "Der Krieg zw. Preussen und seinen Bundesgenossen und Frankreich."
2   London, Public Record Office (PRO), Foreign Office (FO) 64, 703, nr. Metz, 10 October 1870, Capt. Henry Hozier to Granville.

regiments. Because they were new, none of them had time to develop full reserves, which meant that thirty Prussian regiments in 1870 would go to war with one-third of their strength untrained; thirty to fifty men per company knew little or nothing about the Prussian rifle or tactics.[3] In sum, the French and Prussian armies were opposites. Although the number of French soldiers serving with the colors in peacetime outnumbered the Prussians 400,000 to 300,000, the addition of 900,000 Prussian reserves and *Landwehr* would bury the French army under an avalanche of German troops. Everything would turn on the speed with which these formations could be mustered. Quantity would overcome quality. As a German officer assured a French colleague in 1869: "*Vous serez vainquers le matin, mais la victoire sera à nous le soir grâce à nos réserves*" – "you may win in the morning, but we will win in the evening with our reserves."[4]

Many French generals ignored the menacing overhang of Prussian manpower, consoling themselves with the thought that France's *grognards* or "old grumblers" – grizzled veterans of the Crimean, Italian, and Mexican campaigns – would perform far better than Prussia's green recruits or hastily recalled reservists. And yet there was much surprising evidence to contradict even this view for those willing to face it. In his anonymously published *L'Armée Française en 1867*, General Louis Trochu laid bare the flaws of the French system. French soldiers, who habitually reenlisted and soldiered into their fifties and sixties, were simply too old, too jaded, and too cynical. Plucked from their villages and families at a young age, the *troupiers* had become coarse and impenetrable in an all-male society. Despised by their officers and indifferently supplied even in their peacetime barracks, they had become habitual scroungers or *débrouillards*, a practice that all too often crossed the line into thievery. Jean-Baptiste Montaudon, a French officer who had seen discipline collapse in the Franco-Austrian War of 1859 when thousands of French soldiers pretended to "lose" their units to scavenge or escape the fighting, called French soldiers "vermin" and "parasites."[5] Trochu called them "whoremongers" – "*fricoteurs*" – and pleaded for stricter discipline. An astonishing number of French soldiers in the 1860s were alcoholics who eased the boredom of garrison life with hard drinking. Because troopers took a dim view of drinking alone – a practice they called "acting Swiss" – individual tippling tended always to widen into a torrent. In this respect at least, republican sneers about the "corrupting life of the barracks" seem to have been on target. Trochu asserted that French soldiers literally drank the entire day, beginning with wine (*un pauvre*

3   G. von Bismarck, *Kriegserlebnisse 1866 und 1870–71*, Dessau, 1907, p. 90.
4   Vincennes, Service Historique de l'Armée de Terre (SHAT), Lb1, "Renseignements Militaires."
5   Gen. Jean-Baptiste Montaudon, *Souvenirs Militaires*, 2 vols., Paris, 1898–1900, vol. 1, pp. 488–9.

larme – "a little teardrop"), progressing to spirits (*le café, le pousse-café*), climaxing with a gut-searing brandy (*le tord-boyaux* – "the gut-wringer"), and ending with *la consolation*, a sweet liqueur that the French soldier sipped as he lay in his bunk contemplating the next day's exertions. Far from imbuing the army with an *ésprit de corps*, the French system tended to destroy it, fresh-faced youngsters succumbing to the bad habits of their elders.[6]

The impression made by the Prussian army was altogether different. Though the French disparaged the short-service Prussian force as an "army of lawyers and oculists" – *pauvres bourgeois de 40 ans* – the Prussians were actually extraordinarily fit, well trained, and disciplined. To begin with, all Prussian males were literate and numerate; they were the product of compulsory primary schools that were not adopted in France until the 1880s. They could be shown models, drawings, and maps, and involved in complex tactical exercises. Their three years of military service were so intense and well-organized that they had only to meet four or five times a year as reservists and none at all as *Landwehr* men to refresh their skills.[7] Once conscripted, Prussians took more target practice than their peers in other armies, and practiced small-unit fighting in camp and in tutorials, where veterans described the pace and confusion of combat to green recruits.[8] Their military education continued off the parade ground. *Dienstliche Vorträge* or "service lectures" echoed through the Prussian barracks after troop exercises. Fresh from the yard or obstacle course, still sweating into their fatigues, Prussian recruits were lectured by their NCOs, big, wooden men, who woodenly drove home the virtues of discipline, obedience, and order: "*Der Soldat soll das Vaterland gegen äussere Feinde verteidigen, und die Ordnung im Innern beschützen*" – "The soldier must defend the fatherland against external enemies and also uphold domestic order."[9] Indoctrination like this took root in young minds, yielding a ferocious discipline that would serve the Prussian army well in the harsh winter campaign of 1870–71.

For all of their military experience, the French lacked this psychological strength, which General Trochu frankly admired in a lecture to the French artillery school at Metz in 1864: "The Prussian army has the best morale in Europe because the sentiments of patriotism and honor are so well-developed *even among ordinary soldiers*."[10] Trochu lamented the absence of similar sentiments in the French army. Because the troopers were assumed to be bumpkins or sots, they were continually punished. The pettifogging character of French

6 Gen. Louis Trochu, *L'Armée française en 1867*, Paris, 1870, pp. 76, 86–98. Roger L. Williams, *Napoleon III and the Stoffel Affair*, Wortland, 1993, pp. 43–4.
7 PRO, FO 64, 703, nr. Metz, 10 Oct. 1870, Capt. Henry Hozier to Granville.
8 Geoffrey Wawro, *The Austro-Prussian War*, Cambridge, UK, 1996, pp. 24–5.
9 Friedrich Freudenthal, *Von Stade bis Gravelotte: Erinnerungen eines Artilleristen*, Bremen, 1898, p. 20.
10 Trochu, *Armée française*, pp. 10, 14–15, 22.

discipline eventually bred a fearless indifference. Ordered to perform fatigues, soldiers would slouch away, muttering "let me die in peace."[11] A Prussian visitor to Metz in 1865 noted that French soldiers went through their exercises chatting casually with their friends, often falling so deep into conversation that they did not hear the commands of their officers. The Prussian officer was particularly impressed by the demonstration of a new French rifle. While an NCO displayed the weapon and described its parts, he was gradually drowned out by the burble of private conversations, at long last provoking the intervention of an officer, who stomped into the ranks and roared: "*Silence! Vous n'êtes pas à la foire!*" – "Silence! You're not in the barracks!"[12] Another Prussian observer, present at French troop exercises in Paris, noted that they began late and were frequently interrupted so that the officers could adjourn to a nearby café for refreshment.[13]

French sources were at least as skeptical. When the French army's general inspector visited the 99th Infantry Regiment at Aix-en-Provence in July 1869, he noted dirty rifles and kit, troops lolling unsupervised in the shade of their gymnastics equipment, choristers who could not sing, a fencing instructor who could not fence, and a disturbing number of NCOs either in jail or *cassé*, busted down to private for various crimes. One of them – Corporal André – had let a thief out of jail so that they could sneak into Aix together to "drink up" the stolen money. *Absence illegale* and insubordination were chronic problems in the French army. The army inspector concluded his visit to the 99th – an altogether typical regiment – with a plea that the officers find a way to "moralize" (*moraliser*) their undisciplined rowdies. About the only thing the French troops did well that day in Aix was shooting ("outstanding at all ranges"), which, incidentally, would have been regarded by the fabulously anarchical French infantryman as proof that in everything that *really* mattered, he was the best.[14] Hardened by long service and dubious role models, French troops were casual and irreverent, everything the Prussians were not. However, there was much truth and wisdom (and insight into the French mind) in the saying of Marshal Thomas Bugeaud, who had shaped the French army in the 1840s: "Our soldier always swallows the ruler lengthwise, but rarely sideways."[15] Indiscipline, in other words, was a sport, kept within reasonable bounds by the troops themselves, and converted in battle to a ruthless calm and efficiency.

11 Trochu, *Armée française*, p. 92.
12 Walter von Bremen, ed., *Denkwürdigkeiten des preussischen Generals der Infanterie Eduard von Fransecky*, Leipzig, 1901, p. 205.
13 Graf Alfred von Waldersee, *Denkwürdigkeiten*, 3 vols., Berlin, 1922, vol. 1, p. 69.
14 Munich, Bayerisches Kriegsarchiv (BKA), B 949, captured regimental diary, "99e de Ligne: Ordres du Régiment – 2. Baon." Aix, 14 July 1869, Gen. Comte de Noüe.
15 Feldmarschall von Hess, "Rescension: Trochu," *Österreichisches Militärzeitschrift* (ÖMZ) 2 (1867), pp. 415–18.

The sins of the French army would not have escaped the notice of the French war ministry, which held a lottery every year to select conscripts and then reaped handsome profits selling exemptions to frightened draftees. The fact that even poor peasant families would scrape together 2,400 francs ($7,200) to buy a son or husband out of military service suggested that something was amiss in the French army. Bourgeois conscripts fairly ran for the exits, leaving the enlisted ranks with the uneducated dregs of rural society. Like dregs in any vessel, these had an inconvenient tendency to rise to the top. Because the low pay and pensions and slow advancement of the French army attracted few officer candidates, fully two-thirds of French infantry and cavalry officers in 1870 had been promoted from the ranks. Naturally the level of education and culture was appalling; Waldersee, no snob, noted that foreign attachés recoiled from the "coarse, uneducated society" of even high-ranking French officers. French officers were also old in comparison with their Prussian equivalents; clambering through the ranks, these men had first had to make sergeant, then waited ten years to make second lieutenant, and so on. Incredibly (to a Prussian), the average age of a French lieutenant in 1870 was 37, a captain 45, and a major 47. And those were the *average* ages; in the battles of 1870, the Prussians would capture French junior officers in their fifties and sixties. These men were ten to thirty years older than their Prussian peers, physically unfit, intellectually blank, and, in the judgment of a French contemporary, all too often "apathetic and inert," having endured too many disappointments in their own lives to take much interest in those of their men.[16]

One of Napoleon III's adjutants painted an even grimmer picture: French senior officers were "torn by favoritism and rivalries," and junior officers "shut their mouths and stupefied themselves in the café;" NCOs were "jealous and critical, sentiments that they passed to their men."[17] The Prussian army was of an altogether finer caliber. Senior officers, in some cases, were as divided and disputatious as the French; but they were closely watched by Moltke, who never hesitated to sack or reassign uncooperative commanders. Junior officers were young, educated, and bolstered in wartime by "one-year volunteers," university students permitted to serve one year instead of three and mobilized in emergencies. Noncommissioned officers were career professionals; they were proud men drawn from the middle ranks of society, indifferently paid, but assured a large pension and a lucrative government sinecure upon retirement. Prussian privates were the fruit of universal conscription, healthy, educated, and easily made into soldiers.[18]

---

16 Montaudon, vol. 1, pp. 216–17, vol. 2, pp. 27–8. Waldersee, vol. 1, pp. 69–70. PRO, FO 64, 703, Versailles, 23 October 1870, Capt. Henry Hozier to Granville.
17 *Papiers et Correspondance de la Famille Impériale*, 10 vols., Paris, 1870, vol. 4, p. 119.
18 Montaudon, vol. 1, pp. 216–17, vol. 2, pp. 27–8. PRO, FO 64, 703, Versailles, 23 October 1870, Capt. Henry Hozier to Granville.

Clearly France's "old grumblers" were not all that they were cracked up to be, which made some approach to Prussian methods and troop strength after 1866 essential. To rejuvenate the French army and flush out the hard-drinking *grognards*, Marshal Adolphe Niel, the French war minister from 1867–69, stopped paying bounties to entice reenlistments. The immediate effect was unanticipated and disastrous; thousands of old veterans abruptly retired at a moment when as many as 20,000 of the 80,000 French conscripts called every year were buying their way out of military service. In theory, the army was supposed to replace these men with substitutes; in practice, the millions raised by the sale of exemptions were deposited in a fund kept secret from the legislative body, the *dotation de l'armée*, which was regularly tapped by Napoleon III to buy gifts for his cronies or settle their gambling debts.[19]

With the strength of the French army in decline and the pool of con-scribable twenty-year-olds shrinking as the French population stagnated in the 1860s, Niel desperately attempted a French equivalent of the Prussian reserves and *Landwehr*. Niel's Military Law, sent to the legislative body in 1868, extended French military service from seven to nine years (five years active duty and four in the reserve) and provided funds for the recruitment and training of 400,000 *gardes mobiles*, part-time soldiers who would be mus-tered in wartime and sent wherever needed.[20] Unfortunately, the reserve force would need several years to accumulate, and the *Garde Mobile* ran aground in the legislative body, where Napoleon III's liberal opposition stripped away most of its funding. Voting with Thiers's liberals, Gambetta's republicans slashed Niel's *Garde Mobile* down to the bare bones. A reserve army that was supposed to have conscripted all able-bodied males not taken in the annual drafts for a period of five years and trained annually for twenty consecu-tive days counted barely 90,000 men by 1870. To allay republican fears of "the corrupting life of the barracks," these men exercised just fourteen days a year, none of them consecutive, so that the men could sleep in their own beds. To assuage fears that the *Garde Mobile* might become yet another instru-ment of Napoleonic militarism, the *mobiles* were forbidden to deploy beyond their native regions, making them not *mobile* at all. With their officers cho-sen by local mayors and prefects (another sop to the politicians) and their NCOs recalled from retirement, discipline was execrable, and the *mobiles* were armed with an obsolete rifle that had been rejected by the regular army five years earlier.[21] Although Napoleon III and Leboeuf would call the *mobiles* in July 1870, they were far from ready, and would arrive too late to render

19 Waldersee, vol. 1, pp. 63–4.
20 "Zur Heeres-Reorganisierung," ÖMZ 2 (1867), pp. 131–2.
21 Geoffrey Wawro, *Warfare and Society in Europe, 1792–1914*, London, 2000, pp. 104–5. Michael Howard, *The Franco-Prussian War*, orig. 1961, London, 1981, pp. 33–5. Gen. Louis Jarras, *Souvenirs*, Paris, 1892, pp. 35–7. Montaudon, vol. 2, pp. 32–4, 52–4. *Journal Officiel de l'Empire Français*, 24 March 1870.

assistance to the 400,000 French regulars pinned under Prussia's million in eastern France.

Planning and organization were other Prussian strengths not conspicuous in the French army. General Helmuth von Moltke's great general staff in Berlin was a European phenomenon. Comprised of sixty rigorously prepared officers, the best and the brightest of the Prussian *Kriegsakademie*, the Prussian general staff was famed for the precision and accuracy of its intelligence and war-planning.[22] Moltke also greatly improved the fighting effectiveness of the Prussian army in the years after his appointment as staff chief in 1857. To facilitate mobilization, he discarded the army's extraterritorial organization, which had scattered Prussia's 330 infantry battalions across the kingdom as a police force, and put it on a territorial footing instead, with each battalion permanently garrisoned in one of ten corps districts, seventeen after 1866. To facilitate deployments, he diverted military spending from fortresses to railways and steadily brought even private railway companies under military control. In practice, this meant that state and private railways were constructed in militarily useful regions and provided with rolling stock, platforms, and sidings suitable for large troop movements. Moltke was among the first European generals to entrust his entire correspondence to the electric telegraph, cutting notification times and, in two instances, the Danish War of 1864 and the Austro-Prussian War of 1866, synchronizing the opening moves from his office in Berlin. In an age when most field commanders felt chained by the telegraph ("there is nothing worse than campaigning with a wire in your back," an Austrian general had famously complained in 1859), Moltke at once recognized the potential of the telegraph to coordinate vast "encirclement battles" or *Kesselschlachten* by multiple pincers.[23]

All of these theoretical and technical innovations combined in Prussian war-planning. Whereas the Austrians had struggled to devise a plan of campaign for their war with the Prussians in 1866, Moltke had promptly implemented one drawn up well before the war, rushing his army along three rail lines to envelop the slow-mobilizing Austrians at Königgrätz. In a postwar analysis of the Prussian victory, Austrian Field Marshal Heinrich Hess asserted that Moltke had revolutionized warfare: "Prussia has conclusively demonstrated that the strength of an armed force derives from its *readiness*. Wars now happen so quickly that what is not ready at the outset will not be made ready in time... and a ready army is twice as powerful as a half-ready one."[24] To ready Prussia for a war with France, Moltke dispatched teams of Prussian general staff officers to France in the years after 1860; travelling in mufti, they studied France's eastern forts, mapped Alsace and Lorraine,

22 Arden Bucholz, *Moltke and the German Wars 1864–1871*, New York, 2001, pp. 16–20, 51–3.
    Arden Bucholz, *Moltke, Schlieffen and Prussian War Planning*, Providence, 1991, pp. 31–57.
23 Dennis E. Showalter, *Railroads and Rifles*, Hamden, 1975, pp. 40–51.
24 Freiherr von Hess, "Frankreich und Preussen seit Sadowa," *ÖMZ* 2 (1869), pp. 150–4.

calculated the food stocks of every town and district in northeastern France, and made useful contacts. Major Alfred von Waldersee, Moltke's attaché in Paris, cultivated the pretty mistress of Napoleon III's principal aide-de-camp, who provided the Prussian general staff with much useful information on the French army.[25] Using this material in addition to studies of his own, Moltke was able to prepare a stunningly effective plan of attack against France, finding Napoleon III's weak spots and pivoting around his strongholds. By 1869, the Prussian war plan was complete: The Prussians would rush along five rail lines in three groups to "seek the enemy main force, find it and attack it."[26]

The French, alas, had nothing to compare with Prussia's military organization or general staff. Although Niel's Military Law of 1868 had ordained a shift to a Prussian-style territorial system to tighten the regular army and give the *gardes mobiles* some structure to adhere to, the transformation was only beginning in 1870. This left France with an inefficient extraterritorial system in which staffs and regiments were shunted around the country every two or three years. The war ministry deliberately practiced this *non-endivisionnement* or "non-divisioning" of the army to make it a "school of the nation" that would imbue provincial lads with a sense of patriotism by rotating them around their splendid country, from the Alps to the Atlantic, from the Loire to the Pyrenees, or, in the by no means atypical case of the 92nd Infantry Regiment in 1870, from Poitiers to Sidi-bel-Abbes.[27] This extraterritorial system, whatever its social merits, made wartime mobilizations exceedingly complex. Troops had to be returned to their depots to assemble and equip and *corps d'armée* – the skeleton of any modern army – had to be lumped together from staffs and divisions that were presumptive at best. Whereas Prussian corps existed as permanent territorial units that had only to be reinforced with local reservists in wartime, every French attempt to create a formation as large as a corps was an adventure, hence the celebrated complaint of a French brigadier in August 1870: "*Suis arrivé à Belfort; pas trouvé ma brigade; pas trouvé général de division; que dois-je faire? Sais pas où sont mes régiments.*" ("I have arrived at Belfort; can't find my brigade; can't find my divisional commander; what should I do? I don't even know where my regiments are.")[28]

Railways were another organizational tool neglected by the French general staff. Whereas Moltke's staff had a railroad section that synchronized troop movements and maintained the German railways in wartime, the French

25 PRO, FO 64, 703, nr. Metz, 10 October 1870, Capt. Henry Hozier to Granville. Waldersee, vol. 1, p. 54.
26 Gen. Julius Verdy du Vernois, *With the Royal Headquarters in 1870–71*, London, 1897, pp. 10–14. Wolfgang Foerster, *Prinz Friedrich Karl von Preussen: Denkwürdigkeiten aus seinem Leben*, 2 vols. Stuttgart, 1910, vol. 2, p. 132.
27 *Annuaire Militaire de l'Empire Français pour l'année 1869*, Paris, 1870.
28 Col. Joseph d'Andlau, *Metz: Campagne et Négociations*, Paris, 1872, p. 493.

entered the war of 1870 with a skein of public and private rail companies, all of which burdened the others with mountains of paperwork every time a load of men or material was transferred from one line to another. Marshal Niel did assemble a commission in July 1869 to militarize the French railroads and rush the critical line from Verdun to Metz to completion, but died a month later. His successor, General Edmond Leboeuf, dissolved the commission and left the Verdun-Metz line unfinished under pressure from the Ministry of Public Works.[29] Niel's efforts to infuse the French army with Moltke's studiousness also failed. In Prussia, every garrison contained a military society that met to hear lectures and discuss military innovations; in 1868–69 Niel organized *conférences régimentaires* to perform the same function; the seminars fizzled, most French officers sharing Marshal Bazaine's view that "solid footing and a good eye" (*bon pied, bon oeil*) were the only important attributes for an officer.[30]

It was significant that what half-hearted initiatives there were in France did not emanate from the general staff, which, in contrast to Moltke's *Generalstab*, was a seniority-ridden backwater. Although entrance to the French *école d'application* or staff college was as brutally competitive as any graduate school in France, officers could rest on their oars once placed in the general staff's immutable pecking order. Top graduates took the best jobs in Paris and slouched through them for life, delegating most of their functions to civilian bureaucrats in the war ministry; less fortunate officers whiled away the years in provincial garrisons or overseas, laughingly dismissed as "*casanières*" ("convalescents") by their more vigorous regimental colleagues, who rotated past them every two or three years.[31] With the brilliant example of Prussia before him, Niel tried mightily to correct the problem, insisting that staff promotions be "at the choice of the emperor" (*au choix*) rather than by seniority. Though he did finally secure the right to promote *au choix*, he was foiled by the emperor's unerring ability to promote the wrong sort of people and the dogged resistance of the French regiments, which deplored what one officer called Niel's "expansionist tendencies" and frequently refused to accept graduates of the staff college on the grounds that they were "outsiders" unversed in regimental traditions.[32]

Amid this sniping and confusion, French planning, mapping, and wargaming were utterly neglected. Indeed when France went to war with Austria in 1859 to "free Italy from the Alps to the Adriatic," the *état-major* found itself with no maps of *any* part of that vast theater. When General Louis Jarras

29 "Die Rolle der Eisenbahnen im Kriege," ÖMZ 1 (1868), pp. 198–9. Jarras, p. 19.
30 Williams, *Stoffel*, p. 25. L'Ex-Maréchal Bazaine, *Episodes de la guerre de 1870*, Madrid, 1883, p. xi.
31 Andlau, p. 472.
32 Jarras, pp. 474–5. Waldersee, vol. 1, pp. 69–70.

was assigned to the general staff in 1867 at the height of the Luxembourg crisis, he discovered that the staff's only maps of Germany were on an all but useless 1:320,000 scale, four times the scale of Prussian maps of France. Jarras's crude fix – he cut the maps into sections, photographed them, and blew them up to yield a larger scale – was stopped by Niel himself, who decided that it would be cheaper simply to provide French officers with an allowance to purchase road maps in bookshops.[33] When Marshal Achille Bazaine took command of the French III Corps at Nancy, hard by the German border, in 1868, he asked to see maps of his new district and was told that none existed. His requests to Paris for maps were never answered.[34]

In 1869, the French army's own newspaper criticized this lack of even basic competency and the tendency toward "paper-pushing" and "bureaucratic servility" in the French general staff.[35] Much of the problem stemmed from a lack of strong leadership. Moltke's powerful position did not even exist in the French army, rather the general staff was a subordinate unit of the war ministry. Niel was an intelligent, reform-minded minister, but overwhelmed by his administrative responsibilities. In 1869, Napoleon III did briefly consider converting Niel into a Prussian-style general staff chief, but then Niel died on the operating table after a bungled gallstone surgery.[36] By 1870, France still had no general staff chief, rather the emperor – the nominal commander-in-chief – communicated with the army through his chief adjutant, General Barthélemy Lebrun (whose mistress provided the Prussian embassy with much useful military intelligence), and his war minister, first Marshal Niel, then General Edmond Leboeuf. At least as worrisome as the lack of a general staff chief was the lack of war plans. At the climax of the French-instigated July crisis in 1870, the chief of the *dépôt de guerre* in Paris asked the new French war minister – General Leboeuf – which topographical maps would be needed for the coming campaign. To this, Leboeuf replied, "As the emperor still has no plan of campaign, choose whichever regions *you* judge suitable."[37] In the event, no war plan was ever devised, vastly compounding the confusion of the French mobilization.

Tactics provided a final important contrast between the French and the Prussians. In all areas – infantry, artillery, and cavalry – the two armies took different approaches that collided violently and revealingly in 1870. Infantry warfare had been fundamentally changed by the Austro-Prussian War of 1866. In that conflict, the Prussians had used breech-loading rifles to ravage

33 Jarras, pp. 1–5.
34 Bazaine, *Episodes*, p. x.
35 Col. Joseph Andlau, "Die Generalstäbe," ÖMZ 2 (1869), pp. 155–6. Montaudon, vol. 1, p. 482.
36 Williams, *Stoffel*, pp. 46–7.
37 Jarras, p. 7.

the Austrians who had less sensibly armed themselves with a muzzle-loader. Spewing fire at four or five times the rate of the Austrian rifle, the Prussian *Zündnadelgewehr* or "needle rifle" had decided every battle in 1866, crippling every Austrian attack and spreading panic through the Austrian regiments. No less important than the Prussian rifle were Prussian tactics. The Austrians had employed shock tactics by massed battalion columns in 1866. These were still the European standard enshrined in the Napoleonic Wars and reinforced in the Italian War of 1859 when the French had used massed attacks by 600-man battalions to defeat the Austrians. In 1866, the Austrians, who had experimented unsuccessfully with fire tactics in 1859, reverted to shock tactics, consigning four-fifths of every battalion to massed columns in every situation: plains, hills, villages, and even in deep woods. The tactic, which the Austrians had expected to overawe the Prussians with "moral force" and "shock," proved disastrous. Indeed every battle had followed the same dispiriting pattern: A dense column of Austrians would hurl itself with few preliminaries at a line of rapid-firing Prussian infantry, taking grievous casualties.

In 1866, the Prussians had consistently killed, wounded, or captured five Austrian soldiers for every casualty of their own: 5,000 Austrians killed, wounded, or captured at Trautenau, 5,500 at Vysokov, 6,000 at Skalice, and 44,000 at Königgrätz. "Those were slaughters, not battles," a Prussian officer observed after the war.[38] Though only about one in every 250 Prussian bullets actually struck a human being and inflicted a wound – faster loading enabled Prussian infantrymen to blaze away recklessly – 1-in-250 was apparently enough, and the ratio in no way diminished the psychological effect of the breech-loader, which few had predicted before the war.[39] With more than 200,000 intact troops after the disaster of Königgrätz, the Austrians were so demoralized by the incessant fire of the needle rifle that their officers advised an immediate armistice; Emperor Franz Joseph reluctantly agreed. This outcome stunned armies all over the world, and largely explained Napoleon III's unwillingness to intervene in the Austro-Prussian War despite the colossal Prussian gains. The French army in 1866 had been all too similar to the Austrian: It had carried a muzzle-loading rifle and had still practiced shock tactics by massed battalions. Had the French attempted to "seize the Rhine" and dictate to the Prussians after Königgrätz, they too would have been cut down in their "storm columns," a probability that Colonel Eugène Stoffel, Napoleon III's attaché in Berlin, had prefigured in every report.[40] To answer

38 Oblt. Carl Morawetz, "Rückblicke auf unsere Taktik auf dem nördlichen Kriegsschauplatz 1866," ÖMZ 3 (1867), pp. 319–24.
39 Oblt. Leopold Auspitz, "Zur Taktik des Hinterladers," ÖMZ 4 (1867), pp. 191–3. H. Sutherland Edwards, *The Germans in France*, London, 1873, pp. 35–6.
40 Williams, *Stoffel*, pp. 21–2.

the Prussian challenge, Napoleon III held his fire after Königgrätz, named Niel minister of war in 1867, and gave him the broadest possible powers for procurement and reform.

Niel's first acquisition was a new rifle that would counter the Prussian *Zündnadelgewehr*. Prodded by Napoleon III, who took a keen personal interest in the project, Antoine Chassepot and a team of French engineers rushed a breech-loading rifle into service by late 1866. France's model 1866 infantry rifle – nicknamed "Chassepot" – was a marvel and far better than the needle rifle, which had been introduced by the Prussian firm, Dreyse, twenty-five years earlier and was long in the tooth by the 1860s. With an effective range of 1,000 yards and a maximum range of 1,500, the Chassepot thoroughly outclassed the Dreyse, which was effective only to 400 yards and 600 yards in the most experienced hands.[41] The differences by no means ended there. The Chassepot was a lighter, handier rifle that could fire eight to fifteen rounds a minute. The needle rifle, loaded with a clunky bolt action, could manage just four or five rounds a minute, a rate of fire that had been miraculous in 1866 but was already obsolete. Chassepot bullets were another advantage; finely milled and jacketed in linen not paper, they were smaller and more powerfully charged than the needle rifle's, which gave them far more penetrative power. Just how penetrative was ghoulishly demonstrated by an army surgeon in Strasbourg in 1868: The good doctor propped up the corpse of a middle-aged man and had a local infantryman fire into the body five times from various ranges. The impact was terrific, even to a medic accustomed to war wounds; there were "bones smashed out of all proportion to the size of the bullet," veins and arteries crushed, and muscles torn away. Most frightening of all was the disparity between the entry and exit wounds; one was the size of the bullet itself and the other was seven to thirteen times greater. A search for the bullets after the test found none; they had all bored through the corpse, through two mattresses, and deep into the wall of the firing range. *This* rifle had stopping power that was far greater than the needle rifle, which lost much of its thrust through the leaky breech, and often inflicted only light wounds that sometimes allowed casualties to get back on their feet and continue fighting.[42]

The smaller caliber of the Chassepot bullet (11 mm versus 14 mm) enabled French infantrymen to carry more of them. With 105 rounds in their pouches, French infantrymen would be far more effective than the Prussians who could fit no more than 70 rounds in their haversacks. French riflemen would also be unaffected by the plume of sparks and grease that burst from the breech of the Dreyse each time it was fired. The Chassepot breech was sealed with a rubber ring, which was a novel safety feature imported from France's new rubber

---

41 "Zur Heeres-Reorganisierung," ÖMZ 2 (1867), pp. 131–2. Showalter, pp. 77–84.
42 "Wirkungen der Chassepot-Projectile," ÖMZ 1 (1868).

plantations in Indochina. When all of the differences were considered, one better understands the almost erotic admiration German soldiers had for the Chassepot. Holding one for the first time in August 1870, a Bavarian lieutenant called it "a gorgeously worked murder weapon, a dainty little thing."[43]

To augment the fast, long-range fire of the Chassepot, the French introduced another infantry weapon in the 1860s, the Montigny *mitrailleuse*; it was the world's first machinegun. Like the American Gatling gun against which the *mitrailleuse* competed for foreign sales, the *mitrailleuse* was a "revolver cannon," a bundle of thirty-seven gun tubes, each successively detonated by a hand crank. Once the last tube had fired, the gun crew ejected the spent cartridges, slid a box of reloads into the breech, and resumed cranking. In trained hands, the "coffee grinder" (as French troops affectionately called the *mitrailleuse*) could rattle off four or five thirty-seven-round magazines every sixty seconds, which amounted to 100–200 rounds per minute, a blistering rate of fire for the 1860s. Prussian observers, who quailed at the chatter of the *mitrailleuse*, had a different name for the gun; they called it the *Höllenmaschine*, the "hell machine," but shrewdly noted its vulnerabilities. Though an errant *mitrailleuse* ball had notoriously killed a French peasant at 3,000 yards during tests, the maximum range of the gun was generally taken to be 1,200 yards.[44] Hence the four-man crews that served the guns had to be deployed well forward, where, without gun shields or other cover, they were constantly exposed to enemy shell and rifle fire and easily overrun.[45]

What the French needed to do after 1866 was wed the Chassepot and the somewhat over-hyped *mitrailleuse* to new tactics that would fully exploit their features, and this they attempted to do with a seriousness that was lacking in some of their other areas of military administration. Between 1866 and 1870, the French army discarded the shock tactics they had used in 1859 and moved in an altogether new direction. To grasp the reasons for France's defeat in the Franco-Prussian War, it is important to recognize the key differences between French and Prussian tactics as they evolved after 1866. Though impressed by the agility of the Prussians in 1866, the French perceived weakness in the Prussian system. In particular, they criticized the "tendency toward fragmentation" in Prussian tactics, the heretical willingness "to break connections between lines and columns on the battlefield to deliver *partial* attacks." In other words, the French criticized the very quality that had done so much to bewilder, panic, and entrap the Austrians in 1866: the sliding, successive onslaught of twenty-man Prussian platoons, arriving at the

43 BKA, HS 856, "Mein Tagebuch," Wissembourg, 5 August 1870, Landwehr-Lt. Josef Krumper.
44 SHAT, Lb1, *L'independence Belge*, 27 July 1870.
45 Ob-lt. Musil, "Über die Mitrailleuse und den Einfluss der verbesserten Feuerwaffen auf das Heerwesen," ÖMZ 9 (1868), p. 98.

run – seemingly haphazardly – from all directions. In a study of Prussian tactics published in 1868, a French staff officer concluded that Prussia's small-unit tactics enhanced firepower for a moment, but left the Prussian army sprawled awkwardly across the battlefield. A better adversary than the Austrians would have employed massed reserves to counter-attack the small, scattered Prussian units and crush them in detail. This French tactician compared Prussian tactics in 1866 to the tactics adopted by the French Republic in 1792 – "uncontrolled, small columns, converging from all points of the compass" – and predicted that Moltke would be compelled to take his army in hand after 1866 just as Napoleon I had been forced to modify French tactics after 1800.[46]

In fact, Moltke would change little. What the French failed to notice was that Prussian *Auftragstaktik* – "mission tactics" – permitted orderly decentralization, for Prussian troop commanders, fully briefed on the aims of the battle before them, were only *apparently* isolated from one another. In fact, they were operating together, struggling toward a common objective, and were widely spaced only to maximize the fire from their artillery and rifles. The French, with their Cartesian predilection for structure, did not grasp this fact; they saw only chaos in the Prussian tactics and devised an opposite system, one that would permit the stately, controlled development of a battle by senior officers.

French tactics after 1866 emphasized the defensive. Marshal Adolphe Niel, an engineer by training and a man inclined to the defensive in war, resolved to offset Prussia's enhanced firepower by equipping each of his brigades with 1,000 shovels and axes. Under Niel, French battalions were trained to dig three-foot shelter trenches in twenty-five minutes or less. Whereas the Prussians spread their battalions across the battlefield, the French packed theirs into narrow, prepared positions bristling with rifles, *mitrailleuses*, and cannon. According to the new, post-Königgrätz French tactics, the Prussians would be forced to attack the French trenches, where they would be mowed down by the accurate, rolling fire of entire battalions with their artillery. Whereas the Prussians were permitted to fire at will once they came within range of the enemy, French infantrymen were forbidden to fire more than five cartridges at a time. Accuracy was then verified by an officer, who would also give the order to resume fire. It was a disappointingly bureaucratic system given the Chassepot's superior rate of fire, but was intended to conserve ammunition for the French specialty: the *"feu de bataillon."*

Entrenched or lying behind their backpacks, the French infantry placidly awaited the approach of an enemy column and then, at a signal from their officers, opened fire, not at once, but successively. Fire flared on the left wing and rolled like thunder to the right, devastating the ground in front. Careful

46   Col. Ferri-Pisani, "Urteile über den preussischen Feldzug 1866," ÖMZ 9 (1868), pp. 188–9.

observers noted the low priority assigned skirmishers in the new French tactic. Whereas the Prussians routinely pushed eighty skirmishers far in advance of an attacking battalion to make contact with the enemy, throw him off balance, and find his flanks, the French kept skirmishers back with the main body of infantry to exploit the long range of the Chassepot and intensify the *feu de bataillon*. The fact that French battalions routinely detached 300 skirmishers – a veritable army – was less significant than the fact that they were kept on a short leash. This French tendency to huddle skirmishers under the main body of infantry to augment defensive fire would leave units blind and unprotected against swarming Prussian attacks.[47] When a German visitor to the Camp de Châlons asked several French officers whether the reformed army retained the ability to attack, he was told that "tactics have changed completely since 1866. We now fight in the manner of Algerian natives, that is to say, we prefer to *shoot* from a distance rather than close with the bayonet."[48] Organization had something to do with this new "Algerian" style: the smallest maneuver formation in the French army in 1870 was still the battalion. Its only method of attack was a "serried order," which was a crowded line of six companies. The Prussians maneuvered in 250-man companies, often subdividing into platoons; these were much smaller targets than France's serried battalions.[49]

To all appearances, the new French tactics were perfectly rational responses to the military events of 1866. However, they ignored the basic features of Moltke's fire tactics: the widening of the fighting front by scrambling small units and the flanking attack, which would only be facilitated by the narrow, fixed positions selected by French officers. The French ought to have studied Moltke's published analysis of Prussian fall maneuvers in 1869. Moltke's conclusion was that Prussian methods after Königgrätz would be the same as before: "The secret of our success is in our legs; victory derives from marching and maneuvering."[50] This willingness to *move* on the battlefield was a key difference between the French and Prussian armies in 1870. Although French regiments did occasionally practice tactical offensives, they did so in massed battalions. This tactic had worked against jittery, poorly armed Austrian troops in 1859, but would shatter on the battlefields of 1870, where Prussia's artillery and needle rifles would tear the shock columns to pieces, a reprise of 1866.[51] Overall, French experiments with the tactical offensive lacked conviction. An Austro-Hungarian officer sent to observe French

47 "Die taktischen Lehren des Krieges 1870–71," ÖMZ 4 (1872), pp. 18–19. Waldersee, vol. 1, pp. 67–8, 89.
48 SHAT, Lb3, Faits politiques, March 1870, "Correspondance du camp français." "Neue Taktik," ÖMZ 1 (1869), p. 380.
49 SHAT, Lb10, Besançon, 1882, Capt. Zibelin, "Etude sur la bataille de Rezonville/Mars-la-Tour: Travail d'hiver."
50 Capt. Ernst Schmedes, "Die Taktik der Preussen," ÖMZ 12 (1871), pp. 194–6.
51 Anon., "Die neue Feuertaktik der französischen Armee," ÖMZ 3 (1867).

maneuvers in 1869 watched incredulously as the opposing forces settled into fixed positions and refused to attack: "So *this* is how the French maneuver – both sides march to prepared positions and settle in without maneuvering against each other, without using terrain, without shortening and lengthening their fronts."[52]

To avoid this French tendency and restore mobility to the battlefield, the Prussians fine-tuned their successful tactics in 1868, thinning the center of their battalion columns, throwing more skirmishers out front to cover the advance, strengthening the flanks, augmenting the reserves, and resolving never to attack in formations larger than the 250-man company. Prussian battalions practiced the rash transition from march columns to company columns – the standard mode of attack – over and over. Nothing was overlooked to accelerate the process and increase pressure on the enemy. When it was discovered that it took time to separate and reorganize the platoons of various companies during the transition, it was decided to form improvised companies with mismatched platoons whenever necessary. Like the Austrians in 1866, the French in 1870 would come to dread the shouted command *"rechts und links marschiert auf! Marsch! Marsch!"* It was the sound of a Prussian envelopment with platoons fanning out to the left and right to encircle a flat-footed enemy.[53] To find their way across unfamiliar terrain and cohere with the overarching battle plan, all Prussian officers were issued large-scale general staff maps. This was not as basic a precaution as it seemed. Few Austrian line officers had maps in 1866; fewer French ones had them in 1870. These changes informed and articulated the already flexible Prussian battalion as never before, making it, in the words of a French officer, "an intricate machine of small moving parts" that could stream together or divide according to circumstances.[54]

Although wisely conceived, Prussia's infantry tactics were still vulnerable to the law of ballistics, namely that the Chassepot could hit targets at 1,200 yards twice the range of the needle rifle. This "Chassepot gap" meant that every Prussian attempt to encircle the French might conceivably be beaten back before it could come into range. King Wilhelm I was especially susceptible to this pessimistic view; indeed when Moltke's deputy sent Major Alfred von Waldersee to observe the French army in February 1870, he ordered Waldersee to "limit [his] praise of the Chassepot, for the king reacts badly to such reports."[55] In July 1870, *Independance Belge*, a respected Brussels daily, confidently predicted that the Prussian army would not dare attack in the looming war; rather it would hole up in fortifications at Trier, Mainz, and

52　Capt. Ernst Schmedes, "Französische Manöver zu Châlons," ÖMZ 2 (1869), pp. 19–20.
53　Capt. Wendelin Boeheim, "Die Elementar-Taktik der Infanterie," ÖMZ 2 (1867), pp. 241–2.
54　SHAT, Lb5, Sous-Lt. Charles Ebener, "Etude sur la bataille de Wissembourg, 4 August 1870," Longwy, 21 March 1882. Andlau, pp. 451–8. Capt. Ernst Schmedes, "Die Taktik der Preussen beim Ausbruche des Feldzuges 1870," ÖMZ 4 (1871), pp. 4–11. "Über die preussischen Herbstmanöver," ÖMZ 4 (1868).
55　Waldersee, vol. 1, pp. 50–1.

Frankfurt to avoid the Chassepot.[56] This was also the view of many nervous Prussian infantrymen, who had constantly to be reassured (fraudulently), that "the needle rifle is *not* outranged by the Chassepot."[57] Moltke and his generals were much more sanguine. Indeed the reason that they were lumbered with such a mediocre rifle in 1870 was that they had invested so heavily in the procurement of cutting-edge artillery after 1866. The Prussians now relied on breech-loading steel Krupp cannon that fired more quickly and accurately and farther than France's ten-year-old bronze guns, which had been state-of-the-art in 1859, but were already obsolete in 1870.

If properly used, Prussia's Krupp artillery would be the most effective defense against the Chassepot. In the war of 1866, Moltke acknowledged that the Prussians had used their guns exceedingly badly, trailing them in small packets behind each army corps and moving them slowly, if at all, into action. On average, the Prussians had used fewer than half of their cannon in the war, the Austrians all of theirs. This was partly the fault of the guns themselves – many of the Prussian cannon in 1866 had been obsolete smoothbores – and partly the fault of Prussia's inexperienced field commanders, many of whom had never actually experienced war in Prussia's long years of peace after 1815. The Austrian experience in 1866 had been altogether different. Indeed artillery was the single bright spot of the war for the Austrians, who had observed French practice and technology in 1859 and copied them. In the early 1860s, the Austrians had rearmed with a rifled six-pound cannon and resolved to *use* it. Grouping their guns in mobile batteries, the Austrians had pushed them to the front in every clash with the Prussians. This in effect was a reversion to Napoleonic practice, which the more cautious, bureaucratic armies of the Restoration had dispensed with. Napoleon had been famous for strewing the field with his guns – indeed he called them *bouquets* – pushing them into the line of battle to open breaches and help the infantry and cavalry through. The risk of the system was that the guns would be lost, but Napoleon trusted his marshals to fight for every one, and usually reserved a *grande batterie* of as many as 200 guns for his own personal interventions. In 1859, the French, armed with a rifle far inferior to the Austrian Lorenz, had dusted off this Napoleonic tactic and successfully used massed batteries of artillery to blast the Austrians out of their positions at Magenta and Solferino and win the war.

In 1866, the Austrians had employed identical tactics against the Prussians, massing their corps and reserve guns in one or two great batteries – 100 guns in the minor battles, 300 at Königgrätz – to fend off the needle rifle and sweep the field. The Austrians had not only used more guns than the Prussians, they had fired more shells, 118 per gun compared with a Prussian average of just 50.[58]

56 SHAT, Lb1, Faits politiques, *Independance Belge*, 27 July 1870.
57 SHAT, Lb3, Renseignements, 30 July 1870, *Journal de Bruxelles*, Correspondant de Bonn.
58 "Aus dem norddeutschen Bunde," ÖMZ 1 (1869), pp. 385–6.

This had made life difficult for the Prussian infantry, which, in sectors of the Königgrätz battlefield where well-served Austrian batteries were managing 217 shells per gun, had endured bombardments of an almost First World War intensity. Paul von Hindenburg, the future president of the Weimar Republic and a Prussian platoon leader at Königgrätz, found himself in just such a hot sector, losing his company commander, his NCOs, and half his men in a matter of minutes to Austrian shelling.[59] Unfortunately, Austria's infantry tactics were so bad and ineptly applied in 1866 that even superior guns could not rescue the situation. Still, Moltke thought hard after the war. Most of the Prussian casualties had been caused not by Austrian bayonets or small arms fire, but by shell and shrapnel. Infantry was plainly losing its grip on the modern battlefield to the increasingly accurate, rapid-firing, and longer-ranged artillery. Like the Austrians after 1859, the Prussians after 1866 noted the changes and overhauled their artillery, procuring powerful new models and tactics.

The new models, manufactured by Krupp, were relatively big caliber steel breech-loaders. While the mainstay of the French artillery was still the muzzle-loading four-pound gun, with a twelve-pounder for heavy service, the standard Prussian field gun after 1866 was a six-pounder – "six pounds" describing the weight of the projectile – their heavy gun a twenty-four-pounder. This discrepancy in firepower made a difference, but the real advantage of the Krupp guns was their superior rate of fire, range, accuracy, and ordnance. With superior rifling, breech-loading mechanisms and percussion detonated shells, the Krupp guns had three times the accuracy, twice the rate of fire, a third greater range, and many times the destructiveness of the French guns, which had to be loaded at the muzzle and charged with an unreliable time-fused shell that could burst in just two possible zones, a short one, 1,300 yards, or a long one, 2,500 yards, sparing all who found themselves in the broad gap between the zones. In a word, the French guns, though they had performed brilliantly in 1859, were thoroughly outclassed by 1870. This surprised no one in the Franco-Prussian War. France's military attaché in Berlin, Colonel Eugène Stoffel, had warned repeatedly of the superiority of the Prussian artillery after Königgrätz and, in a closely watched arms sale, the Belgian army had rejected the French *Napoléon* (the bronze four-pounder) and rearmed with the Krupp six-pounder in 1867. And yet still the French clung to their bronze tubes with the same tenacity and logic with which they would cling to the quick-firing "seventy-fives" before 1914; the gun would compensate for its weak caliber with a greater mobility.[60] That illusion would be shattered in 1870 as brutally and conclusively as it was in 1914.

In fact, the Prussian six-pounders could be swiftly moved by horse teams to execute Moltke's new artillery tactics. Evincing their usual genius for

59 Gen-Feldmarschall Paul von Hindenburg, *Aus meinem Leben*, Leipzig, 1934, p. 27.
60 Andlau, pp. 466–70.

war, the Prussians did not merely copy the French tactics of 1859 or the Austrian tactics of 1866. Though Moltke admired the devastating work of the Austrian guns in 1866, he also recognized that grand batteries like that wielded by MacMahon at Solferino or Benedek at Königgrätz would not serve the scrambling Prussian infantry particularly well. Stripped of their corps guns, Prussia's riflemen would be exceedingly vulnerable to a better-armed infantry like the French. On the other hand, a too liberal dispersal of the guns across Prussia's seventeen corps would deprive the army command of the ability to direct massive, back-breaking fire at vulnerable points, as the French had done at Solferino and the Austrians had nearly done at Königgrätz. Thus, between the wars, Moltke restlessly searched for the *"goldene Mittelstrasse"* – the "golden mean" – between the conventional dispersal of the guns and their concentration in grand batteries. Though the golden mean was only discovered in the fighting of 1870, it had begun taking shape in Prussian maneuvers of the late 1860s. In brief, the Prussians moved away from *"grossen Batterien"* ("great batteries") and inclined instead toward *"Artillerie-Massen"* ("artillery masses"). The distinction was more than semantic. "Great batteries" were static lines of guns culled from various units in the course of a battle to pulverize an attacking enemy or shatter his defenses. Their weakness was their immobility. Once they had repulsed an attack or opened a breach, they could be moved only with great difficulty and loss of time. "Artillery masses" were dynamic; they were independent batteries of guns that massed where needed, poured in gouts of fire, then limbered up and massed somewhere else, either with the same group of batteries, or with others.

If Prussia's infantry tactics seemed anarchical, this novel use of artillery seemed positively deranged and posed the risk that Prussian batteries would hare off to the wrong points leaving the infantry and cavalry exposed. *Auftragstaktik* mitigated that risk, for Prussian gunners – briefed on the action before them – would be battling toward the same objectives as the infantry. And anyway, the Prussian guns generally stayed close to the infantry, much closer than the French, who, even in peacetime maneuvers, unlimbered and opened fire at extreme ranges, exhibiting no willingness or ability to share the risks of the infantry fight. Prussian gunners unfailingly pressed in behind their infantry, to shorten ranges, improve accuracy, and necessitate fewer changes of position.[61] A French critic called the Prussian artillery of 1870 *"la charpente"* or "framework" of Moltke's army. It shaped every clash with the enemy by softening the point of attack and shooting the infantry through.[62] The great benefit of artillery masses was their mobility,

61 Capt. Ernst Schmedes, "Die Taktik der Preussen beim Ausbruche des Feldzuges 1870," ÖMZ 4 (1871), pp. 4–11, 19–21. "Über die preussischen Herbstmanöver," ÖMZ 4 (1868).
62 SHAT, Lb10, Besançon, 1882, Capt. Zibelin, "Etude sur la bataille de Rezonville/Mars-la-Tour: Travail d'hiver."

their capacity not only to move briskly and opportunistically, but to swarm around a target and subject it to desolating cross fires, what Prussian artillerymen called "*zwei-oder dreifaches Kreuzfeuer.*"[63] The Prussians did not dispense altogether with "great batteries," but clearly favored roving masses of artillery, a trend that would culminate at the battle of Sedan in September.

A final important difference between the French and Prussian armies was their use of cavalry. The war of 1866 taught clear lessons in this regard, lessons that were intelligently applied by the Prussians, largely ignored by the French. Of course it was not easy for European cavalry regiments to reform themselves in the 1860s; they were the most aristocratic units in any army, and had a social and psychological predilection for the old-fashioned tactics of the Napoleonic Wars, namely raids and scouting by the light regiments (hussars and dragoons) and massed attacks in the last phase of a battle by the heavies (cuirassiers and lancers), who would run down weary or disorganized enemy infantry and guns. Yet constant improvements in rifles and artillery had doomed these tactics as early as the 1840s, when it became a risky proposition for saber-wielding hussars to raid any enemy camp that contained a few riflemen and a suicidal one for massed squadrons of cuirassiers and lancers to charge enemy infantry and gun lines. The fate of Lord Cardigan's light brigade at Balaclava in 1854 was an illustrative example of this fact; two-thirds of the 670 hussars and lancers who charged a line of Russian guns were killed, wounded, or blown off their horses. "*C'est magnifique, mais ce n'est pas la guerre,*" was the judgment of a French general who watched the action. And still the European cavalries resisted change. Although bright reformers called for the conversion of heavy regiments into light ones – dragoons and other "mounted infantry" for scouting, skirmishing, and other "light service" – few armies heeded the call. Indeed the opposing cavalries in 1859 and 1866 were little changed from those of 1815. In both wars, heavy or "reserve" regiments comprised the bulk of the cavalry and sat uselessly behind every battlefront waiting for openings that never opened. Equipped with rifles and modern artillery, even exhausted enemy infantry and gunners were able to fend off cavalry attacks with rapid long-range fire. Königgrätz witnessed a cavalry charge every bit as futile and tragic as Cardigan's at Balaclava. As the Austrians retreated from their positions around Sadova on 3 July 1866, two of their three heavy cavalry divisions trotted forward to slow the Prussian pursuit. Although the Austrian heavies – resplendent in their gleaming breastplates and plumed helmets – were trained to form "walls" of galloping horseflesh to smash enemy lines with "shock attacks," they never even reached the Prussians at Königgrätz.

---

63 Capt. Hugo von Molnár, "Über Artillerie: Massenverwendung im Feldkriege," ÖMZ 1 (1880), pp. 288–97.

Instead they lost 30 percent of their strength to long-range artillery fire before panicking and dissolving, a dismal end to a dismal battle.[64]

The Prussian cavalry had been even less effective than the Austrian in 1866. Whereas Austria's storied light units – Polish lancers and Hungarian hussars – had performed credibly in the war, the Prussian cavalry had performed abysmally on all counts. Reserve regiments had failed to intervene in any of the big battles and the light regiments, put to flight by Austria's superior hussars, repeatedly lost touch with the Austrians, leaving Moltke always in doubt as to the route taken by his adversary. Indeed Moltke might never have caught the Austrians at Königgrätz had not a lucky patrol of Prussian *uhlans* (lancers) ambled through the Austrian picket line around Königgrätz in the twilight of 2 July, viewed the vast Austrian encampment around Sadova, and then galloped back to headquarters with the vital intelligence. Informed that the Austrians had foolishly halted with their backs to the Elbe, Moltke marched his armies through the night to trap them. On 3 July he closed the trap, or thought he had, but in the last phase of the battle, when the panic-stricken Austrian North Army dissolved, Moltke signaled urgently for his heavy cavalry to ride the Austrians into the Elbe. In vain, only 39 of Prussia's 350 cavalry squadrons appeared on the field, the rest, lost in the tangle of wagons, caissons, and ambulances behind the lines, never made it to the front.[65]

Moltke never forgave the ineffectiveness of his cavalry in 1866, "*ein nutzloser, kostspieliger Ballast für die Armee*" – "a thoroughly useless drag on the army."[66] Though it took time and some final touches in the fighting of 1870, he successfully suppressed reactionary elements and established a uniquely modern cavalry force that would prove one of Prussia's most potent weapons in the Franco-Prussian War. Bucking tradition, Moltke dissolved or lightened most of the army's cuirassier regiments (only eight remained in 1870) and, with the help of the king's powerful nephew, Prince Friedrich Karl, assigned the Prussian horse an altogether new role for the next war: "far less to deploy in great masses than to be *everywhere* at once."[67] This was an extraordinary statement that foreshadowed German tactics in World War II, the restless scouting and skirmishing that concealed German troop movements and revealed those of the enemy. The "new look" cavalry was solidly established in time for Prussian autumn maneuvers around Glogau in 1869. There the Prussian horse impressed foreign observers with their "ceaseless reconnaissance and cooperation with other arms." They rarely "sought success in independent actions, rather in support of the infantry," a significant change from

64 Wawro, *Austro-Prussian War*, pp. 268–70.
65 Wawro, *Austro-Prussian War*, p. 271.
66 Capt. Ernst Schmedes, "Die Taktik der Preussen beim Ausbruche des Feldzuges 1870," ÖMZ 3 (1871), pp. 194–6.
67 Foerster, vol. 2, pp. 139–40.

1866, when most of the Prussian cavalry had awaited saber charges that never materialized.[68]

The new role for the cavalry was elegantly stated by Colmar von der Goltz, one of Prussia's brightest reformers: "It must encircle the enemy like an elastic band; retire before him when he advances in force, but cling to him and follow him when he retires."[69] To do this, the Prussian cavalry was fundamentally reorganized; of the six regiments assigned to a Prussian army corps, only two were left in reserve for "heavy service;" four were permanently assigned to the infantry for light tasks: as scouts, advance guards, escorts, and rear guards. In practice in 1870, even the reserve regiments were pushed forward, usually combined into *ad hoc* reconnaissance divisions that spread themselves in front of advancing armies to gather intelligence, prepare requisitions, tear up or secure bridges and railways, and drive back every French attempt to reconnoiter the Prussians. These reconnaissance units exercised extraordinary initiative in 1870, another face of *Auftragstaktik*. As they fanned across thirty or forty miles of frontage, they continually subdivided, regiments throwing out squadrons, squadrons throwing out troops, troops throwing out single riders to scour the countryside. The riders themselves were self-reliant, each issued with salami, bread, and forage for three days, which freed them from the necessity of backtracking for supplies.

No less important than Prussian tactics was the improved quality of the Prussian cavalryman. Captain Henry Hozier, a British officer who rode with the Prussians in 1870, was struck by two things: the "intellectual capacity of the Prussian cavalry officer" and the drab, stripped-down efficiency of the Prussian cavalry regiment. Prussian *uhlans*, hussars, and dragoons maintained stronger peacetime squadrons than other armies so as to have sufficient numbers of well-trained, fit men and horses in wartime. In the field, Prussian cavalry troopers emphasized function over form. No time was wasted brushing or burnishing; the men practiced riding and shooting instead. Officers were required to learn French after 1866 – to facilitate an invasion of France – and trained to use maps and assess terrain. Rigorous selection boards weeded out most of the well-connected aristocrats who had traditionally taken commissions in the cavalry and promoted increasingly on the basis of energy, tactical competence, and language skills. In contrast to the munificent French cavalry, the Prussian cavalry after 1866 was remarkably plain. Men and officers alike were given horses by the state and dressed in simple tunics and overalls that enabled gentlemen of little or no means to join a cavalry regiment. In France, as in Britain or Austria, an officer would be expected to supply his

---

68 HHSA, Informationsbüro (IB), 18, 1870 #50, Vienna, 21 Feb. 1870, Beust to Metternich. Capt. Ernst Schmedes, "Die Taktik der Preussen beim Ausbruche des Feldzuges 1870," ÖMZ 3 (1871), pp. 194–6.
69 Hew Strachan, *European Armies and the Conduct of War*, London, 1983, p. 120.

Fig. 1. Prussian cavalry scout reports to a field headquarters, 1870

own horses and splendid uniforms, the price of admission to an elite cavalry regiment. Thus, Prussia's free provision of horses had another salutary, perhaps unintended effect; it made Prussian officers fearless, "whereas," as Captain Hozier put it, "an English officer who has paid 200 guineas for his horse is not."[70]

As in so many other areas, the French saw the changes in cavalry warfare, but did not adjust. France's cavalry went to war in 1870 almost exactly as it had in 1859, in massed, gaily uniformed heavy squadrons. Whereas the Prussians kept just eight regiments of cuirassiers in 1870, the French had twelve. They would have had even more had Niel not dissolved forty-two heavy squadrons as a cost-saving measure during his short tenure at the war ministry. The problem was compounded by the "heaviness" of France's supposedly "light" dragoon and lancer regiments. The lancers were more unwieldy than Prussian *uhlans*, and the French dragoons prided themselves on looking just like cuirassiers, a senseless preoccupation. One of the few changes that the French cavalry did make suggested that they were on the wrong track anyway. In 1868, they stripped the breastplates off of their cuirassiers, sold the surplus equipment to Brazil, and procured thicker, heavier armor for the reserve cavalry. Confronted with enhanced firepower, the French heavies

70   PRO, FO 64, 703, Versailles, 24 Oct. 1870, Capt. Henry Hozier.

were determined to ride right through it.[71] An Austro-Hungarian general staff officer who watched the Prussian army maneuvers at Glogau as well as the French maneuvers at Châlons in 1869 noted a remarkable difference in the two armies' use of cavalry. Whether reconnoitering or attacking, the Prussian horse moved briskly and efficiently; the French cavalry in contrast "were even sloppier and more machine-like than the infantry and artillery." They patrolled and skirmished "very badly," and even executed their specialty, massed attacks in two or more rows, in a "weak and feeble manner," and rarely accelerated beyond a trot to avoid disorganizing their regimental fronts.[72] Inadequately trained and equipped as a scouting force and all but useless as a reserve force because of the two-and-a-half-mile range of modern guns, the unreformed French cavalry would prove a tragically wasted asset in 1870.

71 "Aus dem Lager von Châlons," ÖMZ 3 (1868), p. 77.
72 Capt. Ernst Schmedes, "Französische Manöver zu Châlons," ÖMZ 2 (1869), pp. 19–20.

3

Mobilization for War

Having voted war credits on 15 July, France formally declared war on Prussia four days later. The declaration detonated explosions of patriotic feeling in Paris. The mass demonstrations before Emile Ollivier's *hôtel* on the Place Vendôme, General Jean-Baptiste Montaudon nervously watched. Having declared war in the *Corps Législatif*, Ollivier was the man of the hour; he relished the attention, periodically appear on his balcony to wave to the surging crowds. In Paris, troops were mobbed as they marched to the eastern station. Civilian bystanders pressed in on them from all sides and joined their ranks, shouldering packs and rifles, standing drinks at sidewalk cafés, and bellowing *"à Berlin! À bas les prussiens!"* Citizens thronged the Tuileries Palace day and night waiting for *their* Napoleon to ride out and take command of the army. The French provinces were at least as excited. Troops rolling to the front in railcars recalled that even remote train stations were crowded with spectators yelling encouragement, shoving flasks of wine through the windows, and enjoining the men to rout the "German blockheads" – *"têtes carrés allemands."*[1]

French expectations ran high, and for Louis-Napoleon's troops everything turned on the speed with which they could deploy to the frontiers. Although the French would *eventually* be outnumbered by the Prussians, they would have several weeks in which to strike with their long-service regulars before Prussia could collect its reserves. Whereas the Prussians brought their regiments up to strength in the permanent corps districts and then transported them to the front, the French rushed whatever they had to hand in each of their 120 regimental and battalion depots to the front and only later completed

1   Munich, Bayerisches Kriegsarchiv (BKA), HS 888, Landwehr Lieut. Joseph Dunziger, "Kriegstagebuch der Jahre 1870–71." Gen. Jean-Baptiste Montaudon, *Souvenirs Militaires*, 2 vols., Paris, 1898–1900, vol. 2, pp. 56–7.

the units with reservists and men returning from leave. Though the French approach was fraught with problems – how would reservists and men on furlough actually *reach* their units in the chaos of mobilization? – it did confer a powerful advantage on the French in the first days of the war.[2] The French also assumed that the Prussians would have to make big detachments to the North Sea and Baltic coasts (to defend against French marine landings) and Lower Silesia (to defend against an Austrian "war of revenge").

Initially, then, the odds were in France's favor. French general staff officers estimated that most of their infantry could be deployed to the theater of war within fourteen days, whereas the Prussians would need seven *weeks* to assemble their reserves and allied contingents. "Not a man has moved yet," General Leboeuf's military secretary told a British visitor on 10 July, "but the army can be concentrated on the German frontier in a fortnight."[3] Here was the French army's principal strength: its ability to improvise, to slap together large forces on short notice and ship them off to war. This so-called *système D* – "*on se débrouillera toujours*" ("one always muddles through somehow") – had been consecrated (and raised to new heights of reckless efficiency) by Napoleon III's uncle, who had habitually stolen a march on his enemies by lunging across their borders and collecting men and supplies on the move.

Just such a rolling, marauding French advance was what the Germans feared most. Passing through the Bavarian Palatinate a couple of days after the French declaration of war, a Prussian officer reported that the same worried question was on every peasant's lips: "*Ei, komme se denn endlich?*" – "hey, when will the French get here?"[4] Lieutenant Richard Ris, a Badenese guardsman, noted that his regiment deployed itself defensively behind the Rhine from 16–26 July to stop the French invasion that *everyone* assumed was imminent. Ris recalled frantic hours digging trenches and demolishing the railway bridge at Kehl to slow the French thrust.[5] German worries were groundless, for Napoleon III was not prosecuting the war with anything like the vigor of Napoleon I.

To begin with, Louis-Napoleon had no plan. During the Luxembourg affair of 1867, Marshal Niel had proposed a hasty French invasion of Prussia along the line Thionville-Luxembourg-Trier, a plan that had made perfect sense, gathering as it did French troops in an area of good rail connections and fortifications and thrusting them like a knife on to the open ground between Prussia and the south German states. Unfortunately, in the sleepy atmosphere of the Second Empire *dépot de guerre*, Niel's idea was never

2 Graf Alfred von Waldersee, *Denkwürdigkeiten*, 3 vols., Berlin, 1922, vol. 1, pp. 81, 85.
3 London, Public Record Office (PRO), Foreign Office (FO) 425, 95, Paris, 10 July 1870, Col. Claremont to Lord Lyons. Michael Howard, *The Franco-Prussian War*, orig. 1961, London, 1981, p. 47.
4 G. von Bismarck, *Kriegserlebnisse 1866 und 1870–71*, Dessau, 1907, p. 88.
5 Richard Ris, *Kriegserlebnisse*, Auerbach, 1911, pp. 11–13.

elaborated into a formal plan.[6] In 1868, General Charles Frossard, the darling of the empress and the prince imperial's tutor, had sketched a quite different plan, this one purely defensive. Three French armies, bristling with Chassepot rifles and *mitrailleuses*, would entrench at Strasbourg, Metz, and Châlons to repel a Prussian invasion. In February 1870, after a visit to Paris by Austria's Field Marshal Archduke Albrecht, a Habsburg revanchist unaware of political realities in the new state of Austria-Hungary, Napoleon III gave the Frossard plan a bizarre twist. After uncritically accepting the archduke's empty promise that Austria-Hungary would join a war against Prussia, Napoleon III, guided by General Barthélemy Lebrun, divided his army into two halves. One was placed defensively at Metz and the other was placed offensively at Strasbourg in position to "liberate" south Germany jointly with the Austro-Hungarians. Besides being militarily risky – the French army would be split by the barrier of the Vosges Mountains – the Lebrun twist was based on flawed assumptions. Archduke Albrecht, Emperor Franz Joseph's hoary old uncle and a veteran of 1866, hated the Prussians, but had little influence in the newly constitutional and liberal Habsburg Monarchy, where ethnic Hungarians, eager to mend fences with Bismarck not fight him, dominated. There would, in all likelihood, be no Austro-Hungarian invasion of Prussia or south Germany in 1870, hence the French army was needlessly cut in two.

The plans – Niel's, Frossard's, and Lebrun's – were really not plans at all. They were rough sketches that did not fill in the overarching aims and intermediate objectives urgently needed by the gathering French army. To conform with all three of the plans, Napoleon III broke his army into three pieces, the Army of the Rhine under the emperor himself at Metz, I Corps under Marshal Patrice MacMahon in Alsace, and VI Corps under Marshal François Canrobert at Châlons. The detached corps of MacMahon and Canrobert were really small armies, both with four divisions. And yet no coherent plan of campaign existed; no measures had been taken to coordinate the attacks of the Army of the Rhine and I Corps and bring VI Corps promptly into play. Even General Leboeuf, the French war minister, exhibited a baffling ignorance as to the proper use of the army. On 25 July, as the deployments ground forward, he told the British military attaché in Paris that Canrobert's corps would remain at Châlons until the threat of a Prussian invasion through Belgium had abated and only then would be pushed up to the Rhine.[7] Such considerations made no sense, because this was 1870 not 1914; the French, not the Prussians, were in the best position to strike first.

On 28 July, Napoleon III rose, smoked what would be his last cigarette on his favorite perch above the gardens of St. Cloud, and then made his way down to the imperial train, accompanied by his fourteen-year-old son and his

6   H. Sutherland Edwards, *The Germans in France*, London, 1873, p. 19.
7   PRO, FO 425, 96, #119, Paris, 25 July 1870, Col. E. S. Claremont to Lord Lyons.

quarrelsome cousin Jerôme, for the journey to Metz where he would dramatically place himself at the head of the Army of the Rhine. By now, just ten
days into the war and before the fighting had even begun, Napoleon III must
have been beginning to regret his bellicosity in the matter of Prince Leopold
Hohenzollern. The patriotic fury of the French masses had already begun
to ebb away, replaced by skepticism and the first signs of discouragement.
Parisians greeted the emperor's appointment of his wife as regent coldly. Indeed to ward off popular upheaval, Napoleon III was forced to leave 15,000
sorely needed troops behind in the capital and submit his wife's nomination
to the legislative body with the stipulation that she would neither initiate nor
amend any legislation in the emperor's absence.[8] Even the empress, as reactionary as they came, was appalled by the emperor's unseasonable choice
of garrison commandant for Paris: seventy-five-year-old Marshal Achille
Baraguay d'Hilliers, the dodderer who had destroyed Giuseppe Mazzini's
Roman Republic in 1849, connived in the *coup* of 1851, and now seemed fully
prepared to destroy Paris in case of popular risings against the war or the
emperor.[9]

Napoleon III's high command was also deeply divided. Although he had
no real military experience, Louis-Napoleon insisted on personally leading
France's principal army into battle. Critics ascribed nefarious motives to the
emperor. He needed to appear at the head of his troops to take personal credit
for any victories. The *Armée du Rhin* was his *Grande Armée*, a means of
linking himself in the public mind with his more storied uncle. He feared
Marshals Bazaine and MacMahon, who might gain too much stature from a
French victory and eclipse the Bonapartes altogether.[10] Probably all of these
musings influenced the emperor, which may explain the bizarre construction
of his headquarters staff. France's leading soldiers – Bazaine, MacMahon, and
Canrobert – were exiled to outlying corps while the emperor himself presided
at imperial headquarters with General Leboeuf, now Marshal Leboeuf, as his
major général and Generals Lebrun and Jarras as his *aides-majors-généraux*.

The hastily invented posts of "major general" and "assistant major general" hinted at the emperor's panic. Desperate to piece together a high command without involving France's most celebrated marshals, Louis-Napoleon
needed some formal means to subordinate senior officers like Bazaine and
MacMahon to relative neophytes like Leboeuf and Lebrun. The "major gen-
eralcy" accomplished this, but at a great cost. Bazaine, already angry with the
emperor for making him the scapegoat for the failed Mexican expedition of
the 1860s, was cut to the quick. Expecting an army in 1870, he received a corps

8 Washington, DC, National Archive (NA), CIS, U.S. Serial Set, 1780, Paris, 29 July 1870,
   Washburne to Fish.
9 PRO, FO 425, 96, #178, 28 July 1870, Col. E.S. Claremont to Lord Lyons.
10 Col. Joseph Andlau, *Metz: Campagne et Négociations*, Paris, 1872, p. 8.

instead, and, according to Colonel Joseph Andlau, one of Bazaine's staff officers, "complained bitterly to everyone that he had been humiliated." Even more significant, in view of subsequent developments, was Bazaine's complaint that the emperor had "ignored [the marshal's] political importance." Andlau would later acribe Bazaine's refusal to fight his way out of Metz to relieve the emperor at Sedan to the hurt feelings of July.[11]

Arriving at Metz late in the day on 28 July, Napoleon III repaired to his headquarters in the Hotel de l'Europe to discover yet more bad news: Thirty anonymous letters from soldiers in the French army accusing virtually every one of his marshals and generals of cruelty, treason, or incompetence. Leboeuf, who carried the letters to the emperor, never forgot their dispiriting contents, and recalled that many were written not by disgruntled conscripts, but by fellow French officers. After leafing through the letters, the emperor slumped in the heat of the early evening. Charles Fay, a colonel in the emperor's entourage, recalled the "stifling, crushing warmth" in the cramped dining room that had been hastily converted to army headquarters, and the curious mood of helplessness. Marshal Leboeuf, who had grandly assured the legislative body in March 1870 that he was "not just sitting with his arms crossed," but was drafting plans to "hurl forces to the [German] frontier and carry the war to the enemy before he can carry it to us," now found himself sitting with his arms crossed, awaiting a Prussian invasion.[12] The three doors to the dining room continually swung open and slammed shut; couriers dashed in, shouted their messages and dashed out, adding to the headaches and perplexity within. Outside headquarters, the corridors and lobby of the Hotel de l'Europe swarmed with journalists, tourists, and gawkers, who plucked at the emperor and his marshals whenever they stepped out for a breath of air or a cigarette. "It was under *these* conditions," Leboeuf bitterly noted, "that France embarked on the war."[13]

Later that evening, Napoleon III invited Marshal Achille Bazaine to the imperial headquarters for an informal discussion of the war. That meeting, a chilly affair, portended trouble between the emperor and his chief field commander. Sixty years old in 1870, Bazaine was the most celebrated general in France. The son of a Versailles engineer, he had flunked the entrance exam to the *Ecole Polytechnique* as a young man, enlisted in the army, and struggled through the ranks. A private at age twenty, Bazaine was a colonel by thirty-nine, a general at forty. None of this was due to nepotism, the route of many Napoleonic officers. Bazaine had earned his stars the hard way, always leading from the front. He had organized successful counter-insurgencies in

11 Andlau, *Metz*, pp. 8–9.
12 *Journal Officiel de l'Empire Français*, 24 March 1870.
13 Vincennes, Service Historique de l'Armée de Terre (SHAT), Lb 14, "Extrait de la deposition de Ml. Le Boeuf devant le conseil d'enquete."

North Africa and Mexico, had taken Fort Kinburn in the Crimean War, had commanded divisions at Sebastopol and Solferino, and had been wounded twice, first in Algeria and then in Italy. In 1863, Bazaine had been dispatched to Mexico to shore up the faltering command of Marshal Fréderic Forey. More accolades awaited him there. He replaced Forey, defeated a Mexican field army, and took Mexico City. By 1864, Bazaine was a folk hero in France, a bourgeois risen from the enlisted ranks to conquer an exotic, faraway country. He was made a Marshal of France that year and ordered to complete the "pacification" of Mexico so that Archduke Maximilian of Austria, a French client, could be seated on the throne of the "Mexican Empire."

At the peak of his fame and power, Bazaine's career began to unravel between 1864 and 1866. Although the marshal organized an effective counter-insurgency, he could never totally eradicate the roving guerrillas of Benito Juarez, whose strategy was simply to prolong the war and wait the French out. By 1866, Juarez's strategy paid off; appalled by the mounting cost of the "Mexican adventure," the French legislative body demanded that Napoleon III abandon it. He did so in December 1866, ordering Bazaine and the troops home (and leaving poor Archduke Maximilian in the lurch.) When Bazaine returned to French soil with the last troop transport in March 1867, he made an infuriating discovery. To deflect blame for Mexico from the Bonapartes, Napoleon III had blamed Bazaine (subtly, discreetly, through cabinet members and the press), an insult that the marshal never forgot or forgave. After giving Bazaine leave (and a lovely provincial *chateau* to enjoy it in), Napoleon III attempted to win back the marshal, giving him command of III Corps (Nancy) in 1868–69 and the élite Guard Corps in 1870. None of these attempts at reconciliation worked; when war broke out in July, Bazaine still burned with resentment at the way he had been treated three years earlier.

Napoleon III's rough treatment of Bazaine in July 1870 only exacerbated the situation. As Bazaine was the senior marshal at Metz, Napoleon III gave him temporary command of all units in Lorraine until the emperor's arrival on 28 July. However, the command of what amounted to nineteen divisions of infantry and cavalry was conferred with an explicit ban on "initiatives of any kind without orders from Paris." Adding insult to injury, Napoleon III dispatched Leboeuf and Lebrun to Metz on 24 July and formally subordinated Bazaine, France's most popular marshal, to Leboeuf, "*major général*" in name, but number ten on the army's seniority list of generals, far below Bazaine, who was near the top of the marshals' list. The blow to Bazaine's pride was, as an onlooker put it, "annihilating … it could scarcely have been possible to insult a man more completely."[14]

14 Gen. Charles Fay, *Journal d'un officier de l'Armée du Rhin*, Paris, 1889, pp. 37–8. Andlau, *Metz*, p. 11.

Fig. 2. Bazaine in Mexico

This, then, was Bazaine's frame of mind when he entered the Hotel de l'Europe to confer with Napoleon III, Leboeuf, and Lebrun in the warm evening hours of 28 July. Already irritated, Bazaine became more so when pressed by Lebrun, Leboeuf, and the emperor for "suggestions" for a plan of campaign against Prussia. Bazaine predictably had nothing to suggest. He had always been a "muddy boots general," not a strategist, and now saw no reason to assist the *major général* or the emperor, who had cut him after Mexico. Tired and out of sorts, Bazaine stared blankly at his interlocutors. According to General Louis Jarras, a witness to the scene, the mood was cold and stilted, not at all conducive to the urgent brainstorming that was required.[15]

The Franco-Prussian military balance in late July was exceedingly delicate. France had 150,000 troops grouped along the borders of the Prussian Rhine provinces and the Bavarian Palatinate; the Prussians had as many men packed into a rough square formed by the Saar and the Lauter in the south, the Moselle in the west, and the Rhine in the north and east. Both armies were well-served by railways, but neither would have an easy time attacking the other. A French attack across the Rhine would expose its flanks to the big Prussian garrisons at Mainz and Rastatt; the Prussians faced similar problems. If they passed the Rhine above Strasbourg, they would slam into the best part of the French army assembled around Metz. If they passed beneath Strasbourg, they would run up against the Vosges Mountains, a significant natural obstacle that might shatter their tactical unity. No wonder Napoleon III and his staff pressed Bazaine for answers; the war would unquestionably begin as a series of linked strategic movements with the Prussians trying to break into Alsace-Lorraine, and the French into the Rhineland or Franconia.[16] Someone in the French headquarters needed to mark the way forward, but no one did.

One of the more intriguing documents in the French archives is a letter from Marshal Patrice MacMahon to Leboeuf on 27 July requesting a meeting at Strasbourg or Metz "to decide whether [I Corps] will take new positions on the lower Rhine, or remain in its present position."[17] MacMahon clearly wanted to *do* something with the French army, but was ignored. More administrators than strategists, Leboeuf and Lebrun chose a purely defensive course as the least troublesome one. They would mass the Army of the Rhine in Lorraine and let the Prussians come at them. Empress Eugénie gave powerful support to this attitude. In a private meeting with the Austrian ambassador on 31 July, she confided that "France will prolong the war, convert it into a

15 "Marschall Bazaine und die Rhein-Armee von 1870," *Allgemeine Militärische Zeitung* 46 (1892), p. 363.
16 SHAT, Lb3, "Renseignements," *L'Indépendance Belge*, 31 July 1870.
17 SHAT, Lb1, Strasbourg, 27 July 1870, Marshal MacMahon to Marshal Leboeuf.

war of sieges, to give potential allies time to prepare."[18] Critics of this supine mentality, junior officers who gathered every evening in Metz's *Café Parisien* to speculate upon the great offensive they hoped was imminent, and their more senior colleagues like General Charles Frossard – who proposed a rapid invasion of the Saarland to put the Prussians on the defensive – or General Auguste Ducrot – who proposed a French seizure of Kehl and Landau to sever the Prussians from their South German allies – were rebuffed with Leboeuf's unvarying refrain: "The army needs time to constitute itself."

And yet time was the one thing that the French did not have. As Marshal Niel had always said, France could only compensate for Prussia's superior numbers by *"la promptitude des coups portés"* – "the superior speed with which blows could be delivered."[19] A hasty French attack would not only stun and disorganize the Prussians, it might induce the Austrians, Italians, and Danes to enter the war at France's side. Vienna's *Neue Freie Presse* editorialized in precisely this vein on 23 July, wondering why the French did not "seek a decisive battle before the Prussian deployment was complete." If the emperor and Leboeuf simply sat down to await a Prussian invasion of France, they would squander their only advantage in the war and discourage would-be allies.[20]

On 27 July, the eve of his departure for Metz, Napoleon III met in St. Cloud with Prince Richard Metternich, the Austro-Hungarian ambassador. At the meeting, a last-ditch attempt by the French emperor to win an Austrian alliance, Louis-Napoleon described plans for a bold French offensive into Germany. Two great armies were ready, he assured Metternich: one under Bazaine at Metz, another at Strasbourg under MacMahon. "Soon" they would converge on Mannheim and erupt into Germany, splitting Prussia from its newly annexed territories, paralyzing the southern states, and joining hands with French marines, who would shortly land on Prussia's North Sea and Baltic coasts.[21] Metternich's record of this conversation, dispatched to Vienna that evening, conforms exactly with a "secret plan" overheard by an officer in French headquarters at Metz in late July. According to the plan, allegedly disclosed only to Leboeuf, Lebrun, and MacMahon, the emperor would mass 100,000 troops at Strasbourg under MacMahon, 150,000 at Metz under his own command, and then swing briskly into Germany via Rastatt and Germersheim, cutting off the south German armies and then sweeping north into Prussia. Canrobert would rush forward from Châlons to reinforce the

18 Vienna, Haus-Hof-und Staatsarchiv (HHSA), Politisches Archiv (PA) IX, 95, Paris, 31 July 1870, Metternich to Beust.
19 Andlau, *Metz*, pp. 13–16, 30.
20 *Neue Freie Presse*, 23 July 1870. *Pall Mall Gazette*, 1 August 1870. Eberhard Kolb, *Der Weg aus dem Krieg*, Munich, 1989, pp, 73–5.
21 HHSA, PA IX, 95, Paris, 27 July 1870, Metternich to Beust.

invasion and the French navy would land marines at Kiel and Rostock.[22] Probably this was Louis-Napoleon's intention – hence his promise of a "second Jena" when he left Paris – but dreams of a glorious attack into Prussia were quickly dashed by military reality (the French simply did not have enough troops to mask Prussia's Rhine forts *and* invade Germany) and by the chaos of the French mobilization in July.

Though the first French units made it out to Alsace and Lorraine in reasonable order, the trailing battalions, squadrons, and batteries stuck fast in a jam of railway cars. Compared with Prussia, France simply did not have enough "strategic railways": double-tracked or partially double-tracked trunk lines from industrial and population centers to the Rhine. Whereas the Prussians had six such lines – three from Berlin that swept most of northern and central Germany, and three others from Hamburg, Dresden, and Munich – the French had just four: Paris-Sedan-Thionville, Paris-Metz-Forbach, Paris-Nancy-Hagenau, and Belfort-Strasbourg. A vital fifth line, Verdun-Metz, had been left unfinished, as had double-tracked connections between Thionville and Forbach and Strasbourg and Hagenau that, if built, would have linked the four French railways. Another weakness of the French system was its greater reliance on single tracks that could only handle movement in one direction. Much more of the German network was double-tracked, which meant that the Germans moved an average of fifty trains a day to the French border in 1870, the French just twelve. Because no French train could move more than a single infantry battalion, cavalry squadron, artillery battery, or supply column at a time, it took three whole weeks to assemble an army corps, a task that the better organized Prussians executed in three to seven days.[23]

The logistical difficulties of assembling a field army were at least as nettlesome. Trains had to be run into sidings to await their fellow units and supplies had to be unloaded and distributed to needy formations, which were invariably miles from the railhead. So great was the confusion – supply trucks could not be unloaded fast enough to keep the trunk lines open – that France's principal eastern line, Paris-Forbach, had to be shut down for an entire day in the third week of July to collect, count, and rearrange the disorganized loads of men, horses, guns, ambulances, bridging equipment, munitions, and foodstuffs stranded along the line. Even when rail service was restored, the flow of troops to Lorraine was disappointing. On 27 July, a British journalist at Metz reported, "You cannot conceive the difficulty of uniting even 100,000 men. If even 15,000–20,000 arrived each day it would take a week, but even that number is impossible because the cavalry need horses and the artillery

22 "Der Krieg von 1870–71," *Österreichisches Militärisches Zeitschrift* (ÖMZ) 1 (1871), pp. 239–41.
23 "Die Eisenbahnen im deutsch-französischen Kriege, 1870," ÖMZ 1 (1871), pp. 191–4. SHAT, Lb1, "Faits politiques," 25 July 1870, "Correspondance de Berlin."

need guns. Sometimes thirty wagons roll into the station and, after all the equipment has been taken off, just fifty men step down!"[24]

No wonder French divisions that were supposed to have 9,100 men by the seventh day of mobilization had just 6,500, all with Chassepots, but many without cartridges, which were sent separately. Overall, Napoleon III found himself in late July with just 40,000 men at Strasbourg, not the 100,000 expected, and scarcely 100,000 ill-equipped men at Metz, not the 150,000 regarded as a bare minimum. His reserve at Châlons was even worse off; Canrobert's VI Corps was missing two divisions and as yet had no field-ready cavalry or artillery.[25] The navy was in no position to land marine infantry, because neither the fleet nor the marines had mobilized. Much of the Mediterranean Fleet was visiting Malta, and many of France's 9,000 marines were on summer leave. Twenty-thousand additional marine troops would not be ready until late August at the earliest. Poor communication between France's principal fleets did not help matters. A mobilization order telegraphed from Brest to Oran on 16 July did not find its way to the French squadron at Mers-el-Kebir until 20 July.[26] When Colonel Edward Claremont, Britain's military attaché in Paris, visited the French naval ministry on 31 July to see how their plans for naval attacks on the German coast were shaping up, he found a "great want of direction," stemming chiefly from the emperor's loss of interest in the peripheral operation: "It bored and tired him; he did nothing, yet no one else was empowered to do anything either."[27]

As worrisome as the slow pace of the French mobilization was the rather terrifying lack of reserves. Whereas the Prussians could count on a million reservists and *Landwehr* troops to bolster their permanent front-line strength of 300,000, the French had little behind their 400,000 regulars. An appeal for volunteers in late July fell on deaf ears. In all of France, a country of 35 million, just 4,000 men heeded the call. Though Niel's army reform had created a class of reservists, they were among the first casualties of the slapdash French mobilization, invariably placed at the end of the queue or dumped in an eastern station – the name of which they were not told to preserve secrecy – with no idea where to find their divisions.[28] Though there were some *gardes mobiles*, 250 battalions on paper, they were slow to mobilize. None had rifles, mess kits, or camping equipment, and their morale was awful. Watching the *mobiles* of the Seine – mostly Parisian servants and workmen – parade through Paris

---

24 SHAT, Lb1, "Press Etrangère," *The Globe*, 27 July 1870.
25 BKA, B982, "Notizen über die französischen Armee." Waldersee, vol. 1, pp. 81, 84–5. "Der Krieg von 1870–71," ÖMZ 1 (1871), p. 241. Howard, pp. 69–70.
26 Vincennes, *Archives Centrales de la Marine* (ACM), BB4, 907, Brest, 26 July 1870, Adm. Fourichon to Naval Minister.
27 PRO, FO 27, 1807, 49, Paris, 26, 29 July and 3 August 1870, Col. Claremont to Lyons. FO 425, 96, 230, Paris, 31 July 1870, Col. Claremont to Lyons.
28 SHAT, Lb6, Paris, 6 August 1870, General Dejean to Marshal Leboeuf.

in early August, Britain's military attaché noted that they bawled "Down with the Emperor," "Ollivier, to Cayenne" and other subversive slogans the entire way. Marshal Canrobert, ordered to make soldiers of these men at the Camp de Châlons, recoiled in disgust, concluding in a letter to Leboeuf that their conduct "surpassed my worst expectations." Infected by revolutionaries, the *mobiles* "displayed no admiration for the virile qualities (*mâles qualités*) of the regular army," which had often to be summoned to contain them, and spent most of their time disobeying orders and threatening to break out of camp to march not on Berlin, but on Paris, to overthrow the Bonapartes.

The fact that Canrobert, a Marshal of France and a hero of the Crimean and Italian Wars, felt helpless to punish this bare-faced sedition, suggests the overwhelming magnitude of the problem. He could only console himself with another disbelieving letter to Leboeuf: "the cry '*á Paris*' was chanted over and over in the most ignoble way, and mixed with other seditious shouts." Overall, Canrobert judged that "good elements" in the *garde mobile* probably outnumbered the bad, but were helpless against the "radical agents"– *les méneurs* – who constantly subverted army discipline and wrung new converts from "the sluggish, uncertain, bored mass of *mobiles*."[29] Though the Parisian *mobiles* were the most worrisome, *gardes mobiles* emanating from the provinces were often no better. Typical of the reports from French prefects in July was this one from Limoges: "Upon leaving the department to serve as a nurse in the military hospital at Versailles, [twenty-five-year-old] Jean Beaufils loudly threatened to assassinate the emperor. He vowed that 'if he ever got within range of the emperor he would shoot him down like a dog.'"[30] Little wonder that most of the *mobiles* were left behind in the initial deployment or scattered among the fortress garrisons of Belfort, Thionville, Strasbourg, Verdun, Toul, and Sedan, where it was hoped that they would do less mischief than in the field.[31] All in all, Niel's *garde mobile* was not living up to expectations. An outfit created to double the front-line strength of the French army in wartime would produce scarcely two or three competent divisions in the entire course of the Franco-Prussian War.

Sadly for the French, morale problems and indiscipline were not confined to the *garde mobile*. Even as the army mobilized, the regular troops showed little enthusiasm for the task before them and required constant discipline. Troops marching east to Metz thought nothing of straggling into Luxembourg to buy tobacco, even when forbidden by their officers. This apparently common practice prompted an urgent bulletin from Gramont reminding Leboeuf

---

29 SHAT, Lb4, Camp de Châlons, 1 August 1870, Marshal Canrobert to Marshal Leboeuf. PRO, FO 27, 1809, 60, Paris, 5 August 1870, Col. Claremont to Lord Lyons. Howard, pp. 67–9, 183–4.
30 SHAT, Lb1, Paris, 30 July 1870, Minister of Interior to Minister of War.
31 SHAT, Lb4, Metz, 2 August 1870, Napoleon III to Minister of War. "*Les mobiles ont déja fait preuve d'un ésprit détestable.* They must be dispersed from Châlons."

that each plug of tobacco procured in this manner was technically a violation of Luxembourg's neutrality that might justify a Prussian march through that country into the French flank.[32] On 28 July, the *Journal de Marseille* reported that a battalion embarking that morning for Metz had left without 200 men, who had wandered off to savor "the delights of the city."[33] Virtually every French division reported that the men were refusing to wear the leather shako that the army had adopted in the 1830s; French troops "lost" the decorative hats at every opportunity, chiefly on the road and in railroad cars. Railway officials reported that every platform inhabited by a French infantry unit would be strewn with cast-off shakos after the unit had entrained and the men ignored their NCOs when they were ordered to retrieve the hats. Under pressure like this, the emperor abolished the shako on 30 July, adopting the soft kepi to preempt further "evil acts and manifestations of indiscipline."[34]

But the *troupiers* were only getting started. Once the shakos were gone, the troops began throwing away other things: spare shoes, mess kits, even rifles. In some French units, officers were dispatched to field hospitals to scavenge replacements for Chassepots discarded by their men. A colonel in Frossard's II Corps reported that many of his sullen, hungry men gobbled all of their rations and dumped out the entire contents of their backpacks during the deployment, arriving at Sarreguemines without cartridges, blankets, or the hardtack biscuit and sausage that would see them through a long march. For these violations their officers were usually punished; the men had all too obviously "lost their heads" under the influence of wine and cognac passed up to them in every village they transited.[35] When not actually marching to the front, French infantrymen protested what they called "*corvées*" – a reference to the forced labor owed pre-Revolutionary aristocrats – which usually involved the unloading and distribution of war material at train stations and supply depots. Or they wrote republican newspapers demanding better food, drink, and billets. On 28 July, Saint-Etienne's *l'Eclaireur*, a republican paper, protested the army's gastronomic crimes: "Can it be true what we are hearing: that the good soldiers of Haute-Sâone are not offered bread with their soup? That in fact they are being fed soup alone?"[36]

Other armies needed rum; the French needed bread. Indeed the records of the Army of the Rhine describe a veritable bread crisis in late July, when the emperor personally intervened to establish daily shipments of bread from

---

32 SHAT, Lb3, Paris, 31 July 1870, General Dejean to Marshal Leboeuf.
33 SHAT, Lb3, Metz, July 1870, "Renseignements."
34 SHAT, Lb1, Sarreguemines, 27 July 1870, General Failly to Marshal Leboeuf.
35 SHAT, Lb1, Armée du Rhin, Morbach, 27 July 1870, Col. Chantilly to General Doëns.
36 SHAT, Lb2, Metz, 28 July 1870, 1. Div. to 1. Brigade. Lb3, Metz, July 1870, "Renseignements." Lb3, Châlons, 31 July 1870, Intendance Militaire (VI Corps) to Marshal Leboeuf. *L'Eclaireur*, 28 July 1870.

Paris to Metz.[37] What *this* did to France's already retarded mobilization timetable can only be guessed at. Besides bread, there were chronic shortages of coffee, sugar, rice, salt, and potable water, which frequently triggered mutinous outbursts, inflamed by the wine or *eau de vie* that had to be frequently substituted for water. After settling into their cantonments at Châlons, twelve soldiers of the 100th Regiment paused to admire a statue of the prince imperial and then began methodically smashing the eagles and the crown that adorned it. Private Louis Germain shinnied up the pedestal, grasped the statue of the emperor's only son, and hurled it to the ground to wild shouts of "*à bas la famille impériale! Ollivier à Cayenne et l'Empereur avec lui!*" – "Down with the imperial family! Ollivier to Cayenne and the emperor too!"[38]

Against these startling bouts of indiscipline, Napoleon III would have relied on his élite Guard regiments, but even their vigilance was suspect. As the emperor's 1st Guard Division settled into its camps around Metz at the end of July, their general staff chief wrote a despairing note: "Large numbers of the men leave the camp after 'taps' (*l'appel du soir*) and pass the night drinking at the *cantinières* that have established themselves along the march routes."[39] As they sipped their wine late into the midnight hours, the conversation of the French infantrymen took a pessimistic turn. The Metz correspondent of a Brussels newspaper reported that French troops were convinced that they were destined for a "bloodbath on the Rhine." On 28 July, he watched the massed divisions of the Army of the Rhine as the emperor's proclamation announcing the Franco-Prussian War was read to them and noted a "lack of enthusiasm" in every quarter, only a few isolated cries of "*vive l'Empereur,*" and muttered complaints when the sergeant majors read the emperor's prediction of "a long and difficult war." "*Pourquoi?*" many of the gathered thousands grumbled. "*Quels sont les projets de l'Empereur?*" – "Whatever for? What exactly is the emperor planning?"[40] This would be one of the more corrosive characteristics of the French army in the war, the keen interest taken by enlisted men in strategic questions. Though the troops generally had no understanding of strategy, and nothing to suggest, they were always on the lookout for traps and betrayal. Any delay or misstep on the part of their officers would instantly be ascribed to treason or incompetence, either a deliberate attempt to deliver the army into Prussian hands or the natural ineptitude of feckless aristocrats. This attitude was, as one French brigadier put it in a letter to divisional command, an "incipient evil" ("*fâcheur début*")

37 SHAT, Lb1, St. Cloud, 26 July 1870, Napoleon III to General Dejean.
38 SHAT, Lb3, Camp de Châlons, 30 July 1870, Gendarmerie Impériale, 4e Legion, Arrondonisment du Camp de Châlons.
39 SHAT, Lb3, Garde Impériale, fin Juillet, Chef d'état major to 1. Division.
40 SHAT, Lb2, Metz, Quartier impérial, 28 july 1870, "Proclamation de l'Empereur à l'Armée." Lb4, "Renseignements," 2 August 1870, *L'Indépendance Belge.*

that would only widen in the weeks ahead.[41] All of this weighed crushingly on Napoleon III, whose dynasty was theoretically a *régime du sabre*, a military regime cemented in place by a loyal army. Witnesses who saw him at Metz noted his discomfort. The London *Globe* correspondent wrote on 30 July of Louis-Napoleon's "continuously sad expression." His step was "rigid and inelastic," his face "stamped with suffering." A Belgian reporter described the emperor's "peculiar mood" as a mix of apathy and despair. Napoleon III seemed so frail that when his open carriage rattled through St. Avold on a tour of inspection on 29 July, his adjutants leaned across his body to shield him from flowers thrown down from the balconies.[42]

THE PRUSSIAN MOBILIZATION

Prussia greeted the war with some of the same rapture felt in France. Adolf Matthias, a student at the University of Marburg, recalled waiting hours under a hot sun on 15 July just to catch a glimpse of seventy-three-year-old King Wilhelm I of Prussia when his train passed through from Bad Ems to Berlin. As the royal train rolled through Marburg, the crowd roared its approval: "*Krieg, wir wollen Krieg Majestät!*" – "War, we want war Your Majesty!" Later that evening, Matthias sat in Marburg's beer garden when the telegram announcing France's mobilization was read aloud from the bandstand. "Never," he wrote in his diary, "have I seen such passions as were released by those magic words, *'der Krieg ist erklärkt.'* Officers, civil servants, professors, students, merchants, we all sang *'Heil dir im Siegerkranz,' 'Die Wacht am Rhein,' 'Ich bin ein Preusse, kennt Ihr meine Farben,'* and *'Deutschland, Deutschland über alles.'* Later, when the band was exhausted, we walked over to the *Ratskeller*, where we drank some more, and beat up some English students, who said things that offended our patriotic hearts."[43]

Matthias volunteered for the army the next morning, as did tens of thousands of others. Far more Germans than French volunteered for the war, although initially the performance of volunteers, usually students, justified all of the doubts that the French had about short-service soldiers. Nineteen-year-old Matthias could not even march from his student rooms to the center of Marburg. How would he fare on the roads of France? "I'll never forget my first march with full pack, helmet, rolled coat, flask, cartridges, and rifle. I was supposed to lug all this stuff from my apartment to the *Platz* for parade, but collapsed halfway there and had to ride the rest of the way in a taxi."[44]

41 SHAT, Lb2, Metz, 28 July, 1. Div. to 1. Brigade. Where the conspiracy theories came from is best analyzed by Alain Corbin, *The Village of Cannibals*, Cambridge, MA, 1992, pp. 3–36.
42 *The Globe*, Metz, 30 July 1870. *L'Indépendance Belge*, 29 July 1870.
43 Adolf Matthias, *Meine Kriegserinnerungen*, Munich, 1912, p. 32.
44 Matthias, p. 37.

Fortunately for the Germans, national spirit often compensated for weaknesses of the flesh. A Belgian journalist in Kassel spoke of a palpable "spirit of revolution in Germany... toward national unification at any price." An English correspondent observing the concentration of Steinmetz's First Army at Trier noted "a steady Teutonic determination," and quoted Thomas Carlyle: "we have here the fire good for smelting iron – a fire difficult to kindle, but which hardly anything will put out."[45] Meanwhile, the great blacksmith, the Prussian general staff, had begun recalling reservists and putting the Landwehr on a war footing.

Prussia's gathering storm terrified French officers like Bazaine. On 20 July, the marshal anxiously telegraphed Paris: "the Prussians are putting invalids to work in their public offices and sending every able-bodied man to the front!"[46] A week later, a Parisian journalist in Prussia gasped at the sudden evaporation of "every man between the age of twenty and thirty-eight.... They are all under arms.... The countryside is deserted. Walls of wheat await the absent scythe, and there are soldiers everywhere one looks!"[47] This, of course, was the chief advantage of the Prussian system, its ability to funnel hundreds of thousands of trained civilians into the military on short notice. Though not as quick out of the gate as the French, the Prussians would deploy nearly as quickly, and, in stark contrast to the French, arrive fully equipped with overwhelming numbers.

Unlike Leboeuf, who stumbled unpreparedly into war, Moltke had been carefully planning a war with France since 1866. Prussian war plans took full advantage of Germany's superior railways: five main lines running up to the French border that would permit the Prussian army and its allied contingents to deploy on a long arc from Trier in the north to Karlsruhe in the south.[48] Because the Prusso-German armies would surpass the French in troop numbers by the fourth week of mobilization at the latest, such a deployment gave Moltke the ability to shelter behind the Rhine, Saar, and Moselle in the early days of the campaign, when the French were stronger, and then surge forward to encircle Napoleon III's army once the Prussian mobilization was complete. Unlike the French Army of the Rhine, an uncoordinated mass of twenty-two divisions, Moltke articulated the Prussian main force, cleaving it into three mobile armies. The northernmost was General Karl von Steinmetz's First Army, eight divisions of infantry and cavalry between Trier and Saarlouis. Positioned beneath Steinmetz in the vicinity of Saarbrücken was Moltke's biggest army, the Second Army under Prince Friedrich Karl, the king's nephew, who had also commanded the largest Prussian army at Königgrätz. Of the three

45 *Pall Mall Gazette*, 1 August 1870, "From the German side."
46 Edwards, p. 30.
47 SHAT, Lb2, 28 July 1870, "Presse Parisienne."
48 Howard, pp. 42–4.

Fig. 3. Bavarian infantry mobilize, July 1870

Prussian armies, the Second Army was by far the most cumbersome. It comprised seventeen divisions of infantry and cavalry, a difficult force to maneuver across river lines and fortified country. The southernmost Prussian army, more German than Prussian because it embodied all of the south German units, was the Third Army. Moltke deployed this army of twelve divisions in Baden and the Palatinate around Karlsruhe, and gave command of it to the other hero of Königgrätz, Crown Prince Friedrich Wilhelm, the Prussian king's son, who had swung his flanking army around Benedek's right wing at the climax of the battle in 1866.[49]

This three-part division of the Prussian army positioned Moltke to annihilate Napoleon III wherever he showed himself. If the French emperor concentrated near Strasbourg to invade Baden or defend the line of the Vosges, the Prussian First and Second Armies would swing southwest into his flank and rear. If Louis-Napoleon thrust into the Rhineland or remained at Metz to stand against Steinmetz and Prince Friedrich Karl, the Prussian Third Army would execute the turning maneuver, pushing through the Vosges to threaten

49   Wolfgang Foerster, *Prinz Friedrich Karl von Preussen*, 2 vols., Stuttgart, 1910, vol. 2, p. 132.

the Army of the Rhine's flank and its communications to Paris.[50] Optimal positioning was one thing, gaining the position and advancing briskly out of it was quite another. To do this, Moltke and his staff spent long hours after 1868 assigning each of Prussia's thirteen corps and all of the south German divisions specific tracks and timetables for their moves to the concentration areas. Moltke took a hands-on approach to the work, touring the concentration areas himself in April 1868 to study the ground and facilities. A French officer assigned to shadow Moltke submitted a revealing report, for the areas visited by the Prussian *chef* would be the jumping-off stations of 1870:

> "Moltke has been touring the French frontier since Monday. He first visited Mainz, then Birkenfeld, taking copious notes. Tuesday he slept at Saarbrücken, and took more notes on its heights. Yesterday and today he is at Saarlouis. This morning he rode out in a carriage to view the heights around Vaudevange and Berus. Tomorrow he is bound for Trier, where he will descend the Moselle."[51]

With all of this punctilious planning and touring, Moltke was striving to eliminate the friction and inefficiencies of 1866, when too many Prussian units served by too few railways had tried to bull their way into Bohemia at once. The result had been a jerky, unsynchronized invasion that had offered the Austrians several chances to pounce upon the isolated, poorly supplied Prussian armies as they straggled toward a junction at Königgrätz. This time, Moltke was determined to make the Prussian invasion a smooth, richly supplied extension of the mobilization itself. It would take more than just will-power. That the Prussian mobilization went smoothly in 1870 was a credit to the intelligent organization perfected by Moltke in the years since Königgrätz. Captain Celsus Girl, a Bavarian officer attached to Third Army headquarters, marvelled at the education of his Prussian colleagues. They mobilized efficiently because they had *practiced* mobilization in peacetime. "Prussian general staff officers are singularly well prepared," Girl wrote in July 1870. "They are fast because each Prussian officer on the headquarters staff has done the following exercise: he has arranged railroad transport for a strategic deployment of several army corps from their permanent posts to the concentration area; he has created march tables from scratch and assigned each individual unit transport to a number of different theaters of war."[52] The Prussians were singularly well prepared in other areas as well. They invented the "dog tag" in 1870: an oval disc worn by every soldier bearing his name, regiment, and place of residence. This would speed the identification of casualties and the notification of worried families. To knit army and nation together, they issued each soldier with

50 PRO, FO 64, 703, Versailles, 30 October 1870, Capt. Henry Hozier, "General sketch of the operations of the German armies in France in the campaign of 1870."
51 *Papiers et correspondance de la Famille Impériale*, 10 vols, Paris, 1871, vol. 8, lxi, p. 238. Forbach, 9 April 1868, Capt. Samuel to Marshal Niel.
52 BKA, HS 849, Capt. Celsus von Girl, vol. 3, p. 2.

twelve stamped postcards so that he could write to his loved ones throughout the campaign. In the French army, the field post was, by its own admission, *presque chaos* – "near chaos" – and most enlisted men did not know how to write anyway.[53]

With preparation like this, the Prussian mobilization rolled along much more rapidly than the French. This was all the more impressive because the Prussians had been surprised by the outbreak of war in July. Moltke had actually sent hundreds of his officers on leave on 12 July, and had been forced to claw the men back to their headquarters two days later.[54] Although many German wives, mothers, and children made painful scenes at the barracks and railway stations, many more accepted the war with patriotic fortitude. Twenty-year-old Karl Litzmann, a Prussian Guard lieutenant just out of school, remembered his mother handing him a letter as he boarded his transport in Berlin. It read, "I am pained by the realization that I may never again hold you in my arms, but far greater than my pain is my joy that you too can fight in this war." The last line of the note would chill anyone save perhaps a German of the nineteenth century: "*Es ist nicht nötig dass du wiederkehrst, wohl aber dass du deine Schuldigkeit tust!*" – "It is not necessary that you return from the war, only that you do your duty."[55] Johannes Priese, a private in the Prussian Death's Head Hussars, remembered his father's last words as he left Posen with his regiment in July 1870: "I must not be concerned for my own safety, rather my sole concern must be to fulfill my duty to my people and to my fatherland."[56]

Inspired by sentiments like these, the Prussian mobilization moved briskly forward. It moved less briskly in the south, where the Bavarians, unaccustomed to offensive war planning and caught in the midst of their transition from a muzzle-loading rifle to a breech-loading one, had difficulty keeping to their timetables. They were also encumbered by Prussian misgivings. Doubtful to the last whether the Roman Catholic Bavarians would actually join a Prussian war against France, Moltke refused to provide southern German officers below the rank of general with Prussia's excellent 1:80,000 *Kriegskarten* or "war maps." Indeed the satisfactory performance of the Bavarians and Württemberger in the war is all the more remarkable when one considers that most of their regimental, company, and platoon commanders were plotting their marches with *Reymann's Road Atlas of France*, whose largest scale map was 1:250,000.[57] Nevertheless, throughout Germany, battalions embodied

53 *Journal de Bruxelles*, Bonn, 30 July 1870.
54 HHSA, PA III, 101, Berlin, 14 July 1870, Maj. Welsersheim to War Minister.
55 Karl Litzmann, *Ernstes und heiteres aus den Kriegsjahren 1870–71*, Berlin, 1911, p. 7.
56 Johannes Priese, *Als Totenkopfhusar 1870–71*, Berlin, 1936, p. 15.
57 BKA, B982, Munich, 22 Oct. 1871, Maj. Gustav Fleschuez, "Erfahrungen." BKA, HS 841, "Tagebuch des Unterlt. Adam Dietz, 10. Jäger Battalion, 1870–71." BKA, HS 849, Capt. Girl, vol. 2, pp. 55–8.

their reservists, joined their regiments, and found their place on the railways assigned their corps.

Mobilizations were never simple affairs, even when painstakingly organized by Germans. Josef Krumper, a Bavarian platoon leader, recalled the movement of his company in late July from Augsburg to Germersheim, the concentration area of Crown Prince Friedrich Wilhelm's Third Army. The longest leg of the deployment was covered by rail – 150 miles from Augsburg to Bruchsal – the men "packed like sheep" in the freight wagons, the officers, mobilized civilians, sweating in the second-class carriages and squinting at their wholly inadequate maps of Alsace. At Bruchsal the men debarked at 6 A.M. and began the sixteen-mile march to Germersheim. Sun and rain flattened most of the company; by the first halt at the eight-mile mark, the load was littered with stragglers, men tormented by thirst and blisters. Whenever rain clouds threatened, whole march columns would stop, shrug off their backpacks, and don their coats, a civilian impulse trained out of the more professional French army. Attempts by Bavarian officers to forbid the coats ran up against a drunken wall of defiance; without potable water on the march, the men drank schnapps instead, further retarding their progress. It took two entire days to reassemble the unit and insert it into bivouacs on the French border. There army surgeons treated their first casualties, sunburnt, lame conscripts sick to their stomachs from the offerings of the villages through which they had marched. "In a single day," a German physician reminisced, "One of our men might consume large quantities of milk, beer, must, cider, wine, coffee, cognac, rum ... as well as grapes, apples, peaches, and cherries, most of them unripe."[58] And yet such rambling was an integral part of any deployment, particularly that of a relatively green conscript army like Prussia's. Moltke's genius was his ability to keep the marauding within bounds, and fit every wandering unit into a coherent, punctual plan of campaign.

Most of the Prussian regulars and reservists did better than the Bavarians. By 3 August, Moltke had 320,000 battle-ready troops deployed on the Franco-German border. Tens of thousands of reservists were streaming in behind them. The stage was set for the bloodiest European war of the nineteenth century, a fact that was worriedly noted by the British minister in Darmstadt on 31 July:

> "The present war is one without parallel in the history of civilized nations.... An entire people has been suddenly called from its daily avocations to take a personal part in a struggle, which promises to be the bloodiest and most deadly on record, and in comparison with which, that of 1866 was mere child's play."[59]

---

58 BKA, HS 856, Josef Krumper, "Mein Tagebuch aus den deutsch-französischen Kriege." BKA, B1145, Villeroncourt, 21 June 1871, 2. Infanterieregiment, 2. Bataillonsarzt, Dr. Emil Schulze.
59 PRO, FO 425, 95, Darmstadt, 31 July 1870, R. B. D. Morier to Granville.

4

Wissembourg and Spicheren

By the first week of August 1870, Napoleon III had come under massive pressure to launch an offensive. This was not only the right thing for a Bonaparte to do politically, it was the only way *strategically* for France to preempt Prussia's superior numbers and organization, and, as Gramont continually reminded Leboeuf, the only way for France to lure the wary Austrians, Italians, and Danes into a French alliance.[1] The problem, of course, was that France's advantage in the early stages of a Franco-Prussian war was presumptive and based on nothing more solid than the assumption that a larger peacetime army (France's) could mobilize more quickly than a smaller one that needed reserves (Prussia's). As it chanced, Moltke's army – regulars, reserves, and *Landwehr* – defeated that particular assumption, mobilizing faster than the French, absorbing Louis-Napoleon's half-hearted push across the Saar, and then swarming past it to crack the defensive French positions at Wissembourg, Froeschwiller, and Spicheren and push into France.

Truth be told, offensive operations were the last thing that the French ought to have been contemplating in the first week of August 1870. The synchronization of Gramont's bellicose foreign policy and the army's mobilization had been so utterly neglected that superhuman exertions were now required just to deploy the French army. On 1 August, eleven French guardsmen died of heatstroke marching from Nancy to Metz. Two others, wilting from heat and discouragement, sat down on the side of the road and shot themselves, one in full view of the horrified press corps: "He placed the muzzle of his Chassepot against his right eye and pulled the trigger with his toe. The ball tore off the right side of his face. It was horrible." Metz was still a bedlam of nervous activity, as raw troops and material cascaded in from all

---

1 Eberhard Kolb, *Der Weg aus dem Krieg*, Munich, 1989, pp. 80–2. Joseph Andlau, *Metz*, Paris, 1872, p. 34.

over France. "With each passing day, one discovers that one has been deluding oneself to think that French preparations are complete," the Metz correspondent of *l'Etoile Belge* reported on 1 August. "Two thousand wagons block the streets of Metz this morning, mostly hay, straw, and oats that arrived in the night and await a final destination."[2] The traffic jams were so thick that cavalry and infantry units were put to work day and night as laborers. They would hike down the clogged Metz-Paris railway line until they reached a stalled train, fill their rucksacks and saddlebags with whatever the train was carrying, and then tramp back to Metz where they would dump everything – ammunition, bandages, trenching equipment, mess kits, bales of kepis, tents – on the main square and then retrace their steps.[3] Given the choice of endless fatigues like these or a strike at the Germans, most French soldiers welcomed the latter.

The idea to seize the Prussian town of Saarbrücken was General Charles Frossard's. Sixty-three-years-old in 1870, Frossard was the favorite general of the Bonapartes, the prince imperial's tutor, and commandant of the French II Corps at Metz. Frossard had been urging a preemptive strike at the Prussians for weeks, and finally persuaded the emperor to authorize one on 29 July. Leboeuf wrote the orders the next day, and most of the Army of the Rhine marched the day after that. By 1 August, however, this last-minute French offensive was seeming ill-advised, even risky, for Moltke was busy massing hundreds of thousands of troops to either side of the Army of the Rhine, which now conveniently wedged itself into the tight space between Metz and Saarbrücken. There no longer seemed any point in a French drive east. With 400,000 Prussian troops above and below it, a French advance would merely catch the Army of the Rhine in a vast encirclement and widen the already dangerous gap between the six French corps approaching Saarbrücken and MacMahon's I Corps in Alsace. At this late date, it would have been wiser for Napoleon III to stay put at Metz, connect with MacMahon, and improvise a line of defense against the imminent Prussian offensive. However, the emperor felt constrained to attack *something* before the inevitable retreat. The lonely Prussian 16th Division at Saarbrücken – detached from Steinmetz's First Army to hold the line of the Saar – was a tempting target. Still, no one held out much hope for the operation. Even Frossard, once a great proponent of a drive into the Palatinate and Hessia, now treated the Saarbrücken attack as little more than a "repositioning" of the French army for a forward defense of Alsace-Lorraine.[4] For their part, the Prussians ascribed no importance at all to the attack on Saarbrücken: "The time had passed when [the French] might have

2   Vincennes, *Service Historique de l'Armée de Terre* (SHAT), Lb4, Metz, 1 August 1870, "Renseignements."
3   SHAT, Lb1, "Presse Etrangere," *l'Indépendance Belge*, Metz, 27 July 1870.
4   Michael Howard, *The Franco-Prussian War*, orig. 1961, London, 1981, pp. 80–2.

taken advantage of their over-hasty mobilization," Moltke coolly observed. Indeed Frossard's "reconnaissance in force" seemed to be nothing more than a public relations stunt, because Saarbrücken, wedged into the gap between the Vosges and the Eifel, was a logistical dead-end for an army encumbered with 6,000 wagons of ammunition and engineering equipment.[5]

Nevertheless, the entire Army of the Rhine shuffled dutifully forward on 31 July. Their march carried some units through formerly French territory that had been ceded to the Prussians in 1815. Writing from a little village near Forbach, the colonel of the French 67th Regiment reported, "This place was made Prussian by the treaties of 1815, but since the people sympathize with France, all the males have been deported to Pomerania to prevent desertions. The villages around here contain only women and children."[6] By 2 August, each of the French corps had advanced about ten miles on good German roads wide enough to take four columns abreast. Even at this early date, they clashed with Prussian patrols at every step. A platoon of General Louis Ladmirault's IV Corps fought a skirmish with 200 men of the Prussian 70th Regiment that is noteworthy only because it was carefully recorded by a French junior officer (a rare event in the laconic French army) and because it shed light on the tactics and culture of the rival armies.

As they pushed up against the Prussian border, Lieutenant Camille Lerouse's platoon bumped into a company of Prussian infantry resting in a wood. As Lerouse advanced *en tirailleurs* – in a skirmish line – the Prussians attacked out of the wood in their superior numbers and tried to surround and annihilate the French – *"de nous englober"* – before they could retreat. Flanked on both sides and with Prussians swarming in behind him, Lerouse ordered his men to lie flat and scrape what cover they could from the oat furrows around them. *Une pluie de balles* – "a rain of bullets" – ensued. Once the Prussians halted under the superior fire of the Chassepot (and the superior marksmanship of the French), Lerouse ordered his men forward ten meters, where they knelt and resumed firing. Now the Prussians broke, running away in all directions. A lone Prussian officer, "ashamed by the flight of so many of his men from such a small French force," stood waving a flag and shouting "rally" two hundred yards away. Lerouse himself aimed a Chassepot at the officer: "He fell dead at my second shot." A single French platoon had routed an entire Prussian company! This was plainly going to be an altogether different war than that of 1866. For Lieutenant Lerouse, the after-action wind-down was as interesting as the skirmish itself: his platoon received visits from their brigadier general, their regimental colonel, and their battalion major. Each paid a sort of feudal tribute to the warriors: General Golberg gave fifty francs,

5   Helmuth von Moltke, *The Franco-German War of 1870–71*, New York, 1892, pp. 10–11. SHAT, Lb4, Paris, 1 August 1870, Ministère de Guerre.
6   SHAT, Lb3, Morsbach, 29 July 1870, Colonel of 67th Regiment to 3. Division commandant.

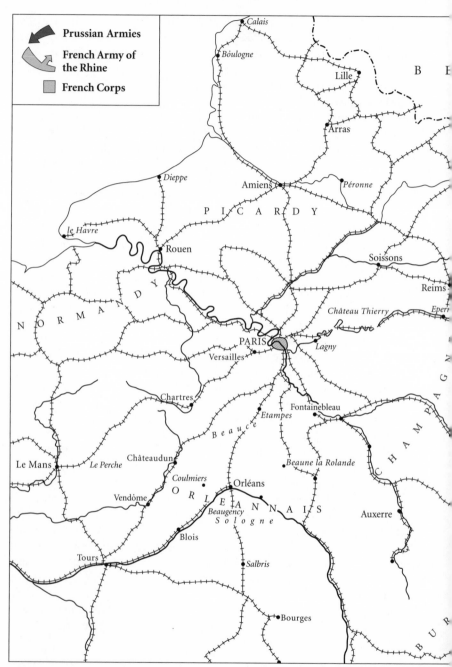

Map 2. Frossard's thrust to Saarbrücken

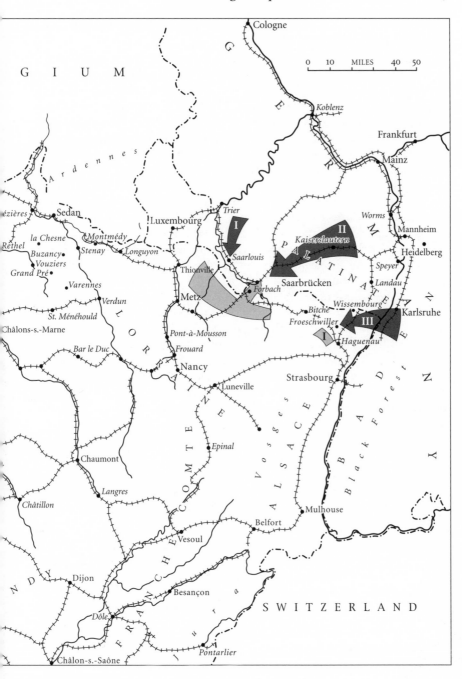

Colonel Giraud gave five, and Captain Dupuy de Podio gave five more.[7] For French *troupiers* of the line, sixty francs – $180 today – was a king's ransom; it would keep Lerouse's platoon in wine and prostitutes for weeks to come.

On 2 August, six divisions of Bazaine's III Corps and Frossard's II Corps broke into Saarbrücken, encountering little resistance from three retiring companies of the Prussian 40th Regiment. The French swept into the town, in the words of one of Frossard's officers, "with aplomb, as if exercising at the Camp de Châlons."[8] Casualties were light – eighty-three Prussians killed and wounded, eighty-six French – just enough to embarrass Napoleon III, who had distributed handbills before the battle assuring his men that the needle rifle was so inferior to the Chassepot that French troops would have time to duck beneath the Dreyse's slow-moving bullet.[9] Saarbrücken was intended to serve as the fourteen-year-old prince imperial's *baptême de feu*. As such, it was a fizzle. When Napoleon III and Prince Louis left their carriage three miles from Saarbrücken to review their passing troops from horseback, they recoiled from the spectacle: Three miles of ground littered with discarded packs, blankets, pouches, mess kits, and cartridges. Wearied by their long march to the front, Frossard's men had simply dropped everything but their rifles in the road. In a deposition taken at his court of inquiry after the war, Marshal Leboeuf recalled that the emperor stopped the nearest battalion in its tracks and attempted to chaff the men in the avuncular tones of Napoleon I. The men brushed impatiently past him, dully intoning: "*Ah, mon Empereur, ôtons-nous nos sacs, ôtons-nous nos couvertures...*" – "Ah, my Emperor, we are dropping our packs; we are dropping our blankets..." Asked to explain this astounding degree of indiscipline at a time when the war was not even going badly for the French, Leboeuf replied:

> "Revolution was gnawing continuously at the Army of the Rhine. In July, I had precise, reliable information that there were sixty agents of the Socialist International in the army. They were always spreading demoralizing rumors: that we had no bread, no ammunition, that the French soldier was too heavily laden. Entire regiments would throw away their cartridges in protest, demanding wagons to carry them."[10]

Little of this demoralizing conduct made the official histories. Instead, Prince Louis Bonaparte had his baptism of fire (excitedly scouring the field for spent cartridges and shrapnel balls); the emperor had himself sketched seated on a horse (for the first time in years, grimacing with pain from his hemorrhoids), and rows of happy troops were turned out to cheer the emperor

---

7 SHAT, Lb4, Histroff, 1 August 1870, Lt. Lerouse to Capt. Dupuy de Podio, "Rapport sur le combat de Histroff, le 1er Août 1870."
8 SHAT, Lb4, Saarbrücken, 2 August 1870, General Bastoul to General Frossard.
9 Andlau, p. 34.
10 SHAT, Lb14, "Extrait de la déposition de Ml. Le Boeuf devant le Conseil d'Enquete."

and the prince imperial. The French press, which had very limited access to headquarters and the front, gullibly hailed the *"victoire de Sarrebruck,"* and published gory engravings of French *mitrailleuses* soaking the Saarbrücken heights in German blood.[11] Of course little blood was shed on either side, and before long even the bloodthirsty French public began to doubt. Frossard's three-page *Rapport à l'Empereur*, describing the "great victory" was read skeptically when placarded around France on 5 August as was the promise of the newspaper *France* that Saarbrücken "inaugurated a new epoch of history." Summarizing it all, Britain's military attaché in Paris remarked that "the French have the keenest sense of the ridiculous and cannot help but laugh at this."[12]

More seriously, Saarbrücken further corroded relations between Napoleon III and Marshal Bazaine. Although Bazaine was the senior general in the push to Saarbrücken, he was pointedly humiliated again, this time relegated to a supporting position behind Frossard, who, in the terse judgment of the Prussian general staff, was the inferior general: "inexperienced, a political creature and a zealot."[13] Even the wording of the orders from Leboeuf seemed calculated to wound Bazaine's pride: "the emperor commands Frossard with II Corps to cross the Saar and take Saarbrücken with two of Bazaine's divisions in reserve." Personally insulted, Marshal Bazaine also questioned the usefulness of the battle: "*Quel était le but de cette opération?*" – "Whatever was the *aim* of that operation?" Bazaine later inquired. "Saarbrücken was an important point only if one seriously intended to invade Prussia or force an entry into Bavaria," but not if one planned simply to abandon it after the battle.[14] Joseph Andlau, a French staff officer critical of Bazaine, nevertheless testified that the marshal did attempt to convert Frossard's pointless operation into a real enveloping attack with three French corps against the 40,000 Prussian troops gathered in the vicinity of Saarbrücken. Once again, Bazaine was ignored by the emperor, who wanted to manage operations himself and had no intention of launching a real offensive. "Annoyed by the fibs and trifles of the emperor, Bazaine withdrew into his corps, increasingly ignoring his surroundings."[15] Indeed from Saarbrücken forward, Bazaine, once an enterprising *troupier*, began to emit the quarrelsome, obstructive memoranda that would characterize his command style in the weeks ahead. When ordered by Leboeuf to arrange a council of war with Frossard on 31 July – at Frossard's headquarters, not Bazaine's – the Marshal replied: "How can I advance? I

11 H. Sutherland Edwards, *The Germans in France*, London, 1873, pp. 36–7. Theodor Fontane, *Der Krieg gegen Frankreich 1870–71*, 4 vols., orig. 1873–76, Zurich, 1985, vol. 1, pp. 155–6.
12 PRO, FO 27, 1809, Paris, 5 Aug. 1870, Claremont to Lyons. SHAT, Lb4, Paris, 2 August 1870, Minister of the Interior to all prefects. Andlau, pp. 24–6. Fontane, vol. 1, p. 156.
13 Wolfgang Foerster, *Prinz Friedrich Karl von Preussen*, 2 vols., Stuttgart, 1910, pp. 141–2.
14 F. A. Bazaine, *Episodes de la Guerre de 1870 et le Blocus de Metz*, Madrid, 1883, pp. 11–18.
15 Andlau, pp. 24–6.

still have no ambulances.... I also need horses and medicine. It's just too risky."[16]

The Prussians, who had never planned to defend the left bank of the Rhine until their mobilization was complete, were amazed by all of this French fumbling. Prince Friedrich Karl, commander of the Prussian Second Army, dismissed Louis-Napoleon and Frossard as *"Kinder der Halbheit"* – "children of half-measures." The *Berlin Post*, noting the strategic uselessness of the Saarbrücken thrust, compared Napoleon III to "that Roman Emperor, who led his legions to gather seashells on the shores of Britain." After exhausting and disorganizing their army to seize "the line of the Saar," the emperor and his generals now yielded the line without a fight, falling all the way back to the Moselle. It was extraordinary conduct.[17] A French officer close to the emperor observed that Napoleon III was proceeding exactly as he had done in Italy in 1859, "randomly, making things up as he went along."[18] The emperor's fateful order to General Pierre Failly's V Corps at Sarre-Union gave more evidence of his confusion. Failly's 30,000 troops were the hinge between Napoleon III's Army of the Rhine and MacMahon's I Corps in Alsace. Unless direly needed, Failly ought to have remained in constant contact with MacMahon, who potentially faced an enveloping attack by the entire Prussian Third Army. And yet Napoleon III and Leboeuf carelessly ordered Failly to join the attack on Saarbrücken, effectively stripping MacMahon of support in the battles at Wissembourg and Froeschwiller several days later.[19]

Happily, none of this was apparent on 2–3 August, when Frossard's brigades in Saarbrücken made the most of their emperor's distraction. They spent a pleasant day at rest, drank up 15,000 liters of beer, and then evacuated Saarbrücken in the rakish style of the *Grande Armée*, with requisitioned sausages and loaves of bread skewered on their bayonets.[20] How to explain French blundering before and after the battle? Perhaps it stemmed from overconfidence. General Louis Jarras interviewed fourteen Prussian prisoners taken at Saarbrücken and circulated their revelations through imperial headquarters. Many of the Prussian captives were demoralized before the battle even commenced. They were married men with wives to support. Some had "thrown down their arms" without fighting; they considered the French "too redoubtable" and the Chassepot too "frightening." They were disorganized and lacked essential supplies, and – Jarras's conclusion – *on ne compte que médiocrement sur la victoire* – "counted hardly at all on victory in the war."[21]

16 SHAT, Lb3, Metz, 31 July 1870, Marshal Leboeuf to Marshal Bazaine. St. Avold, 31 July 1870, Marshal Bazaine to Marshal Leboeuf.
17 Foerster, vol. 2, p. 142. *Berlin Post*, 10 August 1870.
18 Andlau, p. 30.
19 SHAT, Lb3, Metz, 30 July 1870, Marshal Leboeuf to Marshal Bazaine.
20 Fontane, vol. 1, pp. 152–3.
21 SHAT, Lb4, Metz, 3 August 1870, Gen. Jarras to Marshal Canrobert. Metz, 3 August 1870, Gen. Jarras, "Rapport sur l'intérrogatoire de 14 prisonniers prussiens."

If the Prussians captured at Saarbrücken did not count on victory, Moltke certainly did. By 2 August his three armies were ready. After pulling the 16th Division back from Saarbrücken to safety, the 50,000 men of Steinmetz's First Army moved into the space between Trier and Saarlouis on the right flank of Prince Friedrich Karl's Second Army (134,000 men), which had crossed the Rhine and marched most of the way to Kaiserslautern. (Friedrich Karl's appearance with six infantry corps and three divisions of cavalry just thirty miles from Saarbrücken explained the haste with which Frossard abandoned the place after the clash on 2 August.) As in 1866, Moltke left a wide gap between his principal armies, to facilitate their supply and movement and create the "pockets" that the widespread armies would surround and seal in the decisive *Kesselschlachten* ("pocket battles.") Königgrätz in 1866 had been the first of the genre, all but destroying the Austrian field army; Moltke planned more in this campaign. Hence, Crown Prince Friedrich Wilhelm's Third Army (125,000 men) drew up not on Second Army's left, but fifty miles to the south, around Landau and Karlsruhe. This was a gamble, because it isolated Crown Prince Friedrich Wilhelm's four corps, who would spend several days walled off from the rest of the Prussian army by the Vosges Mountains. But, as in 1866, when Moltke had not hesitated to detach the crown prince's Second Army to create the conditions for a strategic envelopment of the Austrians, rather recklessly placing the wall of the Sudeten Mountains between Crown Prince Friedrich Wilhelm and Prince Friedrich Karl's First Army, Moltke saw that this risk also could be minimized by a rapid Prussian advance. This would press the French into a "pocket" and unite the three Prussian armies in a concentric, mutually supporting invasion of French territory.

That was the rather neat theory. In practice, as one might expect, the Prussian invasion was quite a bit more difficult. It was complicated at every step by logistics, personal rivalries within the Prussian chain of command, and the fury of the Chassepot rifle. After skirmishing with French outposts on 25 July, a Prussian officer judged the French rifle "amazing." Just three French infantrymen had sufficed to hold up his entire column with well-aimed, nonstop fire at 1,200 paces.[22] As the Prussians advanced in greater numbers, the carnage would only increase. Terrain determined the order of Moltke's attacks. With the First and Second Armies separated from Napoleon III's base in Lorraine by the forested defiles of the *Pfälzerwald*, a hilly extension of the Vosges, it fell to the Third Army, which encountered Marshal MacMahon's I Corps on the flat ground between the Rhine and the Vosges, to begin the attack. On Moltke's maps, the problem was simple enough. Indeed he worked it out in accordance with his *Denkschrift* of 1868–69, which had given shape to this Franco-Prussian war. With an army of 125,000, the Prussian crown prince would hammer Marshal MacMahon's corps of 45,000 out of its defensive

---

22 SHAT, Lb1, 25 July 1870, "Renseignements militaires."

positions at Wissembourg and Froeschwiller, pass through the Vosges, and then wheel north, forcing Napoleon III's Army of the Rhine to make front either to the south or to the east. The French would have to confront the Prussian Third Army sweeping up from Alsace or the Prussian First and Second Armies rolling in from the Saar. If they divided their forces, they would be beaten in detail. If they massed them, as Benedek had done in 1866, they would be hit in the front, both flanks, and the rear by the converging Prussian armies. It looked to be the perfect *Kesselschlacht*.[23]

Much of this looming threat was lost on the French, whose reconnaissance in the war was deplorable. In contrast to the Prussian cavalry, which had fundamentally reformed after Königgrätz and taken the motto "*weniger in grossen Massen aufzutreten, als überall mit der Kavallerie zu sein*" ("better to be everywhere with one's cavalry than stuck in big masses"), most of the French cavalry remained stuck behind the lines in massed divisions.[24] Few French squadrons scouted, a curious fact noted by a war correspondent on 30 July: "At the moment, nothing could be less aggressive than the French army. Inhabitants of the entire border region, though accustomed to regular Prussian visits, have not seen a single French dragoon in more than ten days."[25] Those that did see French dragoons were unimpressed by their work ethic. Charles Ebener, an officer with the French II Corps, recalled seeing just one patrol of French cavalry scouts during the entire deployment of 1870. "Several squadrons rode forward to our cantonments on the frontier, ate a long lunch, questioned some local farmers about the 'remarkable features' of the area, and then rode back whence they had come."[26]

Leboeuf at Metz was effectively blinded by this inactivity. On 31 July, he vented his frustration in a letter to Canrobert: "Twenty-four hours have passed without a scrap of intelligence on Prussian troop movements in north or south.... I hear only vague talk of large numbers at Trier and Bitburg."[27] In fact, Leboeuf and the emperor received most of their intelligence from the newspapers, from Swiss, Belgian, and British war correspondents, whose clippings they saved, underlined, and filed every day in fat dossiers labeled "*renseignements*," a term reserved in better days for military intelligence. Notice of the impending Prussian attacks on Spicheren, Wissembourg, and Froeschwiller came not from French cavalry screens, but from raw conjecture, interviews with Prussian prisoners, and the police chief at Wissembourg, who was astonished by the sudden appearance of large bodies of Prussian infantry outside his village on 3 August, a concern that he shared with his prefect,

---

23 Moltke, *The Franco-German War of 1870–71*, pp. 8–14. Foerster, vol. 2, pp. 132–41.
24 Foerster, vol. 2, pp. 139–40.
25 SHAT, Lb3, 30 July 1870, "Renseignements." From *l'indépendance Belge.*
26 SHAT, Lb5, Longwy, 21 March 1882, Lt. Charles Ebener, "Etude sur la bataille de Wissembourg, 4 Auguste 1870."
27 SHAT. Lb3, Metz, 31 July 1870, Marshal Leboeuf to Marshal Canrobert.

who eventually forwarded it to the ministry in Paris, which then sent it to Metz.[28]

Alarmed by these scraps of intelligence, Leboeuf and the emperor began nervously to dismantle the offensive concentration they had begun at Saarbrücken, pulling back their *corps d'armée*, and spreading them in a defensive cordon along the eastern rim of France. General Louis Ladmirault's IV Corps, ordered to advance and seize Saarlouis after Saarbrücken, now reverted to a purely defensive role blocking the Moselle valley and the corridor to Thionville. Without even awaiting orders, Frossard yielded Saarbrücken on 5 August and hiked back to the more defensible line of Forbach and Spicheren. Bazaine retreated with III Corps from Sarreguemines to St. Avold. Failly, previously committed to the Saarbrücken attack with V Corps, now retraced his steps to the Alsatian citadel of Bitche. MacMahon remained on the eastern slope of the Vosges at Froeschwiller in Alsace, where his I Corps formed an elongated, brittle link with General Félix Douay's VII Corps at Belfort. France's reserve, General Charles Bourbaki's Guard Corps and Marshal François Canrobert's VI Corps, moved up behind the cordon: the Guards to St. Avold, VI Corps to Nancy.[29] A campaign that had begun with frothy promises of a "second Jena" now passively awaited a Prussian invasion. Having placed his generals on the defensive, Leboeuf merely warned them to expect *"une affaire serieuse"* – "a serious affair" – in the first days of August, a warning that seriously understated the Prussian threat.[30]

THE BATTLE OF WISSEMBOURG, 4 AUGUST 1870

In a telegram to Crown Prince Friedrich Wilhelm's headquarters on 4 August, Moltke reiterated that he was seeking to "bring the operations of [the Second and Third] Armies into consonance." Both armies must advance to join in "the direct combined movement" against Louis-Napoleon's principal army.[31] Blumenthal and the crown prince complied, pushing their army steadily westward in the first days of August. Moltke landed his first blow in Alsace, where the Prussian Third Army rammed into Marshal Patrice MacMahon's I Corps in two stages, a small "encounter battle" at Wissembourg on 4 August and an orchestrated clash at Froeschwiller two days later. Although MacMahon commanded a "strong corps" of 45,000 men – "strong"

28 SHAT, Lb4, Metz, 3 August 1870, Gen. Jarras to Marshal Canrobert. Metz, 3 August 1870, Gen. Jarras, "Rapport sur l'interrogatoire de 14 prisonniers prussiens." Metz, 3 August 1870, Marshal MacMahon to Marshal Leboeuf. Paris, 1 Aug. 1870, Ministère de Guerre.
29 Howard, pp. 85–8.
30 SHAT, Lb5, Metz, 4 August 1870, Marshal Leboeuf to all corps and fortress commandants. Lb3, Metz, 30 July 1870, "Renseignements."
31 Helmuth von Moltke, *Extracts from Moltke's Military Correspondence*, Fort Leavenworth, 1911, p. 182.

because it contained four divisions instead of the usual three – the marshal had strong responsibilities. Expected to hold the line of the Vosges, threaten the flank of any Prussian attack toward Strasbourg, maintain contact with Douay's VII Corps in Belfort, yet never lose touch with the Army of the Rhine to his north, the marshal needed every man that he had, and then some.

To cover his vast sector of front, MacMahon placed his four divisions in a wide square, one division and headquarters at Haguenau, a second division at Froeschwiller, a third at Lembach, and a fourth at Wissembourg, a charming little village on the Lauter river, which was France's border with the Bavarian Palatinate. By means of this rather ungainly placement of his divisions, MacMahon simultaneously defended the border with Germany, kept contact with Failly's V Corps, and still had two divisions far enough south to threaten the flank of any Prussian push toward Strasbourg or Belfort. Still, ten to twenty miles of rough country separated each of the four French divisions, a dangerous separation partly necessitated by shortages of food and drink, which forced MacMahon to scrounge among the local population. If MacMahon took the initiative, he would have time to close the gaps and join the units in battle. But if MacMahon were attacked on any of the corners of his square, none of the French divisions would have time to "march to the sound of the guns." They were too far apart, a fact brutally driven home to the 8,600 troops of MacMahon's 2nd Division at Wissembourg on 4 August.

Marshal MacMahon's 2nd Division, commanded by sixty-one-year-old General Abel Douay – Félix Douay's brother and president of the military academy at St. Cyr before the war – had only arrived in Wissembourg late on 3 August. MacMahon hurriedly shoved Douay forward after receiving Leboeuf's vague warning of "a serious affair." Although the French had built Wissembourg into a formidable defensive line in the eighteenth century – a network of towers, moats, redoubts, and trenches along the right bank of the Lauter – Marshal Niel had abandoned the fortifications in 1867, removing their guns and maintenance budgets. Decay followed swiftly in the warm, moist shelter of the Vosges: A war correspondent at Wissembourg in 1870 found the walls crumbling, the moats filled with weeds and rubbish, the *glacis* already sprouting elms and poplars.[32] Still, the place had considerable tactical importance if the Germans came this way. Wissembourg was an important road junction for Bavaria, Strasbourg, and Lower Alsace and, after looking it over, General Douay's engineers recommended that Wissembourg be cleaned up and defended as a "pivot and strongpoint" for operations on the frontier, a recommendation that Douay passed back to I Corps headquarters.[33] Ultimately,

32 Alexander Innes Shand, *On the trail of the war*, New York, 1871, p. 50.
33 SHAT, Lb5, Mersebourg, 19 Dec. 1870, "Notes rédigées sous forme de rapport au Col. Robert, ancien Chef d'Etat-Major de la Division Abel Douay, par le Chef de Bataillon Liaud, du 2e Bataillon du 74 de Ligne." Lb5, Longwy, 21 March 1882, Lt. Charles Ebener, "Etude sur la bataille de Wissembourg, 4 Auguste 1870."

Douay's great misfortune was to have landed at the last minute in the exact spot chosen by Moltke for the invasion of France. Seeking to pin the Army of the Rhine with his First and Second Armies while swinging Third Army into Napoleon III's flank, Moltke wired Crown Prince Friedrich Wilhelm late on 3 August: "We intend to carry out a general offensive movement; the Third Army will cross the frontier tomorrow at Wissembourg."[34]

The Prussian Third Army's seizure of Wissembourg on 4 August was as good an indictment of French intelligence and reconnaissance in the war as any. When General Douay inspected the town on 3 August, he had no inkling that 80,000 Prussian and Bavarian troops were closing rapidly from the northeast in response to the Prussian Crown Prince's order of the day: "It is my intention to advance tomorrow as far as the River Lauter and cross it with the vanguard."[35] Indeed the Prussians had been masters of the *Niederwald*, the sprawling pine forest that ran along both banks of the Lauter and cloaked the Prussian approach, for weeks. French infantry officers could not recall a single French cavalry patrol entering it. What intelligence Douay received on 3 August came not from the French cavalry, but from Monsieur Hepp, Wissembourg's subprefect, who warned that the Bavarians had already seized the Franco-German customs posts east of the Lauter and that large bodies of German troops were in the area. Still, Douay retired that evening without pushing his eight squadrons of cavalry across the Lauter to reconnoiter.[36] Only on the morning of the 4th did Douay finally send a company of infantry across the river. No sooner had they touched the left bank than they were thrown back by Prussian cavalry. This was interpreted as nothing more serious than an "outpost skirmish" in the French camp. Reassured, General Douay ordered morning coffee at 8:00 A.M. and wired the results of his reconnaissance to MacMahon at Strasbourg. Relieved that there was still time to mass his corps on the frontier, MacMahon made plans to move his headquarters to Wissembourg the next day.[37] Even as his telegraph operators tapped out this intention to Leboeuf at Metz, the first Prussian shells were exploding in Wissembourg and General Friedrich von Bothmer's Bavarian 4th Division was splashing across the Lauter. In the Chateau Geisberg, Abel Douay's, hilltop headquarters above Wissembourg, confusion was total.

Central forts of the "Wissembourg lines" in the eighteenth century, the twin towns of Wissembourg and Altenstadt still possessed redoubtable fortifications for an infantry fight: moats, loopholed stone walls and towers, and

34   F. Maurice, *The Franco-German War 1870–71*, orig. 1899, London, 1914, p. 76.
35   Maurice, p. 76.
36   SHAT, Lb5, Longwy, 21 March 1882, Lt. Charles Ebener, "Etude sur la bataille de Wissembourg, 4 Août 1870." Maurice, pp. 74-7.
37   SHAT, Lb5, Strasbourg, 4 August 1870, 9 A.M., Marshal MacMahon to Marshal Leboeuf. Lb5, Mersebourg, 19 Dec. 1870, "Notes rédigées sous forme de rapport au Col. Robert, ancien Chef d'Etat-Major de la Division Abel Douay, par le Chef de Bataillon Liaud, du 2e Bataillon du 74 de Ligne."

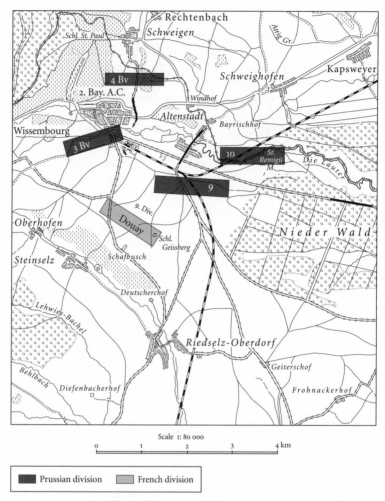

Map 3. The Battle of Wissembourg

an elevated bastion just behind and to the right on the Geisberg. Douay had posted two of his eight battalions, six guns, and several *mitrailleuses* in the riverfront towns of Wissembourg and Altenstadt on the 3rd. He arrayed the rest of his infantry, his cavalry, and twelve cannons on the slopes above the twin towns. As the Bavarians swarmed over the Lauter, every French gun, deployed in a line from Geisberg on the right along to Wissembourg on the left, poured in a seamless curtain of fire. The French infantry, all veterans with Chassepots, adjusted their sights and commenced firing with devastating effect. Nikolaus Duetsch, a Bavarian lieutenant casually inspecting his platoon in Schweigen on the left bank of the Lauter, recalled his amazement when one of

Fig. 4. *Turcos* firing toward Wissembourg

his infantrymen suddenly threw up his arms and cried, *"Ich bin geschossen"* – "I'm hit!" And he was. "The bullet came from the Wissembourg walls, more than 1,200 meters away."[38] Closer in, every French bullet struck home as the Bavarians, emerging from the morning fog in their plumed helmets, struggled through thickly planted vineyards and acacia plantations to reach the Lauter.

For the first time, the Bavarians heard the *tac-tac-tac* of the *mitrailleuse*. These rather primitive "revolver cannon" did not traverse their fire across the field like late nineteenth-century machineguns, rather they tended to fix on a single man and pump thirty balls into him, leaving nothing behind but two shoes and stumps. Needless to say, the gun had a terrifying impact out of all proportion to its quite meager accomplishments as a weapon. ("One thing is certain," a Bavarian infantry officer wrote after the battle, "few are wounded by the *mitrailleuse*. If it hits you, you're dead.")[39] Johannes Schulz, a

38 Munich, Bayerisches Kriegsarchiv (BKA), HS 842, "Tagebuch des Leutnants Nikolaus Duetsch zum Feldzuge 1870–71."
39 BKA, HS 846, Maj. Gustav Fleschuez, "Auszug aus dem Tagebuch zum Feldzuge 1870–71."

Bavarian private hustling toward Altenstadt, later described the carnage in the Bavarian lines. The French artillery and rifle fire was so intense and accurate that every Bavarian attempt to form attack columns on the broken, marshy ground before Wissembourg was shot to pieces. Schulz's own platoon leader was punched to the ground by a bullet in the chest; miraculously, he rose from the dead, saved by his rolled greatcoat, which had stopped the bullet. As the Bavarians wavered, Schulz recalled the blustery appearance of his regimental colonel, whose shouted orders showed just how deeply Prussian tactics had penetrated the Bavarian army in the years since 1866: "Regiment! Form attack columns! First and light platoons in the skirmish line! Swarms to left and right!" That first attempt to cross the Lauter and break into Wissembourg was brutally cut down by the *Turcos* of the 1st Algerian Tirailleur Regiment, who worked their Chassepots expertly from the ditch, the town walls, and the railway embankment, which formed an impenetrable rampart along the front and eastern edge of Wissembourg. Though ten times stronger than the defenders, the Bavarians wilted, the officers shouting "*nieder!*" – "get down!" – the wild-eyed men breaking formation and crawling away in search of cover, terrified by their first sight of African troops. Schulz remembered the conduct of his battalion drummer boy; shot cleanly through the arm, the boy screamed over and over, "*Mein Gott! Mein Gott! Ich sterbe fürs Vaterland!*" – "My God, my God! I'm dying for our Fatherland!"[40]

It had rained in the night and the morning was hot and humid; fog rose from the fields. Most of the Bavarians and Prussians, hacking their way through man-high vines, recalled never even seeing the French; they merely heard them, and fired at their rifle flashes. Adam Dietz, a *Jäger* armed with Bavaria's new Werder rifle, every bit as good as the Chassepot, bitterly concluded that the Prussian tactic of *Schnellfeuer* – "rapid fire" – was impossible when the troops were lying prone: "Rapid fire is not so rapid when you're lying flat because it takes so long to reload; you have somehow to reach into your cartridge pouch, find a cartridge with your fingers, eject, load, aim, and only then, fire."[41] Clearly the French – the *Turcos* and two battalions of the 74th Regiment – were having a better time of it, standing behind cover in Wissembourg and Altenstadt, loading, aiming, and firing as quickly as they could. Only the Prussian and Bavarian artillery limited the losses. Several German guns crossed the Lauter on makeshift bridges and joined the infantry assault, blasting rounds into the wooden gates at close range and giving an early glimpse of the bold tactics conceived after Königgrätz. The rest, deployed on the left bank of the Lauter, shot Wissembourg into flames, dismounted the *mitrailleuses*, and pushed the French riflemen off the town walls. For this, they

40 BKA, HS 868, 4 August 1870, "Kriegstagebuch Johannes Schulz."
41 BKA, HS 841, "Tagebuch des Unterlt. Adam Dietz, 10. Jäger Baon."

could thank the French artillery; firing an unreliable, time-fused projectile and standing too far back from the action, the French guns, after some initial success, caused little damage on the Prussian side.[42] Still, with the outskirts and canals of Wissembourg choked with Bavarian dead, it was an inauspicious start to the war.

Luckily for thirty-nine-year-old Crown Prince Friedrich Wilhelm, Prussian tactics never relied on frontal attacks. They groped always for the flanks and the line of retreat, and Wissembourg was no exception to this rule. Even as Bothmer's division foundered in Wissembourg and Altenstadt, General Albrecht von Blumenthal, the Third Army chief of staff, was directing the Bavarian 3rd Division against the French left and swinging the Prussian V and XI Corps into Douay's right flank and rear. From the rising ground behind the Lauter, Blumenthal and the crown prince could make out Douay's tent line with the naked eye. It was clear that the French general had no more than a division with him, and that he was dangerously exposed, what soldiers called "in the air," with no natural features protecting his flanks, no reserves, and no connection to the other divisions of I Corps.

Abel Douay did not live to recognize the utter hopelessness of his situation. Riding out to assess the fighting in Wissembourg, he was killed by a shellburst as he stopped to inspect a *mitrailleuse* battery at 11 A.M. By then the Prussian envelopment was nearly complete. The Prussian 9th Division, leading the V Corps into battle, had crossed the Lauter at St. Remy, taken Altenstadt, and stormed the railway embankment at Wissembourg, taking the embattled Algerians between two fires. Six more Bavarian battalions swarmed across the Lauter above Wissembourg, closing the ring. Though surrounded, the French held on, blazing away along the full circumference of their narrowing ring on the Lauter, while the French batteries above fired as quickly as they could into the swarms of Bavarians and Prussians on the riverbank. Ultimately it was the *Wissembourgeois*, not the French troops, who ran up the white flag. Faced with the certain destruction of their lovely town, the inhabitants emerged from their cellars and demanded that the 74th Regiment open the gates and let the Germans in. Here was an early instance of the defeatism that would plague the French war effort from first to last. Major Liaud, commander of the 74th's 2nd battalion, bitterly recalled the interference of the townsfolk, who pleaded with his men to end their "useless defense" and refused even to provide directions through their winding streets and alleys. When Liaud sent men onto the roofs of the town to snipe at the Germans, he was scolded by the mayor, who reminded him that the French troops "were causing material damage" and needlessly prolonging the battle. The battle ended abruptly when a crowd of

---

42 SHAT, Lb5, Longwy, 21 March 1882, Lt. Charles Ebener, "Etude sur la bataille de Wissembourg, 4 Août 1870."

determined civilians advanced on the Haguenau gate, lowered the drawbridge, and waved the Bavarians inside.[43]

If victory belonged to the Germans, it was not immediately apparent to the troops. Indeed the brave French stand in Wissembourg knocked the wind out of the Bavarians, and left them gasping for most of the afternoon, leaving the Prussians to complete the envelopment. Captain Celsus Girl, a Bavarian staff officer who rode back from the Lauter at the climax of the battle, was amazed to discover the roads east of the river clogged with Bavarian stragglers (*Nachzügler*) too frightened by the sounds of battle to advance. "There were clusters of men beneath every shade tree on the Landau Road.... Most were just scared, trembling with 'cannon fever'.... Nothing would move them; they answered my best efforts and those of the march police with passive resistance." And this was the better of the two Bavarian corps; after inspecting General Ludwig von der Tann's Bavarian I Corps before the battle, Blumenthal and the crown prince had judged it incapable of fighting and left it in reserve, far behind the Lauter.[44] Though the Bavarians were a disappointment, raw German troop numbers carried the day. As the French guns and infantry on the Geisberg tried to disengage their embattled comrades below prior to a general retreat, they were themselves engulfed by onrushing battalions of the Prussian V and XI Corps, which worked around behind the Geisberg, pushed the French inside the chateau, and then stormed it.

Fighting raged for an hour, with French infantry, barricaded inside every room and on the roof, firing into the masses of Prussians assaulting the ground floor. Considering Prussia's military reputation, a French officer was appalled by the crudity of the Prussian attack: Wave after wave of Prussian infantry broke against the walls of the chateau and its outbuildings. The largely Polish 7th Regiment was mangled, losing twenty-three officers and 329 men.[45] On the slopes below the Geisberg, Prussian, and Bavarian troops from Wissembourg joined the attack, pushing uphill through the remnants of the French 74th Regiment. A Bavarian sergeant took the Chassepot from the hands of a French corpse on the hillside and was amazed to find the rifle sights set at 1,600 meters, an impossible shot with the Prussian needle rifle or the Bavarian Podewils.[46] The battle for the chateau stalled until gunners of the Prussian 9th Division succeeded in wrestling three batteries onto an undefended height just 800 paces from the Geisberg. At that range they could not miss, and white flags shortly appeared on the roof. Among the casualties of this

43 SHAT, Lb5, Mersebourg, 19 Dec. 1870, "Notes rédigées sous forme de rapport au Col. Robert, ancien Chef d'État-Major de la Division Abel Douay, par le Chef de Bataillon Liaud, du 2e Bataillon du 74 de Ligne."
44 BKA, HS 849, Capt. Celsus Girl, "Erinnerungen," pp. 30–5.
45 SHAT, Lb5, Longwy, 21 March 1882, Lt. Charles Ebener, "Etude sur la bataille de Wissembourg, 4 Août 1870."
46 BKA, HS 841, "Tagebuch des Unterlt. Adam Dietz, 10. Jäger Baon."

last bombardment was the Duc de Gramont's brother, colonel of the French 47th Regiment, whose left arm was ripped off by a shell splinter. Two hundred Frenchmen surrendered as the rest of Douay's division fled westward, abandoning fifteen guns, four *mitrailleuses*, all of the division's ammunition, and 1,000 prisoners. Abel Douay, by now a rigid corpse on a table in the Chateau Geisberg, had never stood a chance. He had stood in a bad position against twenty-nine German battalions with just eight of his own. Marshal MacMahon did not learn of the disaster until 2:30 P.M., when he resolved to collect the survivors of Douay's division and lead a "fighting retreat" through the Vosges passes to Lemberg and Meisenthal, where he would be better positioned to unite with the Army of the Rhine and Canrobert's VI Corps. The collection point would be a little village on the eastern edge of the Vosges called Froeschwiller.[47]

There would be no retreat, fighting or otherwise, for the companies of Algerian *tirailleurs* and the 300 men of the French 74th Regiment still trapped inside Wissembourg. There the fighting sputtered from house to house, though most Prussian and Bavarian infantry simply strolled in through the Landau or Haguenau gates and looked around curiously. A thirsty Bavarian private recalled accosting the inhabitants of the town and demanding beer and cigars. While engaged on this errand, he bumped into a squad of Prussians with red French army trousers flapping from their bayonets. He remembered wondering how they had got there. The Prussians yelled "three cheers for the Bavarians" – "*vivat hoch ihr Bayern!*" – as they ran laughing past.[48] General Blumenthal's adjutant, a dour Mecklenburger, did not share those comradely sentiments; he rode in through the Haguenau gate – "furious, silent, cold" – searching for the Bavarian unit that had stolen his favorite horse that morning. A Bavarian officer sat and watched the young mayor of Wissembourg, the official who had caused the French garrison so many problems. Clearly not an Alsatian, he was a "thirty-six-year-old man with black hair and a Mediterranean face." As bullets ricocheted around the *Marktplatz*, the mayor, still apparently determined to spare the town "material damage," stood holding the French flag and demanding to speak with the Prussian commander-in-chief. No one paid any attention to him.

Most of the German troops were riveted by their first sight of Africans; they peered curiously at the dead or captured *Turcos* "as if at zoo animals," and hesitantly touched their "poodle hair."[49] Leopold von Winning, a Prussian lieutenant, described the "amazement" of his Silesians, who "stared disbelievingly at the Algerian *tirailleurs*, some of them blacks with woolly hair, others Arabs with bronze skin and sculpted features." The Prussians and Bavarians

47 SHAT, Lb5, Haguenau, 4 Aug. 1870, 2:30 P.M., Marshal MacMahon to Napoleon III.
48 BKA, HS 868, 4 Aug. 1870, "Kriegstagebuch Johannes Schulz."
49 BKA, HS 849, Capt. Girl, "Erinnerungen," pp. 30, 41.

crowded around the *Turcos*, making faces, barking gibberish and pantomiming madly, even offering cigars or their flasks in the hope of a word.[50] The poor *Wissembourgeois*, offered protection by the French the night before, now felt the dead weight of war. Column after column of German troops entered the town demanding bread, meat, wine, wood, straw, forage, and rooms for the night. Bothmer's divisional staff settled into Wissembourg's only hotel and were pleased to find the dining room table already set for Douay's officers.[51]

On the Geisberg, Prussian troops combed through the abandoned French tents, and General Douay's luxurious bivouac became the object of curious pilgrimages from both banks of the Lauter. Gebhard von Bismarck, an officer in the Prussian XI Corps, later described the scene:

> "Next to [Douay's] staff carriage was an elaborate, custom-made kitchen wagon, with special cages for live poultry and game birds ... but the troops were most interested in two elegant carriages on the edge of the camp, the contents of which were scattered far and wide: suitcases, men's pajamas and underwear, and women's things too, undergarments, corsets, crinolines and peignoirs. Our *Rheingauer* laughed and laughed."

Douay's headquarters provided more than titillation. Captain Bismarck and the other Prussian officers were "astounded by the French maps." They were of poor quality on an all but useless scale. Junior officers had none at all, a startling contrast with the Prussian army – though not the Bavarian – where even lieutenants were provided with the best large scale maps. "We went through the knapsack of a French officer and found only a copy of *Monde Illustré* with its "*vue panoramique du théatre de la guerre*," scale 104:32 centimeters. I still have it, surely one of the crudest means of orientation ever used by an army at war."[52] While the professionals interrogated French prisoners and scrutinized their maps, their conscripts drank in the sights and smells of war. Most were unnerved. Franz Hiller, a Bavarian private, never forgot the scene on the Geisberg after the battle. Dead and wounded men lay everywhere. Many of the corpses were decapitated, or missing arms or legs. Hiller observed that inexperienced men like himself invariably paused to peer inside the wagons full of mutilated corpses, then staggered back in shock. This was the real "baptism of fire," rendered even more poignant for Hiller by a sad discovery: "I saw the corpse of a young Frenchman and thought 'what will his parents and family think and say when they learn of his death?' His

50   Leopold von Winning, *Erinnerungen eines preussischen Leutnants aus den Kriegsjahren 1866 und 1870–71*, Heidelberg, 1911, pp. 76–80.
51   BKA, HS 846, Maj. Gustav Fleschuez, "Auszug aus dem Tagebuch zum Feldzuge 1870–71."
52   G. von Bismarck, *Kriegserlebnisse 1866 und 1870–71*, Dessau, 1907, p. 103.

pack lay ripped open at his side; there was a photograph of him. I took it, and have it to this day."[53]

Both the Prussians and the Bavarians studied French tactics at Wissembourg, carefully noting their strengths and weaknesses. Bavarian Captain Max Lutz concluded that the French tactics, supposedly created for the technically superb Chassepot, were actually ill-suited to the French rifle. Instead of exploiting the Chassepot's range, accuracy, and rate of fire by lengthening their front, the French had massed their troops in narrow positions that were easily crushed by artillery fire, demoralized, and outflanked. The French thus put themselves at a double disadvantage: They could not take Prussian attacks between cross fires and could not themselves launch enveloping attacks. They were, as Lutz put it, always *"zu massig aufgestellt"* – "too compactly formed."[54]

After Wissembourg, the *Berlin Post* waxed grandiose on the significance of the battle. "The German brotherhood in arms has received its baptism of blood, the firmest cement." Wissembourg had blazed "the path of nationalism" for Prussia and the German states.[55] The Prussian *Volkszeitung* took the same line, generously crediting the Bavarians: "the Bavarians have decisively defeated the enemies of Germany . . . the battlefield bears witness to their unwavering fidelity."[56] The truth, of course, was altogether different. Like poor Lieutenant Bronsart von Schellendorf, hunting furiously for his stolen *Grauschimmel* among the unruly Bavarians, the Prussians had turned an intensely critical gaze on their new south German ally before the smoke of the battle had even lifted. What they found was an undisciplined Bavarian army that had performed abysmally in 1866 (as an Austrian ally) and still seemed unprepared for the tests of modern warfare.

Bavarian march discipline was scandalous, at least as bad as French. The south Germans left far more stragglers in their wake than the Prussians. Whereas Prussian units could march directly from their rail cars into battle, the Bavarians needed days to sort themselves out. Every march route traversed by the Bavarians in the early weeks was left littered with discarded equipment, much of which was missed in battle, another problem for the south Germans.[57] "Our troops have no fire discipline," a Bavarian officer confessed after the battle. "The men commence firing and transition immediately to *Schnellfeuer*, ignoring all orders and signals until the last cartridge is out the barrel." Excitement or panic partly explained this, as did a trade-union

53 BKA, HS 853, Franz Hiller, "Erinnerungen eines Soldaten-Reservisten der 11. Kompanie Infanterie-Leib Regiment, 1870–71."
54 BKA, B 982, Munich, 22 November 1871, Capt. Max Lutz, "Erfahrungen."
55 London, Public Record Office (PRO), FO 64, Berlin, 13 August 1870, Loftus to Granville.
56 PRO, FO 64, Berlin, 16 August 1870, Loftus to Granville.
57 BKA, B 982, Munich, 3 December 1871, Maj. Theodor Eppler, "Erfahrungen."

mentality that did not prevail in the Prussian army: "[Bavarians] feel that they have done their duty simply by firing off all of their ammunition, at which point they look over their shoulders expecting to be relieved. Many [Bavarian] officers also subscribed to this delusion." Bavarians rarely attacked with the bayonet and proved only too willing to carry wounded comrades to the rear in battle, leaving gaps in the firing line. After the war, Prussian analysts discovered that Bavarian infantry had needed to be resupplied with ammunition at least once in every clash with the French, a hazardous, time-consuming process that involved conveying crates of reserve cartridges into the front line and distributing them. The Prussians, who nearly always made do with the ammunition in their pouches, marveled that Bavarians averaged forty rounds per man per combat, no matter how trivial. In the Prussian army, such exuberance was frowned upon; *Terraingewinn* – conquered ground – was the sole criterion of success. For this, fire discipline was essential. In the ensuing weeks, the Prussian criterion would be hammered into the Bavarians.[58]

Having picked Wissembourg clean, the Germans moved off in pursuit of MacMahon's 2nd Division. Even Bavarian officers shied at the excesses of their men as they slogged through a cold, pelting rain. The passing French troops had churned the dirt roads to the west into quicksand. Many of the Prussians and Bavarians lost their shoes in the slime, and marched on in their socks, cold, wet, and miserable. The Bavarians looted every house or shop they passed, often ignoring their officers, who had to wade in with drawn revolvers to force them back on the road. The Prussian XI Corps – comprised mainly of Nassauer, Hessians, and Saxons annexed after 1866 – had its own crisis as scores of *Schlappen* and *Maroden* – "softies" and "marauders" – fell out and refused to go on. Ultimately, as in the Bavarian corps, they were all raked together and pushed down the roads to Froeschwiller, perhaps by the example of the largely Polish Prussian V Corps, which plowed stolidly through the rain, earning the grudging admiration of a Bavarian witness: "*gute Marschierer.*"[59]

In Metz on 4 August, Louis-Napoleon roused himself and dispatched an enquiring telegram to General Frossard at Saarbrücken: "*Avez-vous quelques nouvelles de l'ennemi?*" – "Have you any news of the enemy?"[60] Indeed he had. The Prussian First and Second Armies were on the move, so swiftly and in such strength that Frossard had already abandoned his post on the Saar and pulled back to Spicheren, an elevated village commanding the Saarbrücken-Forbach road and railway. By the end of the day, Napoleon III had frozen

---

58 BKA, HS 846, Maj. Gustav Fleschuez, "Auszug aus dem Tagebuch zum Feldzuge 1870–71." B 982, Munich, 3 December 1871, Maj. Theodor Eppler, "Erfahrungen."

59 BKA, HS 846, Maj. Gustav von Fleschuez, "Auszug aus dem Tagebuch zum Feldzuge 1870–71." HS 868, "Kriegstagebuch Johannes Schulz." HS 849, Capt. Girl, "Erinnerungen," pp. 31–5.

60 SHAT, Lb5, Metz, 4 August 1870, 9:05 A.M., Napoleon III to Gen. Frossard.

with fright. Ladmirault, still creeping forward on Frossard's left, was urgently pulled back; Bazaine was ordered to remain at St. Avold, the Imperial Guard at Metz. Failly's V Corps, Napoleon III's only link with MacMahon, was forgotten in the hubbub at Metz. It remained at Saargemuines without orders, an oversight that would doom MacMahon two days later.[61] By now, Marshal Leboeuf's command was turning in circles. The emperor pestered him with messages and the empress, in Paris, thought nothing of waking the *major général* in the middle of the night with urgent telegrams that usually began "I did not want to wake the emperor and so I have cabled you directly..." Leboeuf may well have wondered whose sleep was more important, but groggily rose and replied anyway.

THE BATTLE OF SPICHEREN, 6 AUGUST 1870

Moltke meanwhile watched the developments in Alsace closely. His plan in 1870 was as simple as in 1866, "to seek the main forces of the enemy and attack them, wherever they were found."[62] The aim was a great pocket battle, in which the three Prussian armies would curl around Napoleon III's Army of the Rhine and destroy it. General Charles Frossard's occupation of Saarbrücken had played into Moltke's hands; indeed the Prussian staff chief had fervently hoped that Frossard and Bazaine would push their attack deeper into German territory, where they could have been set upon with a minimum of friction by all three German armies. Moltke understood that a battle south of the Saar would be far more difficult, requiring the Prussians to get the Third Army through the Vosges and the First and Second Armies over the Saar and the rolling, forested ground beyond it. Though the desired battle north of the Saar never materialized – Napoleon III and his subordinates sensing the danger beyond the river – Moltke still liked his chances south of the Saar. He would push Prince Friedrich Karl's Second Army through Saarbrücken and into the heart of Frossard's new position at Spicheren and Forbach. The ensuing battle for Forbach – a principal French supply dump – and the neighboring French ironworks of Stiring-Wendel would suck in additional French corps, creating a compact target for Moltke's pincers: Steinmetz's First Army turning south from Tholey and Crown Prince Friedrich Wilhelm's Third Army bending north from Alsace. Although the Prussian Third Army, slowed by Bavaria's clumsy mobilization, was not yet through the Vosges, it was far enough along after Wissembourg that Moltke felt free finally to unleash the First and Second

61 SHAT, Lb5, Metz, 4 August 1870, 1:20 P.M., Marshal Leboeuf to Marshal Bazaine. Metz, 4 August 1870, 5:15 P.M., Napoleon III to Marshal Leboeuf. Boulay, 4 August 1870, 8 P.M., Marshal Leboeuf to Napoleon III. St. Cloud, 4 August 1870, 11:20 P.M., Empress Eugénie to Marshal Leboeuf.
62 Fitzmaurice, pp. 107–8.

Armies, confident that the crown prince would defeat MacMahon and close up on the main army's left for a decisive battle east of Metz.

Moltke's plan, of course, was to engage Frossard and Bazaine on the left bank of the Saar with his largest force – Prince Friedrich Karl's Second Army – and then envelop the two French corps and all who might "march to the guns" with Steinmetz's 40,000 troops, who would cross the river at Saarlouis and strike into the French flank and rear. The plan had excellent prospects, not least because Napoleon III's orders for 7 August had four of his corps concentrating in the Saarbrücken-Forbach-Sarreguemines triangle. The four corps – Frossard's, Bazaine's, Ladmirault's, and Bourbaki's, the cream of the French army – would be ripe for the picking.[63] The problem was Steinmetz. A hero of 1866, when he had slashed through formidable Austrian positions at Skalice, facilitating the junction of Moltke's three armies at Königgrätz, seventy-four-year-old Steinmetz was well past his prime by 1870. Indeed some thought him senile; he was not Moltke's choice for an army command, but he remained a popular figure – the quintessential Prussian – and a dear friend of King Wilhelm I. Like the Blücher of legend, Steinmetz campaigned in an unadorned uniform and private's cap, and expressed himself in the rough language of the common man. Closer examination of Steinmetz's feat in 1866 should have raised doubts about the general. Had the Austrians only fought better from their elevated positions at Skalice, they might have annihilated Steinmetz's corps; as it was, he nearly annihilated it himself, marching his divisions into the ground after the battle in his haste to win the war single-handedly. Indeed Steinmetz had not even appeared at the climactic battle of Königgrätz; his corps was so wasted by battle and forced marches that Moltke had been forced to rest it on the crucial day.

On 5 August 1870, Steinmetz again took matters into his own hands. Though ordered by Moltke to cross the Saar on Prince Friedrich Karl's right and feel for the French flank, Steinmetz decided on his own initiative to take the shortest line to Frossard's new position at Spicheren. Hungry for a fight and scornful of Moltke, Steinmetz wheeled his two corps south on to roads that had been earmarked for the seven corps of Second Army. For a nineteenth-century army that sustained itself on carted supplies of food and ammunition, a logistical blunder like this could be as catastrophic as a lost battle. As Stein-metz's march columns shouldered into the crowded space between Saarlouis and Saarbrücken, they cut Prince Friedrich Karl off from his forward units and barred his path.[64] Thus began a ludicrous episode in the Franco-Prussian War: the smallest of the three Prussian armies, never intended to play more than a supporting role, blocked the principal army's way forward and ventured off to battle with 60,000, potentially 120,000 French troops. To Moltke's

63 SHAT, Lb6, Metz, 6 August 1870, Marshal Leboeuf to Marshal Bazaine.
64 Foerster, vol. 2, pp. 144–7.

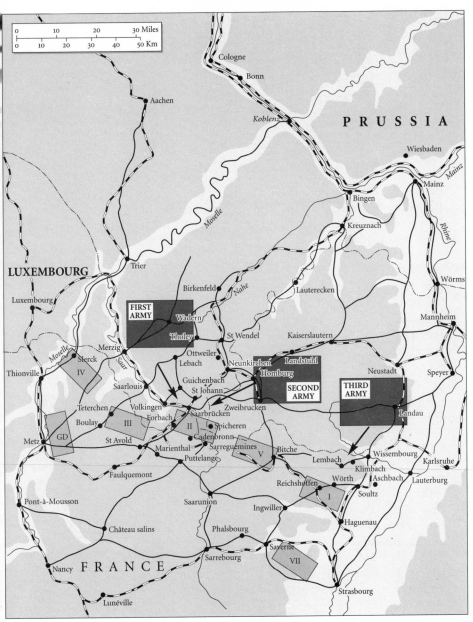

Map 4. Moltke strikes, 5–6 August 1870

amazement, Steinmetz was risking a large fraction of the Prussian army and ruining the attempted *Kesselschlacht* on the Saar. Major Waldersee's diary entry – "headquarters is beginning to regret [Steinmetz's] appointment" – was the understatement of the war.[65]

Steinmetz all along believed himself to be operating in the fighting spirit of that most famous of Prussians, Gebhard von Blücher. The enemy was retreating; therefore, *someone* needed to cling to him and keep contact. If Moltke and Prince Friedrich Karl were not up to the task, he was. In fact, Friedrich Karl, in constant contact with his forward units, had ordered his cavalry divisions on 5 August to "hang on the [French], make prisoners, and report constantly." Pushing ahead in the patient, methodical style of Moltke, the Second Army commandant was fixing the contours of the Army of the Rhine before closing the trap. When he received news of First Army's plunge, he was no less flabbergasted than Moltke: "Steinmetz has fatally compromised my beautiful plans."[66]

Although it was Steinmetz who weaved into Prince Friedrich Karl's path, the First Army commandant actually had little to do with the bloody battle that flared up on the Spicheren heights south of Saarbrücken on 6 August. Spicheren was the work of one of Steinmetz's divisional generals, Georg von Kameke, who, after crossing the Saar on the 6th, spied Frossard's new position at Spicheren and Forbach and mistakenly assumed that the French general was in full retreat. To engage what he took to be Frossard's rear guard, Kameke threw his two brigades into the teeth of one of France's most redoubtable natural positions: the wall of hills running between Spicheren and Forbach.[67]

Frossard, who had yielded Saarbrücken because of its indefensibility, had no intention of yielding Spicheren too. Bazaine stood nearby with four divisions and the position was excellent, classified as a *"position magnifique"* in the French army survey. Standing in Spicheren and looking down the heights toward Saarbrücken was like standing atop a green waterfall. Steep fields of waving grass plunged into deep woods that, far below, tumbled into the Saar valley. Spicheren's only weakness was the ease with which it could be flanked. Because the Prussians had massive forces arrayed along the Saar, some of their divisions would be able to penetrate above and below the plateau to engage Bazaine and force Frossard down from Spicheren. To counter the threat, Frossard placed only one of his three divisions on the Rote Berg, the central height. The other two divisions and their cavalry were placed lower down by Forbach, where they would be positioned to repel any Prussian attempt

65 Alfred von Waldersee, *Denkwürdigkeiten*, 3 vols., Berlin, 1922, vol. 1, p. 88. Moltke, *The Franco-German War of 1870-71*, pp. 22–9.
66 Foerster, vol. 2, pp. 146–7.
67 Gen. Julius Verdy du Vernois, *With the Royal Headquarters in 1870-71*, London, 1897, pp. 56–7.

to prise Frossard out from the left. Frossard's right wing seemed adequately covered by Jean-Baptiste Montaudon's division – the nearest unit of Bazaine's III Corps – at Sarreguemines, just seven miles from Spicheren. Overall, the French held the stronger hand on 6 August; that a battle was fought there before the arrival of Second Army in strength was due to entirely to the "fog and friction" of war: Steinmetz's turn south slowed Prince Friedrich Karl's advance and Kameke's impulsive attack went in without any reference to the overarching plans of Moltke or the army commanders.

Frossard, a graduate of the *Ecole Polytechnique* and an exacting engineer (his siege works had strangled the Roman Republic of Mazzini and Garibaldi in 1849), was an intelligent officer undone at Spicheren by a curious, unorthodox Prussian tendency first detected by the Austrians in 1866. Whereas the French army, like most armies, engaged in set-piece contests, never giving battle without adequate troops to hand, the Prussians had a rougher approach, which they had amply demonstrated in the Austro-Prussian War. At Vysokov and Jicin, preludes to Königgrätz, small Prussian advance guards had probed into heavily defended Austrian positions, engaged them, and only slowly reinforced themselves. Bismarck's first words to Moltke at Königgrätz defined the practice: "How big is this towel whose corner we've grabbed here?" The Prussians grabbed first and asked questions later. Once the enemy was firmly engaged, he could be rolled up from the flanks. Thus, for the Austrians and later the French, it was often impossible to know whether one was engaged in a "reconnaissance in force" against a small detachment or a real battle. Often the Prussians themselves did not know; they were literally blundering into an enemy and feeling him out, like a cop patting down a suspect. Of course, one of the changes made by the Prussians after 1866 was to reassign this function to the cavalry, hence the long screen of light and heavy squadrons that preceded every infantry formation. But Steinmetz had shortcircuited this critical reform on 5 August, when he veered across the path of the cavalry screen and pushed his infantry into the van. He was plainly more comfortable with the brutal methods of 1866. If his infantry gained a foothold, more units would rush in, but sporadically, only slowly lengthening the line. Loud periods of violence would alternate with bewildering moments of calm. Frossard, criticized after Spicheren for not summoning Bazaine's four divisions soon enough, was just the latest victim of these creeping Prussian tactics.

The creeping commenced at midday on 6 August, when the first of Kameke's two brigades shook out its guns and began bombarding the Rote Berg, the reddish, ironstone nose of the Spicheren position, which bulged into the Saar valley and overlooked the road from Saarbrücken. Soon three batteries of Krupp cannon were at work, firing explosive shells 2,000 yards on to the Rote Berg, where General Sylvain de Laveaucoupet's division, ordered by Frossard to hold the plateau, waited in their shelter trenches. With much of Laveaucoupet's division under cover and his view of the French obscured by the forests that grew up the sides of the Spicheren hills and the slag heaps and mills of Stiring-Wendel, Kameke had no idea that he was facing an entire corps. He continued to believe that he faced nothing more than a rearguard – despite the volume of artillery fire raining down on him – and thus thought nothing of sending the six battalions of General Francois's 27th Brigade into the teeth of the French position.

Francois extended four of his battalions along a three mile front and kept two in reserve. His right, feeling for the French left, worked its way up the Forbach railway, along the edge of the Stiringwald. His left, several thousand paces to the east, struck into the woods at the base of the Rote Berg. While Francois's half-Prussian, half-Hanoverian brigade staggered forward in company columns, they came under heavy artillery fire, far heavier than would have been expected from a rearguard. The Hanoverians advancing along the Forbach railway embankment passed under the curtain of shellfire at Stiring only to collide with an entire French brigade. Hundreds were struck down by Chassepot rounds. It was an inauspicious start to the war for these recently annexed "Prussians." One-fifth of them were married men with children – as yet only the Prussians resorted to this severe practice – and Hanoverians taken prisoner by the French avowed that "their hearts were not in the fight."[68] Francois's left wing fared no better than the right; the two Prussian battalions sent against the Rote Berg ran into a gale of Chassepot and *mitrailleuse* fire as they trooped into the woods below the height. Frossard's 10th Chasseurs had hidden themselves in the wood and fired quickly into the clumsy Prussian columns, cutting down dozens of frightened men in an instant. By one o'clock, Kameke's attack had stopped dead. The feet of the Spicheren heights – Stiring-Wendel and Gifert Wood – were littered with Prussian dead and wounded. Exhibiting again that bull-headed spirit, which had seen him through Svib Wood, one of the bloodiest episodes of the battle of Königgrätz, Francois gathered his last five reserve companies and personally led them into Gifert Wood. These men – more Hanoverians of the 74th Regiment – crossed most of the way through the wood, but were halted on the reddish, ironstone slope of the Rote Berg by French fire. Only Kameke's divisional artillery, now closing up behind the infantry in large numbers, prevented Francois from being swept away. Indeed, it was these resourceful Prussian guns, pushing through the woods and the potato fields beyond, that most impressed the French. Prussian "artillery masses" maintained a constant shellfire that filled the French trenches with dead and wounded and discouraged counter-thrusts.[69]

Now came another of those bewildering pauses characteristic of Prussian operations. While Francois desperately clung to the corners of the French

68 SHAT, Lb8, Metz, 11 Aug. 1870, Gen. Jarras, "Rapport sur l'interrogatoire des prisonniers."
69 SHAT, Lb6, Bernay, 28 Nov. 1877, Lt. Coudriet., "24e Regt. De Ligne: Participation du Regiment à la journée de Spickeren."

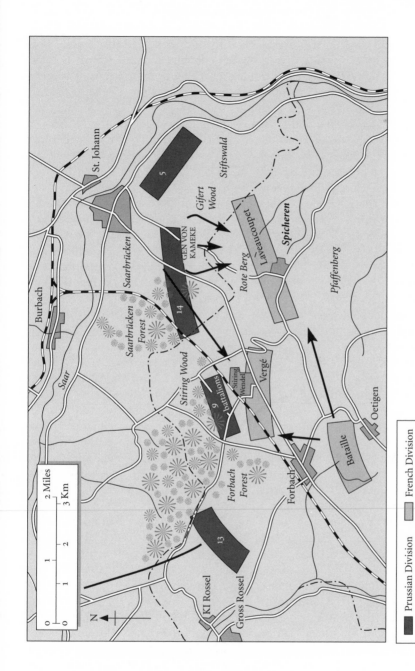

Map 5. The Battle of Spicheren

Prussian Division   French Division

position and awaited reinforcements, Frossard wondered just exactly how many men he was facing. Every French counter-attack that formed above Francois's huddled companies was blown back by Kameke's vigilant artillery. Resourceful French gun teams that ventured down the height to shorten their ranges and obviate the Krupp's advantage were instantly brought under counter-battery fire and chased away. By early afternoon five abandoned French guns languished in no-man's-land. They would be First Army's first trophies of the war if only Kameke could scale the Rote Berg.

Help was on the way. By mid-afternoon, Kameke's 28th Brigade, commanded by General Wilhelm von Woyna, had relieved the exhausted remains of Francois's 74th Regiment at Stiring and fanned out along the wooded ridge above the ironworks, taking the single brigade that Frossard had posted there in a cross fire. As the battle of Spicheren sputtered back to the life with the arrival of these fresh troops, Francois rose on the Rote Berg, drew his sword, and led his men on to the bare red slope. Within seconds the general was dead, ripped by five bullets. Many of his men met the same fate, the rest fell back into the Gifert Wood. By 3:00 P.M., Kameke's 14th Division was reeling; to deal the knockout blow, General Laveaucoupet ordered his 40th Regiment to counter-attack into Gifert Wood. They drove in with bayonets, pushing Francois's demoralized survivors before them. On Spicheren height, Frossard permitted General Charles Vergé to launch his second brigade at Woyna's troops in Stiring, knocking the freshly arrived Prussians almost all the way back to Saarbrücken. Had Frossard only strengthened these counter-attacks and continued them, he might have dealt a stinging defeat to the Prussians. But Frossard fully shared the French penchant for defensive tactics introduced after Königgrätz. Just as Laveaucoupet refused to leave the shelter of Gifert Wood and pursue Francois's survivors across the open ground toward Saarbrücken, so Frossard refused to leave Spicheren and the safety of his *position magnifique*. Having expelled the Prussians, he sat down to wait.

"Battle is slaughter," Clausewitz had written forty years earlier. If you shy from it, "someone will come along with a sharp sword and hack off your arms."[70] This was a warning that Frossard should have heeded. As he reined in his counter-attacks, the Prussians were sharpening their sword. Having reached the outskirts of Saarbrücken on the 6 August, Prince Friedrich Karl and his leading units, Konstantin von Alvensleben's III Corps and August von Goeben's VIII Corps, heard the sounds of battle from Spicheren and immediately began shifting troops to the front. Battalions were sent by rail along the Forbach line at half hour intervals; other units were sent on foot along the arrow-straight *Route Impériale*; Goeben's 9th Hussars galloped forward with two batteries of guns to help stem the rout below Stiring and

---

70 Carl von Clausewitz, *On War*, orig. 1832, Princeton, 1976, p. 260.

the Gifert Wood. The contrast between the French and Prussian styles was remarkable; whereas French generals exercised little initiative and seldom strayed from fixed positions and lines of communication, Prussian generals joined a battle at a moment's notice, even if this meant moving with only a fraction of their total strength and none of their supplies. Odd battalions could be brigaded together, supplies and ammunition shared out. The main thing was to increase numbers at the point of attack and put pressure on the enemy.

General Alvensleben himself rode the rails to Saarbrücken with a battalion of the Prussian 12th Regiment. No sooner were his horses taken off than he galloped forward to the battlefield and relieved Kameke of his blundering command. Surveying the human wreckage of the day – lines of dead and wounded in Prussian blue on the Rote Berg, the Gifert Wood and along the Forbach railway – Alvensleben understood that the battle would have to be begun all over again. He would have to work efficiently, for Bazaine had finally agreed to lend Frossard Jean-Baptiste Montaudon's division. If Montaudon marched all out, he could still make Spicheren in time to intervene in the battle.[71] While a brigade of the Prussian 5th Division retook the Gifert Wood, nine more battalions, tumbling off their trains and march routes in no kind of order from Alvensleben's III Corps and Goeben's VIII Corps, stretched the attack along the entire edge of the height. Charles Vergé's division in Stiring was finally dislodged and forced back on Forbach with heavy losses: 1,300 killed and wounded.

French facility with the rifle was demonstrated by Vergé's prodigious consumption of ammunition that day, 146,000 cartridges. That this expenditure by a single division represented one-third of the entire French war industry's daily production was at least as unsettling as the fact that fewer than one round in seventy-five actually struck a Prussian. Clearly the problem of fire control had still to be worked out.[72] Lieutenant Prospère Coudriet of the French 24th Regiment admired the discipline and cohesion of the Prussian attacks under this withering if not always accurate French fire. Though the Prussians ascending toward Spicheren were attacking into a semi-circle of converging fire from two entire French regiments and a Chasseur battalion, the Prussians plowed grimly ahead, their company columns preceded by long lines of skirmishers, which used the ground well to evade French defensive fire and pour in salvos of their own. Coudriet particularly admired the skill with which the Prussian skirmish line – the only shield against the Chassepot – was maintained. As Prussian fusiliers fell, they were swiftly replaced by ordinary infantry; 250-man companies would widen their intervals and sprint

71 J. B. Montaudon, *Souvenirs Militaires*, 2 vols., Paris, 1898–1900, vol. 2, pp. 4–7.
72 SHAT, Lb6, Metz, 10 Aug. 1870, Gen. Vergé to Gen. Frossard. Lb4, Paris, 1 Aug. 1870, Gen. Dejean to Marshal Leboeuf.

forward to replace the casualties. By this rolling, firing advance, the Prussians ground inexorably uphill, first through woods, then potato fields, then the rusty gravel of the Rote Berg.

On the iron mountain, the ground was so steep that soil and grass would not hold on the gravel slopes, and most of the Prussian wounds were to the head, hands, or feet, the only body parts exposed to an entrenched enemy firing straight down the vertical.[73] Against defensive fire like that, the Krupp guns were an essential strut. At Spicheren, Prussian gun teams pushed to within 1,200 yards of the French trenches – a considerable feat on the steep slope – and demolished them with explosive shells and shrapnel. Prussian shells burst in twenty or thirty jagged shards; Prussian shrapnel scattered forty zinc balls at bullet speed. This was hard to take in large doses. French senior officers rushed in where the fighting was hottest, one remarking "wavering among the troops" – "*hesitation chez les soldats*" – wherever the Prussian guns concentrated.[74] Coudriet of the 24th recalled seeing his regimental colonel torn apart by shell fragments as he directed fire from behind a breastwork on the Rote Berg. At last the French line began to give, pulled by the roughly one-third of French effectives who were reservists, none of whom had been with their regiments for more than a week when the Prussians struck.[75] By 6 o'clock – when many of the Prussian units had been on their feet for thirteen hours – Alvensleben had accumulated a substantial reserve of seven battalions, all from his own corps. Although he had no idea where Montaudon's division was, he had to assume that French supports were in the vicinity.

To shatter what remained of Frossard's corps before the arrival of reinforcements, General Alvensleben thrust this improvised reserve into the flank of the French position, sending the troops up the Forbach Berg, a hump of the Rote Berg that ran west toward Stiring. This brigade-strength formation, steadily augmented by new arrivals, crested the ridge and staggered into Laveaucoupet's left flank. This combination of overlapping infantry attacks and massed artillery barrages finally broke the French, who backed off the Rote Berg toward Spicheren and then, as darkness fell at 9 o'clock, yielded the entire plateau, flooding in opposite directions down the roads to Sarreguemines and Forbach. The colonel of the French 63rd Regiment voiced what would become a common complaint in the war: "Our men fired their rifles all day to no apparent effect against an enemy who constantly increased his numbers and turned our flanks."[76] This, of course, was the Prussian

---

73 Shand, p. 22.
74 SHAT, Lb6, no date, no name, "Notes sur la part qu'a prise la 63 d'Infanterie à l'affaire de 6 Août 1870."
75 SHAT, Lb6, Bernay, 28 Nov. 1877, Lt. Coudriet., "24e Regt. De Ligne: Participation du Regiment à la journée de Spickeren."
76 SHAT, Lb6, no date, no name, "Notes sur la part qu'a prise la 63 d'Infanterie à l'affaire de 6 Août 1870."

Fig. 5. Prussian infantry struggle on the Rote Berg

operational art in a nutshell: initiative, superior numbers at the chosen point, flanking attacks, and encirclement. Driven from Stiring and the Rote Berg, General Frossard briefly attempted to reform his position in Spicheren and Forbach, but soon learned that the entire Prussian 13th Division, which had crossed the Saar downstream at Völklingen, was marching into his unguarded left flank and rear. The pocket or *Kessel* was closing, yet Frossard had no reserves left to keep it open.

Giving up on the Saar, Frossard ordered a general retreat back to the line of the Moselle. On both roads away from the plateau Frossard's men collided with General Montaudon's march columns, which, having received no orders from Bazaine until 3:30 P.M. and no information from Frossard until 4:00 P.M., were only now wearily arriving at the front after forced marches of eight to fifteen miles. General Armand de Castagny's division, which, like Montaudon's, had belatedly "marched to the guns," halted several kilometers south of Forbach in darkness. The road was a bedlam of panicked troops and overturned wagons. Frossard's men – "starved, thirsty, dropping with fatigue" – were in no mood to continue the fight.[77] Castagny, still striving to reach Spicheren, recalled stopping one of Frossard's generals and asking him "how long did it

77 SHAT, Lb6, Paris, 25 June 1872, Col. Gabrielle to War Minister.

take your brigade to pass this road?" The general stared wildly at him: "*Mais je suis seul; j'ai perdu ma brigade*" – "But I am alone; I have lost my brigade."[78]

Bazaine later called Spicheren a "sad, useless battle," but he bore a large measure of responsibility for the defeat. All four of his divisions could have intervened to snatch victory from defeat; none of them did. Bazaine's adversaries – Alvensleben and Goeben – exhibited the opposite tendency, feeding battalions, squadrons, and batteries into the fight as quickly as they could be made available. Bazaine, of course, needed to be more cautious.[79] His divisions were spread forty miles from St. Avold to Bitche and he could not have known that Spicheren was a major battle until very late in the day. To have reacted earlier and sent large numbers of troops to Spicheren would have narrowed his position and perhaps enabled the Prussians to sweep around Frossard *and* him. He rebuffed Frossard's first call for assistance at nine o'clock in the morning, writing, "Our line is unfortunately very thin, and if this Prussian movement is serious, it would be wiser to [withdraw]."[80] That rebuff was hard to justify, for Frossard – himself in doubt as to the severity of the Prussian attack – requested just two brigades, one of Montaudon's for Spicheren and one of Decaen's for Forbach. Two brigades from two different corps would hardly have compromised Bazaine's position. Probably Bazaine's failure had more to do with a lack of acuity or just plain spite; the marshal did not like Frossard, who was the imperial family's favorite general.

Spicheren and Frossard's efforts to excuse the defeat after the war led to the creation of a "*Dossier Frossard*" in the French army archive, where senior officers involved that day were invited to answer Frossard's charges that he had been abandoned by his colleagues. The gist of all the reports submitted is that Frossard himself wavered too long between believing the Prussian attack to be a minor affair and a serious battle. As late as 5:15 P.M. – as Alvensleben was preparing his final push up to Spicheren and Zastrow's 13th Division was descending on Forbach – Frossard, deceived by yet another pause in the action, wired Bazaine: "The fighting, which has been lively, has calmed down.... I expect that I will remain master of this ground and will return the Montaudon Division to you." Bazaine, greatly relieved, was shocked to receive the following telegram just two hours later: "*Nous sommes tournées*" – "we have been outflanked."[81] The irresolution that Frossard displayed at Spicheren simply could not be remedied under the conditions of nineteenth-century warfare. A French division in the field needed two hours to prepare itself for a march and many more hours to execute the march. Time was the

78 SHAT, Lb6, "Dossier Frossard," Paris, 29 Nov. 1870, Gen. Castagny, "Reponse à la brochure du General Frossard en ce qui concerne la Division de Castagny pendant la journée de Forbach." Montaudon, pp. 4–7.
79 Andlau, pp. 41, 50. Howard, p. 92.
80 Montaudon, pp. 4–7.
81 SHAT, Lb6, "Dossier Frossard," Forbach, 6 Aug. 1870, Gen. Frossard to Marshal Bazaine.

critical element, yet Frossard the engineer let it slip away, perhaps, as one colleague snidely noted, because Spicheren "was his apprenticeship in the management of troops."[82]

Impressed by the effectiveness of French tactics on parts of the battlefield, the Prussians marveled at the overall incompetence of their operations. On 7 August, Prince Friedrich Karl wrote Alvensleben and compared Bazaine's floundering at Spicheren with Benedek's in 1866: "As in 1866, the French... let us prise apart several corps to strike at a soft, brittle mass," in this instance, General Charles Frossard's II Corps. Writing to his mother two days later, the Second Army commandant emphasized again the parallels with the Königgrätz campaign: "Everywhere this war is beginning like that of 1866, crushing defeats of isolated corps and great demoralization. The woods about here are full of enemy deserters. The position we took at Spicheren was incredibly strong."[83] Indeed it was, and Prussia's massive casualties at Spicheren ought to have tempered all delighted comparisons with 1866. French marksmanship and the Chassepot were killing Prussians at an unprecedented rate. Whereas the Prussians had routinely killed or wounded four Austrians for every Prussian casualty in 1866, they lost two men for every French casualty at Spicheren. Nearly 5,000 Prussians were cut down in the battle, more than half the number of Prussian killed and wounded at Königgrätz, and this in a relatively minor "encounter battle."

Because of Steinmetz's turn south and Kameke's rashness, the Prussians had absorbed brutal, wholly avoidable casualties. A witness who watched King Wilhelm I tour the battlefield in an open carriage noted that he "appeared stunned" by the unexpected carnage.[84] His only meager consolation was the extent of French losses, surprising given the natural advantages of the Spicheren position. Frossard lost 4,000 men, a sum that included 250 officers and 2,500 prisoners seized in the rapid Prussian envelopment; the latter were put to work burying the French and Prussian dead in mass graves all over the field before being shipped across the Rhine to prison camps. When Frossard reassembled his divisions in the following days, he found that they had lost everything in the retreat: forty bridges, hundreds of tents, and food, clothing, coffee, wine, and rum valued at 1 million francs.

Emperor Napoleon III's cares were far heavier. The Prussians seemed to be snipping off his army corps one after the other. It did seem eerily like 1866, when the Prussians had isolated a succession of Austrian units and chewed them up in frontier battles, draining Benedek of much needed strength in

---

82 SHAT, Lb6, "Dossier Frossard," Paris, 29 Nov. 1870, Gen. Castagny, "Reponse à la brochure du General Frossard en ce qui concerne la Division de Castagny pendant la journée de Forbach."
83 Foerster, vol. 2, pp. 145–7.
84 Friedrich Freudenthal, *Von Stade bis Gravelotte*, Bremen, 1898, p. 106.

the days before Königgrätz. Alarmed by the defeats at Wissembourg and Spicheren, the emperor informed Bazaine that he would "pull in Marshal MacMahon's corps and concentrate the army in a more compact manner."[85] With the Prussian armies spreading, as MacMahon worriedly put it, "like an oil stain" between the French corps, Napoleon III and Leboeuf belatedly tried to close the gaps. They were too late; MacMahon was about to be inundated.

85   SHAT, Lb 6, Metz, 6 August 1870, Marshal Leboeuf to Marshal Bazaine.

5

Froeschwiller

After Wissembourg, General Abel Douay's battered division – now commanded by General Jean Pellé – had reeled away to the southwest in the direction of Strasbourg. After pulling itself together on 5 August, Crown Prince Friedrich Wilhelm's Third Army moved off in Pellé's baggage-strewn wake. Having lost contact with MacMahon, the Prussian crown prince wanted to scour the ground east of the Vosges before turning into the mountains to join the Prussian First and Second Armies on the other side.[1] To do this, he made a difficult change of front southward: the Bavarian II Corps scrambled down the road to Lembach on the right, the Prussian V Corps and XI Corps descended on Woerth and Soultz in the center, and the Württemberg and Baden divisions – commanded by the Prussian General August von Werder – moved up on the left at Aschbach.

The roads were difficult with ascending ranges of wooded hills that only occasionally opened on to fields of corn or tobacco before the woods or vineyards closed in again. At first, the crown prince and his staff chief, General Albrecht von Blumenthal, assumed that MacMahon was running for cover in the fortress of Strasbourg. Late on the 5th, however, a *Totenkopf* hussar rode through Woerth, noted barricades on the road to Froeschwiller, dismounted, swam across the Sauer, had a long look at MacMahon's sprawling position, and galloped back to headquarters.[2] By late evening, the crown prince and Blumenthal were fully apprised: MacMahon was not at Strasbourg; on the contrary, he had scarcely moved from the positions he had held during the battle of Wissembourg. He was still at Froeschwiller, like Spicheren, one of the French army's *positions magnifiques*. Blumenthal and Crown Prince

---

1 Frederick III, *The War Diary of the Emperor Frederick III 1870–71*, New York, 1927, pp. 29–30.
2 Johannes Priese, *Als Totenkopfhusar 1870–71*, Berlin, 1936, pp. 30–8.

Friedrich Wilhelm were pleasantly surprised. Froeschwiller could be encircled by a large army. That evening they began to plot a *Kesselschlacht* involving the entire Third Army for 7 August.[3]

Driven from Wissembourg on the 4th, MacMahon resolved to stand at Froeschwiller, which he considered a strong position and a hub of France's eastern communications. If it fell, the Prussians would be able to seize control of the Bitche-Strasbourg railway as well as the principal roads passing through the Vosges. This, in turn, would isolate the French garrison at Strasbourg and make it easier for the Germans to supply their large armies in France.[4] The chief defect of Froeschwiller was its vulnerability to a flanking attack. Though redoubtable against a frontal assault, Froeschwiller was easily turned from the south by a large army, and large numbers of troops were something that the Germans had in abundance in 1870. Against MacMahon's corps of 50,000, Crown Prince Friedrich Wilhelm had an army of 100,000 descending on Froeschwiller in three great columns. MacMahon ought to have abandoned the position and withdrawn through the Vosges, but he needed time to collect Pellé's division and still hoped to combine with other French troops in the area to counter-attack the Prussians and recover the ground lost at Wissembourg. Early on 6 August he ordered General Pierre de Failly, commander of the French V Corps, to make his 30,000 troops ready for one of two eventualities: either an attack on the Prussian Third Army as it passed through the Vosges defiles or a bold envelopment of the Prussian crown prince if he dawdled at Wissembourg.[5] Given the numerical odds against MacMahon, this was admirable pluck, but misguided. The Prussians rarely dawdled, and were far too thorough to turn into the Vosges without first making sure of MacMahon.

Froeschwiller was an imposing obstacle with clear fields of fire in all directions. The village perched above the Sauer river and overlooked the important road junction of Woerth, where the plain of Alsace began to rise into the wooded Vosges. Like Spicheren, it wrung every advantage from the Chassepot rifle, because Froeschwiller and its neighboring village of Elsasshausen sat at the heart of a semicircular position on the right bank of the Sauer, flanked by Eberbach on the right and Langensoultzbach on the left. The four villages were linked by a lateral road and easily reinforced. Prussian attacks into this bowl of fire would be impeded by the Sauer, as well as the vines and hop plantations crowded onto the slopes below the French position. On a pre-war staff ride, Marshal MacMahon had paused to study the position and declared: "One day

---

3   Munich, Bayerisches Kriegsarchiv (BKA), HS 849, Capt. Girl, "Einige Erinnerungen," p. 43.
4   Vincennes, Service Historique de l'Armée de Terre (SHAT), Lb 6, Saverne, 7 Aug. 1870, Marshal MacMahon to Napoleon III.
5   SHAT, Lb 6, Camp de Froeschwiller, 6 Aug. 1870, Marshal MacMahon to General de Failly.

I would like to greet the Germans here; not even a field mouse would come out alive."[6] In the hours after Wissembourg, MacMahon gave shape to the greeting, ranging the five divisions he had with him across the Froeschwiller heights. To anchor his left, where the Froeschwiller position merged into the wooded Vosges at Langensoultzbach, MacMahon deployed General Auguste Ducrot's 1st Division, with Jean Pellé's 2nd Division – mauled at Wissembourg – in reserve. He assigned the center at Froeschwiller and Elsasshausen to General Noel Raoult's 3rd Division, and his most vulnerable point, the unsecured right wing that straggled into open fields at Morsbronn, to General Marie-Hippolyte de Lartigue's 4th Division and a weak division of the French VII Corps, which had marched up from Belfort.

Like many nineteenth-century battles, Froeschwiller began as a chance encounter, in this instance, a day earlier than the crown prince and Blumenthal had intended. Advance units of the Prussian V Corps, the Baden-Württemberg Corps, and the Bavarian II Corps, prowling south toward Strasbourg on muddy roads churned up by a night of rain, literally bumped into the French position on 6 August. Mounting toward Langensoultzbach on the French left, General Friedrich von Bothmer's Bavarian 4th Division came under heavy, accurate fire from Ducrot's veterans. Entering Woerth, at the foot of the powerful French position, advance parties of the Prussian V Corps and General August von Werder's Baden-Württemberg Corps drew the concentrated fire of Raoult's entrenched division. Hearing the sounds of battle, the Prussian XI Corps swerved off of its own line of march to slide in beside V Corps and Werder at Spachbach and Gunstett.

Trailing the army at Soultz, Crown Prince Friedrich Wilhelm and General Blumenthal were appalled by the noises of battle drifting over from the west. They had not wanted a battle on the 6th, and worried that impulsive officers at the head of the march columns might blunder into a trap with just a fraction of Third Army, much as Steinmetz and Kameke were doing at Spicheren.[7] Blumenthal sent frantic messages to the front ordering restraint, but the messengers – stalled on bad roads blocked in both directions by men, guns, horses, supplies, and ambulances – arrived too late to halt the fighting. Froeschwiller had found its Kameke: Prussian V Corps commandant General Hugo von Kirchbach. Finding the French in strong positions on the Sauer, the sixty-one-year-old Kirchbach simply bulled into their midst. Like most of his peers, Kirchbach was a veteran of the Austro-Prussian War, which had rewarded even the most reckless Prussian strokes. At Vysokov and Skalice in 1866, Kirchbach had cracked through powerful Austrian positions against

---

6 Oskar Becher, *Kriegstagebuch eines Vierundneunzigers aus dem Kriege 1870–71*, Weimar, 1904, p. 8.
7 Field Marshal Albrecht von Blumenthal, *Journals of Field Marshal Count von Blumenthal for 1866 and 1870–71*, London, 1903, pp. 87–8.

long odds and received the *Pour le Mérite* – Prussia's highest decoration for valor – for his efforts. Four years later, there was no stopping him. He deployed his entire artillery – sixty Krupp guns – in a line at Woerth and launched the brigades he had with him on to MacMahon's killing fields.

The Poles and Germans of the Prussian 9th Division were first into the breach. Passing through Oberdorf and Spachbach, they tramped toward the Sauer, floundered across, and walked into a cross fire. Lieutenant Leopold von Winning of the Prussian 47th Regiment was one of the only platoon leaders to survive the assault. Intersecting streams of fire tore the Prussian attack columns to shreds. Winning watched another lieutenant disintegrate before his eyes, seized by a burst of *mitrailleuse* fire that tore away his feet, legs, chest, and face. Mounted officers, targeted by the sharp-shooting French infantry, were struck down at once. Those that survived frantically dismounted, splashing down beside their men in the water meadows.[8] Gradually the Prussian columns thinned into skirmish lines that lapped against the the French position. Further progress was impossible. Dug in on the high ground, the French were all but invisible from below, and the Prussians, armed with primitive rifles and paper cartridges, found it impossible to lie flat. They would have soaked their cartridges on the wet ground; thus, all along the line, the Prussians crouched or kneeled awkwardly, offering easy targets to the French.

The Baden-Württemberger tried to push their own attack over the Sauer to relieve the Prussians, but were blocked by the river itself, twenty-feet wide and five-feet deep, it slowed the attack to a trickle. While agitated engineers ran through Woerth ripping doors and gates from their hinges and pulling up garden fences to throw across the Sauer, shrapnel, *mitrailleuse*, and Chassepot fire from a still invisible enemy took a steady, demoralizing toll. Wilhelm Sohn, a private in Württemberg's 2nd Regiment, remembered standing with three friends waiting for a bridge; one-by-one his three comrades fell over clutching painful wounds. None ever saw an enemy. Finally Sohn and his depleted company marched across the cold Sauer, through the marshes on the other side, and up the Froeschwiller heights. Sohn's Württemberger used the Prussian tactics introduced after Königgrätz. They "swarmed," one section kneeling and firing to cover the advance of another "swarm."

Of course, some of the swarms never swarmed; the Prussians discovered that the most difficult aspect of an infantry attack is not leading the men across the fire-swept field, but persuading them to leave their cover and attack at all.[9] And in the funnel-shaped area below Froeschwiller, even smartly delivered attacks crumbled in the French cross fire. Sohn watched as nearly

8   Leopold von Winning, *Erinnerungen eines preussischen Leutnants aus den Kriegsjahren 1866 und 1870–71*, Heidelberg, 1911, p. 92.
9   Col. Karl Maywald, "Die Lehren des Krieges 1870–71," *Österreichische Militärische Zeitschrift* (ÖMZ) 2, 1873, pp. 109–10.

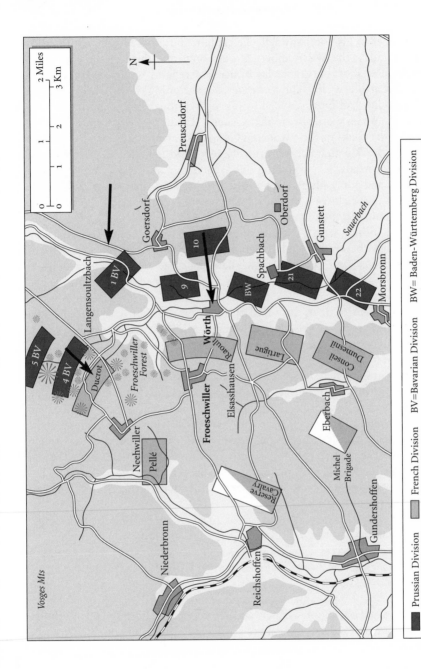

Map 6. The Battle of Froeschwiller

Prussian Division   French Division   BV=Bavarian Division   BW= Baden-Württemberg Division

every officer in his company fell, the captain and most of the platoon leaders. By midday, the Württemberger were only one-third of the way up to Froeschwiller; most of the men lay in shallow trenches with their faces buried in the dirt, artillery, rifle, and *mitrailleuse* fire ripping overhead. Sohn's 250-man company had been reduced to just eighty-four men in ninety minutes of combat. When word spread that General Raoult's Algerian *tirailleurs* had fired into the backs of the advancing German swarms after being overrun on the Sauer, the Württemberger furiously separated the African prisoners and bashed their heads in.[10] Watching this scene from an orchard, Private Franz Härle reached for a plum. As he raised himself on one elbow, he heard a Chassepot crack above him and felt the round tear through his mouth – in one cheek and out the other.[11]

Armed mostly with Podewils rifles, unimproved relics of the 1866 war, the Bavarians barely held their own on the right wing of the Prussian advance. Bothmer's 4th Division, which had spearheaded the German attack at Wissembourg, led in this attack as well. The experience was dreadful, as bad as anything on the Lauter. The Bavarians, who had not slept or eaten properly for two entire days, advanced through woods that literally fell down under the hurricane of French fire. Marshal MacMahon possessed 130 guns at Froeschwiller, and every single one them seemed to be trained on this spot. Trunks and branches snapped and the earth exploded. Johannes Schulz, an enlisted man in the Bavarian 9th Regiment, was shot in the leg and lacerated by a shell fragment as he moved forward. He watched his battalion disintegrate as Ducrot's men – mostly combat veterans of the Crimea, Italy, Mexico, and Algeria – mowed down their adversaries with well-aimed shots. Schulz's battalion commandant fell, then his company commander (wounded, the captain was propped against a tree by his orderly only to receive a better-aimed round through the heart), then his platoon leader. Schulz's best friend, kneeling beside him, was shot in the mouth. He lay stunned with his teeth shattered and blood gushing onto his tunic.

Major Gustav Fleschuez, who joined an attack by Bothmer's 7th Brigade, recalled that it was the invisibility of the French that most unnerved the men. Hundreds of Bavarians fell without even a glimpse of the enemy, only a riot of muzzle flashes flaring along the Froeschwiller ridge. For half-drunken men – the Bavarians had been given only wine in the morning – the experience must have been surreal.[12] Command was impossible because of the din of the battle, which drowned out shouted orders and even drum and horn signals. Visibility came and went as palls of gunsmoke settled and lifted on the field. Thus, the

---

10 Paul Dorsch, ed., *Kriegszuge der Württemberger im 19. Jahrhundert*, Stuttgart, 1913, pp. 293–5.
11 Paul Dorsch, *Noch ein Schwabenbuch*, Stuttgart, 1911, pp. 25–6.
12 BKA, HS 856, Landwehr Lieut. Josef Krumper, "Mein Tagebuch."

Fig. 6. The Bavarians attack Froeschwiller

German troops had "no sense of where or how the battle was going."[13] Under physical and mental strain like this, the Bavarians gave up, and ran back across the Soultzbach, only some of their officers entreating them to rally: *"Nur schiessen, solange ihr könnt!"* – "Just fire, as long as you can!"[14] Fleschuez, one of those diehard officers, was shot in the chest as he urgently conferred with a colleague. He fell down, gasping for air but otherwise unharmed; he had been saved by his wallet, which he had tucked into his breast pocket before the battle.

For the Germans, the prematurely launched battle of Froeschwiller was slipping away. Indeed had the French counter-attacked in the early afternoon, they would probably have won. As at Spicheren, however, they remained on the defensive, determined to wring every advantage from the Chassepot. For the Germans, this was fortunate, not least because the army command was still absent, somewhere on the road between Soultz and Woerth. To gather information and direct the battle in their absence, Crown Prince Friedrich Wilhelm and Blumenthal sent Prussian adjutants forward at midday. Two of them arrived at Diefenbach to find General Ludwig von der Tann, who had commanded the Bavarian army *against* the Prussians in 1866, resting his

---

13 BKA, HS 846, Maj. Gustav Fleschuez, "Auszug aus dem Tagebuch zum Feldzuge 1870–71."
14 BKA, HS 868, "Kriegstagebuch Johannes Schulz."

Bavarian I Corps. Because it was precisely this lack of energy that had doomed the Bavarians in 1866, the Prussians ordered Tann forward, an order he refused. "The Prussians want to sacrifice us Bavarians to spare themselves," Tann grumbled loudly to a colleague.[15] Hearing this, Captain Celsus Girl, a Bavarian who had also ridden up from the Third Army headquarters, reminded Tann that Prussian units were fighting and dying all around them. The Bavarians *had* to fight. In a revealing exchange recounted in none of the war's official histories, Tann and his entourage pounced upon Girl: "You love the Prussians so much that you've forgotten how to be a Bavarian." In this case, "being a Bavarian" meant doing nothing. Tann, who had been general staff chief of the Bavarian army for more than ten years before the war, belatedly observed that his ill-trained infantry did not know how to operate with the artillery, hence could not be thrown against the French positions. It took four couriers from army headquarters to budge Tann, who finally succumbed in the early afternoon to the following formulation: "In the name of His Majesty the King of Bavaria, the Crown Prince of Prussia orders that the [Bavarian] I Corps deploy all of its forces without further delay to support and exploit the gains made at such heavy cost by the Prussians." (The normally imperturbable crown prince was reported to have leaped in the air, stamped around his command post, and pounded the table after Tann's third refusal.)

Even when Tann agreed to attack, it was difficult to rouse the Bavarian troops, who were transfixed by the shell-torn corpses around Woerth and the clatter of the French rifles and *mitrailleuses*. Some flatly refused to attack. Ordered to dismount and push their gun carriages through the plowed fields below Froeschwiller, gunners of Tann's 2nd Brigade shook their heads. Noticing that Tann's ammunition wagons were lagging behind the infantry, who were expending their cartridges at the usual rate, Girl rode back to find the caissons stuck in the mud, full of "lazy peasant conscripts," who would not get down to push or even walk. Rebuked again by Crown Prince Friedrich Wilhelm – "engage the enemy *properly* and drive him back" – Tann eventually did launch an attack with the one division he had to hand, but with disastrous results.[16] While his 1st Brigade attacked straight up the Froeschwiller heights, covering the ground with killed, wounded, and shirkers, his 2nd Brigade received orders to turn the French left. Veering toward Langensoultzbach, this 2nd Brigade cut directly across the path of the 1st Brigade, stopping all progress on a fire-swept slope without cover. The Prussians watched incredulously as the Bavarian *Hellblauer* – the "light blues" – dissolved in panic; hundreds ran back to the Sauer to battles of another sort with furious officers, who rode into the stream to beat the men back to the right bank with their sabers. Those Bavarians

---

15 "*Die Preussen wollten nur uns Bayern d'ran setzen, nun sich selber zu entlasten.*" BKA, HS 849, Capt. Girl, "Einige Erinnerungen," p. 47.
16 Frederick III, p. 36.

who valiantly pressed the attack into the woods below Froeschwiller were forced to their knees by the ripping French fire. Private Lorenz Waas of the Bavarian 11th Regiment wrote that even on their bellies the men could get no closer to the French than 150 yards. The Chassepot and *mitrailleuse* fire was too intense. Gradually Tann's corps, like Hartmann's, slid backward, awaiting progress by the Prussians.[17]

At midday, the Prussian XI Corps, marching to the guns, pitched in at the opposite end of the field, on the left wing, beside the Prussian V Corps and Werder's Baden-Württemberg Corps. These men, mostly Saxons, groped for the unanchored right wing of the French position around Morsbronn, but fared even worse than the Prussians or Bavarians. Although faced with a thinner line of French infantry – one-and-a-half divisions spread across two miles of front – the Saxons had trouble coming to grips with the long-range fire of the Chassepot. Private Oskar Becher recalled the frustration of his officers as the attacking columns staggered under the shrieking, snapping fusillade: "*Kerls, was man so hört, das tut einem nichts!*" – "Boys, if you can *hear* it, it can't harm you!" Chestnuts like these from the old veterans did little to reassure the new recruits, who, as Becher put it, "waved back and forth like a field of grain with every shell and bullet that passed overhead."[18] The Prussian 87th Regiment splashed into the Sauer at Spachbach, directly beneath the thickly defended French position at Elsasshausen. Even veterans of Königgrätz judged the fire beyond belief. Spachbach shook and rattled under detonations of French shrapnel, and the men had difficulty fording the Sauer, which had overflowed its banks on both sides. As they wallowed along the right bank, up to their waists in water, the nonstop chatter of the French *mitrailleuses* ringing in their ears, the Prussians had to repel repeated, battalion-strength French counter-attacks. Captain Gebhard von Bismarck of the Prussian 21st Division called these bayonet charges "nightmarish." Already terrified by the volume of fire, the Prussians quailed at the ululations of the Algerian troops, who trilled and sang as they fired low into the floundering Prussians. With a desperate heave, much of Bismarck's regiment gave ground, floundering back across the Sauer, where many of the panic-stricken troops had to be shot down by their own officers to stem the rout.[19]

As at Wissembourg and Spicheren, Prussia's Chassepot-slashed infantry attacks had to be rescued by the artillery, which ran forward to evict the French from Woerth and prop up Kirchbach's shattered attacks. A French officer on MacMahon's right observed after the battle that "I Corps was beaten more than anything else by the unceasing, unanswerable Prussian artillery."

17 BKA, HS 889, Lorenz Waas, "Erlbenisse aus der Militärdienstzeit." HS 849, Capt. Girl, "Einige Erinnerungen," pp. 51–3.
18 Becher, pp. 8–15.
19 G. von Bismarck, *Kriegserlebnisse 1866 und 1870–71*, Dessau, 1907, pp. 108–10.

Effective at 4,000 yards, the Prussian guns opened gaping wounds in the
French lines from well beyond the range of the French cannon. Whenever
a French gun opened up to reassure MacMahon's troops, it was instantly
silenced by counter-battery fire.[20] Few French *mitrailleuses* survived into the
afternoon.[21] One of Raoult's generals noted that his brigade would never
have been dislodged from its fine position at Froeschwiller were it not for
the "decimating action" of the Prussian artillery, which killed so many of
his officers that command of the unit became impossible.[22] Ducrot insisted
that his 1st Division would have easily polished off the Bavarian II Corps
with counter-attacks across the Soultzbach had it not been for the arrival of
several Prussian gun batteries, which hammered his men all the way back to
Froeschwiller, uncovering MacMahon's left wing.[23]

As the French receded, the Prussians established themselves on the right
bank of the Sauer, and the two Prussian corps, sporadically assisted by the
Bavarians, pressed the attack on Elsasshausen and Froeschwiller. Though
the French were wilting, they still fought bitterly, and tactical unity among
the Germans broke down completely in the river crossing and the fire storm
on both banks. Officers threw together companies on the spot by grabbing
various men with the epaulets of their corps – yellow for V Corps, red for XI
Corps – and pushing them forward.[24] In the Bavarian sector, officers tried
the same trick less successfully. Ludwig Gebhard, a Bavarian major, observed
"great shirking" in both Bavarian corps. In the woods below Froeschwiller,
Captain Celsus Girl, another Bavarian, met with whole platoons of his countrymen streaming to the rear; the pretext was always the same – stretcher-
bearing or prisoner escort – but Girl noted that there were never fewer than
four or five healthy Bavarian escorts for every prisoner or wounded comrade.
Girl saw a drummer of the elite Bavarian lifeguards cowering behind a tree,
wildly beating the attack signal over and over, driving the remnants of his battalion to certain death. Girl's observations, set down after the battle, convey the
essential truth that every battle is a skein of personal crises only loosely joined
by a plan of operations. While Girl confronted 200 stragglers, ordering them to
reform and attack Froeschwiller, he watched a "crazed, red-faced" Bavarian
infantryman stamp through the woods "as if on the hunt." He was indeed
hunting *Schwarzen* ("blacks"), the dark-skinned French Berber troops, whom
the Germans suspected of every atrocity: backstabbing with their *yatagans*,

20 SHAT, Lc2/3, Sedan, 1 Sept. 1870, Col. Louis Chagrin de St. Hilaire, "Aprés la bataille."
21 Capt. Hermann Thünheim, "Die Mitrailleusen und ihre Leistungen im Feldzuge 1870–71,"
    ÖMZ 4, 1871, pp. 253–4.
22 SHAT, Lb6, Camp de Châlons, 16 Aug. 1870, General Lefebvre, "Rapports des officiers
    généraux sur la bataille de Froeschwiller."
23 SHAT, Lb6, Lorrey, 12 Aug. 1870, Gen. Ducrot, "Rapport sur la journée du 6 Août."
24 Theodor Fontane, *Der Krieg gegen Frankreich 1870–71*, 4 vols., orig. 1873–76, Zurich, 1985,
    vol. 1, p. 242. Winning, p. 92.

shooting the wounded, gouging out the eyes of prisoners with their thumbs, and cutting off the noses and ears of German casualties.[25] Finding a wounded Algerian, the Bavarian would press the muzzle of his rifle against the man's head and blow his brains out, "doubtless," Girl observed, "sending a number of innocents to their eternal sleep."[26]

Troops like Girl's crazed Bavarian were expressing frustration in their own brutal way at the stiff resistance of Colonel Pierre Suzzoni's 2nd Algerian Tirailleur Regiment. Holding the wooded salient below Froeschwiller against the best efforts of two German corps, the Algerians simply would not yield. "We will all die here, if need be," Suzzoni had told his men in the morning, and most of them did. With twenty-nine hundred troops in the morning, the Algerians were reduced to a rump of 250 by the afternoon, enclosed, as one *tirailleur* put it, "in a circle of iron and fire." Suzzoni himself was killed by a shell splinter at 2:30 in the afternoon as were most of his officers. Yet the Africans fought on, calling to each other in Arabic, burrowing into cover, and firing coolly into the fronts, backs, and flanks of the Prussian and Bavarian swarms trying to cross the wood.[27] "There should have been no question of making prisoners of those blacks," Reich Chancellor Bismarck later fulminated. "If I had my way, every [German] soldier who made a black man prisoner would be placed under arrest. They are beasts of prey, and ought to be shot down."[28]

By midday, Crown Prince Friedrich Wilhelm and Blumenthal had finally broken through the jam of wagons, ambulances, and march columns behind Woerth to direct the sputtering offensive.[29] Initially reluctant to fight and distressed by the slow arrival of their troops, the crown prince and Blumenthal now recognized that matters were too far advanced to let go.[30] Sixty-one-year-old General Julius von Bose, commandant of the Prussian XI Corps, was exceeding even Kirchbach in offensive spirit. In 1866, Bose had delivered the first great victory of the Austro-Prussian War, seizing Podol and breaching Benedek's Iser river line to commence the envelopment of the Austrians by three Prussian armies. Circumstances placed him in an identical role at Froeschwiller; streaming across the Sauer at Gunstett, his XI Corps found itself optimally positioned to prise MacMahon from a powerful position and

25 London, Public Record Office (PRO), FO 425, 98, 283, Versailles, 9 Jan. 1871, Bismarck to Bernstorff.
26 BKA, HS 849, Capt. Girl, "Einige Erinnerungen," pp. 54–5. BKA, B 1237, Chaudenay, 21 Aug. 1870, Maj. Ludwig Gebhard. Dresden, Sächsisches Kriegsarchiv (SKA), Zeitg. Slg. 158, Lt. Adolf von Hinüber, "Tagebuch 1870–71."
27 SHAT, Lb6, Bayon, 11 Aug. 1870, Capt. Vienot, "Rapport détaillée sur les incidents de la journée du 6 Août."
28 Otto Pflanze, *Bismarck and the Development of Germany*, 3 vols., Princeton, 1990, vol. 1, p. 483.
29 BKA, HS 858, "Kriegstagebuch Leopold Prinz von Bayern."
30 Frederick III, p. 32.

peel him away from Napoleon III's Army of the Rhine. Watching with a telescope from Froeschwiller, Marshal MacMahon discerned the danger. Although he was pulverizing the Prussians and Bavarians beneath him, MacMahon saw plainly the threat to his right at Morsbronn and Eberbach, where mixed-up swarms of Bose's 21st and 22nd Divisions were meeting scant resistance as they wheeled around the overstretched flank of the French position. Pinned down by fierce Prussian attacks on Eberbach and the Niederwald, General Lartigue's 4th Division and General Gustave Conseil-Dumesnil's weak division from VII Corps had nothing left to repel Bose's turn through Morsbronn.

The German advantage in raw numbers was becoming insuperable as Blumenthal and the crown prince fed more and more troops into battle. By early afternoon, 88,000 German troops were in action against MacMahon's 50,000. On the right, the French reached for their last weapon. Behind Lartigue, on the heights above Morsbronn, stood one of MacMahon's two reserve cavalry divisions. This one, commanded by General Xavier Duhesme, included a heavy brigade of two cuirassier regiments. To throw Bose back and remove his cavalry from a tightening ring of Prussian artillery, Duhesme unleashed his heavy brigade at one o'clock.[31] Led out by General Alexandre Michel, the cuirassiers – resplendent in their polished breastplates and plumed helmets – descended the steep slope at an awkward, lumbering canter, and began running toward Morsbronn. Michel, commandant of the imperial cavalry school before the war, must have bemoaned the broken, semi-wooded ground that shook apart his walls of horsemen and checked most of the momentum that they carried off the hill; Prussian gunfire and rifle volleys flattened the rest. Most Prussian memoirs of the battle recall the scene: the initial fright and the cool reaction. A Saxon of the Prussian 22nd Division could recite the actual orders long after the battle. As the ground shook with the approach of 1,200 cuirassiers – heavy men on heavy horses – Prussian platoon leaders strung their men out in loose skirmish lines: *"Kavallerie 400 Schritt, kleine Klappe, den Mann auf die Brust gehalten. Legt an! Feuer! Schnellfeuer!"* – "Cavalry at 400 paces, put the man's chest in your sights. Aim! Fire! Rapid fire!" The Prussian volleys erupted – drowning out the thunder of the French charge for an instant – and then elided into rapid fire, as each man reloaded, waited for the powder smoke to lift, scanned the field for targets, and fired individually.[32]

This was, of course, a radical change in tactics. Before the adoption of the breech-loading rifle, it had been customary for European infantry to form squares or throw themselves to the ground at the approach of cavalry to avoid the saber blows and make the horses shy. Now they simply stood in lines and

---

31   SHAT, Lb6, Colombey, 12 Aug. 1870, Gen. Duhesme to Marshal MacMahon, "Sur les opérations de la Division de Cavallerie du 1er Corps."
32   Becher, pp. 13–15.

blazed away.[33] A Prussian infantry officer in the Niederwald, the wood that separated Elsasshausen and Eberbach, directed the fire of his men at Michel's heavy brigade when it passed briefly into range. He remembered the strange music the German bullets made when they pinged off the French breast-plates.[34] Hemmed in by rifle and shrapnel fire, Michel's brigade disintegrated; 800 of 1,200 horses or riders were cut down, none made it to within fifty yards of a Prussian infantry company. After the battle, the Prussians were surprised to find hundreds of dead French lancers but few dead cuirassiers. The new steel breastplates procured before the war had served their purpose.[35] (One wonders how the Brazilians fared with the old ones.) The unarmored horses were not so fortunate as the armored men. All movement through the village of Morsbronn stopped as the wounded mounts piled up, shot by Prussian infantry hidden in the buildings until the kicking, writhing carcasses plugged the streets. One Prussian captain recalled ordering his men to cease firing at the trapped, defenseless cavalry, "*denn es sei doch gar so grässlich*" – "because it was just too ghastly."[36] The sacrifice of Alexandre Michel's heavy brigade hardly checked the Prussian advance. In Morsbronn and Eberbach, Prussian officers quickly reorganized their men, changed front to the right, and began to roll up Froeschwiller.

Had all of the French infantry been the seasoned veterans of Sebastopol and Solferino who were inflicting such dreadful losses on the German infantry, Marshal MacMahon might yet have stood his ground. But every French regi-ment contained large numbers of green recruits and forgetful reservists. These were the troops that broke first on MacMahon's vulnerable right wing. At least that was the testimony of Colonel Louis Chagrin de St. Hilaire, who com-manded the French 99th Regiment at Eberbach. Chagrin and his men had endured much in the course of a long and bloody day in expectation of the moment when the Prussian infantry would finally close to take the crests around Froeschwiller and expose themselves to the desolating French "bat-talion fire" introduced after Königgrätz. *Feu de bataillon* was the controlled delivery of aimed salvos by entire Chassepot-armed battalions. After seizing Morsbronn and changing front in the afternoon, the Prussians of XI Corps finally came into range – first skirmish lines, then massed company columns – but just as Chagrin and his captains were giving the order for "battalion fires at long range," they were balked by the greenhorns in their ranks, who ner-vously opened fire, triggering a massive, unaimed, uncontrolled spattering of French musketry, which clouded the entire field in smoke, permitting the Prussians to sprint forward and make their own rifles effective. For an hour,

33 BKA, HS 849, Capt. Girl, "Einige Erinnerungen," p. 82.
34 G. von Bismarck, p. 112.
35 BKA, HS 858, "Kriegstagebuch Leopold Prinz von Bayern."
36 BKA, HS 849, Capt. Girl, "Einige Erinnerungen," pp. 80–1.

Chagrin and his subordinates struggled unavailingly to regain control of the regiment. As the Prussian swarms drew closer, Chagrin's infantry began firing in all directions, even at their own men. Riding over to a group of French infantrymen, Chagrin gaped as they turned their rifles on him and opened fire. Thudding to the ground astride a dead horse, Chagrin watched his would-be assassins shuck off their backpacks and take to their heels.[37]

The Prussian XI Corps's turn around Marshal MacMahon's right flank decided the battle. Thrown back on Eberbach by the flanking attack, General Lartigue's brigades found that their guns and infantry supports had deserted them. This was a phenomenon that Clausewitz had observed years earlier: "When one is losing, the first thing that strikes one's intellect is the melting away of numbers. This is followed by the loss of ground."[38] Seized by panic and disinclined to spend the remainder of the war in Prussia's windy prison camps at Kustrin and Königsberg, Lartigue's infantry, cavalry, artillery, and train ran for their lives; some ran toward the Reichshofen road, others toward Haguenau.[39] With Lartigue out of the way, the divisions of Raoult and Ducrot were now hit *à revers* – in flank and rear – by deadly accurate Prussian shelling and rifle fire. Troops that only moments earlier had seemed prepared to fight to the last man, now threw down their rifles and ran westward, choking the army's principal line of retreat to Reichshofen. Catastrophe loomed as the Prussians and Bavarians rounded the French left as well, using the woods north of Froeschwiller to outflank the massed divisions of Ducrot and Raoult. Hours earlier Raoult had detected the threat and tried to retreat, only to be pushed back into Froeschwiller by MacMahon. Now the Prussians closed their pincers; the units of the French 1st and 3rd Divisions trapped in Froeschwiller continued to resist even as flames from the burning houses engulfed them. General Raoult was shot in the thigh and captured in the town, having refused to leave his men. As he was led away, he would have smelled burning flesh; hundreds of French wounded, crammed into ambulances, had been left behind and burned alive. By five o'clock, a French captain sighed, "the day was irretrievably lost, the rout complete."[40]

General Bose's XI Corps closed in for the kill: Uhlans galloped through the woods between Elsasshausen and Reichshofen to cut off the French retreat and Prussian infantry swarms, using the woods and hops for cover, pushed to within range of the Reichshofen road to pour in rifle fire. All the while, Krupp shells burst along the road, driving the men into the fields and exploding fully loaded French caissons. This was truly *"le diable à quatre"* – "the devil times

37 SHAT, Lc2/3, Sedan, 1 Sept. 1870, Col. Louis Chagrin de St. Hilaire, "Aprés la bataille." Lb6, Neufchateau, 15 Aug. 1870, Gen. Conseil–Dumesnil to Marshal MacMahon.
38 Carl von Clausewitz, *On War*, orig. 1832, Princeton, 1976, p. 254.
39 SHAT, Lb6, Strasbourg, 8 Aug. 1870, Capt. Malingieuil to Gen. Lartigues.
40 SHAT, Lb6, 12 Aug. 1870, Capt. Chardon Heroué, "Rapport sur tous les incidents de la journée de 6 Août."

four." General Ducrot, still trying to fight his way out of Froeschwiller, found himself "swallowed up by tumult and confusion," which was a senior officer's euphemism for mass panic. General Gustave Conseil-Dumesnil, trying to extract his division from Elsasshausen, watched it dissolve completely: "Ringed by exploding shells at 3:30 P.M., the men ran off in groups, streaming away in disorder."[41] Alas, they did not get far. The road to Reichshofen, raked by Prussian shells, was blocked by convoys of French baggage, many of them on fire.[42] Jostled aside and pushed down the southern route to Haguenau by the Prussian breakthrough at Morsbronn and Eberbach, Lartigue's 4th Division found it no better than the Reichshofen road. The men were trampled by the fleeing troopers of MacMahon's two cavalry divisions and repeatedly panicked by a steady drizzle of Prussian shells.[43]

Neatly disengaged by Bose's flanking attack, the Prussian and Bavarian units in the center and on the Soultzbach now scrambled to their feet and pushed up to Froeschwiller and Elsasshausen. Some French units continued to fight valiantly, including the survivors of the 2nd Algerian Tirailleurs, who earned a record number of *Légions d'Honneur* that day for conspicuous valor, multiple wounds, tenacious defense, and the heroic rescue of comrades under fire.[44] Riding forward to survey the field, Crown Prince Friedrich Wilhelm noted that "the French dead lay in heaps, and the red cloth of their uniform showed up everywhere the eye fell."[45] Analyzing Froeschwiller and Spicheren after the war, an Austro-Hungarian officer held them up as examples of all that was wrong with the wholly defensive French tactics introduced after Königgrätz. Both MacMahon and Frossard huddled their entire corps in trenches and breastworks, making themselves vulnerable to turning maneuvers and completely ceding the *Vorfeld* – the ground between the opposing forces – to the enemy. At Froeschwiller, as at Spicheren, the Germans took full advantage of this, successfully scouting the French position on the 5th, then kicking it in on the 6th.[46] Was it not significant that Johannes Priese, the Prussian hussar who discovered the French position at Froeschwiller on 5 August, swam across the Sauer to evade French sentries in Woerth only to discover that there were no French sentries in Woerth? They were all dug in on the Froeschwiller heights.[47]

Emerging in the open after a harrowing day in the woods, the Bavarians opened fire with everything they had. A single battalion of Tann's 2nd Regiment ran through 56,000 cartridges, inflicting fewer than 200 French

41 SHAT, Lb6, Neufchateau, 15 Aug. 1870, Gen. Conseil-Dumesnil to Marshal MacMahon.
42 SHAT, Lb6, Lorrey, 12 Aug. 1870, Gen. Ducrot, "Rapport sur la journée du 6 Août."
43 SHAT, Lb6, Strasbourg, 8 Aug. 1870, Capt. Malingieuil to Gen. Lartigues.
44 SHAT, Lb6, Ambulance de Mannheim, 16 Aug. 1870, Maj. Mathieu.
45 Frederick III, p. 40.
46 "Die taktischen Lehren des Krieges 1870–71," ÖMZ 4, 1872, pp. 18–20.
47 Priese, pp. 30–8.

casualties. Union infantry in the American Civil War had required a record-setting 1,100 pounds of lead and powder to kill a single Confederate. The Bavarians seemed determined to break that record.[48] Indeed most of MacMahon's 11,000 dead and wounded were struck down by the Prussian artillery, which also produced masses of unwounded and demoralized prisoners. (To the delight of their Prussian captors, many of the French POWs referred to Napoleon III as "the old woman;" Marshal MacMahon was "the pig" – "*le cochon.*")[49] Startled by the apparition of German troops on both flanks and in their rear, 9,000 French troops surrendered and thirty guns were lost, the equivalent of an entire division with its artillery. MacMahon's statement after the battle that the withdrawal from Froeschwiller was accomplished "without too much inquietude" wildly misrepresented the draggletailed retreat.[50] Since the French were better armed and better positioned than the Prussians in the battle, French tacticians later puzzled over the Prussian success. What they found was precisely what the Austrians had found in 1866, namely that German tactics were loose and opportunistic; they sought fissures and flowed into them with little regard for tactical orthodoxy. French generals at Froeschwiller had waited the entire day for the German skirmishers to give way to massed columns of infantry. They never had; instead, the entire German army had skirmished, sometimes well, sometimes badly, but always well enough to permit huge masses of reserves to come up and curl around the French flanks, usually concealed by woods and hills. Pounded throughout by the heavy-caliber Prussian artillery, the French had prematurely expended their reserves in counter-attacks, trying to push the Germans back out of range. This rendered them still more vulnerable to the final Prussian attacks, which would come in crushingly on both flanks, often disbanding entire French brigades and divisions.[51]

Doubtless much of the suffering was owed to Kirchbach's impetuosity in the morning. Had the attack gone in a day later under the eyes of Blumenthal and the crown prince, V Corps would not have been shredded, and the French might have been turned out of their position more cheaply.[52] Still, it was a German victory that sheared MacMahon's I Corps away from Napoleon III's Army of the Rhine with nothing to fill the gap. Writing two days after the battle, the British military attaché in Paris blasted the French emperor's mismanagement: "Never was there a more dangerous and faulty strategy than to occupy such an enormous line of frontier without a single reserve to fall back upon."[53] In fact, a reconcentration of the sprawling French army had been

48 BKA, B 1145, Munich, 11 June 1871, Landwehr Lt. Johann Geiger.
49 Frederick III, p. 43.
50 SHAT, Lb6, Saverne, 7 Aug. 1870, Marshal MacMahon to Napoleon III.
51 SHAT, Lb8, Metz, 10 Aug. 1870, "Manière de combattre les Prussiens."
52 BKA, HS 849, Capt. Girl, "Einige Erinnerungen," p. 65.
53 PRO, FO 27, 1809, Paris, 8 August 1870, Col. Claremont to Lyons.

resolved upon before the battle, when the emperor had authorized MacMahon to command the French V and VII Corps in addition to his own, but this was all undertaken too late to affect the outcome at Froeschwiller. Even Failly, deployed around Bitche and Saargemuines, was too far away to assist in any meaningful way. In this respect, it was perhaps a good thing that Kirchbach and Bose launched the battle when they did. Had they waited another day, Failly might have been able to reinforce MacMahon. But such is always the role of chance in war.

If Spicheren and Wissembourg cracked the door into France, Froeschwiller knocked it off its hinges. MacMahon was not merely dislodged from the defensible crests of the Vosges and cut off from the Army of the Rhine by the bulk of the Prussian Third Army, he was effectively stripped and disarmed. "I have today completely defeated Marshal MacMahon, putting his troops to utter and disorderly retreat," Crown Prince Friedrich Wilhelm wrote in his diary after the battle.[54] In frantic telegrams to Paris, Metz, and Châlons after Froeschwiller, MacMahon revealed that his divisions had abandoned all of their tents, field kitchens, mess kits, cooking pots, food, and rifle and artillery ammunition in the panicky retreat. For the next week or so, the French I Corps would be good for nothing. Crown Prince Friedrich Wilhelm could now pursue MacMahon at his leisure or close the gap between himself and Moltke's two armies near Metz.[55] Even Francophiles had to admit the essential truth of a Berlin editorial published after the battle:

> "While Louis-Napoleon flaunts his Saarbrücken laurels, the scattered fugitives of MacMahon's army will arrive to convince their terrified countrymen of the difference between theatrical glitter and solid reality. The neutrals will also reflect more seriously than ever whether it is wise to expose themselves to the hazards of a war that has already taken such a decided turn."[56]

54 Frederick III, p. 31.
55 SHAT, Lb7, Saverne, 7 Aug. 1870, Marshal MacMahon to Marshal Canrobert. Sarrebourg, 8 Aug. 1870, Marshal MacMahon to Marshal Leboeuf.
56 *Berlin Post*, 10 August 1870, in PRO, FO 64, 690, Berlin, 13 August 1870.

6

Mars-la-Tour

As Bismarck had anticipated, France's potential allies in Europe were the first to blench at the news of Spicheren and Froeschwiller. Stunned by the speed of the Prussian attacks, first the Austrians, then the Italians, and finally the Danes stood down, quietly refusing to intervene in a war that the Prussians now looked certain to win.[1] French citizens, fooled by censorship and wild rumors, reacted less surely. Indeed on the day of Spicheren and Froeschwiller, two French swindlers were able to perpetrate a sensational hoax. As crowds of Parisians surged around the Bourse awaiting war news that they assumed would be delivered first to the stock exchange "for the benefit of money-changers and speculators," one of the two swindlers stationed himself in the entrance of the Bourse while the other, disguised as a courier, rode a lathered horse through the crowd, waving a paper and shouting "official dispatch!" The two accomplices met and the well-dressed one, posing as a spokesman for the Bourse, shouted the "war news" at the top of his lungs: "There has been a great battle, a great French victory, 25,000 Prussians have been captured, including the crown prince and forty guns."

Elihu Washburne, the U.S. ambassador to France, noted that "a spark of fire falling upon a magazine could not have produced a greater explosion." The crowd went mad; people clasped one another, kissed, danced, and sang. Within minutes all of the streets and boulevards around the Bourse were jammed with people waving flags and bellowing the *Marseillaise*. The happy news spread like wildfire across the city. A famous opera diva was recognized, hauled from her carriage in the Rue de la Paix, and forced to sing the national anthem over and over. Inside the Bourse, French shares surged on the news, netting the two swindlers a handsome profit on beaten-down shares purchased

---

[1] Eberhard Kolb, *Der Weg aus dem Krieg*, Munich, 1987, pp. 69–78. Michael Howard, *The Franco-Prussian War*, orig. 1961, London, 1981, pp. 120–1.

that morning. By early afternoon, the exhausted crowd learned in the same whispering way that it had all been a hoax; their joy turned to wrath as French shares plummeted back to earth. Hundreds of furious men broke into the stock exchange and "threw the brokers head over heels out the doors and windows." Hundreds more descended on Emile Ollivier's palace in the Place Vendôme; when the chief minister and architect of the war appeared on the balcony to calm the crowds, they roared their hatred, and demanded an immediate end to all press controls. Ollivier darted indoors; it was left to French troops to clear the streets. The next morning – 7 August – all that the French newspapers admitted was this: "The corps of General Frossard is in retreat; there are no details."

At noon on 7 August, Empress Eugénie placarded Paris with a short bulletin: "Marshal MacMahon has retreated to his second line. Everything will be reestablished there.... No more quarreling, no more divisions! Our resources are immense. Fight on with firmness and France will be saved."[2] Privately, the empress was less confident. She ventured into Paris from St. Cloud to monitor the crisis and, according to a friend, she implored her husband to "do *something* to check the Prussian advance" and reassure public opinion.[3] Ollivier did the same, deploring the army's retreat and reminding the emperor that the "strategic situation [was] beginning to impinge on the political situation."[4] Washburne, the American ambassador, observed that "only the rain keeps the mobs off the streets in greater numbers. Everywhere people are reading newspapers and talking agitatedly."[5] With revolution crackling in the air, Ollivier placed Paris under a state of siege and ordered all adult males to report for military service in one of the two national guards: *mobiles* for the men under thirty, *sédentaires* for men aged thirty to forty.[6]

Unfortunately for Ollivier, the mob-suppressing rain would not last forever; it stopped three days after Froeschwiller, when the *Corps Législatif*, recessed for the summer, reconvened in emergency session to consider the war. Originally scheduled for mid-August, the legislative session was pushed up by Eugénie because of public excitement. With the Palais Bourbon ringed by troops, who could barely restrain crowds that ran along the *quai* in both directions and jammed the Pont de la Concorde and the vast *place* on the other side, a diplomatic observer called it "one of the most extraordinary sittings since the Revolution of 1848, if not since the Great Revolution [of 1789]."

2   London, Public Record Office (PRO), FO 27, 1809, Paris, 7 Aug. 1870, Lyons to Granville.
3   Vienna, Haus-Hof-und Staatsarchiv (HHSA), PA IX, 95, Paris, 7 and 8 Aug. 1870, Metternich to Beust.
4   Vincennes, Service Historique de l'Armée de Terre (SHAT), Lb7, Paris, 7 Aug. 1870, Ollivier to Napoleon III.
5   Washington, DC, National Archives (NA), CIS, U.S. Serial Set, 1780, Paris, 8 Aug. 1870, Washburne to Fish.
6   PRO, FO 27, 1809, Paris, 8 Aug. 1870, Lyons to Granville.

The republican revolution that would explode a month later and oust the Bonapartes was already discernible in the violent debate. The speaker's attempt to open the session in the usual way – with reference to the "Emperor of the French and the Grace of God" – was drowned out by the sixteen republican deputies shouting "let's have no more of *that!*" Ollivier, the first speaker, was not even allowed to speak. Jules Favre, loudly assisted by thirty allies, berated him: "France has been compromised by your imbecility! Come down from there!" Ollivier meekly complied, while Emmanuel Arago adumbrated a new republican strategy of "total defense": "Ministers get out of the way! Henceforth the *people* will see to their own security despite your feeble efforts!" How "total defense" would actually be accomplished was explained by Favre: Napoleon III and the "wretched generals" would resign their commands and return to Paris, where they would be tried. The legislative body would assume "full powers," and prosecute the war through a "committee of fifteen." It was all so redolent of the Reign of Terror of 1793–94, when the Jacobins and their "committee of twelve" had seized power in precisely this way (and tried and executed a number of "wretched generals.") While another republican demanded the recall of *Major Géneral* Leboeuf to explain the defeats, Thiers, a liberal, ventured to pin the blame higher up, on "those who have governed us, whose incapacity is peerless."[7] All semblance of order dissolved; Favre and a dozen companions charged the ministerial benches and shook their fists in Gramont's face. The *mamelukes* of the right shouted that the republicans were guilty of treason and must be arrested at once. "There were one hundred men screaming at one another," the speaker vainly, inaudibly ringing his bell to restore order. The British ambassador called it "the most tumultuous and disorderly [parliamentary sitting] ever witnessed in France."[8]

Had Ollivier's government been tougher it might have cracked down on Favre, Gambetta and the other republicans, who were wildly overplaying their hand. Public opinion in France ran against the republicans, and Ollivier had an entire regiment of French regulars camped next door to the legislative body in the gardens of the Quai d'Orsay. But the chief minister had lost heart, and imperial support. That evening the empress demanded his resignation and named a new government to manage the crisis. The new chief minister was General Charles Cousin de Montauban. Cousin de Montauban – "Count Palikao" since 1860 when he had thrashed the Manchus at Pa-li-kiao and reopened China to European trade – by no means represented a break with the past. Much closer to the emperor than Ollivier, Palikao was, as a British analyst put it, a man of the "extreme right ... acceptable only because Ollivier

7   PRO, FO 425, 97, 13, Paris, 12 Aug. 1870, Lyons to Granville.
8   NA, CIS, US Serial Set, 1780, Paris, 12 Aug. 1870, Washburne to Fish. PRO, FO 425, 97, 10, Paris, 11 Aug. 1870, Lyons to Granville.

was widely detested." There was little public support for Palikao; he would merely "keep up a semblance of imperial institutions" while the Army of the Rhine reorganized. "If France sustains another defeat," the British ambassador warned, "revolution will be inevitable."[9]

Ollivier was not the only casualty of 9 August. At Metz, Napoleon III agreed to relinquish command of the Army of the Rhine and give it to Marshal Achille Bazaine. It was high time; the emperor's headquarters was turning in circles after Spicheren and Froeschwiller. On 7 August, while Marshal Leboeuf cabled the war minister in Paris that "the emperor has decided to reconcentrate the army at Châlons," the emperor himself was cabling the empress that "a withdrawal to Châlons has become too dangerous; I will be more useful here at Metz with 100,000 troops."[10] Clearly a firm hand was needed on the rudder, but the faltering, time-consuming way in which Louis-Napoleon effected the change of command at one of the critical junctures of the Franco-Prussian War undercut its effectiveness. Advised by his wife to widen Bazaine's authority, but not excessively, Napoleon III at first merely named Bazaine commander of an embryonic "Army of Metz." This new formation implied the continued existence of the "Army of the Rhine" – Bazaine, MacMahon and Canrobert together – still commanded by the emperor and Leboeuf, the "major general." Only when the legislative body tried to impeach Marshal Leboeuf on 11 August did the emperor finally agree to remove him, along with General Barthélemy Lebrun. Yet two days passed before this was done, and when it was done, Napoleon III ordered Bazaine to accept General Louis Jarras, Leboeuf's principal deputy, as his new general staff chief and to "absorb into your staff all of the officers formerly employed by Marshal Leboeuf."[11] Bazaine's command was not off to a good start.

On 14 August, while Prussian cavalry units were thrusting in behind the massed Army of the Rhine, cutting the telegraph wires between Paris and Nancy and scouting the Moselle bridges above and below Metz, Napoleon III grudgingly elevated Bazaine to the post of "generalissimo." More than a week had passed since the defeats at Spicheren and Froeschwiller, yet only now did Bazaine exercise command over every unit in the French Army of the Rhine. Or did he? Having promised to remove himself to Châlons or Paris, the emperor lingered on at Metz, clinging to the title of commander-in-chief at the empress's behest.[12] Louis-Napoleon's vacillation – he informed Palikao

9   PRO, FO 425, 97, 10, Paris, 11 Aug. 1870, Lyons to Granville. FO 27, 1809, Paris, 9 Aug. 1870, Claremont to Lyons.
10 SHAT, Lb7, Metz, 7 Aug. 1870, Leboeuf to Dejean. Metz, 7 Aug. 1870, Napoleon III to Eugénie.
11 SHAT, Lb1, Metz, 12 Aug. 1870, Napoleon III to Marshal Bazaine. Lb7, St. Cloud, 7 Aug. 1870, Eugénie to Napoleon III.
12 PRO, FO 27, 1810, Paris, 12 Aug. 1870, Claremont to Lyons. HHSA, PA IX, 96, Paris, 16 Aug. 1870, Metternich to Beust.

three days after Spicheren that he "planned personally to resume the offensive in a few days" – effectively stifled Bazaine, who gave vent to his frustration in a revealing exchange on the 13th. Informed by one of the emperor's adjutants that Louis-Napoleon wanted to begin shifting the Army of the Rhine from the right bank of the Moselle to the left, Bazaine shot back, "*Ah, oui, hier c'était un ordre, aujourd'hui c'est un désir; je connais cela, c'est la même pensée sous les mots différents!*" – "Ah, yes, I see, yesterday it was an 'order,' today it's a 'desire'; I recognize what this is, the same old methods dressed up in different words."[13]

Bazaine's churlish tone in this and later exchanges implicated him as much as the emperor in the French defeat. Though his ascendancy was clear in the days after Froeschwiller, he did not make a single operational disposition until late on 13 August, when, at long last, he ordered the four corps around Metz to put the Moselle between themselves and the advancing Prussians. All of this was too little too late; Bazaine's irascibility was a factor, as was his unwillingness to work with General Louis Jarras, the new staff chief. "Bazaine," a witness wrote, "had as little contact as possible with Jarras, whom he considered 'the emperor's man.' He never consulted him, never confided in him, but lacked the courage to get rid of him."[14] Bazaine's contacts with others were at least as sterile: General Charles Bourbaki, the commander of the Guard Corps, recalled meeting with Bazaine two days after Froeschwiller to get his agreement to one of two possible courses, a heavy counter-punch from the east bank of the Moselle or a "fighting retreat to Paris to receive fresh forces and resume the attack." The marshal seemed paralyzed, "utterly preoccupied with all of the miseries afflicting France." His only reply to Bourbaki was a languid "*vous avez peut-être raison*" – "perhaps you're right." Subsequently, he did nothing.[15]

Nor did Bazaine take up modifications recommended by Bourbaki and Leboeuf in a damning exposé of French tactics at Spicheren and Froeschwiller. Whereas the French infantry had regularly wasted their fire at ranges exceeding 1,000 yards, the Prussians had used the wooded, rolling ground of Alsace-Lorraine to push within range of the French, reinforce themselves with artillery and reserve troops, and then launch "decisive strokes" with their relatively poorly armed infantry.[16] Three thousand copies of the Bourbaki-Leboeuf brochure went out to every corps, but Bazaine, the fighting soldier, did not express himself on the matter. Like Benedek in 1866, he buried his head in the comforting trivia of camp life: "By tomorrow, tell me how many mess kits and utensils you need, " he wrote Frossard on the 11th. "Tell your

---

13 Joseph Andlau, *Metz: Campagne et Négociations*, Paris, 1872, pp. 52–3.
14 Andlau, p. 123.
15 SHAT, Lt12, Paris, 28 Feb. 1872, "La déposition de M. le Gl. Bourbaki devant la comm. d'enquête."
16 SHAT, Lb8, Borny, 12 Aug. 1870, General Bourbaki.

officers to profit from the time [at Metz] to purchase all the little essentials needed in their bivouacs," he wrote Ladmirault.[17] Sifting through revelations like these after the war, Austro-Hungarian analysts would place the blame for the French defeat squarely on Bazaine, not the all too obviously feckless Louis-Napoleon: "Bazaine has tried to blame the defeat on the emperor's late transfer of command; in fact, the defeat was chiefly owed to the unconscionable inactivity of the vain, vacillating marshal."[18]

Ultimately, the vacillation at Metz in August 1870 may have cost the French the war. While Napoleon III and Marshal Bazaine dithered – neglecting even to destroy key bridges above and below the city that would facilitate the Prussian envelopment – Moltke was busy surrounding the 200,000 French troops gathered around Metz. France's only hope was to extricate these first-rate troops – the cream of the French army – from the "Moselle pocket" fashioned by Moltke and unite them with MacMahon's corps and tens of thousands of new troops that were being raised and equipped elsewhere in France. Had the French been able to reconstitute this combined army of 400,000 men at Châlons or Paris, the Prussian invasion might have stumbled and disintegrated deep inside hostile territory. The toll in lives and money of conventional and guerrilla wars might have splintered the fragile German coalition; the French – who by mid-August were pressing *everyone* into service, including park rangers and firemen – might have prolonged the war and won a favorable settlement, one without annexations or even indemnities.[19] Interestingly, strategic considerations like these made little impression on Bazaine or Louis-Napoleon, who, aside from posting staff officers in the belfry of Metz cathedral to watch for the Prussian advance, did little to monitor Moltke's movements or intentions. Leboeuf did not react at all when advised by French intelligence officers on 9 August that Third Army's maps showed the the the three Prussian armies uniting at Bar-le-Duc after enclosing the Army of the Rhine.[20] When General Louis Trochu recommended on 10 August that the emperor pull the Army of the Rhine back to Paris, he received no answer. Poor Trochu, who would shortly be charged with the defense of Paris and the presidency of all France, foresaw the outcome of the war with astounding clarity:

"For us to defend Paris successfully, a relief army is essential, to gather in the units mobilizing in the provinces, to prevent the Prussians from completely investing the city, and to keep open the southern roads and railways that will feed and arm the city. *You* are the relief army, yet you are being systematically enveloped by three enemy armies that have only briefly paused to evacuate

---

17 SHAT, Lb8, Borny, 11 Aug. 1870, Marshal Bazaine to Generals Frossard and Ladmirault.
18 "Der Krieg 1870–71," *Österreichische Militärische Zeitschrift* (ÖMZ) 2 (1871), p. 129.
19 PRO, FO 27, 1811, Paris, 9 and 14 Aug. 1870, Claremont to Lyons. HHSA, PA IX, 96, Paris, 16 Aug. 1870, Metternich to Beust.
20 SHAT, Lb7, Nancy, 9 Aug. 1870, Capt. Jung to Marshal Leboeuf.

their wounded, reform their columns and prepare the decisive concentration. One of the three enemy armies has the mission to turn you. The enemy is willing to take heavy casualties to do this, by pouring in substantial, continuously augmented forces. If you remain too long [at Metz], you will be encircled and France will lose the army that is her last hope."[21]

If Bazaine knew that he was France's last hope, he certainly did not show it. The marshal let an entire week pass before he ordered the first troops out of Metz on 14 August; two days later, Napoleon III left the fortress and rattled away to the west to join Marshal MacMahon at Châlons. The two men were belatedly acknowledging that Châlons was the perfect place from which to execute a fighting retreat into the Paris fortifications, or across to the left bank of the Loire, where a relief army for Paris could be constituted as a dagger in Moltke's flank.[22] As the emperor crested the Amanvillers ridge behind Metz – a broad shoulder of hills that would shortly be the scene of the war's decisive battle – he asked the names of the two picturesque hamlets on the road down to Gravelotte. Local legend had it that he sat and brooded when told the answer: "Moscow and Leipzig."[23] He ought to have brooded: The French military defeats at Moscow in 1812 and Leipzig in 1813 had unraveled his illustrious uncle's First Empire; Gravelotte would unravel his.

Behind the emperor, inside the bowl of hills formed by St. Privat, Amanvillers, and Gravelotte, the Army of the Rhine also brooded. Metz was already so full of refugees – local peasants terrified of Prussian conscription, looting, and reprisals – that the gates had been closed to all newcomers. "Return to your homes, or continue your route into France," the fortress commandant unhelpfully advised.[24] Colonel Joseph Andlau, a staff officer in Bazaine's headquarters, observed that even at this early date the army felt "*demi-vaincu*" – "half-beaten."[25] It was easy to see why: A corps like Louis Ladmirault's had been marched into the ground for no apparent reason. First pushed forward to support the invasion of Prussia at Saarbrücken, it was then pulled back, pushed forward, and then pulled back again. Writing on 9 August, Ladmirault described the fatigue and demoralization of his troops: "My men have been marching for five days, yesterday under drenching rains. We have had little sleep, and the horses and gun carriages are horribly worn-out by all the mud and exertions. We need a long rest in a peaceful camp under the walls of Metz."[26]

---

21 SHAT, Li6, Paris, 10 Aug. 1870, General Trochu to General de Waubert de Genlis. SHAT, Lc1, Paris, 13 Aug. 1870, Eugénie to Napoleon III.
22 Charles Fay, *Journal d'un Officier de l'Armée du Rhin*, Paris, 1889, p. 57.
23 Friedrich Freudenthal, *Von Stade bis Gravelotte: Erinnerungen eines Artilleristen*, Bremen, 1898, p. 130.
24 SHAT, Lb8, Metz, 10 Aug. 1870, "Avis du Préfet."
25 Andlau, p. 53.
26 SHAT, Lb7, St. Barbe, 9 Aug. 1870, Gen. Ladmirault to Marshal Leboeuf.

The Prussians, preceded everywhere by their restless cavalry patrols, observed the wandering of the French army. Unchecked by Louis-Napoleon's retreating generals, the three Prussian armies had raced ahead in the intervening week. Steinmetz had crossed the Nied and marched most of the way to Metz. Prince Friedrich Karl had seized the critical bridge at Pont-à-Mousson and pushed his cavalry patrols across the Moselle and up to the walls of Toul on the left bank. Even more impressive was the progress of Crown Prince Friedrich Wilhelm and Blumenthal, who had made it through the narrow Vosges to arrive at Lunéville and Nancy. Along the way, German troops showed little sensitivity in their dealings with the French population. Taught basic French phrases by their officers, they invariably resorted to German; not "*du sel,*" but "*Salz zum salzen.*" French protests were impatiently countered with a forceful shake of the head and three outstretched fingers: "*Nix comprend!*" The Germans took what they could, muttering the old soldier's motto: "*Der Deutsche hasst den Franzmann, doch seine Weine trinkt er gern*" – "The German hates the Frenchy, but loves his wine."[27] For the French peasantry, the emperor's continuing "strategic withdrawals" were a calamity, a fact noted by a Saxon lieutenant in a village near Metz: "I am shocked by the misery that war brings to the peasants. . . . Every village in these parts has been eaten out by successive echelons, leaving the locals with nothing, yet ever more troops arrive needing food." Scrounging and stealing in this way – "*à la guerre comme à la guerre,*" Prussian officers would console the crestfallen villagers – Moltke's three Prussian armies ground forward, positioned for a vast, sweeping encirclement of the French army.[28]

When word reached Moltke on 13 August that the French were only beginning their retreat across the Moselle, he scratched his head in puzzlement. This was all too reminiscent of 1866, when Benedek had most improbably offered battle at Königgrätz with his back to the Elbe. Why would the French deploy in *front* of the Moselle? In 1870, as in 1866, Moltke had to consider the possibility that the enemy was really contemplating a counter-attack. He thus subtly altered his plan of campaign: Steinmetz was ordered forward to engage the Army of the Rhine while two of Prince Friedrich Karl's corps were detached to threaten the French flank. If the French stood their ground or attacked, Moltke hoped that Steinmetz and a fraction of Second Army would suffice to contain them. If they withdrew across the Moselle, the more likely outcome, he would swing the bulk of the Second Army and, eventually, the Third Army into their flank and rear.

On the French side, a war of wills smoldered between Bazaine and Empress Eugénie. Ordered by Napoleon III to retreat across the Moselle and toward Verdun on the 13th, Bazaine refused to budge: "The enemy is approaching and

27 Munich, Bayerisches Kriegsarchiv (BKA), HS 856, Landwehr Lt. Joseph Krumper.
28 Dresden, Sächsisches Kriegsarchiv (SKA), Zeitg. Slg. 158, Lt. Hinüber.

will be observing us in such a way that a crossing to the left bank could be most unfavorable for us." For a man who would write lyrically in his memoirs of the defensive superiority of the Meuse and Aisne lines and the "impenetrable massif of the Ardennes," this was an odd line to take.[29] Bazaine now preferred to stand and fight at Borny. At first, the emperor gave Bazaine complete freedom, but then, prodded by the empress, who warned that Steinmetz and Friedrich Karl might work around Bazaine's northern flank, the emperor, in his irresolute way, seemed to order Bazaine to retreat: "You must therefore do everything you can to effect [the retreat] and if you feel in the meantime that you must undertake an offensive movement, you must make it in such a way that it does not impede the passage [to the left bank.]"[30] In fact, as Britain's military attaché correctly surmised on the 14th, Bazaine really *had* to retreat. By not contesting Nancy or Frouard, the fortified position at the confluence of the Moselle and the Meurthe, Bazaine had surrendered a principal supply line without firing a shot. Because Metz relied as much on the Paris-Nancy railway as it did on its own, "Bazaine has no choice now but to retire to Châlons by way of Verdun."[31]

Bazaine did not see the urgency. He halted the French retreat on 14 August and fought a half-hearted battle on the right bank of the Moselle at Borny. The Prussians also wobbled undecidedly into the battle, though for different reasons. Reproved by Moltke and the king after Spicheren, Steinmetz himself did little to ignite it. Instead, Borny, like Spicheren and Froeschwiller, was triggered by aggressive subordinates, in this case General Karl von der Goltz of Dietrich von Zastrow's VII Corps. As the rump of Bazaine's army, General Claude Decaen's III Corps and one of Ladmirault's divisions, began sliding east to west across the Moselle, Goltz's 25th Brigade swarmed through the woods around Borny to engage them in the late afternoon. Both sides exchanged fire until nightfall, when Bazaine, harried by sixteen Prussian battalions and seven batteries, finally broke off the inconclusive fighting. For the second time in the war, Steinmetz arrived too late to direct his own army. He hove into Colombey at 8:30 P.M., as the firing sputtered out all along the line.[32] In terms of casualties, the French fared better than the Prussians; fighting from prepared positions with numerical superiority, they inflicted 4,600 casualties against 3,900 of their own. The losses, heavy for a rearguard action, suggested the fury of the fighting, as Goltz's outnumbered gunners and riflemen bit deep into Bazaine's ankles while Bazaine and his generals

29 F. A. Bazaine, *Episodes de la guerre de 1870 et le blocus de Metz*, Madrid, 1883, p. viii.
30 SHAT, Lb9, Metz, 13–14 Aug. 1870, Napoleon III to Marshal Bazaine. Paris, 13 Aug. 1870, Eugénie to Napoleon III. Borny, 13 Aug. 1870, Marshal Bazaine to Napoleon III.
31 PRO, FO 27, 1811, Paris, 14 Aug. 1870, Col. Claremont to Lyons.
32 Theodor Fontane, *Der Krieg gegen Frankreich 1870–71*, 4 vols., orig. 1873–76, Zurich, 1985, vol. 1, pp. 321–2.

wildly kicked them off. Overall, Borny was another French strategic reverse. Claude Decaen, III Corps commandant for just thirty-six hours, was killed and replaced by Bazaine. The marshal was only too happy to abandon his command responsibilities and return to his old corps at Borny, where he rode bravely around the field swinging his saber until a piece of shrapnel wounded him in the shoulder and forced his return to Metz, where more precious hours had been lost.

Tactically, Decaen, Bazaine, and Ladmirault failed to exploit good opportunities at Borny, and made nothing of Leboeuf's reminder circulated after Froeschwiller and Spicheren: "Stand on the defensive only until the enemy halts and appears shaken, then pass promptly over to the attack, each battalion in platoon columns preceded by skirmishers."[33] By neither counter-attacking nor retreating, the French played into Moltke's hands. They slowed their own retreat to Verdun and gave the Prussian Second Army time to bring up its laggards, reach the Moselle and begin crossing.[34] King Wilhelm I of Prussia rode along the Noisseville plateau east of Borny on 15 August and was amazed by the sluggishness of the French; observing the bulk of the French army still in and around Metz, the king ordered Moltke to rush Second Army across the Moselle south of the fortress and hasten the advance of Third Army toward Toul and Châlons. With the Prussians on their neck, a French withdrawal from Lorraine would be more complicated than ever.[35] None of this seemed to make an impression on Bazaine, who squandered a few more hours on the 15th touring Borny under a white flag. What struck him most about the visit was not the looming Prussian menace, but the rapacious efficiency of the *lorrain* peasant, who, only hours after the last shots had been fired around Borny, had robbed every corpse on the battlefield:

"Knapsacks were emptied out, anything not of value – papers, letters, books, pictures – was scattered about, but all money had disappeared. To steal the ring from a wounded officer, those wretched Lorrainers had cut off his fingers without even bothering to remove the glove.... I only regretted that as a noncombatant [under a white flag] I could not pick up a rifle and shoot those squalid peasants, who were looting every corner of the field not physically occupied by Prussian outposts."[36]

In Paris, bad news from the front exacerbated the political situation. "Insurrections are imminent," the empress warned her husband.[37] Although

---

33 SHAT, Lb7, Metz, 9 Aug. 1870, Napoleon III, "Dispositions génerales applicables à un Corps d'Armée."
34 SKA, Zeitg. Slg 158, Lt. Adolf von Hinüber, "Tagebuch 1870–71," pp. 14–17.
35 J.-B. Montaudon, *Souvenirs Militaires*, 2 vols., Paris, 1898–1900, vol. 2, pp. 95–7. Fontane, vol. 1, p. 304.
36 Bazaine, *Episodes*, p. 156.
37 SHAT, Lb7, Paris, 9 Aug. 1870, Eugénie to Napoleon III.

Eugénie had persuaded the doddering Marshal Achille Baraguay d'Hilliers to relinquish command of the now critical Paris garrison, she lost valuable time in choosing a successor. Her first choice was sixty-one-year-old Marshal François Canrobert, a talented officer and friend of the Bonapartes. But Canrobert, whose corps had already entrained for Metz, begged off after a day of meetings in Paris. More days were lost while Eugénie ignored the popular choice, General Louis Trochu, a critic of the pre-war army, opting instead for General Jules Soumain, commander of the suburban forts, and then, finally, General Joseph Vinoy.

Vinoy's appointment on 14 August to command XIII Corps was a curious episode, for the Paris garrison had previously been designated VIII Corps. When the British military attaché made inquiries as to the nature and whereabouts of corps VIII through XII, he learned that they did not in fact exist: "Palikao is throwing dust in people's eyes; there are no more men." While Vinoy busied himself with his largely fictitious army, Trochu was sent to Châlons to take command of an even more vaporous unit, the French XII Corps. There, in the legendary Camp de Châlons, seat and proving ground of the peacetime French army, Trochu found twenty-three mismatched battalions of largely unarmed *gardes mobiles*. The army had not even given them the Chassepot; instead, the *mobiles* were issued with the despised *fusil à tabatière* – the "snuff box rifle" – a crudely reengineered 1850s-era muzzle-loader now loaded through a snuff box-like contraption on the breech. Naturally it took a bigger cartridge than the Chassepot, which would complicate French logistics later on.[38] Offered these shabby reserve troops by the empress on 10 August, the emperor refused to take them: "*Je refuse les bataillons de mobiles*" – "I reject the mobile guard battalions."[39] Though chronically short of troops, he wanted no contact with *these* men.

Having wasted an entire week at Metz, Bazaine finally began the retreat to Châlons on 15 August. The last French units around Borny crossed to the left bank of the Moselle and the bulk of the army, already across, began the arduous march up and away from Metz. It was hard going in the *wrong* direction on this of all days, the *Jour Napoléon*, a national holiday commemorating the Bonapartes. No one but the Prussian invader had much to celebrate. The French emperor himself passed a last mournful day with his army, waiting impatiently at Gravelotte for his Guard cavalry to come up from Metz to escort him along the road to Verdun. When the Guard dragoons finally arrived, there was not a squadron among them fresh enough to lead the emperor out that night. He would have to wait till morning, another dangerous

38 PRO, FO 27, 1810, Paris, 12–13 Aug. 1870, Claremont to Lyons. FO 27, 1811, Paris, 14–15 Aug. 1870, Claremont to Lyons.
39 SHAT, Lb8, Metz, 10 Aug. 1870, Napoleon III to Eugénie.

postponement that nearly drove Bazaine, anxious to be rid of Louis-Napoleon, to distraction.[40]

As night fell on the 15th, the Army of the Rhine sprawled wearily along the road west: the two cavalry divisions at Jarny and Mars-la-Tour, Frossard's corps at Vionville, Canrobert's at Rezonville, Bourbaki's at Gravelotte. Ladmirault's divisions had just crested the Amanvillers ridge after trudging up the steep, winding roads from Metz. The Third Corps, now commanded by Leboeuf, trailed behind them. After touring Borny, Bazaine recrossed the Moselle and rode up to Gravelotte, where he slept in the *Maison de Poste*.[41] Napoleon III spent the night in a grubby *auberge* and woke at dawn on 16 August. At 4:30 A.M. he emerged from his rooms, climbed into his coach, and sank heavily into the cushions. "Fatigue, sadness, and worry were written on his face," a witness recalled. "The scene was so lugubrious that it cut most of us to the heart: the emperor distancing himself from his soldiers at the very moment that they girded for battle." Bazaine snapped a salute as the emperor and prince imperial trundled off, then turned to his staff to "express his satisfaction unequivocally." He was finally *"maître de ses actes"* – "his own master."[42] For the 16th, the new master rather disappointingly ordered rest in the morning – to replenish rations and ammunition and sort out confusion in his supply trains – and a "possible" march in the afternoon.[43] He was paying the price of a week's lethargy. Because the Prussian cavalry was now raiding up to the Verdun and Sedan roads with impunity, he could not simply pack his wagon trains of food, forage, and wounded off to the west. He had to send them with armed escorts, which immensely complicated the logistics of the retreat. Placed end-to-end, Bazaine's supply trains stretched forty miles in length. No wonder soldiers called them *impedimenta*. French fighting units that rose at 4:30 A.M. on the 16th ready to march sat idle for most of the day as chuck wagons, ambulances, and *voitures pontonniers* – bridging equipment – rolled past.[44] Reaching Verdun at midday, the emperor repaired to a hotel for lunch and a rest, assuring the mayor that Bazaine was right behind him and would arrive the next day: *"Bazaine me suit... il arrivera demain."*[45]

Bazaine would not arrive the next day, nor the day after. His torpor, which would be the basis of republican accusations of treason after the war, was a great gift to the Prussians. Having fought their way in from the Rhine, the three Prussian armies were spread across a vast theater of war. Steinmetz's vanguard

40 Andlau, pp. 64–6.
41 Fontane, vol. 1, pp. 327–28.
42 Andlau, pp. 65–6.
43 SHAT, Lb10, Gravelotte, 16 Aug. 1870, Marshal Bazaine, "Instruction." Paris, 16 Feb. 1872, Col. d'Ornant to Marshal Leboeuf.
44 PRO, FO 27, 1811, Paris, 19 Aug. 1870, Col. Claremont to Lyons. Andlau, p. 483.
45 SHAT, Lc1, Paris, 14 March 1903, General de Vaulgrenant to General Pendezec.

was at Borny, but the rest of the First Army straggled back to the Nied. The Third Army, still chasing MacMahon, whose bedraggled army was strung out from Joinville to Châlons, had just made Nancy.[46] Only the Second Army found itself within striking distance of Bazaine, yet only a fraction was immediately available. Prince Friedrich Karl's left wing – the Prussian Guards and IV Corps – were too far south to be any use at all. The IX and XII Corps were far to the east, which left only the two cavalry divisions – whose patrols had nearly netted Napoleon III on the road to Verdun – and the III and X Corps, which had begun pushing guns and infantry across the Moselle on the 14th.

Moltke was gambling again. In 1866, he had spread his three armies wide and funneled them through the Sudeten Mountains to envelop the Austrians in Bohemia. For several days, the massed Austrian North Army could have attacked the Prussian armies in detail, but had missed the opportunity, allowing itself to be encircled and nearly annihilated at Königgrätz. Now Moltke tried the same risky trick against the French; for several days in mid-August, the Second Army, pivoting near Metz on the three corps of the First Army and two of its own, was vulnerable to a concentrated French attack on the hinge of the movement while the southernmost corps, too far away to be of any use, swung across the Moselle.[47] The Third Army at Nancy, bound for Châlons and Paris, could not even be considered for a battle at Metz. The Second Army in the center had been broken into mobile packets that could take the various roads west to intercept Bazaine if he had used the ten days since Spicheren to move his army to Verdun.

In his haste to get the Second Army up to the Moselle and across it to clinch some *future* battle, Moltke could only hope that Bazaine would not seriously attack the Prussian III and X Corps, which, crossing the Moselle at Pont-à-Mousson and neighboring bridges, were the vulnerable pivot of Moltke's wheel around Metz. Bazaine's forbearance at Borny and his decision to defend neither Nancy nor Frouard had been a great relief. At Borny, Steinmetz's little First Army had survived a scrape with the entire Army of the Rhine, and the evacuation of Frouard meant that the Prussians could troop up to the Moselle and cross it just about anywhere they liked without bothering to defend their flanks or rearward communications. By 15 August, Moltke had four Moselle bridges working day and night at Dieulouard, Pont-à-Mousson, Pagny, and Novéant. Still, the Prussian armies were stretched thin; that the French failed to detect this fact, nor any of the activity on the Moselle, furnished yet another indictment of their cavalry, who, having skirmished with the Prussians as far westward as Mars-la-Tour on the 15th, pulled back to Vionville for the night without verifying the strength or direction of the Prussian thrust.

46 SHAT, Lb10, Joinville, 16 Aug. 1870, Marshal MacMahon to Gen. Dejean and Marshal Bazaine.
47 F. Maurice, *The Franco-German War 1870–71*, orig. 1899, London, 1914, pp. 132–3.

THE BATTLE OF MARS-LA-TOUR, 16 AUGUST 1870

Free to run their guns up in the night and deploy within range of Bazaine's bivouacs on the Verdun road, the Prussians did just that. While their infantry struggled up the roads behind them, four Prussian batteries opened fire on General Henri de Forton's cuirassier division, resting from the previous day's exertions in the fields south of Vionville, early on 16 August. The officers had just sat down to breakfast at long tables; many of the troopers were still dozing under canvas, the rest were bent over the campfires spooning soup into their bowls when Krupp six-pound shells began falling in their midst.[48] With the Prussian gunners zeroing in on the bright silver and table-cloths of the French mess, Forton's division swung into the saddle and rode away from the bombardment, bulling through General Frossard's II Corps in their haste and racing past a startled Bazaine near Gravelotte. Marshal Bazaine, doubtful as ever, assumed that Moltke was trying to maneuver him away from the Metz fortress works to crush him in the open field. In fact, Moltke, still short of troops, was trying to locate Bazaine and push him back on Metz to stop his "strategic withdrawal" toward Marshal MacMahon and General Trochu's reserve army at Châlons. While three Prussian divisions – the 5th, 6th, and 20th – marched grimly toward the Rezonville plateau, a low ridge that carried the Verdun road away from Metz, Bazaine established headquarters at Gravelotte and strung three corps in a protective semi-circle around it: Canrobert's VI Corps and Frossard's II Corps above and below the road at Rezonville, Bourbaki's Guard Corps in the gap between Rezonville and Gravelotte. It was an odd deployment; throughout 16 August Bazaine would enjoy overwhelmingly superior troop numbers. His men were rested and eager to fight; Leboeuf's III Corps and Ladmirault's IV Corps, having finally extricated themselves from Metz and the narrow, sinuous defiles up to Amanvillers, were ideally positioned to slide in at Vionville and Mars-la-Tour, which would have extended Bazaine's right wing and enveloped the advancing Prussian columns. Yet Bazaine considered none of these options, rather he sat down to wait, leaving Mars-la-Tour, Prince Friedrich Karl's eventual objective, to the Prussians. In his first real test, Generalissimo Bazaine was proving a colossal disappointment to many, including France's luckless diplomats, one of whom had written three days earlier, "The looming battle before Metz is absolutely vital; we must prove to our friends and enemies that France can still win."[49]

Determined to bring the war to a rapid conclusion, Moltke and Bismarck were seeking to prove the opposite. The instant that Moltke assured himself

---

48 SHAT, Lb10, "Rapport sur la part que le 2e Corps d'Armée a prise dans la bataille de Rezonville, le 16 Août 1870."

49 SHAT, Lb9, Florence, 13 Aug. 1870, Malaret to Gramont.

that the French were retreating, he threw three infantry divisions across the Moselle and called everything else up by forced marches. To keep the French from reaching Verdun and the line of the Meuse, Moltke directed the X Corps toward Maizeray, the III Corps to Mars-la-Tour. To contain the French in the meantime, he scrambled his 5th Cavalry Division up to the Metz-Verdun road, provoking the skirmishes of 15 August.[50] But Moltke was still at Herny on the 15th, a village twenty miles east of the Moselle. He assumed that Prince Friedrich Karl would encounter only a rearguard at Rezonville and had no plans for a major battle on the 16th. That would happen once the bulk of the Second Army had come up, the First Army had resumed its march, and Bazaine had been hauled in from the west. The battle of Mars-la-Tour, like the battles before it, was launched by Prussian subordinates persuaded that they were implementing Moltke's overarching mission or *Auftrag*. This *Auftragstaktik* was a key aspect of Prussian war-fighting, but was not without its dangers. Aggressive subordinates, determined to be first in on the action, had piled up unnecessary casualties in every clash with the French thus far. They had prevailed only by building up superior numbers against isolated French corps. But if they stumbled here, in the face of the entire Army of the Rhine, they might suffer a catastrophic defeat. Such considerations made little impression on the III Corps commandant General Konstantin von Alvensleben. Though his 5th Division had only staggered into the village of Gorze at 2 A.M. on 16 August, collapsing wearily in the streets after a twelve-hour march, Alvensleben woke the men just three hours later and sent them through the Gorze Forest toward Vionville, where the westbound French traffic appeared thickest.

Mars-la-Tour was a battle that the French should have won. Alvensleben launched the battle without Moltke's direction and with little support. Two Prussian divisions of the X Corps would join the attack, but, having crossed the Moselle above Alvensleben, they were echeloned far to the south, and would not reach the field until late afternoon. In the meantime, Bazaine had four entire corps perfectly positioned to demolish Alvensleben and any other forward units. That the French failed to pluck this easy victory was more proof of Bazaine's confusion, and the general lack of initiative among senior officers.

Although warned by his cavalry that there were masses of French troops and guns along the road from Gravelotte to Mars-la-Tour, General Alvensleben believed that they were just rearguards of the retreating Army of the Rhine. To chop the rearguard away from the main force that was presumably slipping away to Verdun, Alvensleben ordered his 5th Division to pin the French in Rezonville, while his 6th Division flank marched as quickly

50 Maurice, p. 134–6.

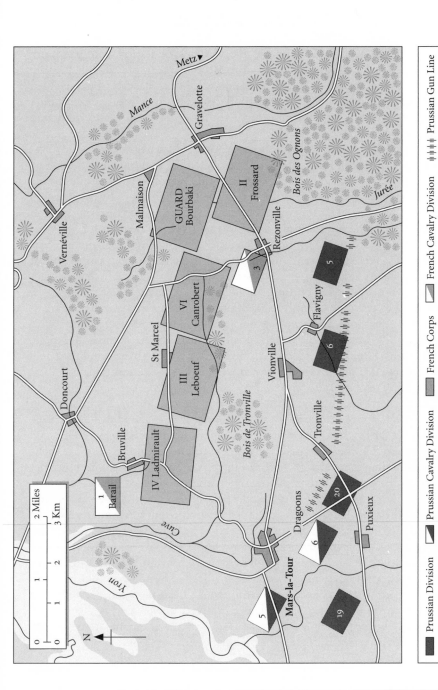

Map 7. The Battle of Mars-la-Tour

■ Prussian Division ◣ Prussian Cavalry Division ■ French Corps ◺ French Cavalry Division ╫╫╫╫ Prussian Gun Line

153

as it could to Mars-la-Tour to bar the road west. General Ferdinand von Stülpnagel's 5th Division, Brandenburgers from the heart of Prussia, advanced in company columns on a broad front and were shot to pieces by the assembled guns and infantry of Charles Frossard's II Corps. In a reprise of the early hours of Spicheren, the French poured fire into the Prussian columns, inflicting punishing casualties.

As his 5th Division reeled backward, Alvensleben began finally to appreciate just how profoundly he had miscalculated. Were it not for his artillery, he would have been swept away. French after-action reports spoke dreadfully of the "terrible fire," the "hail of projectiles" laid down by the Prussian six-pounders.[51] By 11 A.M., ninety Prussian guns had massed on rising ground south of Vionville and Flavigny. Their intense fire prevented both Canrobert and Frossard from exploiting Stülpnagel's repulse. Just how intense was shortly discovered by French surgeons and stretcher-bearers: 60 percent of French soldiers wounded by the Prussian artillery were struck in the back and the neck as they lay flat on the ground. One of Frossard's reserve brigades, lying in the grass well behind the front line, lost sixty officers – thirty in each regiment – without firing a shot.[52] Canrobert's brigades were pelted with shells; one of the first to die was the posthumously famous commander of the French 10th Regiment, Colonel Charles Ardant du Picq, who was killed by a shellburst, a fate that his theory of war would attribute to insufficient "moral action" on the part of the hesitant French generals.

Canrobert's gun line was crushed by the heavier, more accurate Prussian guns, which landed "remarkably accurate, perfectly regulated shell and shrapnel fire on the [French] batteries." Opening the intervals between the French guns or moving them brought the briefest respite; soon the Prussian shells were thumping in again with "astonishing precision."[53] At the time, however, none of this was much comfort to Alvensleben, who must have felt as if he had blundered into a wasp nest. To take pressure off his 5th Division and buy time for the arrival of the X Corps, still miles to the south, Alvensleben halted his 6th Division at Tronville, two miles short of Mars-la-Tour, and renewed the attack on Frossard from the west at 11:30 A.M. Covered by the Prussian gun line south of Flavigny, the 6th Division waded into the midst of the entire French army; they briefly took Vionville, but were forced out by cross fires of shell and shrapnel from Canrobert's VI Corps north of the village and Frossard's II Corps, which had regrouped further east at Rezonville. General Buddenbrock's 6th Division took a few hesitant steps toward Rezonville before breaking off the unequal fight.

51 SHAT, Lb10, "Rapport sur la part que le 2e Corps d'Armée a prise dans la bataille de Rezonville, le 16 Août 1870."
52 Maj. Johann Nosinich, "Der Krieg 1870–71," ÖMZ 4 (1872), p. 157.
53 SHAT, Lb10, au Camp, 18 Aug. 1870, Lt.-Col d'Artillerie to Gen. Lafont.

With the Prussians entirely at their mercy, the French generals failed to finish them off. Frossard later blamed Canrobert for leaving him alone against Alvensleben for most of the day. Canrobert blamed Ladmirault for "advancing too slowly" and uncovering his flank.[54] Of course no one's flanks were more exposed than Alvensleben's, and midday was his hour of extreme danger. General Konstantin von Voights-Rhetz's X Corps was still several hours away, and Alvensleben had spent his entire strength and reserves. His two weakened divisions, huddled in the fields between Tronville and Flavigny, were easy prey for General Louis de Ladmirault's IV Corps, marching to the guns near Mars-la-Tour, Leboeuf's III Corps at St. Marcel, Canrobert's VI Corps in the fields north of Vionville, Frossard's II Corps at Rezonville, and Bourbaki's Guard Corps at Gravelotte. But Bazaine, who worried that Alvensleben's reckless attack was a feint to lure him away from Metz and its forts, stubbornly restrained his generals.

General Charles Bourbaki, closest to Bazaine at Gravelotte, angrily chafed at the pressure to do nothing. When Bazaine's nephew Georges rode breathlessly up to the Guard headquarters at 12:45 P.M. and told Bourbaki to "assure the retreat; the marshal is a prisoner," Bourbaki must have experienced a momentary surge of hope, quickly dispelled when yet another defensive reminder came in from Bazaine's headquarters in the *Maison de Poste*: "Detach a division to cover the Bois d'Ognons and the Ars ravine." The fact that Bazaine had ordered Bourbaki to "assure the retreat" at a moment when the French were clearly winning says much about the marshal's predisposition.[55] Marshal Leboeuf, until recently *major géneral* of the army, disappointed in the clinch. Hearing the thunder of the French and Prussian cannonades in the morning, he had urged Bazaine at Gravelotte to "join the army immediately... and not squander the present advantage."[56] This proved that the French were aware of their local superiority. And yet Leboeuf did nothing on his own initiative; he let three hours pass, then mounted up at midday, peered in the direction of the battle and told his anxious staff that he "would wait for orders from [Bazaine.]"[57] A Prussian general in his position would have marched instinctively to the front.

Though spared an annihilating French counter-attack, the Prussian III Corps had to endure hours of shelling from the massed guns of Canrobert and Frossard. For the Prussians, there was some comfort in the defective French fuses – French shells regularly detonated high in the air or long after

54 SHAT, Lb10, "Rapport sur la part que le 2e Corps d'Armée a prise dans la bataille de Rezonville, le 16 Août 1870." Bivouac sous Metz, 19 Aug. 1870, Gen. Texier to Marshal Canrobert, "Rapport."
55 SHAT, Lt12, 28 Feb. 1872, "Déposition de General Bourbaki."
56 SHAT, Lb10, Bagneux, 16 Aug. 1870, Marshal Leboeuf to Marshal Bazaine. "... *il est essentiel que nous ne perdions pas cet avantage et votre retard le compromet.*"
57 SHAT, Lb10, Paris, 16 Feb. 1872, Col. D'Ornant to Marshal Leboeuf.

they had hit the ground, permitting troops to scamper away to safety – but just some. The sheer volume of French fire more than compensated for the failure of random shells.[58] With morale wilting even in the toughest units, Alvensleben resorted to a desperate expedient. He ordered the nearby 12th Cavalry Brigade to gallop forward and attack Canrobert's gun line. Acutely aware that he was embarked on a suicide mission, a modern day Charge of the Light Brigade, General Friedrich Wilhelm von Bredow delayed as long as was politic, and then grudgingly led the charge by six squadrons of uhlans and cuirassiers at 2 P.M. His last words before setting off were marvelously Prussian: "*Koste es, was es wolle*" – "it will cost what it will."[59]

With Canrobert's gunners firing *mitrailleuse* balls, shrapnel and canister into the massed horsemen, Bredow's cavalry charge ought to have been a slaughter, but the general made clever use of the undulating ground rising up to the Rezonville position. Hidden by low-lying clouds of powder smoke, his squadrons rode through gullies and depressions and exploded into Canrobert's position. "Von Bredow's Death Ride" was a rare instance of a successful cavalry charge against modern rifles and artillery. Though Bredow lost 420 of his 800 men – one of whom was Bismarck's son Herbert, who fell wounded – he overran Canrobert's corps artillery, panicked his trains, and caused Bazaine to sink even deeper into his defensive redoubt around Gravelotte. Forton's cavalry division, which had embarrassed itself in the morning, briefly rode in on Bredow's flank and rear, but was dispersed, not by Prussian lances and sabers, but by the indiscriminate fire of Canrobert's nervous infantry, who shot down 154 of their own cuirassiers in a matter of minutes.[60] Watching the melée from Tronville, a Hanoverian gunner was in no doubt as to the efficacy of Bredow's charge: "We had been routed by the blinding French fire; all of our battery horses were dead and we were about to be overrun when Bredow's cavalry flashed by; they saved the day because [our] brigade was beaten."[61]

Nevertheless, the raw superiority of French numbers seemed unbeatable even in the absence of firm leadership. While Bredow's last attacks buffeted VI Corps, Ladmirault and Leboeuf, having finally left the Sedan road and marched to the guns, were sliding in beside Canrobert at Mars-la-Tour and Vionville. Here the decisive blow should have been landed. To his right, Ladmirault had General François du Barail's entire cavalry division. Ladmirault's flank was secure against any threat, and there before him at Tronville was Alvensleben's, a few battered infantry battalions and a division

58   Richard Berendt, *Erinnerungen aus meiner Dienstzeit*, Leipzig, 1894, pp. 62–4.
59   Karl Litzmann, *Ernstes und heiteres aus den Kriegsjahren 1870–71*, Berlin, 1911, p. 12.
60   SHAT, Lb9, General Henri de Forton, "Rapport sur la part prise le 16 Août par le Division à la bataille de Rezonville."
61   Berendt, p. 67.

of Prussian cavalry wincing at the nonstop clatter of the French *mitrailleuses* and rifles. In this critical sector, the French had 20,000 more troops than the Prussians. But Bazaine never even approached Mars-la-Tour. One of his staff officers thought it curious that the marshal passed the entire battle at Rezonville and Gravelotte – the left wing of his position – instead of the crucial right wing, where the French could have won the battle and exploited it to maximum effect.[62] Even more curious was Bazaine's letter to the emperor after the battle, in which he took credit for a decisive "turning movement" that he had neither ordered nor executed: "We triumphed toward midday, when Leboeuf and Ladmirault arrived on the field and turned the enemy's left under my orders."[63]

In fact, Bazaine's corps commandants received no such direction, and reverted to the defensive reflexes that had been drilled into them since Königgrätz. Advised by his lead *divisionaire*, General François Grenier, that the Prussian III Corps was still in fighting condition, Ladmirault called off the attack toward Tronville and deployed his men defensively around Mars-la-Tour. Leboeuf's III Corps, poised to clear Vionville, was halted by Bazaine himself, who ordered Leboeuf's troops to join the defensive huddle around Gravelotte. With little to do there, Leboeuf had the bright idea of sending his corps down the road to Ars-sur-Moselle to cut off an eventual Prussian retreat. The men marched for a mile before they were overtaken by an angry Marshal Bazaine on horseback, who ordered Leboeuf back to Gravelotte. The entire march and counter-march were opportunistically raked by the Prussian guns at Flavigny, which left 500 would-be assault troops dead or writhing on the turnpike.[64] In his reports, General Bourbaki, commandant of the Guard Corps, expressed his amazement that Bazaine spent most of the day shut inside the post office in Gravelotte, concerned with nothing more than his line of retreat to Metz.[65]

Ladmirault's moment was lost. Between 3:30 and 4 P.M., the first units of General Konstantin von Voights-Rhetz's X Corps arrived on the field. Originally ordered to march for the Meuse to intercept a retreating Bazaine, X Corps had swerved north to reinforce Alvensleben. The troops, a mixed bag of "New Prussians" – Frisians, Oldenburger, Hanoverians, and Brunswicker – shambled heavily into battle. They had been marching up the hot, chalky roads from Pont-à-Mousson and Thiaucourt for twelve hours. The 20th Division established itself at Tronville, shoring up Alvensleben's left wing, while General Schwarzkoppen's 19th Division went promptly over to the attack, driving into what they thought was Ladmirault's flank at Mars-la-Tour. In fact, it was

62 Andlau, p. 73.
63 SHAT, Lc1, Gravelotte, Marshal Bazaine to Napoleon III and General Dejean.
64 SHAT, Lb10, no date, Gen. Nayral. Montaudon, vol. 2, p. 98.
65 SHAT, Lt12, 28 Feb. 1872, "Déposition de General Bourbaki."

his front. In thirty minutes of violence, the French *feu de bataillon* did its murderous work. Reinforced by General Ernest de Cissey's division, Grenier poured volleys into the Prussian swarms, knocking them down before they could even make their needle rifles effective. Schwarzkoppen's first brigade lost 60 percent of its strength, 45 percent killed, including the general and colonels leading the assault. Prussian batteries that rode up to give supporting fire were picked off by the Chassepot: "The bullets hit us from ranges we thought impossible," a Prussian gunner later wrote. "The mass of them more than compensated for the inaccuracy."[66]

To finish the Prussians off, General Cissey ordered his 2nd Brigade to form battalion columns and charge with the bayonet, more proof that the French army, as developed after 1866, really had no viable means of *attack*. The men, shrewd southerners from the Tarn, performed an interesting stunt. Herded into storm columns by their officers, they roared "*en avant*" at the top of their lungs, but stubbornly refused to advance. "*Tout parle, personne ne bouge*" – "everyone was talking, no one was moving," a lieutenant in the 57th Regiment observed. Here was a critical difference between the French and Prussian armies. German troops, in this and subsequent wars, could be ordered to do just about anything; they would take monstrous casualties if need be. French troops were far more discriminating. Informed of the devastation wrought by the needle rifle in 1866, they refused to attack it, especially when their senior officers refused to put themselves in harm's way. (Lieutenant Camille Lerouse of the 57th remembered urging his regimental colonel, Marie-Adrien Giraud, to lead the battalions from the front; Giraud refused.) In this way, the defensive tendencies of the general staff and senior officers were reinforced by the troops themselves, who preferred in every instance to rely on the superior range of the Chassepot. Cissey's brigade, opposed by a single Prussian regiment, did finally attack, the *troupiers* led forward by junior officers well-known to the men – "*oui, oui, mon Capitain, en enfer si vous voulez!*" – but the results could only have reinforced France's preference for the defensive. As the French closed on the Prussians, they made their own shooting more effective but also came into range of the needle rifle. After exhausting their ammunition, the French were rolled back by a Prussian counter-attack: "They swarmed over us, yelling like barbarians." Lieutenant Lerouse became another of the thousands of casualties that day; shot in the foot and through both legs, he collapsed in the grass near Mars-la-Tour.[67]

The battle was a stalemate, thanks largely to the now indomitable Prussian gun line, which counted twenty-one batteries by the end of the day and stretched two miles from Flavigny round to Tronville. This "grand battery" of

---

66 Howard, p. 158. Berendt, pp. 62–7.
67 SHAT, Lb4, Lille, Aug. 1870, Lt. Lerouse to Maj. Dupuy de Podio, "Rapport."

130 guns was nearly as big as the legendary Austrian gun line at Königgrätz and more potent.[68] Prussian gunners observed their shells "tearing holes" in the French columns as they fended off late-afternoon counter-attacks.[69] Though they had held the keys to victory all day, the French had never used them. Steinmetz's failure to move his First Army across the Moselle after Borny had given Bazaine a golden opportunity to mass his entire force against a fraction of Prince Friedrich Karl's, thrash it, and then run for Verdun. In a war of missed French opportunities, this was perhaps the most grievous. General Bourbaki recalled that 5 P.M. was "undoubtedly the moment for a general advance. Bazaine had only to suggest this and we would have ... driven the Prussians into the Moselle."[70] Colonel Joseph Andlau, a member of Bazaine's staff, remembered his own consternation at the marshal's passivity: "it was clear that we had superior numbers against two isolated enemy corps."[71] As an Austrian officer put it, Mars-la-Tour was one of those "half-victories" (*"Halbsiegen"*) that competent generals know how to exploit.[72] The Prussians, with a jackal's nose for weakness, had one last stab at victory as evening descended at 6 P.M. General Albert von Rheinbaben ordered his 5th Cavalry Division to ride northwest and press in hard on Ladmirault's flank. The Prussians executed the maneuver on the grassy plain between Mars-la-Tour and the Yron, a stream that ran under the Verdun road a mile west of the battlefield. As they rode in on Ladmirault, Rheinbaben's light and heavy brigades – hussars, dragoons, lancers, and cuirassiers – collided with Du Barail's entire cavalry division, which Ladmirault had posted on his flank for precisely this eventuality. A whirling, clanking, creaking mêlée ensued while forty squadrons did battle: The saber cavalry hacked away, the lancers thrust with their pikes, and the dragoons fired their carbines into the ruck of struggling men and horses.

Elsewhere the Prussian infantry advanced in rushes under cover of darkness. The French 70th Regiment was panicked and routed by a line of Prussian skirmishers, who walked boldly up to the French in the failing light crying "we are French, cease firing." Once the French had lowered their rifles, the Prussians raised theirs and fired rapidly into the massed companies. The result was a general panic on the French side that raced through VI Corps and much of the rest of the army. Prussian uhlans compounded the chaos by galloping through the French retreat crying *"Vive la France! Vive l'Empereur"* before impaling men on their lances.[73] Night fell on this pandemonium, and

---

68 Capt. Hugo von Molnár, "Über Artillerie: Massenverwendung im Feldkriege," ÖMZ 1 (1880), pp. 295–96.
69 Berendt, pp. 63–4.
70 SHAT, Lt12, 28 Feb. 1872, "Déposition de General Bourbaki."
71 Andlau, pp. 73–4.
72 "Der Krieg 1870–71," ÖMZ 2 (1871), pp. 130–1.
73 SHAT, Lb10, "Rapport du 70 de Ligne sur le combat du 16 Août."

both sides gradually broke off the slaughter, the French retiring on their main body around Gravelotte, the Prussians holding the ground at Mars-la-Tour and Vionville. Interestingly, although Bazaine still had vastly superior numbers, he made no move for Verdun. Instead he put himself at the head of a single battery of Guard artillery and rode out to cover Frossard's retreat from Rezonville.[74] This was a reprise of his conduct at Borny and was one of the least useful things that he could have been doing under the still promising circumstances. Benedek had exhibited the same self-destructive tendencies in the Königgrätz campaign, seeking refuge in administrative trivia or minor combats far below his level of responsibility. Bourbaki later attributed the French defeat in large part to Bazaine's hands-off command style: "I spent the entire day in complete ignorance of Marshal Bazaine's intentions, or of any ultimate objective."[75]

Overall, Bazaine's comportment perplexed Austria's military attaché in Paris, who at that very moment was sitting down to write his minister: "France can win *only* if Bazaine avoids decisive battle in Lorraine and retreats to Paris, putting the Meuse and Marne between himself and the Prussians."[76] With Metz and its garrison in their path, Bazaine on the Marne, and 200 hostile miles to Paris, the Prussian army would have been stretched to the breaking point. Unfortunately, Marshal Bazaine would not appreciate the wisdom of this strategy. He was inclined to call the day a draw and leave it at that, informing the emperor that he had driven off the Prussians by "turning their right" with the III and IV Corps.[77] This was a shameless fabrication. In truth, both armies had fired off all of their ammunition and inflicted enormous casualties: 16,500 Prussians fell, 16,600 French. The officers were decimated by the "encounter battle": 626 Prussian officers killed or wounded, 837 French.[78] The Prussians could sustain these losses better than the French; indeed a French spy in Moltke's headquarters was amazed to overhear Moltke and Roon assuring each other that "they were not troubled by losses of even 20,000 men because they received continuous reinforcements" from Germany.[79] France, with a much smaller army than Prussia's, was not so richly endowed with manpower. Perhaps that explained Bazaine's odd decision not to contest the Verdun road, which he yielded to Prince Friedrich Karl that night, ordering his corps to fall back on Gravelotte and leave the field to the Prussians.[80] The next day, the

74 Fay, pp. 85–6.
75 SHAT, Lt12, 28 Feb. 1872, "Déposition de General Bourbaki."
76 HHSA, PA IX, 96, "Der Krieg zwischen Preussen und seinen Bundesgenossen und Frankreich."
77 SHAT, Lb10, Gravelotte, 16 Aug. 1870, Marshal Bazaine to Napoleon III.
78 "Die Schlacht bei Vionville," ÖMZ 3 (1871), pp. 89–91.
79 SHAT, Lb12, Metz, 20 Aug. 1870, Armée du Rhin, Etat Major Géneral, "Renseignements."
80 Montaudon, vol. 2, p. 98.

British military attaché described the greater significance of Bazaine's decision with remarkable prescience:

"The importance of the French being able to concentrate at Châlons is enormous because the Army of the Rhine will then become an excellent nucleus upon which the forces which are being organized in the rear can form themselves. Three hundred thousand men could therefore be placed in line at Châlons, or fall back to better positions. If Bazaine is cut off, it would be a regular disaster, for there would be no force left to rally round, and nothing could then stop the march of the Prussians on Paris."[81]

No trophies were taken at Mars-la-Tour – no battle flags, *aiglons*, or guns – and both the French and Prussians claimed victory, but there is little doubt that the real loser was Marshal Achille Bazaine, who snatched defeat from the jaws of certain victory. Everything was in Bazaine's favor: Metz's fortifications and garrison of 30,000 ought to have pinned down at least 90,000 Prussian troops, who should have been forced to surround the fortress and block punches at Moltke's lines of communication. As it was, the sheer bulk of Metz and its outlying forts blocked Steinmetz's advance and left seven divisions of Second Army alone against Bazaine's twenty for an entire day.[82] Yet Bazaine made nothing of the opportunity, restraining every offensive impulse that percolated up to his post at Gravelotte. This was all the more remarkable in view of the fact that Bazaine had decided to linger at Metz after being persuaded of its powerful defensive possibilities by the fortress commandant, General Grégoire Coffinières de Nordeck. Coffinières had called Metz a *"position inexpugnable"* from which Bazaine could "sally at his leisure to beat the enemy armies in detail, with an assured refuge at his back."[83] There would never be a more promising chance to sally than 16 August, yet Bazaine let it slip. After the battle, General Heinrich Antonovich Leer, Russia's top academic strategist, marveled that Prince Friedrich Karl had crossed the Moselle and seized the road to Verdun so easily: "In theory, against a modern fortress like Metz with a 30,000-man garrison and ... an army of 100,000 or more on its flank or rear, you would need at least 600,000 men to neutralize the fortress and army."[84] Friedrich Karl had accomplished the feat with just 60,000. For all the bravery of his men, Bazaine should have hung his head in shame.

Tactically, Mars-la-Tour was another victory for the Prussian artillery. One French infantry officer called the battle a "massive artillery duel," and the Prussians clearly won it, using gun masses to offset their small troop numbers and keep French counter-attacks at bay. Mars-la-Tour saw the first

81 PRO, FO 27, 1811, Paris, 17 Aug. 1870, Col. Claremont to Lyons.
82 Maurice, p. 153.
83 Andlau, p. 70.
84 "General Heinrich Antonowitsch Leer über den Krieg 1870–71," ÖMZ 4 (1874), pp. 41–51.

extensive use of Prussian *"Artillerie-Massen,"* batteries of guns that separated from their infantry or cavalry brigades to join improvised gun lines wherever needed. By the end of the day, these various improvised lines stretched two miles from the edge of the Gorze forest through Flavigny to Tronville. Even under heavy shrapnel and Chassepot fire, the Prussian gunners restlessly closed their ranges, in pointed contrast to the French gunners, who invariably drew back under fire. This had something to do with the Prussian code of *Waffenbrüderschaft* – "armed brotherhood" – which required every soldier to sacrifice himself for another, regardless of regiment or branch of service. Gunners, in other words, had to give up their lives for infantrymen and vice versa, no excuses tolerated. Though many Prussian infantry officers – pitted against Chassepots and *mitrailleuses* – would regret the loss of their artillery to the gun lines, the advantages in terms of massed, crossing, concentric fire proved decisive by day's end.[85] General Henri de Forton's 3rd Reserve Cavalry Division was panicked at the start of the battle by a "hailstorm" of Prussian shells, and beaten in the afternoon by what Forton called Bredow's *"goum*-like tactics."[86] *Goums* were Algerian irregular cavalry, who used speed and deception to overrun their enemies, very much in the style of Bredow. Philippe Zibelin, one of Canrobert's junior officers, marveled at the deadly work of the Prussian gun line at Flavigny, which rocked VI Corps back on its heels for the entire day. Zibelin, who had watched the Prussian attacks on Vionville and Rezonville in the morning, also praised the "superior initiative" demonstrated by Prussian company commanders, who maneuvered their swarms deftly and "used the rolling ground to shield their men from the worst effects of the Chassepot." Overall, Zibelin attributed Prussia's battlefield victories to a quality completely lacking in French tactics, what he called the "principle of successive efforts." Every Prussian probe was instinctively joined and reinforced by other units, creating broad, deep flanking attacks that the French could not withstand.[87]

Paris drew all the wrong conclusions from the battle. Count Palikao assured the legislative body on 16 August that the Army of the Rhine was ready to "reconcentrate" at Châlons.[88] Gramont's replacement at the foreign ministry, Prince de la Tour d'Auvergne, told foreign ambassadors that Bazaine had cleared the road west and "assured his retreat behind the Marne." As an attaché at Bazaine's headquarters passed on the same information, it would

85 SHAT, Lb10, "Rapport sur la part que le 2e Corps d'Armée a prise dans la bataille de Rezonville, le 16 Août 1870." Capt. Hugo von Molnár, "Über Artillerie: Massenverwendung im Feldkriege," ÖMZ 1 (1880), pp. 295–96. Berendt, pp. 62–7.
86 SHAT, Lb10, 24 Oct. 1872, General Henri de Forton.
87 SHAT, Lb10, Besançon, 1882, Capt. Zibelin, "Etude sur la bataille de Rezonville/Mars-la-Tour. Travail d'hiver."
88 PRO, FO 27, 1811, Paris, 16 Aug. 1870, Col. Claremont to Lyons.

appear that even Bazaine thought that this was the case.[89] The false omens did nothing for Napoleon III's depressed regime, which appeared to have abandoned all hope of victory. Before the result of Mars-la-Tour was known in Paris, Tour d'Auvergne begged the British ambassador to form a "league of neutrals" that might secure an armistice for which the French would posit only two conditions: territorial integrity and maintenance of the Bonaparte dynasty. Everything else would presumably be negotiable: cash indemnities, reparations in kind, disarmament and colonial concessions.[90] The Second Empire was tottering before the fall.

89 HHSA, PA IX, 95, Paris, 17 Aug. 1870, Metternich to War Minister. 18 Aug. 1870, Metternich to Emperor Franz Joseph.
90 PRO, FO 425, 97, Paris, 16 Aug. 1870, Lyons to Granville.

7

Gravelotte

As the fighting flickered out around Mars-la-Tour and Vionville, Moltke, King Wilhelm and Bismarck, wedged between the march columns of the Saxon XII Corps, finally crossed the Moselle at Pont-à-Mousson. Prince Friedrich Karl had crossed earlier in the day and spent much of it at Gorze trying to direct the seesaw battle and its aftermath.[1] With his usual perspicacity, Moltke grasped the larger significance of Mars-la-Tour. Bazaine was marooned, divided from the French hinterland by most of the Prusso-German army.[2] Moltke immediately stopped the race to the Meuse and directed his IV, VII, VIII, and XII Corps to wheel into line beside Alvensleben and Voigts-Rhetz at Rezonville and Gravelotte. To reduce Steinmetz's potential for mischief, Moltke shifted VIII Corps to the Second Army and ordered Steinmetz to stand in place near Gravelotte with his sole remaining corps while the rest of the Prussian army pivoted north of him. Though hard days were ahead – Bazaine had a friendly fortress at his back and a strong defensive position – Moltke was groping for a decisive encirclement. He would either envelop Bazaine on the skirts of Metz, push him into the fortress to starve, or drive him north to Luxembourg, where, according to the laws of war, the French army would have to lay down its arms.[3] Bazaine's thinking ran shallower; the marshal pondered until 10 P.M., when he and his general staff chief, General Louis Jarras, finally issued a dispiriting set of orders from their rooms in Gravelotte:

---

1 Dresden, Sächsisches Kriegsarchiv (SKA), Zeitg. Slg. 107, Adolf Leopold von Tschirschky, "Militärische Lebenserinnerungen," pp. 274–5.
2 Helmuth von Moltke, *The Franco-German War of 1870–71*, New York, 1892, pp. 48–50. Gen. Julius Verdy du Vernois, *With the Royal Headquarters in 1870–71*, 2 vols., London, 1897, vol. 1, pp. 72–3.
3 Michael Howard, *The Franco-Prussian War*, orig. 1961, London, 1981, p. 164.

"Because of the enormous ammunition consumption by our infantry and artillery, we shall retreat to a new position on the plateau of Plappeville. The movement shall commence tomorrow the 17th [of August] at 4 A.M."

According to Colonel Joseph Andlau, the French officers and troops were "stupefied" by the order: "At Borny, [Bazaine] had argued the necessity of limiting the engagement to hasten the redeployment to Verdun.... Now, tonight, after a victorious battle...when the road to Verdun had been secured with the blood of 20,000 men, we *retreated*! Toward *Metz!*" Major Charles Fay, another of Bazaine's staff officers, shared Andlau's frustration, noting that the army "could have made it to Verdun after [Mars-la-Tour], because the first Prussian reinforcements did not appear the next day till three o'clock in the afternoon."[4] Even if one accepted Bazaine's view that the road to Verdun was too risky, the roads northwest to Sedan were wide open. Colonel Marie-Edouard d'Ornant, Niel's senior aide-de-camp and now Leboeuf's, rued Bazaine's passivity on 17 August: "God only knows what might have been the result had we delivered a second battle" on the heels of Mars-la-Tour. According to d'Ornant, the Prussians were clearly overextended, and the Army of the Rhine had more than enough food and ammunition to fight and continue the retreat to Verdun: "It would have been easier to push the army forward than pull it back to Metz."[5] General Bourbaki was even blunter: "throughout the day and night of 16 August the routes to Verdun were open; Bazaine could have got away to unite with MacMahon *had he wanted to.*" The last words were underlined by Bourbaki, who suspected that Bazaine was conspiring to separate himself from the meddling emperor and empress at any cost.[6]

Of course Bazaine had his reasons; to reach Verdun at this late date, he would have had to abandon most of his supplies and baggage, and would have offered his flank to the Prussians, both risky propositions. Moreover, if overtaken by the Prussians *en rase campagne* – in open country – he would have had the worst of all worlds: insufficient supplies and ammunition for a long battle and no refuge behind the detached forts of Metz. Weighing all of these factors, Bazaine chose what he believed was the safest course, a retreat to Plappeville, one of Metz's outlying forts.[7] Still, the marshal's letter to the emperor on 17 August substantiated Bourbaki's claim that Bazaine *wanted* to remain at Metz. "I will resume my march [toward Verdun] in two days if possible, and will not lose time, unless new battles thwart my arrangements."[8]

4   Charles Fay, *Journal d'un officier de l'Armée du Rhin*, Paris, 1889, pp. 100–1.
5   Vincennes, Service Historique de l'Armée de Terre (SHAT), Lb11, 1872, Col. d'Ornant.
6   SHAT, Lt12, 28 Feb. 1872, "Déposition de General Bourbaki."
7   F. A. Bazaine, *Episodes de la guerre de 1870 et le blocus de Metz*, Madrid, 1883, pp. 156–7.
8   SHAT, Lb10, Plappeville, 17 Aug. 1870, Marshal Bazaine to Napoleon III.

With the Prussians massing around him, Bazaine must have known that he would not have "two days" to regulate his affairs. His inexplicable dawdling eroded morale in the Army of the Rhine, and fledged a conspiracy theory among the troops that went like this: aristocratic French officers – in cahoots with Prussian reactionaries and Parisian republicans – were trying to kill the men by herding them back to the dangerous ground they had just vacated with the loss of 17,000 dead and wounded. (*"Pourquoi cette fuite? C'était bien la peine de nous faire tuer, pour nous ramener, où nous étions auparavant."*)

Paranoids saw their conspiracy theory confirmed the next day when Bazaine gave orders for an immense bonfire at Gravelotte. With the Prussians streaming up from the Moselle bridges in ever greater numbers, Bazaine, who had used the 16th to push his supplies and wounded along the road to Verdun, now pulled them back. Most of the wounded were simply left in their ambulances for the Prussians; the supplies were driven into the square in Gravelotte, heaped up, and burned. Everything that made military life worth living went into the blaze: cases of wine, sacks of coffee, cuts of beef, loaves of bread, coats, trousers, shoes, blankets, and tents. Because Bazaine had chosen Metz as his refuge in part to save his supplies, the fire must have struck everyone as inconceivably depressing, particularly the long-suffering *grognards*, who grimly humped their seventy-pound packs past the flames on their return to Metz.[9]

By late afternoon the redeployment was complete. Bazaine had selected the "Amanvillers position," a six-mile ridge above Gravelotte that blocked the approach to Metz from the west. Now that the armies were fighting with "reversed fronts" – the Prussians with their backs to France, the French with theirs to Germany – Bazaine could place this formidable obstacle between himself and the Prussians. The position seemed strong from a distance but was flawed. Though the left wing at Gravelotte could be anchored on the hills and ravines that plunged steeply down to the Moselle, there was nothing fixing the right wing at St. Privat. The elevated village, defended by Marshal Canrobert's VI Corps, was "in the air," that is, it had no natural obstacles barring attacks from the right. Nor did Bazaine send over extra artillery to compensate for the weakness, or even warn his corps commanders of the Prussian advance, which was reported to him by lookouts in Metz cathedral and Fort St. Quentin and by hundreds of peasants fleeing ahead of Moltke and his plundering quartermasters. Like Benedek before the climactic battle of Königgrätz, Bazaine abandoned his army at its supreme moment, hiding himself in the fort at Plappeville to indulge, as one officer put it, *"un fatalisme tout arabe"* – "a thoroughly Arab fatalism."[10]

9 Joseph Andlau, *Metz: Campagne et Négociations*, Paris, 1872, pp. 77–83.
10 Andlau, pp. 84–5.

A no less pathetic scene was underway in Châlons, where Napoleon III and his weary entourage had finally arrived to confer with Marshal Patrice MacMahon, newly arrived from Alsace, and General Louis Trochu, commandant of the roughshod French XII Corps. These were the only senior French officers available, because the rest of the army was turning at bay near Metz. Early on 17 August, Napoleon III chaired a council of war to discuss the military situation. Prince Jerôme-Napoleon, Louis-Napoleon's ambitious cousin, opened the meeting with a brutally frank *exposé* of the emperor's position:

> "The emperor has effectively abandoned the government to take command of the army; he is now abandoning the army to Marshal Bazaine. Now he finds himself alone at the Camp de Châlons, without any army at all. What this means is that he has abdicated command of both the government and the army. If he does not wish to find himself in a position where he must really abdicate, he had better retake command of one or the other."

The emperor wearily agreed, suggesting that as it was no longer possible for him to lead the army, he had better "resume the government with a firm hand." Forty-eight-year-old Prince Jerôme, exerting ever more influence over his flagging cousin, insisted that Napoleon III's return to Paris be "preceded by an army general, who must prepare the city militarily and politically for the emperor's arrival." General Trochu agreed to perform the thankless job. This was the surprisingly *reactionary* seed of Louis Trochu's "Government of National Defense," later acclaimed by republican historians. Trochu's only condition was that MacMahon's little army be diverted not to Metz, where it might be lost, but to the defense of Paris, where it could wear the Prussians down and seek for opportunities in a protracted siege. To this, both Napoleon III and MacMahon agreed: Paris was the "proper destination" for MacMahon's army. Once again, the emperor and the empress were working at cross-purposes. In Paris, Eugénie and her war minister, General Pierre Dejean, had already decided that MacMahon would pause only to "reconstitute" his army at Châlons and then march quickly to the relief of Bazaine. Orders to this effect had been sent to MacMahon at midday on 16 August.[11] Informed of her husband's council of war on the 17th, Eugénie rejected its decisions and set the "Army of Châlons" on an entirely different course. That evening General Dejean gave the wobbling emperor his marching orders:

> "The empress has shown me the letter in which you announce that the Army of Châlons will be moved to Paris. I beseech the emperor to renounce this idea, which will look to the public like an abandonment of the Army of the Rhine, which can no longer make its way to Verdun. In three days the Army of Châlons will number 85,000 men, when joined by Douay's corps, it will

11 SHAT, Lb10, Châlons, 16 Aug. 1870, Gen. Trochu to Marshal Bazaine.

have 18,000 more. Can you not launch a powerful diversion (*puissante diversion*) against the Prussian armies already exhausted by their many battles? The empress shares my opinion."[12]

Napoleon III weakly submitted. On the eve of Gravelotte, Prince Richard Metternich wrote Vienna that the French emperor was "deeply depressed ... the prince imperial nervous and ill, the empress in the most frightful condition."[13]

While Napoleon III and Eugénie hatched the idea of a "powerful diversion" to take pressure off Bazaine – a "diversion" that would snowball into the catastrophic battle of Sedan – Bismarck was touring the Mars-la-Tour battlefield late on 17 August. Though glad to be setting the pace of the war, Bismarck was horrified at the artless and gory methods of generals like Kameke, Kirchbach, and Alvensleben, which had made a casualty of his own son. In Rezonville, he had a revealing encounter with one of the hundreds of wounded French officers left behind by Bazaine. When the Frenchman expressed admiration for the Prussian army, Bismarck replied that Prussia would be doing even better, indeed would "win the war in just fifteen days if armed with the Chassepot." He then reflected for some minutes, and added: "but if you had our *generals*, the war would be over as quickly, with the opposite outcome."[14] Bismarck was bitterly pondering a fault line in Prussian military art that would diminish only with the passage of years, the rejuvenation of the officer corps, and the perfection of military technology. Essentially there were two types of officers in Prussia in 1870, and many in between who blended the qualities of both types. One type argued the invincibility of "moral" factors like "will," "guts," and "instinct." (Think of Steinmetz, or Bredow before his "Death Ride" muttering "*koste es, was es wolle.*") The other type exalted science, maneuver, and innovation, to win with a minimum of friction and casualties. That was Moltke's school, and Bismarck's, summed up in the Moltke maxim: "Though great successes presuppose bold risk-taking, careful thought must precede the taking of risks." The continual tension between the two types added to the burdens of Prussian great headquarters in the war.

Nevertheless, though Alvensleben had taken heavy casualties on 16 August, he had stopped Bazaine and turned him back on Metz. This was a favorable outcome for Moltke. He now had time to push two of his three armies into the space between Metz and Verdun to cut Bazaine off from the rest of France. To make sure that Bazaine did not contemplate another bolt for the Meuse, Prince Friedrich Karl ordered another night march in the pre-dawn hours of the 17th. His corps wheeled up to the Metz-Verdun road in the

12 SHAT, Lc1, 17 Aug. 1870, "Conseil de guerre au camp de Châlons."
13 Vienna, Haus-Hof-und-Staatsarchiv (HHSA), PA IX, 95, Paris, 18 Aug. 1870, Metternich to Beust.
14 Andlau, p. 193.

dark and dispatched mounted patrols in all directions to make contact with the French.[15] To Moltke's great relief, the only French troops west of Gravelotte were stragglers and deserters. The entire Army of the Rhine had withdrawn to Bazaine's new position on the Amanvillers ridge.

THE BATTLE OF GRAVELOTTE, 18 AUGUST 1870

Bazaine's retreat to Plappeville and Moltke's wheel to face the position set up the first set-piece battle of the Franco-Prussian War. All previous fights had been "encounter battles" sparked by accidental collisions or impetuous subordinates. This one was anticipated and carefully planned on both sides. While Moltke fanned the 200,000 troops and 730 guns of his First and Second Armies northward from Vionville and Mars-la-Tour, Bazaine settled 160,000 troops and 520 guns into the line of hills that rose between Gravelotte and St. Privat.

The French units on the southern end of the line, General Frossard's II Corps around Point du Jour – a hamlet above Gravelotte – and Marshal Leboeuf's III Corps in the fields to either side of the infelicitously named Moscow and Leipzig farms, dug themselves in to block any chops from Steinmetz at the root of Bazaine's position. General Ladmirault's IV Corps stood to Leboeuf's right, in the open fields of waving grain around Amanvillers. To the right of Ladmirault was Marshal Canrobert's VI Corps, the weakest unit in the Army of the Rhine, which was inexplicably given the most vulnerable sector, the hilltop postion of St. Privat. Canrobert's vulnerability was magnified by his distance from Bazaine's headquarters at Plappeville, where the marshal held Bourbaki's Guard Corps in reserve, four miles from St. Privat. If seriously threatened or turned, Canrobert would have to wait hours for reinforcements.[16]

Early on 18 August, Prince Friedrich Karl ordered his army to attack. Massed in the fields and plowland between Rezonville and Mars-la-Tour, the Prussians formed march columns and wheeled toward the French position. For many units, it was a grisly progress through fields littered with unburied casualties of Mars-la-Tour. Friedrich Freudenthal, a Prussian artillery officer with the IX Corps, cringed at the memory: "It was gruesome; we had to force our horses through rows of corpses, and I'll never forget the sound of skulls cracking beneath our wheels and the dull thump of arms and legs caught in our spokes; all cohesion was lost as our horses frantically shied, trying to find a way around the dead."[17] Second Army's right wing, the largely Hessian IX Corps, marched toward Gravelotte to close the gap between itself and

15 SKA, Zeitg. Slg. 158, Lt. Adolf Hinüber.
16 Howard, pp. 167–8.
17 Friedrich Freudenthal, *Von Stade bis Gravelotte*, Bremen, 1898, p. 127.

Steinmetz's VII Corps, which had been fitfully skirmishing with Frossard through the night. To their left, the Prussian Guards, with the battered III and X Corps in reserve, formed the center of the Prussian advance, the Saxon XII Corps the left wing.

Believing that Bazaine had descended to Metz or turned away to the north, Friedrich Karl initially assumed that the troops and guns visible around Amanvillers were no more than a rearguard. He thus advanced on a narrow front, bunching the Second Army for a frontal assault on the ridge. Arriving on the scene at 10:30 A.M. and moving forward to study the French tent lines and cook fires, Moltke ascertained the prince's error and briskly corrected it, spreading the Second Army wider and redirecting the XII Corps toward Roncourt and St. Privat.[18] Although the Saxons had a hard march ahead of them, they might deal the decisive blow in the battle, cutting around Bazaine's right wing to envelop the Army of the Rhine.

According to Major Alfred von Waldersee – who would succeed Moltke as German General Staff chief eighteen years later – there was no consensus in Prussian headquarters about the wisdom of an assault on Bazaine's redoubtable position. Some generals were for the brusque frontal attack begun by Prince Friedrich Karl, others for a holding action and a gradual turning of the French right once its precise location was determined. Circulating freely in Prussian headquarters on 18 August, American General Phil Sheridan – there as an observer for President Ulysses S. Grant – recalled the general uneasiness: "the ground over which an approach to the French line had to be made was essentially a natural open glacis, that could be thoroughly swept by the fire of the defenders."[19] With unburied dead from Mars-la-Tour filling the air with stink – Sheridan described the king's nauseated bodyguards bundling corpses off the captain's hill at the last minute – no one was particularly eager to renew the attack. While Moltke studied Prince Friedrich Karl's dispositions in his temporary post at Flavigny, War Minister Albrecht von Roon enjoined the king not to attack: "The object has already been attained; the French line of retreat has been cut. To throw them out of a strong position now will entail a useless loss of blood."[20] General Roon was right, as subsequent events would demonstrate, but the battle of Gravelotte had already sputtered into life.

The battle began between Gravelotte and Verneville, where General Albrecht von Manstein's IX Corps shook out its guns and began to rain shells on Ladmirault and Leboeuf at noon. For Manstein, still grieving for a son killed at Spicheren, this was his first chance to sink his teeth into the French.

18 Freudenthal, p. 130.
19 Philip H. Sheridan, *Personal Memoirs of P. H. Sheridan*, 2 vols., New York, 1888, vol. 2, pp. 368–9.
20 Alfred von Waldersee, *Denkwürdigkeiten*, 3 vols., Berlin, 1922, vol. 1, pp. 89–90.

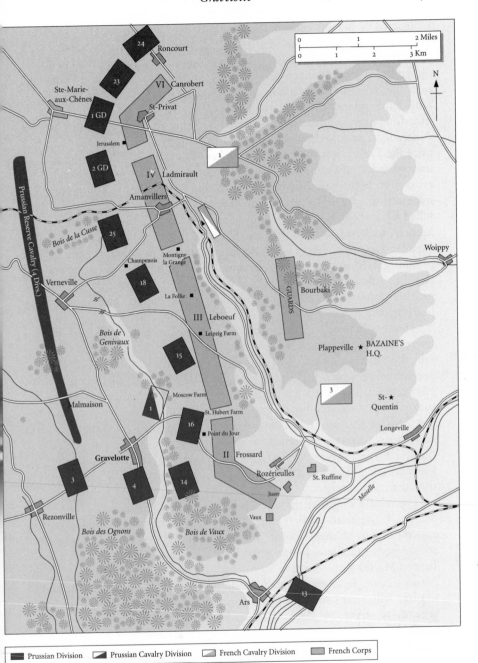

Map 8. The Battle of Gravelotte

Unbriefed by his superiors and unclear as to how many troops he had before him, he ordered up his reserve artillery and prepared an infantry assault with his 18th Division. Leading a battery of cannon to the front, a Prussian officer remembered passing the 18th, lined up in the potato fields around Verneville, their heads bowed, receiving a last blessing from the chaplains. While Manstein's infantry readied themselves, the IX Corps formed a mass of fifty-four guns, which rolled forward to bring the French center around Amanvillers and the French batteries at Montigny la Grange under fire. For once the French got the better of the Prussian artillery. Blundering into an unexpectedly powerful position, Manstein's gun crews were decimated by cross fires. Lieutenant Friedrich Freudenthal watched his five-man crew disintegrate; one was shot through the throat, a second in the chest, and a third killed by a shellburst. As the gun team regrouped, a shell exploded in the limber, butchering three horses and hurling a fourth gunner to the ground at Freudenthal's feet, where he lay screaming, trying to press his entrails back into his gut. Moments later the last gunner fell: Shot in the groin, he crawled twenty yards away and died. Freudenthal signaled desperately for reinforcements, but found that his frightened Hanoverian supports had "melted away like butter."[21]

Hearing Manstein's cannonade, General Steinmetz immediately ordered Dietrich von Zastrow's VII Corps and August von Goeben's VIII Corps to join the faltering attack. This was open defiance of Moltke's order of the previous day, which had transferred the VIII Corps to the Second Army, but very much in keeping with Steinmetz's querulous temperament. As this brazenly reconstituted First Army ground forward, pushing its infantry into the teeth of Frossard's field fortifications at Point du Jour and Leboeuf's at Moscow (*Moscou* in French), it sloughed off 150 Krupp guns, which, in the new Prussian style, worked forward in improvised groups, pounding the French shelter-trenches and loopholed farm buildings to take pressure off of the infantry columns.

Gravelotte would be the septuagenarian Karl von Steinmetz's last hurrah. Moltke, who passed the first hours of the battle on his hill behind Gravelotte, seated on a pile of knapsacks or "walking about, kicking clods of dirt or small stones here and there, his pace pale and thoughtful," was flabbergasted.[22] Indeed Moltke never forgave Steinmetz's artless and suicidal assaults up the Mance ravine. In any attempted envelopment, the trick is to pin the enemy in place with attacks on his heavily armed front only when the flanking force is ready to strike. By lurching at the French lines hours before the Saxons reached the fields below St. Privat, Steinmetz was once again playing into enemy hands, wasting Prussian strength in partial attacks that could not succeed.

21 Freudenthal, pp. 130–2, 135–41.
22 Sheridan, vol. 2, p. 371.

Commanded by Moltke to await the order for a general attack, Steinmetz slipped the leash shortly after 3 P.M., ordering the VII Corps, elements of the VIII Corps, and the 1st Cavalry Division to ascend the narrow road that rose eastward from Gravelotte to Metz. This cobbled road dipped into the Mance ravine and climbed through the heart of Frossard's defenses at Point du Jour and Moscou. Seven Prussian infantry regiments, obstructed by their cavalry and guns, stumbled into the crossing fires of 140 French guns and several divisions of infantry with Chassepot rifles. Against converging *mitrailleuse* bursts and gales of "battalion fire," the Prussians did not stand a chance in this sector. They checked on the lower slopes and fell back on Gravelotte. Ignoring the warnings of Moltke, the king rode forward to see the rout first-hand. Moltke and Sheridan jogged along beside him, Sheridan recalling that the seventy-three-year-old king "berated the fugitives in German so energetic as to remind me forcibly of the 'Dutch' swearing that I used to hear in my boy-hood in Ohio."[23] Just beyond Gravelotte, this perturbed royal headquarters had a famous encounter with Steinmetz. "Why are the men not advancing?" the king demanded. "They have no more leaders; their officers are all dead or wounded," Steinmetz replied. Jostled by fleeing soldiers, the king grabbed at the passing troops and demanded that they return to their units. "They are cowards," he muttered to no one in particular. This enraged Moltke, who burst out: "But the men are dying like heroes for Your Majesty!" The king gave his staff chief an icy look and spat out, "I alone will be the judge of that." Moltke turned and angrily rode away, leaving his royal majesty alone near the Mance ravine.[24]

This was the moment for Bazaine to counter-attack and smash the First Army to bits. On the other end of the line the Prussian Guards were just arriving below Amanvillers where they could do little but lean on their rifles to await the arrival of the Saxon XII Corps on their left. While their guns unlimbered and took up firing positions opposite Ladmirault, the Saxons trooped as quickly as they could through the woods and fields behind them, barging finally into the French outposts at St. Marie-les-Chênes at 3:30 P.M. Together the Saxons and the Prussian Guards assembled their own shifting "artillery mass," 180 guns in all, which worked steadily forward to pummel the increasingly vulnerable divisions of Ladmirault and Canrobert.

The impact of this second great mass of Prussian guns was terrific. While the Saxon Corps wisely gave the bare fields below St. Privat a wide berth and flank marched further north to Roncourt, where they could change front and strike into the flank and rear of Canrobert's position, Amanvillers and St. Privat crumbled under the rain of shells. After the battle, Ladmirault would

---

23 Sheridan, vol. 2, p. 377.
24 Munich, Bayerisches Kriegsarchiv (BKA), HS 849, Capt. Girl, vol. 2, p. 59. Waldersee, vol. 1, pp. 89–90. Verdy, vol. 1, pp. 84–5.

lead efforts to reform the static, defensive French tactics. He found his men "limp and discouraged" at the climax of the fight; they had been psychologically destroyed "by the constant menace of the Prussian artillery...the whistling, bursting, nerve-shattering rain of projectiles."[25] Canrobert's 1st Brigade, Colonel Charles Ardant du Picq's old unit, clung to Ste. Marie-aux-Chênes below St. Privat for a time, but then yielded it to the booming Prussian guns and infantry attacks. Ardant du Picq, who famously (and posthumously) argued that the "moral action" of inspired troops could overcome the "destructive action" of inanimate guns, a foolish view that contributed to the enormous French losses of 1914, would have learned from a scene described by his colleague, Colonel Joseph Vincendon: "Each time the Prussian skirmishers fell back before our heavy fire my men cried '*à la baionnette!*' and attempted to counter-attack; four of them actually vaulted the stone wall and charged the Prussians, only to be mowed down."[26] Here and elsewhere on the battlefield, "moral action" proved worthless against the "destructive action" of Prussia's six-pounders. Two hundred and seventy Prussian cannon raked St. Privat, Amanvillers, and the intervening farms for the entire afternoon and evening, drilling an estimated 20,000 shells into the French positions. This was more than three times the number of French shells fired in the battle.[27] Whole units were butchered; trenches collapsed, buildings caught fire, and roofs caved in on their frightened defenders.

General Ernest Pradier, one of Ladmirault's brigadiers, rued the effectiveness of the Prussian "artillery masses." Thirty-two Prussian guns sank their teeth into Pradier's brigade in the afternoon and shook it until nightfall: "they fired without interruption, smothering us in shells."[28] Another of Ladmirault's officers scoffed that Gravelotte had never been a fair fight: "We were the superior infantry, but that made no difference, for throughout we were just cannon meat (*viande à canons*) for the Prussian batteries."[29] By the end of the day, when the Prussian guns massed most effectively, every French cannon and *mitrailleuse* that opened up was swiftly bracketed and disabled by Prussian shells; even well-hidden batteries behind earthworks were put out of action. Despite superior positions – most German accounts spoke of seeing nothing but French kepis throughout the battle – the French lost thousands of dead, wounded, and missing to the Prussian cannon. Fully 70 percent of French casualties in the battle were caused by this insistent German artillery. (The statistic was reversed in the German regiments, where 70 percent of casualties

25 Andlau, pp. 457–8.
26 SHAT, Lb 11, Metz, 19 Aug. 1870, Col. Joseph Vincendon, "Rapport."
27 SHAT, Lb 9, n.d., Gen. Soleille to Marshal Leboeuf. Lb 11, Gen. Frossard, "Rapport sur l'Affaire du 18 Août."
28 SHAT, Lb 11, Metz, n.d., Gen. Ernest Pradier.
29 SHAT, Lb 11, la Roche sur Yon, 14 Nov. 1873, Baron des Ormières to Duke Daumale.

Fig. 7. Prussian infantry ready to advance on St. Privat

were inflicted by the Chassepot.)[30] As had been observed at Mars-la-Tour, "hitting the dirt" offered little protection. Two French surgeons noted after the battle that 60 percent of French troops with artillery wounds had been struck in the back or neck while lying on the ground. Affirming the energetic philosophy of Ardant du Picq, these doctors concluded that "it is always safer to attack the guns than to lie flat within their range."[31]

By late afternoon, the battle of Gravelotte, so favorable to the French for a time, was turning in favor of the Prussians. Because Bazaine had ignored Canrobert's pleas for reinforcements and was refusing to reload his front line units with shells and cartridges from the reserve, there was no defense against the looming envelopment on the French right.[32] Fixed in place by the Prussian Guards below him, who fought bitterly for Ste. Marie-aux-Chênes, a village at the foot of the Amanvillers plateau, Canrobert was a helpless spectator to the Saxon flank march into the valley of the Orne and up to Roncourt on

30 Maj. Johann Nosinich, "Der Krieg 1870–71," *Österreichische Militärische Zeitschrift* (ÖMZ) 4 (1872), p. 157.
31 SHAT, Li 2, Polygone de Metz, Nov. 1870, Drs. Goujon and Félizet, "Des effets produits par les armes prussiennes."
32 SHAT, Lb 11, la Roche sur Yon, 14 Nov. 1873, Baron des Ormières to Duke Daumale.

his right. Once behind him, the Saxons and whatever cavalry they had with them would be able to sweep through St. Privat and commence the roll-up of the entire French position from north to south. Victorious against Steinmetz, Leboeuf and Frossard would be caught in the late afternoon encirclement and annihilated, Bazaine trapped in the fort at Plappeville.

Such would have been Moltke's plan of attack. Once again, it was defeated by what Clausewitz called the "fog and friction of war." Deceived by the silence of the French guns (all knocked out or chased away by the Prussian Krupps) or merely eager to pluck the laurels of victory before the Saxons, General August von Württemberg deployed the entire Prussian Guard Corps in attack columns and sent them up the steep slope to St. Privat at 5 P.M. Marshal Canrobert's beleaguered regiments could not believe their luck; to cross the "Chassepot gap" more quickly, the Prussian officers had foolishly grouped their men in company columns rather than loose skirmish order. The guardsmen made easy marks; emerging from the smoke and rubble of St. Privat, the French infantry stood, kneeled, or lay flat and opened up with their Chassepots. Lieutenant Paul von Hindenburg, who would command the German army in World War I and preside over the Weimar Republic, rode forward with his battalion commander to observe the French position. He could not believe the intensity of the fusillade; aimed fire came in "like a hurricane." With unlimited targets, the French officers had placed their battalion lines one behind the other to achieve a massive concentration of fire. Communication on the Prussian side was impossible, because the noise drowned out the drums and every shouted command.

Further up the hill, Captain Alfred von Eberstein tried repeatedly to lead his company of the 3rd Guard Regiment into St. Privat. It was impossible; the French battalion fires – augmented by Saxon "friendly fire" plunging in from Roncourt – drove the Prussian columns together, massing thousands of desperate men in tight spaces where every shell splinter and Chassepot ball struck home. Shot in the leg, Eberstein hobbled over to his battalion comman-dant who had been shot in the arm; as Eberstein applied a tourniquet, a shell burst below them, ripping the major in half and wounding Eberstein again. In all, 8,000 Prussian guardsmen tumbled to the ground dead or wounded. Hundreds more tried to desert the front; streaming away from the French fire in wild-eyed panic, they were met by stalwarts like Eberstein who staggered back to his feet and screamed, "*Wer hier nicht bei mir bleibt, den schiesse ich nieder!*" – "I'll shoot down anyone who doesn't stop here!" Eberstein watched as another Prussian officer chased down a fleeing master sergeant and ran him through with his saber.[33]

---

33   Alfred von Eberstein, *Erlebtes aus den Kriegen 1864, 1866, 1870–71 und mit FM Graf Moltke,* Leipzig, 1899, pp. 40–3. Theodor Fontane, *Der Krieg gegen Frankreich, 1870–71,* 4 vols., orig. 1873–76, Zurich, 1985, vol. 1, pp. 427–35.

To the right of the Guards, the Prussian 25th Division, mainly Hessians annexed in 1866, had even less success attempting to batter their way into Ladmirault's positions around Amanvillers. Though every Hessian gun fired more than 100 shells that day, they made less impact than usual on Ladmirault's men, who were entrenched, lying behind breastworks, or barricaded inside stone farm buildings. Without effective suppressing fires, the German infantry had to cross 1,800 yards of mostly uphill open ground to reach the French. It was an impossible task; a Prussian Guard officer operating on the flank of the Hessians, told how his entire battalion was destroyed by Chassepot fire. The men who survived quickly exhausted their ammunition trying to return the "stupendous French fire." As they crawled among the dead and wounded scavenging for cartridges, the French *chasseurs* would counter-attack, pushing them off the height before scampering back to their indomitable lines.[34] A Hanoverian captain watching through his telescope lamented the "colossal losses;" the Hessian attacks on Amanvillers wilted under the French defensive fire and each Prussian move toward St. Privat left rows of dead and wounded men behind it.[35] Officers were blown off their horses, company columns were cut to pieces, and platoons and squads were driven into the grass 600 yards below the village. In little more than half an hour, General August von Württemberg's single corps had lost nearly as many men as the entire Prussian army had lost at Königgrätz four years earlier. Hindenburg recalled his amazement that the French did not counter-attack and annihilate the "shattered, bullet-holed remains" of the Guard Corps.[36] A possible explanation for this French passivity was contained in a letter written after the battle by a French enlisted man:

"Why did our captain not march at the head of the company? Why did he turn command over to a wounded second-lieutenant, leaving us without a *chef* at a critical moment? Why do our staff officers skulk behind the lines, never less than an hour away, descending on the troop columns only after the battle, like birds of prey, scolding and criticizing the brave men who fought the enemy. These gentlemen are farcical, ridiculous."[37]

If French officers, who were much older on average than their Prussian counterparts, were shrinking from fire, and French staff officers were failing to coordinate and energize the fighting, it becomes easier to comprehend the stagnant defensive tactics used by the French infantry. Spared a counterattack, the Saxons deployed as the last Prussian skirmishers fell back from St. Privat. With fourteen batteries of guns, they opened up from Roncourt at 7 P.M.,

34 Fontane, vol. 1, pp. 418–21.
35 Richard Berendt, *Erinnerungen aus meiner Dienstzeit*, Leipzig, 1894, p. 78.
36 Paul von Hindenburg, *Aus meinem Leben*, Leipzig, 1934, pp. 34–7.
37 SHAT, Lb 14, Anon., Au camp devant Metz, 26 Aug. 1870, "Des soldats de l'Armée du Rhin à son excellence M. le Ml. Bazaine."

taking Canrobert, already heavily engaged along his front, in the flank. Minutes earlier, Canrobert had considered counter-attacking the Prussian Guards. Startled by the abrupt collapse of French resistance in Roncourt, he now began to retreat, pulled by his own frightened troops. A subsequent investigation into the cause of the cave-in on the French right wing revealed that many of Canrobert's companies had simply stopped fighting and strolled back to their bivouacs in the midst of the battle to eat and rest. Some of these hundred-man companies had detached as many as twenty front-line troops *"pour faire la soupe"* – "to prepare supper" – while their comrades were in action.[38]

As Canrobert went, so went Ladmirault; uncovered by the retreat of the VI Corps, Ladmirault took heavy fire in his right flank and rear, and watched helplessly as his divisions dissolved in what he called "mass confusion." Flinging away their packs and camping equipment, the men of the IV Corps ran away from the Prussian fire with some troopers halting only to plunder supply convoys parked along the plateau.[39] General Bourbaki, still loitering with his two Imperial Guard divisions near Plappeville, had now to choose between requests for reinforcements from Canrobert and Ladmirault. After battering all day against Ladmirault's corps at Amanvillers, the Prussians had finally made a breach. According to French Major Louis Carré, the breakthrough was accomplished by another of the deceptions for which the resourceful Prussians were becoming notorious. Flattened into the grass by French fire, the Prussians had raised their rifle butts in the air and called *"cessez le feu!"* Confused, the French had ceased firing long enough for the Prussians to rise, race through the fields and open up with their needle rifles.[40]

With the Germans cracking and shivering the French front at all points, Bazaine provided no direction whatsoever; queried by Bourbaki, he replied obliquely, *"Mettre vos troupes en mouvement, quand vous vous jugerez convenable"* – "put your troops in motion whenever you judge it convenient."[41] The phrasing was vintage Bazaine: stilted, vague, and unknowing. Without orders from the generalissimo, Bourbaki sent an adjutant, Captain Louis de Beaumont, galloping hell-for-leather to Fort St. Quentin, which gave a good view of the battlefield. Specifically, Bourbaki wanted to know if the Prussians were seriously threatening Bazaine's left flank around Gravelotte and Vaux. If not, Bourbaki intended to throw his reserve into the fighting around Amanvillers and St. Privat. A few minutes on the walls of Fort St. Quentin and a few words with the local commander satisfied Beaumont that there were no Prussian troops at Vaux and that Steinmetz was being

38 SHAT, Lb 14, Au camp sous Metz, 25 Aug. 1870, Marshal Canrobert, "Note." Lb 13, Metz, 24 Aug. 1870, Anon. To Marshal Bazaine.
39 SHAT, Lb 11, Au camp, 20 Aug. 1870, Col. de Geslin, "Rapport sur l'affaire de 18 Août." Lb 11, Ch. de Sansonnes, 19 Aug. 1870, Gen. Ladmirault to Marshal Bazaine.
40 SHAT, Lb 11, n.d., Maj. Carré, "Rapport sur la bataille du 18 Août 1870."
41 SHAT, Lb 11, Camp de Sansonnet, 21 Aug. 1870, Gen. Bourbaki, "Rapport sur le combat de 18 Août." Lt 12, 28 Feb. 1872, "Déposition de Gen. Bourbaki."

driven back at Gravelotte. By 4:30 P.M. the captain was galloping back to Bourbaki, who had ridden forward to Amanvillers to view the action. Halfway home, Beaumont overtook Bazaine, who was himself returning from Fort St. Quentin to Plappeville with his staff. Recognizing the captain, a Second Empire grandee conspicuous in the green and scarlet uniform of the Empress's Own Dragoons, Bazaine stopped him and asked: "*Capitaine de Beaumont, où allez-vous?*" – "I am returning from Fort St. Quentin," Beaumont replied. "I was there on orders from General Bourbaki." Bazaine thought for a moment, and then said: "Since you are returning to General Bourbaki, tell him this." Beaumont later recorded that "the ensuing order so shocked me that I made a note of it as well as the conversation that followed."

Beaumont's notes, produced at Bazaine's court of inquiry after the war, describe Marshal Bazaine's floundering at the climax of the battle of Gravelotte. Although the French still had the upper hand, Bazaine refused to see it. "Go tell General Bourbaki that he ought to warn Marshal Canrobert that he is falling back." The imprecision and pessimism of the order "stupefied" Beaumont, who, in his own words, "could not make sense of it." Ladmirault had just advised Bourbaki that the Prussian Guards were beaten and victory in sight. "*Monsieur le Maréchal*," Beaumont blurted out. "Would you permit me to repeat the order that you have just given, to make sure that I have understood it?" Bazaine nodded. "Is it Marshal Canrobert who should retire after notifying General Bourbaki, or is it General [Bourbaki] who should retire after notifying Marshal Canrobert?" Bazaine pondered, leaving one of his colonels to answer: "It is General Bourbaki who must advise Marshal Canrobert that he is no longer supporting him, and then he should retreat to his bivouacs." After marching most of the way to Amanvillers, Bourbaki was to return to Plappeville at the height of the battle without firing a shot. Beaumont was thunderstruck, Bazaine suddenly roused, "*Mais certainement! Les Prussiens ont voulu nous tâter et la journée est finie. Maintenant, je vais rentrer*" – "Yes, just so! The Prussians wanted to have a go at us and the day is done. Now it's time to retire."[42]

While Bazaine finished with Beaumont, Bourbaki continued to juggle competing demands for his troops from Ladmirault and Canrobert. Without a clear directive from the army commander, he worried that his corps would be frittered away, "*paquet par paquet*." While Bourbaki deliberated, Bazaine actually rode past him and said nothing. He merely glanced at the Imperial Guards, massed in their march columns, and then turned down to Plappeville, where he rode disconsolately around the walls of the fort before vanishing inside.[43] Showing little initiative himself, Bourbaki rather timidly sent one of his divisions to Ladmirault, but kept the other back. It was too little too late; as Bourbaki rode with his guardsmen toward Amanvillers, they were swept

42 SHAT, Lb 11, Paris, 22 March 1872, Conseil d'Enquete, "Déposition de Capt. de Beaumont."
43 Andlau, p. 92.

back by a flood of panicked troops, some from Ladmirault's corps, others from Canrobert's, and the wreckage of François du Barail's cavalry division, which had formed up to oppose the Saxon advance only to be blasted by the Prussian artillery.[44]

The French retreat quickly degenerated into what Bourbaki bitterly called a "*dégringolade*," a tumbling, riotous rout. Without delineated lines of retreat, rallying points, or even orders, officers had no way to direct their men. Staff officers who went to Plappeville for guidance were coldly rebuffed by Marshal Bazaine: "You had your positions; you should have defended them; if you now find yourselves in trouble, it is your own fault." Colonel Joseph Andlau, who witnessed the debacle, later suggested an explanation for Bazaine's bizarre behavior: "Having assigned the men good positions, Bazaine refused to give further orders or even formulate a plan because such measures would have exposed him to criticism if they had failed." Andlau found it revealing that in all of his correspondence Bazaine referred to Gravelotte not as a "battle," but as a "defense," as if the "*défense des lignes d'Amanvillers*" were a shrewdly conceived operation ruined by bumbling subordinates.[45]

Marshal Bazaine plainly never even considered using his superior position and massed numbers at Gravelotte to maneuver and deal the scattered Prussians a heavy blow. Writing to Canrobert on the morning of the battle, Bazaine had ordered the marshal to hold St. Privat "in such a way that will permit the right wing to change front and occupy new positions behind it." This was a roundabout way of saying "in such a way that will permit the right wing to *retreat*."[46] Before the battle even began, in other words, Bazaine assumed that he was going to draw or lose the contest. The human impact of this pessimism and diffidence was tragic and unending as night fell. Aimless, frightened French units mingled and thousands of men hid in the woods that lined the slopes down to Metz. French troops on the forward edge of the plateau, many of whom had been barricaded inside farm buildings, now pleaded with passing troops to blow holes in the walls and set them free. The lucky ones wriggled out through cracks, leaving their rifles and packs behind.[47] Though VI Corps fought bravely to the end, counter-attacking for every gun and *mitrailleuse* overrun by the Prussians and Saxons, Canrobert's divisions went to pieces in the retreat, littering the ground behind St. Privat with cast-off rifles and more than 1,000 unopened crates of cartridges.[48] Even the unvanquished French troops around Point du Jour eventually gave way

44 SHAT, Lb 11, Camp de Sansonnet, 21 Aug. 1870, Gen. Bourbaki, "Rapport sur le combat de 18 Août."
45 Andlau, p. 97–101.
46 SHAT, Lb 11, Plappeville, 18 Aug. 1870, 10 A.M., Marshal Bazaine to Marshal Canrobert.
47 SHAT, Lb 11, Au camp, 19 Aug. 1870, Gen. Sanglé-Férriere, "Rapport."
48 SKA-Abg. Potsdam, Nr. P 967, Teandelize, 22 Aug. 1870, "Relation über die Theilnahme des XII Armee-Corps an die Schlacht von St. Privat la Montagne, am 18. Aug. 1870." SHAT, Lb 13, St. Martin, 23 Aug. 1870, Gen. Jarras to all corps commandants.

as Prussian skirmishers worked behind Moscou and St. Hubert in the failing light and began to shoot Leboeuf's men in the back. The Third Corps and Frossard's II Corps joined the general retreat down to Metz. Only the exhaustion of Moltke's army prevented a vigorous pursuit, which might otherwise have destroyed Bazaine's army before it reached the safety of the entrenched camp.[49]

Bazaine's conduct throughout the battle was extraordinary. He issued only one or two minor orders and never went forward from Plappeville to direct or even observe the fighting around Amanvillers or St. Privat.[50] When officers appealed for instructions, he greeted them all with the same unhelpful refrain: "Your general has been placed in very strong positions; he must defend them."[51] His general staff officers boiled with frustration; trained to collect and distribute information, they were forbidden to go forward. Major Charles Fay, one of those officers, whiled away the hours at Plappeville studying Bazaine. He found it extraordinary that the generalissimo never even considered riding forward to direct the battle. Instead the marshal slumped in his office, busying himself with trivial paperwork amid a strange silence caused by winds that carried the noises of battle away from Plappeville.[52] Only once did Marshal Bazaine bestir himself. At 2 P.M. he rode with five officers to Fort St. Quentin, which overlooked Gravelotte and the fighting around Point du Jour. Though Steinmetz was attacking this sector, witnesses recalled pointing out the much larger (and visible) threat to the northern end of the line where a German ring of fire was closing around St. Privat and threatening to engulf Canrobert and seal off Bazaine's last line of retreat, the road northwest to Briey and Sedan. Bazaine, inspecting a battery of twelve-pound fortress guns as if he were on a peacetime staff ride, showed little interest. When pressed by a subordinate, he looked up and dispensed the usual advice: "They are in good positions; they must defend them." He reflected for several minutes, then uttered one of his few orders of the day. It was less than momentous: "Send two batteries of the artillery reserve to guard the route to Briey, if it is still possible."[53]

Although he had 120 guns and 30,000 elite troops in reserve, Bazaine did nothing with them. Indeed he forbade his generals to dip into the army's ammunition reserve, which effectively disarmed many front-line units that had fired off all of their ammunition in the first phase of the battle or lost it to the Prussian artillery.[54] When General Bourbaki sought permission to engage in the afternoon, Bazaine hauled him back. After the war, many officers testified against Bazaine. One of them, Captain Jean-Paul Lacaze, an artillery officer

49 SHAT, Lb 11, Au camp, 19 Aug. 1870, Gen. Sanglé-Férriere, "Rapport."
50 SHAT, Lb 11, Metz, n.d., Marshal Leboeuf, "Rapport sur la bataille de St. Privat."
51 Andlau, p. 86.
52 Fay, p. 114. SHAT, Lb 8, Rémilly, 3 March 1872, A. Gauder to M. Rolles.
53 Andlau, pp. 87–9.
54 SHAT, Lb 11, la Roche sur Yon, 14 Nov. 1873, Baron des Ormières to Duke Daumale.

in Plappeville, found it "bizzare" that Bazaine was even in Plappeville – two or three miles from anywhere – and wondered if it were not "rather strange" that Bazaine ducked back into the fort "at the exact moment – 4 o'clock or 4:30 – when the entire Prussian effort was being hurled at [St. Privat]."[55] Strange indeed: A study of the letters and telegrams Bazaine drafted or dictated in the late afternoon of 18 August reveals just how strange.

At 4:15 P.M., when Steinmetz was thrusting Zastrow's corps up the road from Gravelotte in the wake of Goeben's, Bazaine sat down in Plappeville to compile a list of the generals and colonels killed that day. He transmitted the list to the emperor above a note that read, "At this very moment, an attack with considerable forces led by the King of Prussia himself is striking all along our front lines." One would have thought that curiosity alone would have carried Bazaine to the front lines. At 5:11 P.M., while the bloody fighting continued above Gravelotte and the Prussian Guards were attacking up the slopes from Ste. Marie-aux-Chênes to St. Privat, Bazaine wired a florid, self-congratulatory account of the battle of Mars-la-Tour to France's Minister of the Interior in Paris: "We captured 600 prisoners that day, and a battle standard." Between 5:30 P.M. and 8:20 P.M., the hours that decided the battle, when Steinmetz threw the king's last divisions into the cauldron at Point du Jour and the Saxons flanked Canrobert on the left and bashed in the entire French position, Bazaine traded telegrams with Napoleon III on the subject of provisioning arrangements at Verdun. "Shall I leave the vast quantities of stores that are already at Verdun there?" Louis-Napoleon queried. At 8:20 P.M., while the Germans overran the French position and Bazaine's army dissolved, Marshal Bazaine initialed and posted his last message of that fateful day: "I had no idea that there were such large stocks at Verdun. I think that it would probably be best to leave only those things that I will need should I ever succeed in reaching the place."[56]

Bazaine's efforts to defend his bizarre conduct after the war were unconvincing. He made no mention of those damning letters and telegrams, nor mercifully did his court of inquiry. As for the encounter with Captain Louis de Beaumont, he asserted for a time that Beaumont had "misunderstood" him. He had really said "*rester*" ("remain in place"), not "*rentrer*" ("retire"), but others came forward to verify that Bazaine had audibly said "retire," to more than one of Bourbaki's adjutants. Odder still was Bazaine's attempt to recast entirely the incriminating encounter with Captain Beaumont on the road between Fort St. Quentin and Plappeville. At his court of inquiry, he claimed that he had spoken to Beaumont thus: "*Dites bien à Bourbaki de rester où il est, de se mettre en rapport avec Canrobert et de ne pas s'engager à la légère*" – "Tell Bourbaki very plainly to stay where he is, make contact

55 SHAT, Lb 11, Paris, 4 April 1872, Conseil d'Enquete, "Entrevue Bazaine."
56 SHAT, Lb 11, Plappeville, 18 Aug. 1870, Marshal Bazaine to Napoleon III.

with Canrobert, and not engage lightly."[57] This was all too obviously a lie, because Bazaine never spoke or wrote in that direct Moltkean style, rather he rambled deviatively. If properly led, the Army of the Rhine might have won the battle of Gravelotte and altered the course of the war. Given Bazaine's disastrous leadership, it was little wonder that he was tried and scapegoated after the war.

As Bazaine's position crumbled, Steinmetz sought to administer the *coup de grâce*. Indulged by his old friend the king, Steinmetz, who had already slaughtered many Prussian battalions in his fruitless attacks across the Mance ravine, now ordered more. It was a sign of the limits of Moltke's power that he remained silent while Steinmetz ordered what remained of Goeben's VIII Corps as well as General Eduard von Fransecky's II Corps to strike again at Point du Jour and Moscou. Fransecky recalled the preparations for the attack; he, Goeben, Zastrow, Kameke, and Woyna dismounted near Gravelotte, spread a map on the ground, hunkered around it, and peered up at the terraced French position. It was decided that Goeben would make for Moscou, Fransecky for Point du Jour.[58] Goeben's attack, with sturdy East Prussian troops, broke down in rare panic, the men starting up the road but then dissolving as accurate, unsuppressed fire descended again from Frossard and Leboeuf. (Most of the French *mitrailleuses* fired more than 600 rounds in the battle, which was an unnerving volume of fire even for the most hardened Prussian troops.)[59]

The panic intensified as Prussian shells, fired blindly from Gravelotte, burst among their own troops. When Fransecky marched in behind Goeben's shaken brigades, the panic and confusion were at fever pitch. General Fransecky himself was accosted by dozens of crazed troops shouting, "*Excellenz, unsere eigene Brüder schiessen auf uns!*" – "Excellency, our own brothers are shooting at us!" As Fransecky tried to calm and sort out the troops, his gunners and infantrymen, deceived by the failing light, opened fire on the silhouettes above them. These were the East Prussians of the VIII Corps who were trying to extricate themselves from Frossard's grip. With a convulsive heave, they broke for the rear; Fransecky and his staff were picked up and borne fifty yards by the mass of fugitives. Thereafter, the general whirled in circles trying to stem the rout; he remembered vividly a wounded horse that clung to him "like a dog" through the entire sad episode, limping after him wherever he turned.[60] A second wave of panic coursed through Gravelotte, Prussian conscripts elbowing past the startled king bellowing "all is lost!"

57 SHAT, Lb 11, Paris, 4 April 1872, Conseil d'Enquete, "Entrevue Bazaine."
58 Walter von Bremen, ed. *Denkwürdigkeiten des preussischen Generals der Infanterie Eduard von Fransecky*, Leipzig, 1901, p. 509–12.
59 SHAT, Lb 11, Metz, n.d., Lt-Col. Maucourant.
60 Bremen, p. 516.

On the Mance road, clots of disbanded Prussian infantrymen huddled behind overturned wagons and ammunition cars firing wildly into their own men who tried in vain to reach the safety of their lines as night fell.[61]

Curiously, French officers at the head of the ravine observed the same signs of panic and demoralization among their own troops. At 7 P.M., Frossard's 8th Regiment pushed forward from its reserve position to relieve the 23rd Regiment at Moscou Farm, which had exhausted its ammunition repulsing Steinmetz's mad attacks. Arriving under heavy fire at the Moscou position, the men of the 8th found that their comrades of the 23rd would not yield their trenches and stone walls. Though their rifles and pouches were empty, they dared not retire across the open ground behind them which was being blasted by Krupp shells. General Gaspard Pouget, waiting behind the lines for the return of the 8th, watched incredulously as his entire brigade bunched and burrowed into the ground around Moscou. It was a rare instance of *retardaires* or stragglers at the front rather than the rear of an army.[62] Many of them would have been better off retiring. Ascending to Moscou the next day, General Julius Verdy was astonished to see the French shelter-trenches still bristling with troops and rifles. He rode closer under a white flag to discover that the men were dead, killed by overhead bursts of shrapnel: "they lay there as if still in the ranks, their rifles pushed forward over the parapet as if ready to fire."[63]

Though thousands of exhausted German troops joined in Prussia's anthem of victory as darkness descended – "*Nun danket alle Gott*" – more hours would pass before King Wilhelm I would finally accept that Gravelotte was indeed a Prussian victory. From his post near the Mance ravine, where Phil Sheridan found Wilhelm slumped "on an uncomfortable seat, made by resting the ends of a short ladder on a couple of boxes," it seemed more like a bloody defeat.[64] Twenty thousand Prussians had fallen to nudge the French off of their ridge line. Fransecky's II Corps, Moltke's last reserve, had been chopped up and dissolved in panic. The king's own Guard Corps had been senselessly thrown away at St. Privat, scores of aristocratic cousins killed or wounded in the fighting. Most of the Prussian wounds were agonizing, the Chassepot rounds having a tendency to tumble through the body smashing bones, tearing tissue, and blowing exit holes four times bigger than the entry wound. All of the German casualties mentioned the "razor pain" of the French bullet.[65] Marshal Bazaine's army, far from being decisively enveloped, had escaped to fight again, and fallen back on Metz with relatively slight losses of 12,000. As

61 Anton von Massow, *Erlebnisse und Eindrücke im Kriege 1870–71*, Berlin, 1912, pp. 24–30.
62 SHAT, Lb 11, Metz, 21 Aug. 1870, Gen. Pouget to Gen. Bataille.
63 Verdy, vol. 1, pp. 82–3.
64 Sheridan, vol. 2, p. 377.
65 Maj. Johann Nosinich, "Der Krieg 1870–71," ÖMZ 4 (1872), p. 157.

penance for a badly executed battle, King Wilhelm I insisted that he would bivouac with his troops on the plateau. Eventually coaxed back to Rezonville for the night, he slept fitfully in a dirty cottage on an iron camp bed.[66]

Despite the king's misgivings, Gravelotte could in no way be interpreted as a French victory. Generalissimo Bazaine had stumbled badly, remaining blind throughout the contest to the larger significance of his army or the necessity of combining with MacMahon's growing Army of Châlons. At noon on 18 August, Bazaine sent MacMahon and Failly telegrams that encapsulated his failings as an army commander. To MacMahon: "I presume that the Minister of War has given you your orders. Your operations are absolutely beyond my zone of action and I therefore fear that any instructions I give might send you in the wrong direction." To Failly's wandering VII Corps: "I cannot reply one way or another to your requests for instructions.... It is really up to you to match your marches to events."[67]

The result of this strange apprehensiveness – one imagines the great Napoleon turning in his grave – was a French strategic disaster; the Prussian armies had joined hands across the Moselle completely severing France from its principal army. Prussia's *National-Zeitung* did not exaggerate when it called Gravelotte "an event of the greatest importance as regards the issue of the war. The reconcentration of the French army is rendered impossible, the road to Paris opened." Indeed by holing up at Metz, Bazaine "had lost the capacity to defend his country."[68] And for what? Before the battle even started, the marshal had been informed that Metz contained fewer than 800,000 Chassepot rounds, hardly a day's worth of fire, and even less in the way of artillery shells and food.[69] This last shortage was no small consideration in the French army. As a great general of the Revolution once lamented, "*Mes lapins n'ont pas de pain; pas de pain, pas de lapins; pas de lapins, pas de victoires*" – "my rabbits have no bread; no bread, no rabbits; no rabbits, no victories."[70] Without adequate stocks of bullets, shells, or bread, Metz would be a trap, not a refuge.

66 Waldersee, vol. 1, p. 90.
67 SHAT, Lb 11, Metz, 18 Aug. 1870, Marshal Bazaine to Marshal MacMahon. Metz, 18 Aug. 1870, Marshal Bazaine to Gen. de Failly. Lc 1, Paris, 14 March 1903, Gen. de Vaulgrenant to Gen. Pendezec.
68 *National-Zeitung*, 18 Aug. 1870.
69 SHAT, Lb 10, Fiquoumont, 17 Aug. 1870, Gen. Soleille to Marshal Bazaine. Lb 10, Plappeville, 17 Aug. 1870, Marshal Bazaine, "Note." Bazaine direly concludes: "*Metz n'a plus aucun ressource pour l'armée.*" Massow, p. 32.
70 Louis-Jules Trochu, *L'Armée française en 1867*, Paris, 1870, pp. 106–7.

8

The Road to Sedan

Bismarck slept in a hayloft after Gravelotte, woke the next morning and rode across the battlefield with American General Phil Sheridan. Sheridan recalled that they swigged from a bottle of brandy while riding through the "awful carnage." The "sight was sickening to an extreme," and the chancellor veered squeamishly into the gaps between the corpses on the way up to Moscou and Leipzig.[1] Lower-ranking Prussians were not so fortunate; they spent the day after Gravelotte burying their dead and dragging their wounded to makeshift field hospitals. For many, already pushed to the limit by fear, thirst, hunger, and exhaustion, burial duty, not combat, was the most harrowing experience of the war. The men dug mass graves and filled them with 9,000 decomposing corpses. For at least one German officer, the memory was inexpugnable, pursuing him even in his sleep long after the war: "The battles, the shooting, the freezing winter bivouacs: all those things I've long since forgotten, but not the interment of the dead at St. Privat; that was so ghastly that it *still* wakes me in the middle of the night."[2]

Bazaine meanwhile awoke from his lethargy and finished herding his broken army off the plateau of Amanvillers. Defeat and retreat seemed to enliven the marshal. In the course of 19–20 August, the 140,000-man Army of the Rhine retreated to Metz, staking out a vast semicircular encampment between Plappeville and the Moselle. Though secure for the moment, this mass of men, wagons, horses, and batteries – discreetly renamed the "Army of Metz" to reflect its reduced ambit – was acutely vulnerable to bombardment, and difficult to feed and water.[3] An International Red Cross representative who breasted

1   Philip H. Sheridan, *Personal Memoirs of P. H. Sheridan*, 2 vols., New York, 1888, vol. 2, pp. 381–4.
2   Richard Berendt, *Erinnerungen aus meiner Dienstzeit*, Leipzig, 1894, p. 78. Dresden, Sächsisches Kriegsarchiv (SKA), Zeitg. Slg. 158, Lt. Hinüber.
3   Joseph Andlau, *Metz: Campagne et Négociations*, Paris, 1872, p. 102.

the heights of Amanvillers on 21 August noted that the Prussians had already circumvallated Metz with ramparts and trenches, blocked the westbound roads, torn up railways in and out of the city, and seized all food, drink, and livestock from the surrounding villages.[4] Bazaine's defeat and retreat to Metz had darkened France's already dim strategic situation. Now the marshal's large army was blocked in Metz by 300,000 Prussian troops, while the rest of Moltke's force moved against Paris, the political nerve center of France.[5]

Paris remained blissfully ignorant of the battle, the Prussians having cut the telegraph lines out of Metz late on 18 August. Bazaine's written account of the battle would not reach Paris until the 22nd. When challenged by Jules Favre on 20 August to explain Prussian newspaper accounts of a great battle at Gravelotte, Count Palikao was forced to admit that he had no information.[6] This ignorance fostered grand illusions. In the Austrian embassy – a handsome palace in the Rue de Grenelle given to the Austrians by the Bonapartes in a not so subtle bid for friendship – Prince Richard Metternich continued to believe that Bazaine had slipped away to unite with MacMahon at Châlons or Reims. Hence Metternich still liked France's chances in the war, particularly if Bazaine and MacMahon could be reunited and attached to a "third army forming on the Loire."[7] If this happened, the weary Prussian army might eventually be fought to a standstill. Unfortunately, by retiring on Metz, Bazaine had ruined that hopeful scenario. Moltke's task was now much easier; he had only to shut Bazaine inside Metz with a fraction of his army and then set off in pursuit of MacMahon with the rest. The pursuit was simplified by Bazaine's passivity. Without the Army of the Rhine before it or on its flank, Crown Prince Friedrich Wilhelm's Third Army was completely free in its movements. It could seek battle with MacMahon in the open field or, if MacMahon remained at Châlons or Reims, march directly on Paris by the valley of the Aube to turn him out of either position.[8]

Bismarck, meanwhile, was coming under considerable foreign pressure after Gravelotte. On 21 August, Austria's ambassador wired Vienna that "the moment is come to stop the struggle and begin diplomatic negotiations."[9] That same day, Prince Jérôme-Napoleon traveled to Florence with his Piedmontese wife to enlist the Italian government in the cause of peace. Italy's foreign minister, Emilio Visconti-Venosta, formally invited the British and Austrians to join in a "league of neutrals" to help Italy "maintain the integrity

4   F. A. Bazaine, *Episodes de la guerre de 1870 et le blocus de Metz*, Madrid, 1883, p. 157.
5   Charles Fay, *Journal d'un officier de l'Armée du Rhin*, Paris, 1889, p. 122.
6   London, Public Record Office (PRO), FO 27; 1812, 22 Aug. 1870, Lyons to Granville.
7   Vienna, Haus-Hof-und Staatsarchiv (HHSA), PA IX, 95, Paris, 19 Aug. 1870, Metternich to Beust.
8   PRO, FO 27, 1812, Paris, 22 Aug. 1870, Col. Claremont.
9   Eberhard Kolb, *Der Weg aus dem Krieg*, Munich, 1989, pp. 106–11. HHSA, PA IX, 95, Paris, 21 Aug. 1870, Metternich to Beust.

of France... and preserve Europe from calamity." To Britain's ambassador, Visconti-Venosta confided, "the dismemberment of France will destroy the balance of power and sow the seeds of future wars."[10] Russia, whose benevolent neutrality in all three German wars of unification had been a crucial factor in their success, was finally showing signs of unease with Moltke's lightning victories. In the days after Gravelotte, Britain's ambassador in St. Petersburg noted that the Russian press, public and army were "alarmed by the colossal force and large extension of territory acquired by Prussia." Russia's foreign minister, who resented Bismarck's growing fame, demanded a European congress to settle the war. Only the United States announced "strict neutrality;" the European powers seemed to be positioning themselves for a confrontation with what Britain's minister in Stuttgart called the mounting "arrogance and self-sufficiency" of the Germans, who now hinted that they wished to shift their western frontier from the Rhine to the Moselle, "or perhaps even the Argonne."[11] Hermann von Thile, who ran the German foreign ministry during Bismarck's absence at the front, appeared "anxious and suspicious," worried that the Austrians and Russians might combine with the British and Italians to roll back Berlin's gains.[12]

Safely ensconced in Metz, Marshal Bazaine began to recover his bounce. In a letter to MacMahon he seemed happy to report that "we are once again on the defensive."[13] This was Bazaine's favored role, for it forced the enemy to take all the hard decisions. On 20 August, his headquarters issued a plucky communiqué that made light of Prussia's devastating victories: "One of France's armies is now concentrated around Metz. The other is at Châlons under two of the most popular names in the French army, Marshal MacMahon and General Failly." Stretching credulity to the limit, the bulletin concluded that "our adversaries must now despair of their predicament, for they find themselves overextended everywhere." To fill the widening gaps in the Prussian line, Berlin was allegedly "drafting every German below the age of thirty-one and laying bare Germany's Baltic and North Sea coasts." This, Bazaine's headquarters triumphantly concluded, "has exposed Prussia to attacks by our fleet."[14]

THE FRANCO-PRUSSIAN WAR AT SEA

That last hopeful exhortation would have been news to the French navy, which at that very moment was chugging harmlessly around the North Sea and Baltic

---

10 PRO, FO 27, 1812, Florence, 22 Aug. 1870, A. Paget to Lyons. FO 425, 97, London, 17 Aug. 1870, Granville to Lyons. FO 425, 97, Florence, 30 Aug. 1870, A. Paget to Granville.
11 PRO, FO 425, 97, Stuttgart, 27 Aug. 1870, Gordon to Granville.
12 PRO, FO 64, 690, Berlin, 27 Aug. 1870, Loftus to Granville. FO 425, 97, Paris, 16 Aug. 1870, Lyons to Granville.
13 *"Nous sommes donc de nouveau sur la defensive."* Vincennes, Service Historique de l'Armée de Terre (SHAT), Lb 11, Metz, 18 Aug. 1870, Marshal Bazaine to Marshal MacMahon.
14 SHAT, Lb 9, Metz, 20 Aug. 1870, "Correspondance du Quartier General."

in search of coal and a mission. To be sure, the French navy had begun the war with high hopes, determined to deal a decisive blow in the struggle with Prussia. For this it was well-equipped. France's 470 ship navy was second only to England's in 1870, and nearly ten times the size of Prussia's. The large number of French hulls permitted Napoleon III to maintain a global empire that stretched from Vietnam to Martinique. For war with another great power, he relied on his forty-five ironclad battleships, frigates, and floating batteries. The Prussians, latecomers to sea power, had only five ironclads to guard a 600-mile coast, their new naval base at Wilhelmshaven, and flourishing ports at Bremen, Hamburg, Lübeck, Rostock, Stettin, Danzig, and Königsberg.[15]

Initially, Napoleon III had planned to use his fleet to land a corps of infantry – 9,000 marines and 20,000 reservists – on the Prussian coast. Forty-eight-year-old Prince Jerôme-Napoleon had been talked about as the probable commander of the expedition, with General Louis Trochu as his staff chief and, in view of the prince's reputation as a tyro, his "mainspring."[16] These troops, even under Jerôme-Napoleon's command, posed a substantial threat. Militarily, Prussia relied on swift communications for its deployments, but found many of its critical roads and railways within striking distance of the sea. The French navy noticed this; among the files of Admiral Martin Fourichon, commander of France's North Sea squadron in 1870, is a North German railway map given to him by the French naval minister in August 1870. The minister had traced the following railroads in red ink: Memel-Königsberg-Berlin, Stettin-Berlin, Stralsund-Berlin, Flensburg-Hamburg, and Bremen-Hanover.[17] The import was plain enough: If France's "siege fleet," fourteen flat-bottomed ironclad batteries with heavy guns, could nose along the German littoral shelling the ports and French marines could fight their way on to Germany's strategic railways, Moltke would have to modify his plan of campaign and make big troop detachments for coastal defense. In July, French agents had approvingly noted Prussian plans to deploy no less than 160,000 troops to the seacoast. The *Junkers* were particularly worried that the French would pour troops into Pomerania to raise the Poles against the Germans.[18]

Economically, Prussia's expanding population and industry relied heavily on imports and exports, so heavily that the cash-strapped Prussian war ministry had spent 10 million talers ($120 million today) on coastal defenses in the two years before the war. Seven hundred ships tied up every day at a big harbor complex like Rostock-Warnemünde; any blockade of these ports would jolt the German economy and slow the import of essential raw materials.[19]

15 "Stärke der französischen Marine," *Österreichische Militärische Zeitschrift* (ÖMZ) 4 (1867), p. 114. Lawrence Sondhaus, *Preparing for Weltpolitik*, Annapolis, 1997, pp. 92–6.
16 PRO, FO 27, 1807, Paris, 26 July 1870, Col. Claremont to Lyons.
17 Vincennes, Archives Centrales de la Marine (ACM), BB4, 907, Paris, Aug. 1870, *Liebenows Eisenbahnkarte von Nord-Deutschland*, Adm. Rigault to Adm. Fourichon.
18 SHAT, Lb 4, Strasbourg, 1 Aug. 1870, Capt. Jung to Marshal Leboeuf.
19 ACM, BB4, 907, 7 July 1868, "Les ports de guerre de l'Allemagne du Nord."

Politically, the French foreign ministry considered successful landings on the German coast the essential precondition for aid from Denmark's respectable navy and its 50,000-man army. "We must embark an expeditionary force at once if we wish to obtain a Danish alliance," France's minister in Copenhagen wrote Gramont on 4 August.[20]

Given the prospective rewards of even a small expedition, Colonel Edward Claremont, Britain's military attaché in Paris, marveled at the way in which Louis-Napoleon let the opportunity slip. France's Mediterranean Fleet – twelve ironclads destined for Brest and then the North Sea – was unluckily ordered to Malta for a port call on 4 July, the very day that the Franco-Prussian crisis began to simmer. It would take three full weeks to redirect the ships to Brest – partly because telegraphed orders were taking a full week to bounce between Paris, Mers-el-Kebir, and the fleet – nearly as long to begin cancelling leaves and drafting conscripts.[21] The Mediterranean Fleet, commanded by sixty-one-year-old Admiral Fourichon, would not reach the North Sea until the second week of August, too late to dent Moltke's invasion of France, and too late to begin a sustained naval operation in the North Sea, which would become unnavigable in October. At first, Claremont attributed this fumbling to the emperor's lack of interest – "the naval expedition ... bored and tired him, he did nothing" – but later discovered infighting between Jerôme-Napoleon and Admiral Charles Rigault, the French naval minister, who flatly refused to entrust France's splendid new fleet to the emperor's cousin. There were other political complications; General Trochu complained to Claremont of British and Russian pressure on Denmark to remain neutral, but without Danish bases and support, French plans to "raise the Danes of Schleswig-Holstein against Prussia" receded into the realm of fantasy.[22] By 3 August, Colonel Claremont was reporting that "no expeditionary force will be sent to the Baltic, only a feint." For the French, this was a failure with strategic consequences. It permitted the Prussian mobilization to rush unchecked up to the French border and subtracted nothing from Moltke's overwhelming troop numbers. Yet according to Claremont, it was precisely the need to counter those Prussian troop numbers that paralyzed the French. Every available man and battery of guns was needed on the German frontier: "The Army of the Rhine has absorbed everybody and everything.... There is not a single general officer left over, and only five staff officers."[23]

The French plan to shell and blockade the German coast also faltered. While France's Mediterranean Fleet struggled back from Malta, the emperor's

20 SHAT, Lb 5, Copenhagen, 4 Aug. 1870, M. de Cadore to Gramont.
21 ACM, BB4, 907, Algiers and 16, 28, 29 July 1870, Adm. Fourichon to Adm. Rigault. PRO, FO 425, 95, Paris, 8 July 1870, Col. Claremont to Lord Lyons. Paris, 10 July 1870, Capt. Hore to Lord Lyons.
22 PRO, FO 425, 96, Vienna, 14 July 1870, Bloomfield to Granville.
23 PRO, FO 27, 1807, Paris, 26, 29, and 31 July 1870, 3 Aug. 1870, Col. Claremont to Lyons.

Channel Fleet concentrated in the roads of Cherbourg, resentfully watched by the *Cherbourgeois*, who saw their hopes for the rich August racing season evaporate. First their race course was taken over by France's marine division, and then the race itself, France's Kentucky Derby, was canceled. Seen off by Empress Eugénie, the Channel Fleet, now the "Baltic Squadron," put to sea and steamed away to the northeast with sealed orders on 24 July.[24] Sixty-two-year-old Admiral Louis Boüet-Willaumez, who had drafted a plan to land 40,000 troops on the Prussian coast at the height of the Luxembourg crisis three years earlier, was given command of the squadron: four 7,000 ton ironclad frigates with ten-inch guns and several corvettes.

Both French squadrons, Boüet's beating up the Frisian coast and Fourichon's returning from the Mediterranean to the North Sea, immediately felt a shortage that would stymie their operations until they were abandoned in September: coal. Boüet, whose larger fleet burned 350 tons of coal a day, was so obsessed with the commodity that he began and ended virtually every report with an accounting of the *"question du charbon,"* the "coal question." Fourichon's smaller fleet burned 200 tons a day, yet carried only 250 tons in its bunkers. Needless to say, both fleets required continuous replenishment, but rarely found it in the inhospitable waters of the North Sea and the Baltic, where some coal could be had from the Danes or the British on Heligoland, but most had to be shipped hundreds of miles from Dunkerque, the nearest French stockpile.

Without regular fuel supplies, French naval operations sputtered east and west of the Skagerrak. To stretch their dwindling supplies, both Boüet and Fourichon reduced speed and spent entire days at anchor, hoping that their mere presence would discourage Prussian blockade-runners. At night they would fire up half their boilers and sniff along the German coast. Ironically, the French captains, thirsting for action in Cherbourg, now came to view the appearance of a Prussian ship as a great calamity, for it always necessitated a fruitless chase, which burned yet more irreplaceable *charbon.*[25] On 12 August, ordered by the impatient empress and her naval minister to "land a useful and brilliant blow *somewhere,*" Boüet convened a council of war on board his flagship near Kiel. They studied the entire Prussian coast from Flensburg to Memel, briefly considered an attack on Alsen, but then dropped the idea. "The bay is too well defended, and without landing troops the operation would be pointless."[26] Everywhere the French admirals looked they encountered the same problems – bays that were too shallow to approach in deep-draught frigates and powerful Krupp coastal batteries that could fire out to 4,000 yards, nearly twice the effective range of the rolling French warships.

24 PRO, FO 425, 96, Paris, 29 July 1870, Capt. Hore to Lord Lyons.
25 ACM, BB4, 908, En mer, 29 July 1870, 1 and 5 Aug. 1870, Adm. Boüet to Adm. Rigault.
26 ACM, BB4, 908, Baie de Marstal, 12 Aug. 1870, Adm. Boüet to Adm. Rigault.

Admiral Fourichon's operations in the North Sea were thwarted by the same problems. Like Boüet, he had no charts of this unfamiliar sea, and applied in vain for them at Danish ports. Ordered to attack the Prussian navy in its half-finished base at Wilhelmshaven and plow up the Elbe and Weser to hit Hamburg and Bremen, Admiral Fourichon gnashed his teeth in frustration. No German pilots would guide him through the coastal waters, and Wilhelmshaven was untouchable behind its hedge of submerged mines, cables, chains, and booms. Both the Elbe and the Weser were blocked by the same contrivances and sunken ships, making attacks there too risky to contemplate. Coal problems worsened in the face of hit-and-run attacks by Prussian gunboats and corvettes that, in Fourichon's words, necessitated "a ruinous consumption of coal," first to evade the attacks and then pursue them into the fog or darkness. Ultimately, Fourichon despaired, wiring Paris on the day of Gravelotte that *"rien n'est à faire"* – "nothing can be done."[27] Prussia's three armored frigates could not be prised out of Wilhelmshaven, and without monitors or floating batteries – mothballed after the Crimean War and still under repair – the French navy had a very limited land attack capability. Theirs was a "blue water navy" built to contest the high seas with the British. In the shallow "brown waters" along the Prussian littoral it was less useful. Boüet maintained his leaky blockade only until September, when he and Fourichon, beset by heavy weather and criticism from Paris, withdrew their sputtering squadrons to Cherbourg and Dunkerque for the winter. The Franco-Prussian war at sea was over.

It was just as well that the French marine division was no longer with the fleet, for, after Bazaine's entrapment at Mars-la-Tour and Gravelotte, the marines were urgently needed with France's last field army, the 130,000 troops and 420 guns of Marshal Patrice MacMahon's Army of Châlons. Arriving at Châlons on 16 August, Napoleon III had supervised the melding of MacMahon's battered I Corps to France's only strategic reserve, pieces of the VII Corps and several dozen battalions of *gardes mobiles*. The demoralization of the veterans, who had endured Froeschwiller and the retreat from Alsace, and the indiscipline of the *mobiles*, few of whom wanted to be with the army at all, made for ugly scenes. "It was a lumpish crowd," a staff officer recorded, "vegetating rather than living, hardly moving even if you kicked them, grumbling that we had no right to disturb their sleep."[28]

The disastrous decision to move Marshal MacMahon's Army of Châlons from the safety of Paris toward Metz originated with Empress Eugénie, Palikao, and Eugène Rouher, the emperor's chief confidant. Under pressure from the empress, who feared for the dynasty and wanted Bazaine extricated from Metz at any price, MacMahon reluctantly agreed to a move away from

27 ACM, BB4, 907, Heligoland, 18, 20 and 21 Aug. 1870, Adm. Fourichon to Adm. Rigault.
28 Michael Howard, *The Franco-Prussian War*, orig. 1961, London, 1981, p. 183.

Paris. The march east was ordered by Rouher, who later admitted that he had "no strategic aptitude whatsoever."[29] On 21 August, MacMahon shifted his headquarters to Reims and, from that communications hub, began placing the Army of Châlons on a northerly route to Metz. Charles Kessler, a captain in MacMahon's headquarters, recalled that at the time no one at Reims or Paris knew *anything* about Bazaine's situation, the location of the German Third Army, or the formation of a new Prussian force, the Army of the Meuse. For a time, then, ignorance fostered the delusion that this little army could operate independently against the vast German forces in the vicinity.[30] Encouraged by a dispatch from Bazaine that promised a breakout toward Sedan, MacMahon put his army on the same course, both to join forces with Bazaine and to sidestep the principal Prussian thrust that was expected any day at Châlons.[31] Marshal MacMahon had little confidence in the operation, but could take some comfort in his promotion (by Rouher) to "*general en chef*" and Napoleon III's demotion – in the emperor's own words – to "the marshal"s first soldier, prepared to fight and win, or die trying."[32]

The violent, seesawing first month of the Franco-Prussian War had confirmed Moltke's aphorism that "no plan of campaign survives the first shock of battle." Having planned to sweep Napoleon III's Army of the Rhine into the Metz pocket, Moltke had instead broken it in two with inconclusive results. Much like Benedek's army in 1866, which had slipped through a hole in Moltke's pocket at Königgrätz, Bazaine's army had withdrawn from Gravelotte to good fortifications on the Moselle. MacMahon's forces had evaded the pocket altogether, slipping away to form the core of a new army on the Marne. Thus, Moltke's problems multiplied rather than abated after Gravelotte. He had simultaneously to besiege Bazaine at Metz, probe toward Paris, and seek the decisive battle with MacMahon that had thus far eluded him. To do this, he carved a fourth army out of his three, deployed two of them at Metz and put the other two on the road to Châlons and Paris. The Second Army, which had ballooned to unwieldy proportions in the days before Gravelotte, was shorn of 120,000 men: the Guards, IV Corps, XII Corps, and two cavalry divisions. These units, commanded by forty-three-year-old Crown Prince Albert of Saxony, a veteran of 1866 who had executed the turning maneuver at St. Privat, were melded in a new "Army of the Meuse" and pushed toward Verdun on 23 August, the first stage on the road to Paris.[33]

On Albert's left, Crown Prince Friedrich Wilhelm of Prussia continued his westward march with the 180,000 troops of the Third Army. Already across

---

29 SHAT, Lc 1, Paris, 19 April 1872, "Enquête Parlementaire."
30 SHAT, Lc 1, Paris, 6 March 1903, Gen. Kessler to Gen. Pendezec.
31 Howard, pp. 188–9.
32 *Papiers et Correspondance de la Famille Impériale*, 10 vols., Paris, 1870, vol. 4, pp. 59–63.
33 Gen. Julius Verdy du Vernois, *With the Royal Headquarters in 1870–71*, 2 vols., London, 1897, vol. 1, p. 102.

the Moselle, they reached the Meuse on 20 August, the Marne on the 24th. Meanwhile, Prussia's efficient system of conscription began to replace the casualties of the first month; 150,000 replacements had arrived, and 300,000 more were forming.[34] Thoroughly impressed, French citizens and national guards did little to arrest these transports, or the steady German advance. Arriving in Bar-le-Duc in late August, Prussian troops found that the mayor had placarded the town thus: "Prussian scouts are approaching. Because our town is entirely open it would be useless and even dangerous to defend it. Close ranks and endure this temporary disaster with manly resignation, prudence, and calm."[35] At Metz, Prince Friedrich Karl retained command of the rump of the Second Army as well as Steinmetz's First Army, a combined force of 120,000 that strung itself thinly around the forts: Four corps on the left bank of the Moselle, two on the right. Steinmetz, infuriated at his subordination, would shortly be relieved of command anyway. Named Governor of Posen on 15 September, Steinmetz departed for his new duties, which, to everyone's great relief, lay 500 miles to the east.

In Metz, Bazaine, now surrounded by just six Prussian corps, showed little sign of life. Though he needed several days to reorganize and resupply his troops, he also needed to break out of Metz to regain his operational freedom before the Prussians could bring up yet more reinforcements to improve their field fortifications and seal him in. Colonel Jules Lewal, a member of Bazaine's staff, recalled that the marshal simply ignored an appeal for cooperation from MacMahon received on 22 August. The message, carried through Prussian lines by a French volunteer, who swallowed the dispatch and later extracted it from his feces whenever stopped by the Prussians, made clear that MacMahon was marching toward Metz with 130,000 troops.[36] Yet even if Bazaine left MacMahon to his fate, he would not be safe at Metz for long. His army, blundering from one defeat to the next, was crumbling from within, a fact confirmed by Bazaine's own visits to the troops, and letters received from officers.[37] On 24 August, one French officer wrote: "Our troops need severe discipline; far too many are looters (*pillards*) or stragglers (*trainards*), they sneak out of camp and have begun to defy their NCOs, complaining that they lack things: orders, food, wine, or ammunition." Even normally steady NCOs had begun to defy their superiors. On 23 August, a drunken sergeant of the French 63rd Regiment, scolded by his sergeant major, shakily raised his Chassepot and shot him dead.[38] According to General Frossard, indiscipline

---

34 PRO, FO 64, 690, Berlin, 27 Aug. 1870, Loftus to Granville.
35 H. Sutherland Edwards, *The Germans in France*, London, 1873, p. 80.
36 SHAT, Lb 13, Conseil d'Enquête, 28 March 1872, "Déposition de Col. Lewal." Anton von Massow, *Erlebnisse und Eindrücke im Kriege 1870–71*, Berlin, 1912, pp. 33–4.
37 SHAT, Lb 12, Metz, 21 Aug. 1870, Marshal Bazaine: "Physical condition of troops is satisfactory, moral state less so."
38 SHAT, Lb 12, 23 Aug. 1870, II Corps, 3rd Div.

surged because of the irreplaceable casualties among French officers: "Morale and discipline have begun to slide because many companies have no officers at all." Some regiments were commanded by captains, companies by lieutenants, platoons by corporals. Local mayors complained of rampant crime committed by French troops; one demanded "protection against marauding soldiers, who commit thefts, rapes, plunder gardens, and use ladders to climb into locked houses."[39] Besides the moral deficit, there were the obvious material ones: the Prussians had cut Bazaine's principal aqueducts after the battle of Gravelotte, stopping the flow of potable water to the fortified camp. The Army of Metz and its 12,000 wounded would now have to drink from the semi-polluted Moselle, and suffer the consequences. Only strict rationing would extend the fortress's food more than a month, yet rationing – imposed even as the troops were ordered to increase their labors on the forts, battery positions and terraces of Metz – would erode the morale and fighting quality of the troops, and accelerate the spread of illness.[40]

Faced with these realities, it is remarkable how little Bazaine did. Breaking out ought not to have been a problem, for the system of bridges and detached forts built at Metz in the 1860s enabled him to concentrate his army swiftly on either bank of the Moselle. There he could smash through an isolated fraction of the besieging force, which, to mask the detached forts, had to divide its men and guns between the two banks of the Moselle and spread itself thinly across fifty miles of front. Bazaine's later assertion, "that the blockaded army must not be expected to come to the aid of the one free in its movements," was preposterous, for MacMahon, pinned between the Meuse and the Argonne by superior Prussian forces, was far less free in his movements than Bazaine.[41] Had Bazaine fought clear of Metz, he would have enjoyed intriguing possibilities. He could have marched south between the Moselle and the Seille – the rivers securing his flanks – to Nancy and Lunéville, where, after a pause to rest and resupply the army, he could have taken up defensive positions at Frouard or the Langres plateau.[42] Or he might have marched east into the Vosges to place his large army between Moltke and his supplies and reinforcements. One can only imagine the havoc that the Army of Metz – with its twenty six regiments of cavalry – could have wrought behind German lines, destroying bridges, tearing up railways, plundering convoys, and slowly strangling Moltke's campaign. With such a force – 140,000 men and 440 guns – operating in eastern France, Moltke would have had no choice but to double back on it, releasing MacMahon on the Meuse.

39 SHAT, Lb 13, Metz, 24 Aug. 1870, Anon. to Marshal Bazaine. Lb 12, Ban St. Martin, 21 Aug. 1870, Gen. Frossard to Marshal Bazaine. Lb 12, Ban St. Martin, 21 Aug. 1870, Mairie to Marshal Bazaine.
40 Andlau, p. 173.
41 Bazaine, *Episodes*, p. 163.
42 SHAT, Lb 14, "Extrait de Fay."

Or Bazaine might have used more direct methods; either an attack west through Gravelotte to regain the Verdun road, or a push north toward Thionville. Feeding at the frontier forts and using the inviolable Belgian border to secure one flank, the Army of Metz could have attempted an end-run around the intervening Prussian armies to unite with MacMahon near Sedan. Major Charles Fay recalled that a bolt north was seriously contemplated in headquarters; if the French army had moved fast, it could have smashed through the weak Prussian screen on the right bank of the Moselle, marched to Thionville, pushed a powerful advance guard across the river, and brought the bulk of Bazaine's army over to the left bank before Prince Friedrich Karl could react. In this way, Bazaine could have united with MacMahon and reconcentrated the armies. The garrison at Thionville – anticipating Bazaine's arrival – had already scoured the countryside for supplies, packed three army trains with food and drink, and readied pontoons to bridge the Orne and the Moselle.[43] Speed and daring, however, were needed, precisely what Bazaine lacked. His daily "*bulletin de renseignements*" indifferently noted the progress of Prince Friedrich Karl's trenches, field works, and requisitions: "Today the enemy has occupied Vigneulles.... He is constructing palisades." Instead of planning a breakout, Bazaine spent the week after Gravelotte admonishing his officers for trivial breaches of hygiene and discipline, or just wasting time. Testimony collected after the war describes a rather indolent Bazaine, who worked short hours, gossiped with his nephew, and spent the evenings playing dominos.[44] On 25 August, the eve of the first weak French sortie, Bazaine wrote Canrobert a long letter listing minor infractions committed by his troops the week before at St. Privat.[45] This was a waste of everyone's time. Like Benedek in the days before and after Königgrätz, Bazaine was consoling himself with familiar routines. When a courier slipped through the Prussian lines around Metz with an urgent appeal from MacMahon on 22 August, Bazaine joked, "*De suite, de suite, c'est bien vite*" – "faster, faster, not so fast!"[46]

While Bazaine slumbered, his generals did little to awaken him. At a council of war on 26 August, most of Bazaine's generals advised him to remain inside the forts. First to speak was General Marie-Justin Soleille, keeper of the army's artillery reserve, who argued that since he had only enough shells for a single battle, it made no sense to waste them in a sortie. Rather the army should preserve itself as a "force in being" to influence armistice negotiations that would certainly begin when the Prussians reached Paris. This defeatist view was endorsed by most of the other generals. General Frossard, the thruster of

---

43 *Le Progrès*, 13 April 1872. Andlau, pp. 105, 111–12. SHAT, Lb 14, "Extrait de Fay."
44 SHAT, Lb 13, Conseil d'Enquête, 28 March 1872, "Déposition de Col. Lewal."
45 SHAT, Lb 14, Ban St. Martin, 25 Aug. 1870, Marshal Bazaine to Marshal Canrobert.
46 Andlau, p. 121.

Saarbrücken, now drooped sadly, "agreeing absolutely" with Soleille and asserting that every unit but the Imperial Guard was demoralized and incapable of offensive operations. Though concerned that the army's morale would plummet without action, Marshal Canrobert agreed that "a move away from Metz with our immense columns of guns and baggage would be impossible." Marshal Leboeuf, cold and sulky, spent several minutes defending his own tarnished record in the war before agreeing that "conserving the army intact was the only reasonable course." General Ladmirault observed that it made no sense to leave Metz if there were no ammunition for a prolonged campaign.[47]

The position of General Bourbaki is harder to discern. Although the minutes of the conference – kept by Colonel Napoléon Boyer, Bazaine's loyal aide-de-camp – portray Bourbaki as "concurring absolutely" with the others, Bourbaki later swore that he dissented at the council of war, arguing for a run to the Vosges. He probably did, for he had been assuring Bazaine since 21 August that "morale and health were excellent, food abundant, trains loaded, and infantry and artillery ammunition complete."[48] Marshal Leboeuf, whom Boyer depicted sullenly agreeing to Soleille's plan, later charged that Soleille had grossly underestimated the army's ammunition reserves – "there were 120 rounds for every gun at Metz and powder for 300 more" – and testified that he had "argued heatedly" with Soleille during the two hour conference.

Whereas Bourbaki's concern was freedom of movement, Leboeuf's was food; he recognized that Metz was provisioned for a garrison of 20,000 and a civil population of 70,000. It did not have stores for the 140,000-man Army of the Rhine and its 12,000 wounded, and would therefore be *improved* as a strategic asset if the army were simply removed and the fortress restored to its small but sustainable garrison.[49] Still, the preponderance of opinion at the council of war was for lying up at Metz. Most of the generals grasped eagerly at Soleille's worries about ammunition as an excuse to do nothing, yet Soleille's own reports submitted three days after Gravelotte described an Army of Metz overflowing with cartridges, enough to issue every infantryman 140 rounds with 3.8 million cartridges in reserve.[50] This was plenty of firepower, more than enough to break out of Metz and regain the army's communications with the rest of France. The main concern should have been escape to reinforce MacMahon on the Meuse or fight another day, yet no one wanted this. It was better, as Soleille and Coffinières put it, to renounce all military activity and cultivate the army as a "political factor" in pending peace talks. This was cautious to a fault, for MacMahon was about to be annihilated and the well-armed

47 SHAT, Lb 14, Metz, 26 Aug. 1870, Col. Boyer, "Conférence du 26 Août 1870."
48 SHAT, Lb 14, Santonet, 21 Aug. 1870, Gen. Bourbaki to Marshal Bazaine.
49 SHAT, Lb 14, "Extrait de la deposition du Ml. Leboeuf."
50 SHAT, Lb 14, Déposition Bourbaki, "Conférence du 26 Août 1870."

Army of Metz – reduced to 375 grammes of bread per man per day – was already feeling the first pinch of famine.

Surrounded by doomsayers, Marshal Bazaine made only two feeble attempts to break out in the fortnight between Gravelotte and Sedan. The first, on 26 August, began as a major operation: Bazaine ordered two additional bridges built across the Moselle to carry the three corps on the left bank of the river across to the right. Once assembled around Fort St. Julien, Bazaine's army would punch through the weak Prussian detachments northeast of Metz, abandon their baggage, and run for Thionville, the first leg on the march to Sedan and Paris. Such was the plan; in reality, the sortie of 26 August became a weak jab north that bounced off the Prussian outposts and collapsed back on Metz.[51] Marshal Canrobert, observing the sortie, recalled that it was blunted by foul weather as much as anything else. Cold wind and rain slowed the troops and gave the Prussians time to stiffen their defenses. Yet Bazaine seemed relieved by the failure of the breakout. "*Messieurs*," he declaimed to his assembled corps commanders, "the beastly weather forces stagnation on us again." Of course more "postponements" of the breakout would seal the fate of MacMahon's Army of Châlons, but Bazaine did not seem to care; indeed he did not even confide the news of MacMahon's approach to his generals. "We knew nothing of Marshal MacMahon," Canrobert later testified, "only that he had been beaten at Froeschwiller and had retreated precipitately; in short, we did not even suspect the existence of [the Army of Châlons] because the marshal told us nothing about it."[52]

The second sortie from Metz, on 31 August, was a more serious undertaking, but only slightly. Indeed Bazaine's conduct throughout it was the basis after the war for accusations that he had deliberately "betrayed" the army. Having finally informed his generals of MacMahon's location and predicament, Bazaine massed his army under cover of darkness on the 30th. He then unaccountably delayed his attack with eight entire divisions on the three Prussian battalions at Noisseville. Though the Prussians used the respite on 31 August to reinforce their units on the right bank, they never had more than three divisions against eight French infantry divisions, several brigades of cavalry and 162 guns: some 90,000 men in all. Colonel Joseph Andlau, who stood beside Bazaine at Fort St. Julien in the morning, recalled pointing across the Moselle to the dust clouds stamped up by Voigts-Rhetz's X Corps as it rushed to cross the river at Hauconcourt, directly in the path of Bazaine's escape to Thionville. Bazaine's only comment was this: "*C'est bien, ce sont les troupes de la rive gauche qui arrivent*" – "yes indeed, those are the troops arriving from the left bank."[53]

51 SHAT, Lb 14, La Ronde, 26 Aug. 1870, Gen. Bourbaki. Lb 14, "Extrait Canrobert."
52 SHAT, Lb 14, "Extrait Canrobert."
53 Andlau, p. 151.

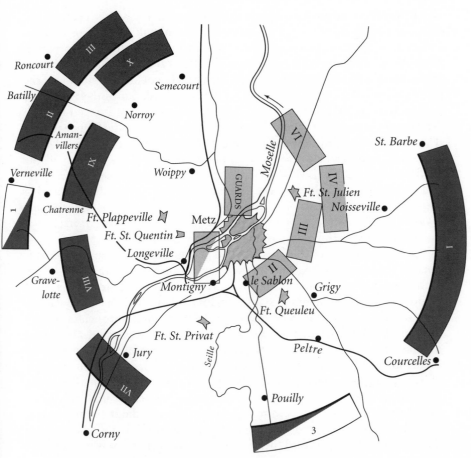

Map 9. Bazaine's sortie from Metz

It was as if Bazaine *wanted* to be stopped in his tracks. Bourbaki, who also saw the marshal at St. Julien on 31 August, found him vague and listless: "I have had a letter from the emperor, informing me that he wishes to extend a helping hand, somewhere in the vicinity of Thionville."[54] In fact, it was Bazaine who ought to have been extending his helping hand to the floundering emperor. Morning turned to afternoon and Bazaine still withheld orders for an attack. To blast away the barricades built by the Prussians on the roads along the right bank, he ordered twenty-four-pound fortress guns removed from Fort St. Julien, lugged to Ste. Barbe and emplaced, an exercise that burned more precious hours. At four o'clock in the afternoon, he finally mounted this new battery position, and fired the first shot at Ste. Barbe. This was the long-awaited signal for a general offensive: Ladmirault's IV Corps into the front of the Prussian position at Ste. Barbe, while Leboeuf's III Corps and Canrobert's VI Corps rolled it up from the flanks at Noisseville and Malroy. If executed in the morning as planned, the French would have bulldozed the small packets of Prussian resistance on the right bank out of their path and broken free. By delaying until the afternoon, Bazaine gave Prince Friedrich Karl time to shift 60,000 troops into the path and flanks of the French march. The French struggled bravely for naught; Bazaine, who commanded from a roadside *auberge* below Ste. Barbe, never committed his reserves to the battle – which he merely called a "lively probe" (*"tentative de vive force"*) – and ordered a retreat the moment Prussian resistance stiffened. Overhearing the marshal's orders, someone cried, *"Ah! Nous sommes perdus! Ce n'est que trop certain, il ne veut pas sortir! On l'avait bien dit"* – "We are goners; he has no intention of breaking out; people were right about him."[55]

Only Bazaine's aversion to escape and maneuver can account for his conduct on the 26 and 31 August. He had every advantage and squandered them all. Many put this down to treachery or intrigues – Bazaine hastening the fall of Napoleon III or withholding troops from his rival MacMahon – but Bazaine's adjutant, Colonel Napoléon Boyer, ascribed it to nothing more nefarious than pessimism, a cloud that hung over Bazaine for the entire campaign. During the fighting of 31 August, Boyer remarked to an army surgeon that "the marshal is attempting a breakout, but is convinced that it will fail."[56] After a full day of battle, Bazaine's angry, dispirited troops were pressed back on Metz again, where they dissolved into undisciplined bands. The retreat itself was interesting; there were no orders to retreat, rather the men did it spontaneously, fed up with Bazaine's half-measures. General Edouard Deligny, who watched the men break up, overheard them asking one another "what is happening?" Because no one had the faintest idea, and "because the troops saw that no one was *doing* anything and that no one was looking after them, they began quietly and peacefully walking back. All the generals and officers questioned said the same thing: "'we marched back because we saw that everyone else was marching back.'"[57] Bourbaki no longer bothered to conceal his loathing of Bazaine: "Thus ended the battle of Noisseville, no measure having been taken to ensure its success."[58] Indeed so half-hearted was Bazaine's push toward Ste. Barbe and Noisseville that Prince Friedrich Karl – girding to intervene at Sedan if needed – did not even bother to cross the Moselle. He left the battle in the capable hands of Manteuffel and Voigts-Rhetz and remained at Briey.[59]

55 Andlau, p. 159.
56 SHAT, Lb 11, Moncel, 22 June 1872, Col. d'Ornant to Marshal Leboeuf. Andlau, p. 157.
57 *Allgemeine Militär-Zeitung*, 28 April 1892.
58 SHAT, Lt 12, 28 Feb. 1872, "Déposition du Gen. Bourbaki."
59 Fay, p. 163.

The 3,000 French wounded struck down in Bazaine's sortie further complicated his position, increasing the demand for water and dwindling medical
supplies in Metz.

At Châlons, MacMahon would have preferred to retire on Paris with its
excellent fortifications and garrison of 150,000, but was dissuaded by political pressure from the empress and Count Palikao. Colonel Louis Chagrin,
commandant of the 99th Regiment, asserted that MacMahon considered a "defensive battle" under the guns of the Paris forts "the only reasonable course"
for his half-green army, but was forced away from the capital by Palikao, who
feared that the arrival of a beaten French field army in Paris might trigger a
rising against the imperial government. Chagrin made the interesting observation that MacMahon ought to have resigned his command, because no general
would have agreed to replace him, and he would have had his way.[60] Other
officers believed that MacMahon genuinely wanted to march east to "coordinate the military efforts that [Bazaine] was allowing to diverge," to ensure
that neither French army was "strategically isolated." In fact, MacMahon's
thinking seems to have been quite a bit more pedestrian; though aware of his
army's flaws, he did not want to mar his reputation by seeming to abandon
Bazaine.[61] Leaving General Joseph Vinoy's XIII Corps with 100,000 *gardes
mobiles* to defend Paris, MacMahon marched.[62] Once Moltke began his wheel
north, speed alone could save the Army of Châlons, but the abrupt change of
line to Mézières and Sedan had completely upset French movements and logistics, making them even slower than usual. The need to avoid the oncoming
Germans and feed his hungry armies impelled MacMahon northward where
the roads climbed steeply through forested defiles and there was only one
overtaxed railway.

Bazaine's surprising inactivity was a great relief to Moltke, who now had
time to improve his lines around Metz and intensify the hunt for MacMahon.
Prussian cavalry patrols, scouting far in advance of the army, had entered
Châlons on 24 August and found it empty save for the charred remains of
Louis-Napoleon's supply dumps. The Third Army, which had been tensing
for several days for a great battle on the Marne, relaxed. Other patrols probed
as far as Reims, questioning mayors and breaking into post offices to seize bags
of mail; thousands of unposted letters were passed back to great headquarters
in the hope that they might furnish clues as to MacMahon's whereabouts,
morale, and intentions.[63] Squeezing between the French forts at Verdun and
Toul, Crown Prince Albert led his new Army of the Meuse across the broad
river in the last week of August and tramped toward Reims and Paris on a
broad front from Ste. Menehould to Vitry-le-François.

60 SHAT, Lc 2/3, Sedan, 1 Sep. 1870, Col. Chagrin, "Aprés la bataille."
61 SHAT, Lc 1, Paris, 14 March 1903, Gen. de Vaulgrenant to Gen. Pendezec.
62 PRO, FO 27, 1813, Paris, 29 Aug. 1870, Col. E.S. Claremont to Lyons.
63 Munich, Bayerisches Kriegsarchiv (BKA), HS 849, Capt. Girl, vol. 2, p. 59.

For many German troops, these were the hardest days of the war. Constant rain pounded the chalky roads into swamps; icy muck filled their boots, and there was little to eat, "*Champagne pouilleuse*" – "wretched Champagne" – being thinly farmed and populated. The men, exhausted by twenty-mile route marches and cold nights in the open, subsisted on rice and whatever they could plunder along the way. Barbarities increased, as German troops robbed and molested the peasants they passed and shot anyone suspected of being a *franc-tireur* or insurgent.[64] MacMahon's move to Reims puzzled everyone in Prussian headquarters; did it portend a defense of Paris from a sheltered position behind the Aisne and the Canal de la Marne or a bold flank march east to relieve Bazaine? According to a staff officer in the Meuse Army, the latter possibility was "not taken seriously by anyone in headquarters."[65] Still, the doubt weighed heavily, for nineteenth-century armies could not be turned on a dime. Crown Prince Albert's march tables would deliver him expeditiously enough to Châlons and Reims, but made no provision for a turn north. If the Army of Châlons used France's northern roads and railways to hasten to Mézières and Sedan, it might hit the Army of the Meuse in the flank or blunder safely past it to take the Prussian Second Army round Metz between two fires, MacMahon's and Bazaine's.[66]

To confront this possibility, Moltke took a calculated risk on 26 August. Prince Leopold of Bavaria witnessed the momentous decision during a supper with King Wilhelm, Bismarck, Moltke, and Roon at Bar-le-Duc late on the 25th. "At the table we talked of nothing but the possible meaning of the French move and prospective moves against it." According to Leopold, "only Moltke's penetrating eyes could settle the uncertain future into a concrete plan."[67] Reacting to sketchy reconnaissance as well as French and British newspaper reports that MacMahon was bound for Montmédy and Metz, Moltke gave orders for first Prince Albert and then Crown Prince Friedrich Wilhelm to begin wheeling their westbound armies around to the north. This was risky on two counts: First, it involved pivoting a large army across a thirty-mile front in the presence of a well-armed, concentrated enemy force. If MacMahon reacted swiftly, he could catch Moltke in the midst of the maneuver and defeat the Meuse and Third Armies separately. Then there was always the risk that Moltke was guessing wrong, that he was embarked on a "*Luftstoss*," a "stab in the air." Were MacMahon simply feinting eastward while retiring on Paris, Moltke would lose an entire week, giving the French

64 G. von Bismarck, *Kriegserlebnisse 1866 und 1870–71*, Dessau, 1907, p. 129. Edwards, p. 79.
65 PRO, FO 64, 703, 30 Oct. 1870, Capt. Henry Hozier, "Sketch of the Operations of the German Army in France." SKA, Zeitg. Slg. 43, 1873, Lt-Col. Karl von Holleben-Normann, "Operationen der Maas-Armee von Metz bis Sedan."
66 Gen. Julius Verdy du Vernois, *With the Royal Headquarters in 1870–71*, 2 vols., London, 1897, vol. 1, pp. 108–16.
67 BKA, HS 858, "Kriegstagebuch Leopold Prinz von Bayern."

precious time to improve their defenses, train recruits and work the foreign embassies. The glacial pace of MacMahon's march east fed this particular fear, for an army evenly spread from Reims to Buzancy seemed capable of anything. Most vexing to Moltke was, as he put it, the "improbability" of the French move. To the Prussian *chef*, a master of strategic movements, it seemed "strange and foolhardy" and therefore improbable that MacMahon and Napoleon III "would leave Paris unprotected and march by the Belgian frontier to Metz."[68] Also troubling was the absence of French cavalry. An eastbound army ought to have secured its exposed right flank with masses of cavalry, but, true to form, the French cavalry hung back, leaving Moltke's patrols to course unchecked (and uninformed) through the Argonne.

A Saxon colonel in Prussian great headquarters later asserted that it required Moltke's "veritable clairvoyance" to make sense of the mystifying French movements and risk the wheel north toward Sedan.[69] Once it was begun, all doubts evaporated. Major Alfred von Waldersee noted the excitement of headquarters in his diary; like spectators at a chess match, the Prussians felt certain that MacMahon was making a disastrous move, what Bismarck judged "a blundering maneuver." Throwing caution to the wind, Napoleon III and MacMahon were leading their last four corps away from Paris and into the crushing embrace of two Prussian armies. Moltke spread his reserve cavalry in wide-ranging patrols to watch and harry the the French I and XII Corps, moving east from La Chesne to La Besace, and the French V and VII Corps, marching from Vouziers to Buzancy. One of these patrols captured Lieutenant Georges de Grouchy carrying MacMahon's complete order of battle and march tables on 28 August.[70] With the Third Army sweeping northward on a broad front from Varennes to Vouziers and the Meuse Army already in place at Dun-sur-Meuse and Buzancy, MacMahon was plunging deeper into Moltke's pocket. The Prussians now controlled every passage through the Argonne and could swiftly mass guns and infantry on any point in MacMahon's rear or right flank. If MacMahon – struggling to move his disorganized units – did not pick up the pace, his army would be pinned between the Meuse and the Argonne and ground to dust.[71]

Even at this early date, Bismarck and Moltke regretted the presence of the French emperor with the Army of Châlons; if captured in the looming

68 Helmuth von Moltke, *The Franco-German War of 1870–71*, New York, 1892, pp. 70–1.
69 SKA, Zeitg. Slg. 43, 1873, "Lt-Col. Karl von Holleben-Normann, "Operationen der Maas-Armee von Metz bis Sedan."
70 Alfred von Waldersee, *Denkwürdigkeiten*, 3 vols., Berlin, 1922, vol. 1, p. 91. Sheridan, vol. 2, p. 394. A. B., "Kriegsgeschichtliche Betrachtungen über den kleinen Krieg," ÖMZ 3 (1876), p. 253.
71 SKA, Zeitg. Slg. 43, 1873, Oblt. Karl von Holleben-Normann, "Operationen der Maas-Armee von Metz bis Sedan." PRO, FO 27, 1813, Paris, 29 Aug. 1870, Col. E. S. Claremont to Lyons. Howard, pp. 196–8.

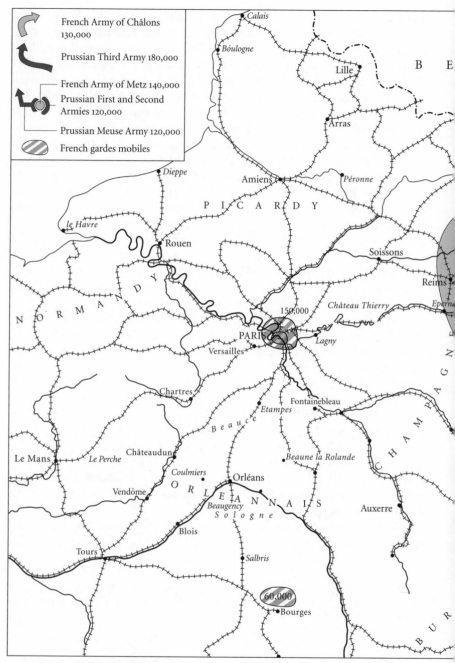

Map 10. MacMahon's march to Sedan and Moltke's wheel north

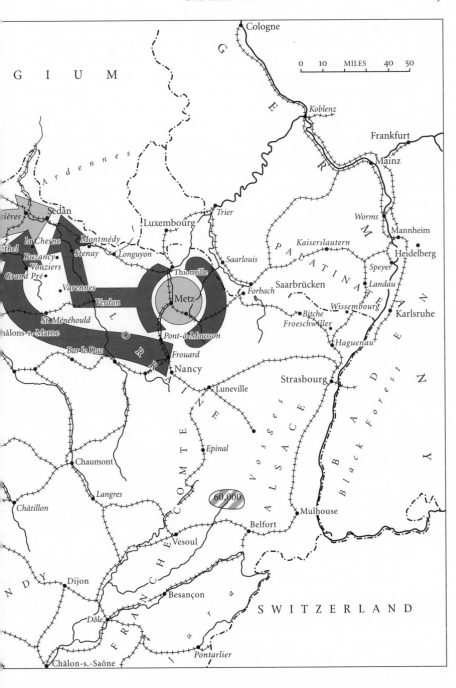

pocket battle, Louis-Napoleon would not be free to arrange the quick peace the Prussians desired. "It will be a great setback for us if we end up capturing Emperor Napoleon," Moltke confided to Prince Leopold of Bavaria on the 25th.[72] Napoleon III's capture might destroy the Second Empire and usher in a more popular republic, condemning the Prussians to a grinding war of attrition. They expected that the "wily old fox" would desert his army on the eve of battle and return to Paris. Scenting victory, the Prussian armies slewed around to the right. Trailing behind them, a British war correspondent noted that Moltke's turn north was physically etched in the countryside; the Germans felled thousands of trees to string telegraph lines along their march routes. Meeting with French peasants near Bar-le-Duc, the Englishman was amazed by their ignorance and susceptibility to wild rumors. One asked him to "describe everything that has happened since our capture of Berlin." The entire village believed that France was winning the war, and that Admiral Boüet had sailed up the Spree and bombarded the Prussian capital.[73]

Though Moltke had to reckon with the possibility of a French attack, he thought it more likely that MacMahon would merely pin himself against the Meuse between Mouzon and Stenay, permitting Saxon Crown Prince Albert to engage the southernmost French corps from the southeast while Crown Prince Friedrich Wilhelm rolled in from the west to close the pocket. Late on 28 August, Moltke ordered the Meuse Army to thrust northward toward Beaumont and the Third Army to march eastward from Buzancy and La Chesne. This was a daring revision of his original maneuver, which had planned to unite the two German armies on the right bank of the Meuse. Realizing that MacMahon was floundering, Moltke now surged in for the kill on the left bank, ordering his armies to join at Beaumont-en-Argonne.[74] Moltke and MacMahon were on a collision course, and the first grating contact occurred on 29 August when General Pierre de Failly's V Corps, the right wing of the French march to Montmédy, slapped into the Saxon XII Corps near Buzancy. After a long firefight, Failly broke off the action and retreated into the Belval Forest, a wood that enclosed the road north to Mouzon, where Marshal MacMahon was supervising the passage of Lebrun's XII Corps to the right bank of the Meuse.

THE BATTLE OF BEAUMONT, 30 AUGUST 1870

Failly, already tarnished by his failure to engage at Froeschwiller, was disgraced by the events of 29–30 August. He yielded his position on the Wiseppe,

---

72 BKA, HS 858, "Kriegstagebuch Leopold von Bayern."
73 Edwards, pp. 84–5.
74 SKA, Zeitg. Slg. 43, 1873, Oblt. Karl von Holleben-Normann, "Operationen der Maas-Armee von Metz bis Sedan."

Fig. 8. The rout of Failly's V Corps at Beaumont

a little stream that curled between Stenay and Buzancy, just as night fell, and herded his tired, dispirited troops on to a bad road through a dark forest. The passage was predictably awful, and when the troops finally emerged from the wood in the clearing around Beaumont, they simply halted, rolled out their blankets, and slept. The troops that filed out of the forest and flung themselves to the ground in successive echelons from midnight until daybreak were unwittingly camping on the very hinge connecting the two approaching German armies. Pushed into the forest south of the village by the left wing of the Meuse Army on the 29th, Failly was brutally awakened on the 30th by the right wing of Third Army: the Bavarian I Corps. ·

Warned to expect a counter-punch from MacMahon at any hour, the Bavarians had been closing warily on the Army of Châlons, occupying every ridge and wood with dragoons and light infantry before dragging the guns and march columns forward.[75] Lieutenant Joseph Krumper recalled the weariness of his platoon as they staggered up the heights beyond Sommauthe at midday and met with a knot of dragoons and general staff officers peering excitedly through a telescope. Even with the naked eye, Failly's horde of *Rothosen* – "red

75 Edwards, p. 99.

breeches" – were clearly visible in the distance with some asleep and others milling about in search of food and drink. As the Bavarians watched, the guns of the Prussian IV Corps opened fire on the sitting target. While the French scrambled to their feet and collected their rifles, the Bavarian 2nd Division rapidly formed battalion columns and marched downhill. Krumper remembered the urgency, the sense that an attack like this on startled, disorganized French troops was an opportunity not to be missed. Though the Bavarians had already covered nineteen miles on foot, they went briskly over to the attack. The men received absolution on the move, the regimental chaplains calling *"Mit Gott, mit Gott!"* as each column rushed past, the officers shouting *"Ladt's G'wehr!"* – "load rifles." Second division struck into Beaumont without firing a shot. Although they took heavy casualties from the Chassepot – Krumper lost seven of twenty-six men in his platoon in the initial rush – they recognized that speed and surprise were their best weapons and simply overran everything in their path.[76]

Fatigued by their long marches, the French had not even bothered to post sentries, nor did they react to warnings from peasants in the morning that "the Prussians were coming." Colonel Valentin Weissenburger of the French 17th Regiment observed that his largely Catalan unit was so worn out by "fruitless marches and counter-marches" that the men would not budge until driven to their feet by volleys of Prussian fire delivered from a range of 500 yards.[77] The men slithered out of their bedrolls and ran toward Mouzon. Weissenburger lost 207 men in the initial rush; other regiments fared worse. The 86th, a Breton regiment, lost 600 men, most on the road to Mouzon, where a jam of baggage cars stopped the fleeing troops in a cauldron of shell fire and shrapnel.[78] The road to Mouzon and the Meuse climbed steeply, and the troops paused to place cannon and *mitrailleuse* batteries, which gunned down 3,400 Germans and checked the pursuit long enough for Failly to conduct most of his corps, minus 7,500 dead, wounded, and missing, to the Meuse.[79]

The shock waves of the German attack and Failly's rout reverbated all the way up to Villers and Sedan, where General Félix Douay's VII Corps was buffeted by panic-stricken stragglers as it crossed to the right bank of the Meuse. The *troupiers* fired at everything that moved, imagining encircling Germans behind every tree and fold in the ground.[80] A Bavarian officer later criticized the French for not punishing the tactical errors committed by the onrushing Germans – a mile-wide gap between the Bavarians and Prussians, the overexcited commitment of reserves – but General Failly, overrun in broad

76 BKA, HS 856, Landwehr Lt. Joseph Krumper. BKA, HS 849, Capt. Girl, vol. 3, pp. 9–18.
77 SHAT, Lc 2/3, 12 Oct. 1870, Col. Weissenburger, "Rapport sur la part prise par le 17e de Ligne à la bataille de Beaumont le 30 Août 1870."
78 SHAT, Lc 2/3, 4 Sept. 1870, Lt-Col. Jacquelot, "Rapport."
79 SHAT, Lc 2/3, Sedan, 4 Sep. 1870, Capt. E. Arnould.
80 SHAT, Lc 2/3, Sedan, 1 Sep. 1870, Col. Chagrin de St. Hilaire, "Aprés la bataille."

daylight, was far too shocked and embarrassed to do anything but flee.[81] At Mouzon, a furious Marshal MacMahon, pressed from the south and the east, ordered Failly and the rest of his army to retire northward to Sedan. He was now cut off from Bazaine, and had little hope of retreating back to Paris via Mézières. Even if he outran the Prussians, he would assuredly lose all of his baggage and ammunition and many of his men and guns as well. That left neutral Belgium as his only viable line of retreat.[82] Though Belgium would be some comfort to the men, who would be interned under pleasant conditions, it would mean the loss of the entire army for the duration of the war. MacMahon would, therefore, have little choice but to make a stand at Sedan, where the fully extended Prussian army would have to finish him off to remove the threat to their flank. As the British military attaché in Paris noted on 29 August, "the fate of the campaign depends on what is about to happen."[83]

Prince Leopold of Bavaria, who had been further north in action against rearguards of the French VII Corps, arrived in Beaumont as evening fell; the village and surrounding fields were littered with French rifles, packs, saddles, coats, wagons, caissons, tents, and assorted equipment. Horses that had been tied to forage lines in the night slumped on their tethers, killed by shell fragments or rifle rounds.[84] General Julius Verdy rode in with Prince Albert of Saxony. Finding a camp table and stools still neatly arranged before Failly's tent, they spread their maps on the table and helped themselves to large portions of sardines, truffled sausages, and *paté de foie gras.*[85] Lieutenant Adolf Hinüber scolded the "unconscionable frivolity of the French" at Beaumont, which had been repaid with 5,700 French dead and wounded scattered along the road to Mouzon and piled thick between full cooking pots around Beaumont. Hinüber leaned over to inspect a dead major who had been shot while inserting his dentures and studying a photograph of his wife. In all, the Germans captured twenty-eight French cannon, eight *mitrailleuses,* and 1,800 prisoners. The French had also abandoned an entire ammunition park of sixty wagons; the Germans found them drawn up in orderly rows in Beaumont, the drivers having cut loose their horses and fled for their lives.[86]

Prussian great headquarters heard and saw some of the battle from their post at Buzancy. There Moltke finally recognized just how tightly he had

81 BKA, HS 982, Munich, 3 Dec. 1871, Maj. Theodor Eppler, "Erfahrungen."
82 SKA, Zeitg. Slg. 43, 1873, Oblt. Karl von Holleben-Normann, "Operationen der Maas-Armee von Metz bis Sedan."
83 PRO, FO 27, 1813, Paris, 29 Aug. 1870, Col. E. S. Claremont to Lyons.
84 BKA, HS 858, "Kriegstagebuch Prinz Leopold von Bayern."
85 Gen. Julius Verdy du Vernois, *With the Royal Headquarters in 1870–71,* 2 vols., London, 1897, vol. I, p. 121.
86 SKA, Zeitg. Slg. 158, Sec. Lt. Hinüber. Dresden, KA, Zeitg. Slg. 43, 1873, Oblt. Karl von Holleben-Normann, "Operationen der Maas-Armee von Metz bis Sedan."

cornered MacMahon. Everyone in the German camp did. With the Crown
Prince of Saxony operating on the right bank of the Meuse and the Crown
Prince of Prussia on the left, MacMahon was wedged in. To encircle him,
Moltke promptly ordered Meuse Army's V and the XI Corps north of Sedan
to place themselves between MacMahon and the Belgian frontier. The Third
Army would approach Sedan on the western side of the river, extending its left
wing to block any retreat toward Paris or Mézières.[87] Posted with Moltke and
Bismarck, General Phil Sheridan attentively watched the Prussians close the
ring: "The German troops moved with … a peculiar swinging gait, with which
the men seemed to urge themselves over the ground with ease and rapidity.
There was little or no straggling, and being strong, lusty young fellows and
lightly equipped – they carried only needle-guns, ammunition, a very small
knapsack, a water-bottle, and a haversack – they strode by with an elastic step,
covering at least three miles an hour."[88] As the Germans tramped quickly
forward, they wondered at the absence of French cavalry. Instead of masking
the retreat of the infantry and guns, the French cavalry used its mobility to
escape the jaws of the Prussian pursuit; one onlooker noted that "MacMahon's
cavalry reached [Sedan] a clear day before the last of his infantry."[89] This gave
the Germans every opportunity to extend their lines, keep contact with the
French, and encircle them. Speaking with an English reporter after the clash
at Beaumont, a Bavarian artillery officer said:

> "I would not be in MacMahon's place for anything. Wherever he goes we shall
> have him within range. We can drive him from point to point, as in a hunt, until
> he is compelled to move in the direction we wish him to take. He is beaten on
> the right and will have to come in front of us directly. If he passes us he will
> meet the Crown Prince [of Saxony], so that one way or the other he is sure to
> be disposed of."[90]

87 PRO, FO 64, 703, 30 Oct. 1870, Capt. Henry Hozier, "Sketch of Operations of the German
    Army in France."
88 Sheridan, vol. 2, p. 398.
89 Edwards, p. 120.
90 Edwards, p. 98.

9

Sedan

As the French reeled away from Beaumont in the direction of Sedan, where Marshal MacMahon hoped to find a temporary refuge, Moltke scribbled orders for 31 August: The Meuse Army would march down the right bank of the Meuse, extending its right wing all the way to the Belgian border; the Third Army was to surge ahead on the left bank to Sedan, seize whatever bridges it could, begin crossing, and push troops into the space between Sedan and Paris.[1] While Moltke worked, so did Bismarck, reminding Brussels of its obligation to disarm and intern any French troops that crossed the Belgian border. If the Belgians permitted the French to regroup on their neutral territory, the Prussians would invade. By late on 31 August, a French withdrawal to Belgian soil had become all but impossible anyway, for the Saxons and the Prussian Guards had extended themselves north and east of Sedan, the Prussian 6th Cavalry Division north and west at Mézières. South of Sedan, the Bavarians had advanced to Bazeilles, Wadelincourt, and Torcy, the Prussian IV Corps to Frénois, the Prussian XI and V Corps to Donchéry, enabling Moltke to push vanguards across the Meuse to block MacMahon's escape in every direction and begin the famous *Umgehung* or envelopment.[2] French engineers sent from Sedan to blow up the Donchéry bridge discovered that all of their gunpowder and blasting caps had been evacuated to Mézières; scouring Donchéry for replacements, they were chased off by Prussian skirmishers.[3] From high ground on the left bank of the Meuse, Moltke could see the entire French camp on the other side. "Now we have them in a mousetrap," Moltke assured the king late on 31 August. As he spoke, troops of the XI Corps were crossing

1   Helmuth von Moltke, *The Franco-German War of 1870–71*, New York, 1892, pp. 84–8.
2   Munich, Bayerisches Kriegsarchiv (BKA), HS 849, Capt. Girl, vol. 3, pp. 28–30.
3   Vincennes, Service Historique de l'Armée de Terre (SHAT), Lc 2/3, Sedan, 1 Sept. 1870, Col. Louis Chagrin, "Aprés la bataille."

the Meuse and pulling up MacMahon's only westbound railway. In Donchéry, hungry Prussians swarmed joyously into abandoned French supply trains to feast on their contents: sausages, hams, bread, butter, jams, sugar, sardines in oil, red and white wines, and cases of champagne.[4] For many, this would be their last supper. On the grassy slope above Frénois, Prussian enlisted men were staking out a luxurious enclosure, where the King of Prussia, Bismarck, and Moltke would invite the princes of Germany, the foreign attachés and the international press corps to watch the trap snap shut on 1 September.

For an officer who just days earlier had written that "the Prussian system consists of concentrating forces to maneuver decisively in great masses," Marshal Patrice MacMahon was showing precious little discernment in his deployments around Sedan.[5] The position, three parallel ridge lines descending to the Meuse, was tailor-made for what was fast becoming a Prussian specialty, the "*Zirkel-Schlacht*" or "circle battle," in which German troops would surround an enemy army and demolish it with masses of artillery and converging infantry attacks. By not contesting the line of the Meuse and then deploying his army defensively on the triangle of inner ridges northeast of Sedan, MacMahon maximized Moltke's advantage. Though the Meuse and the old fortress would have offered protection to an eighteenth-century army – covering its flanks and rear and permitting it to project its entire power north or east – the long range of Moltke's Krupp guns stripped the *position magnifique* of all of its historic advantages. The Prussian chief could either pummel the French from the left bank of the Meuse, or cross to the right bank, march his armies on to the outer ridges around the inert French mass, encircle it, and then commence its destruction. Instead of having a broad river and fortress works across his front, MacMahon would find them in his rear, like Benedek at Königgrätz. The deployment was, in the words of a French participant, "*trés défecteuse*" – "very defective" – not least because it contained no obvious line of retreat.[6] The entire defensive triangle above Sedan measured no more than fifteen miles. With 120,000 troops and 700 guns, the Germans would have little trouble engulfing such a small space, and each step forward would shrink the battlefield some more, multiplying the power of the Prussian guns and increasing pressure on the French.[7] General Auguste Ducrot actually advised MacMahon to deploy two or three miles further north, on the forested heights around Floing, St. Menges, and Illy, where the French could have repulsed a Prussian attack and then conducted a fighting retreat to the west. MacMahon, exhausted by the chaotic retreat from Beaumont, refused, the occasion for

---

4   G. von Bismarck, *Kriegserlebnisse 1866 und 1870–71*, Dessau, 1907, p. 130.
5   "*Papiers et Correspondance de la Famille Impériale*," 10 vols., Paris, 1870, vol. 2, p. 63.
6   SHAT, Lc 2/3, Sedan, 1 Sept. 1870, Col. Louis Chagrin, "Aprés la bataille."
7   Capt. Hugo von Molnár, "Über Artillerie Massenverwendung im Feldkriege," *Österreich-ische Militärische Zeitschrift* (ÖMZ)1 (1880), p. 296.

Ducrot's famous protest: "But here we are in a chamber pot, about to be shitted upon."[8]

General Ludwig von der Tann, commander of the Bavarian I Corps, began the battle at 4 A.M., when he sent his 2nd Division across the railway bridge into Bazeilles. This attack went in sooner than Moltke would have liked, for much of the Prussian army was still marching to the front, but Tann, whose troops had fought abysmally in 1866 and indifferently at Froeschwiller, would not be denied this chance at redemption. The action, which committed unskilled Bavarian troops to bloody house-to-house combat, was later the source of controversy because of the tremendous and avoidable casualties. Shelled by the French guns at Balan and fired at from houses, roofs, trees, and steeples, the Bavarians were cut to pieces in the early hours.[9] Although Prussia's official history of the war later credited Tann with "holding the French fast" at Bazeilles and permitting Moltke to envelop the Army of Châlons from the flanks, it seems that Tann was really the victim of his own personal thirst for glory as well as garbled orders.[10] At least one witness overheard General Albrecth von Blumenthal – the Third Army staff chief – order Tann "to delay the French withdrawal toward Mézieres." But Blumenthal later denied this: "I would never have given such an order; it would have been folly."[11] Folly it must have appeared to the Bavarian regiments pinned in the foggy streets and alleys of Bazeilles at daybreak, fired on from every angle by covered French infantry, marines (the troops held back from the Baltic had found their way here from Cherbourg), and even civilians, many of whom dug out shotguns and hunting rifles to snipe at the easy targets.

General Barthélemy Lebrun's XII Corps had reacted swiftly to the Bavarian thrust, occupying Bazeilles with a division that broke into small parties to retake and hold the shops and houses overrun by the Bavarians at first light. Artillery would be needed to dislodge them.[12] This early outburst startled the Prussian troops of the XI Corps massing at Donchéry for an attack on the French positions at Floing and Illy. Because the Meuse looped upward between Sedan and Donchéry, the men had to march six miles north before they could turn eastward into the French position. Gebhard von Bismarck, an officer in the Prussian 87th, recalled the "taut nerves and anxiety" of his men as they trooped along the oxbow, listening to the roar of the cannonade and the hacking of rifle fire: "Suddenly a man stepped out of the company column before me, scrambled up the Meuse embankment and – with backpack,

8 SHAT, Lc 2/3, 1871, "Bataille de Sedan: Documents historiques concernant le Gen. de Wimpffen."
9 BKA, B 1240, Capt. Balduin Winckler, "Relation über das Gefecht bei Sedan."
10 BKA, B 1123, n.d., Gen. Tann, "Bericht über die Teilnahme I. bayerischen Armee-Corps an der Schlacht von Sedan."
11 BKA, HS 849, Capt. Girl, vol. 3, pp. 32–4.
12 SHAT, Lc 2/3, Paris, 2 Aug. 1872, Gen. Lebrun to Navy Minister, "Rapport au Ministre."

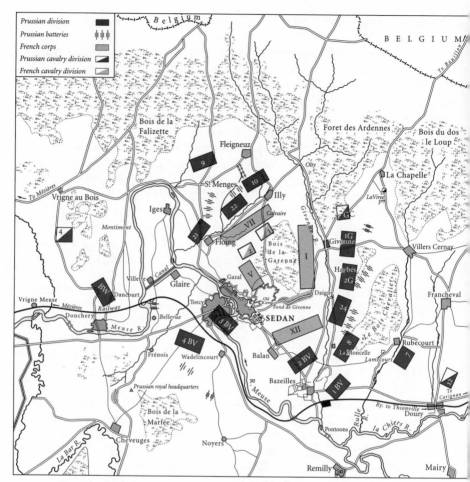

Map 11. The Battle of Sedan

bedroll, and rifle – threw himself into the water below. There was a loud splash, the water closed over him, the rings dissipated, and then *nothing*. He never surfaced. The men gaped for a long time; they were nauseated, by this, and by the grinding pressure on their nerves."[13] Far above on the height of Donchéry, their mastermind, General Blumenthal, felt no such pressure. Though weakened by diarrhea, he scanned the field with his telescope and pronounced it "unmistakably evident that we [will] win."[14]

13 G. von Bismarck, pp. 132–3.
14 Field Marshal Albrecht von Blumenthal, *Journals of Field Marshal Count von Blumenthal for 1866 and 1870–71*, London, 1903, p. 111.

LA GARDE PRUSSIENNE A LA BATAILLE DE SEDAN, DANS LA MATINÉE DU 1ᵉʳ SEPTEMBRE.

Fig. 9. The Prussian Guards close the pocket at Sedan

North of Bazeilles, the first units of the Meuse Army hove into view at La Moncelle and Daigny, outer ridges facing the French troops east of Sedan; they were Saxon advance guards, and General Auguste Ducrot's I Corps gamely met them with counter-attacks that continued all morning as the Meuse Army struggled to attach itself to the Third Army and Ducrot labored to throw them back. Riding out to investigate this unexpected battle, Marshal MacMahon's horse was blown out from under him by a shellburst. Helped to his feet, the sixty-two-year-old marshal found that he could not mount a horse, or even walk. A shell fragment had lacerated his leg. As his strength ebbed away, MacMahon appointed General Ducrot acting commander of the Army of Châlons.

The Prussians were busy all along the line. With the French distracted by the slow spread of fighting northward from the XII Corps's positions at Bazeilles to the I Corps's positions at Daigny and Givonne, the Prussian V and XI Corps crossed the Meuse at Donchéry, trooped up to the Sedan-Mézières road, and then divided. The XI Corps smashed its way into Floing, and the V Corps ascended to Fleigneux, where it would join hands with the Prussian Guard Corps approaching from the east and close the ring around France's last army. The *Kesselschlacht* was shaping up nicely, and not a moment too soon for the German infantry, who did not have another march in their legs. To catch MacMahon, most units had been marching thirteen or fourteen hours a day for several days on end, many of them without food. These were the original *"Kilometerschweine"* – "kilometer pigs." An officer in the 1st Württemberg Regiment recalled that only the steady beat of the drums kept his hungry men going; wincing against the pain, fatigue, and hunger, they shuffled up to the Meuse and across, one man calling, "Someone give me a piece of bread so that I can remember what it is to eat."[15]

Although Ducrot's first order upon assuming command was "retreat to the west," the two Prussian corps behind him were positioned to block that retreat. The withdrawal was stillborn anyway owing to confusion in French headquarters, where General Emmanuel Wimpffen, who had been rushed out from Paris to relieve the disgraced Failly after Beaumont, insisted that he, not Ducrot, was the *real* acting commander of MacMahon's army. Wimpffen, commandant of Oran before the war and sixteenth on the army's seniority list, refused to take orders from Ducrot, who stood twenty-six places below him. While Ducrot ordered retreat from the closing pocket on the premise that the army's artillery and the Sedan fortress guns would slow the German advance from the southeast long enough for the French infantry and cavalry to break out to the northwest, Wimpffen, flourishing his *lettre de commandement* from Count Palikao, ordered the army to stand and fight in the positions it had already occupied around Sedan.[16] With the German Meuse Army folding in from the northeast and the Third Army from the southwest, the French had no viable options anyway. If they tried to push back from Bazeilles or Daigny, they would only entangle themselves in their supply trains and rear echelons while the Germans swarmed in from all directions. If they tried to break out in any direction without artillery support, they would be shot to pieces. Overall, it seemed best to stand pat and slug it out. Thus, by midmorning the battle was raging all along the front from Donchéry, through Bazeilles and up to Illy.[17]

The crucial problem for the French was one already identified in the campaign; their artillery was no match for Prussia's. MacMahon's decision to deploy the army in a defensive triangle above Sedan – Félix Douay's VII Corps between Floing and Illy, Ducrot's I Corps from Givonne to Daigny, Lebrun's XII Corps from Daigny to Bazeilles, Wimpffen's V Corps in reserve and in the gap between Douay and Ducrot – meant that the troops would be at the mercy of the more powerful and accurate Prussian artillery. If the French infantry had felt like "cannon meat" at Mars-la-Tour, they would feel like mincemeat here, where the Prussian shells screamed in unanswered from

15 Paul Dorsch, ed., *Kriegszuge der Württemberger im 19. Jahrhundert*, Stuttgart, 1913, p. 306.
16 SHAT, Lc 2/3, 1871, "Bataille de Sedan: Documents historiques concernant le Gen. de Wimpffen."
17 SHAT, Lc 2/3, Fays-les-Veneurs, 5 Sept. 1870, Gen. Wimpffen to Gen. Palikao.

more than a mile away. When the Bavarians finally cleared Bazeilles at midday and pushed closer to Sedan, their gun line joined a thickening ring of Prussian batteries extending from Tann's new position at Balan to the Saxon batteries above Daigny to the masses of Guard artillery at Givonne to the V Corps guns at Fleigneux, whose roar merged with that of the XI Corps guns thumping away above Floing. It was a circle of fire the like of which no French *troupier* had ever seen. Twenty thousand Prussian shells exploded in this narrow space in the course of the day, harrowing up the soul of every French soldier.[18]

Wimpffen, freshly arrived from Paris, soon grasped that standing still was not really an option. Yet in rather unhelpful contrast to Ducrot, who was tugging northwest, Wimpffen pushed southeast. If he could mass sufficient troops opposite Tann's exhausted and relatively undisciplined Bavarians, the Army of Châlons might pierce the Prussian envelopment and slip through to Carignan for an eventual reunion with Bazaine at Metz. It was an improbable plan, but, given the masses of Prussian troops in the rear of the French army, the one that may have offered the most hope. Conditions on the German side suggest that Wimpffen might even have succeeded. Most of the Bavarian infantry were out of ammunition and not eager to be replenished. A Bavarian sergeant recalled that many German troops simply went to ground in Balan and Bazeilles, passing the day guzzling the wine and cider that they found stacked in every cellar.[19] Lieutenant Josef Krumper described the extreme demoralization of his Bavarians at La Moncelle, when they detected the quickening volume of fire from Wimpffen's guns. The "ground trembled" and the "shells passed like storm winds." The men felt as if "they were on the lip of a volcano," and gradually left their positions in the open to crowd inside the stout walls of the Chateau Moncelle. Assisted by other officers, Krumper entered the chateau to drive the troops back outside, but found the Bavarians, joined by leaderless Saxons of the 107th Regiment, "swilling everything in the house that contained alcohol." With sabers in hand, the German officers beat the men outside, and then lost more valuable time barricading the doors and windows of the house, not against Wimpffen's looming breakout, but against another break-in by their own men. While Krumper worked, he watched a drunken Saxon reel back and forth across the courtyard shouting for a corkscrew.[20]

While Wimpffen readied his blow and begged Napoleon III to come from Sedan to lead the thrust through Balan and Bazeilles, the German guns and infantry were laying waste the entire French front. At 1 P.M., while Wimpffen's

18 Theodor Fontane, *Der Krieg gegen Frankreich 1870–71*, 4 vols., orig. 1873–76, Zurich, 1985, vol. 2, p. 226.
19 BKA, HS 850, Sgt. Bernhard Görner, "Tagebuch des Krieges 1870–71." BKA, B 1240, Châlons, 8 Sep. 1870, Col. Walther to II Corps Cdo.
20 BKA, HS 856, Landwehr-Lt. Josef Krumper.

men pushed the Bavarians out of Balan, the Germans began infiltrating the crack between Douay's VII Corps and Ducrot's I Corps. Creeping in behind the withering barrage of the Prussian XI Corps's ninety guns at Fleigneux, the Prussians wrested the Calvaire d'Illy from demoralized remnants and drove thousands of French stragglers in the direction of Sedan. From General Douay's perspective, this was the crisis of the battle, and eerily similar to the clash that had killed his brother at Wissembourg. German guns and troops at Illy poured fire into the rear of his otherwise formidable defensive position, effectively disengaging the Saxon 22nd Division, which was assailing his front.[21] To the end, Douay's men put up a good fight. Oskar Becher, a Prussian *Feldwebel*, reminds us that even in an "artillery battle," attacking infantry must take ground, which is never an easy task. As Becher's platoon swarmed toward the western edge of the Bois de la Garenne in skirmish order, they were ripped by French shell and rifle fire.

> "Left and right my men fell...I saw my best soldier killed by three bullets.... Our colonel died in the storm, shot twice at 200 yards. I remember trying to flatten myself in the furrows of the potato fields and then crawling among the dead and wounded to scavenge cartridges, which I threw to my men. I found a piece of sugar in a Frenchman's backpack and sucked on it while hearing the hiss of the Chassepot rounds, *pfft, pfft.*"

When another Prussian unit attacked along Becher's flank, he brought his men to their feet and rushed forward again. The platoon plunged into a French trench, meeting no resistance. Every man inside had been killed or wounded by the Prussian shrapnel and shell fragments. Turning to his squads, Becher gave an order that, in any other army, would only have been phrased by an officer, more evidence of Prussia's military excellence: "*Nur vorwärts, die Stellung ausnützen*" – "Keep moving, let's wring every advantage from this position."[22]

The fortress of Sedan itself, the foot of MacMahon's defensive triangle, was the only obstacle that held against the German attacks. Lieutenant Karl Leeb, a light infantryman in the Bavarian II Corps, later described an entire day spent battering weakly against the railroad embankment and palisades at Torcy. Ordered to lead his platoon into the Sedan suburb, Leeb found that more than half of his thirty men simply refused to follow him. "*Vorwärts Leute!*" – "forward men!" Leeb implored, but most of the troops skulked under cover. As the French pulled back under fire from Prussian guns at Frénois, Leeb herded his small band up to a house close to the southern gate of Sedan, where

21 SHAT, Lc 2/3, Sedan, 3 Sept. 1870, Gen. Douay, "Rapport sur la role du 7 Corps dans la bataille de Sedan."
22 Oskar Becher, *Kriegstagebuch eines Vierundneunzigers aus dem Kriege 1870–71*, Weimar, 1904, p. 20.

Fig. 10. The French surrounded

the men spent most of the battle sheltering from the French fire. When they finally moved, it was not to storm the nearby Porte de Paris, but to flee the "friendly fire" of German batteries on Frénois, which ignored Leeb's white flag and pounded his hiding place with shells. A Bavarian major in Torcy later testified that dozens of his men were killed by the German guns, their heads torn off or their backs filled with shrapnel balls and shell splinters.[23] This was in large part because King Wilhelm I had vengefully ordered every available gun turned on the fortress once he learned that Emperor Napoleon III was inside Sedan. Still, some batteries behaved more sensibly than others. When a Bavarian officer rode up to Frénois to order the Prussians to stop firing, he discovered that the offending guns belonged to a Württemberg regiment. In broad Swabian tones, the Bavarian was told that he would simply have to endure the shelling like everyone else: "We've dragged these damn cannon all over France without taking a shot at anything; now we're going to fire, and no one's going to stop us."[24]

23 BKA, HS 846, Maj. Gustav Fleschuez.
24 BKA, HS 857, "Tagebuch des Oberlts. Karl Leeb, k. b. 5. Jägerbataillon."

Elsewhere on the battlefield, it was all but impossible for French troops to stand their ground. By midday, the Prussian Guards, the Saxons, and the Bavarians had mounted 222 guns along the front from Floing round to Bazeilles. The shellfire was heavy and unceasing. French troops at the bottom of the triangle fell back on Sedan. Troops at the top plunged into the Bois de la Garenne, seeking sanctuary under the tall trees. The German artillery and infantry ground forward, each incremental advance improving the accuracy of their guns. Arranged in a rough semi-circle, the German guns were densely massed and firing into the French from both flanks and from the front: from every angle possible, in other words, without the danger of firing at each other.

At Floing, double French trench lines had held the Germans off for most of the day, but by early afternoon, Ducrot too was shattered by the pounding of the German cannon, big batteries wheeling in from the west as well as seventy-eight guns firing non-stop from the left bank of the Meuse. As the men of his I Corps trickled backward to Sedan, they uncovered Douay's left flank, permitting thousands of German troops to pour into the gap between Floing and Illy. Arriving in the hinge between his I and VII Corps at midday, General Wimpffen – a veteran of Balaclava and Solferino – was "horrified" by the intensity of the Prussian artillery fire: "In just ten minutes I saw three entire [French] batteries destroyed."[25] Prince Leopold of Bavaria made the same observation from the German side of the hill: "Every French attempt to mount a battery, *mitrailleuse,* or counter-attack was immediately shattered by our artillery," which would bracket the target with ranging shots and then obliterate it with battery fire. At noon, General Jules Forgeot, the Army of Châlons's *chef d'artillerie,* decided to withdraw the French guns altogether. As the gunners limbered up and trotted away, the jilted infantry, "comprehending nothing of their situation," began themselves to retreat, ignoring the commands of their officers.

With the Prussians pressing in from all sides, General Douay recalled searching for a battery of guns at 1:00 and finding none: "The division had been abandoned; there was nothing left but a single *mitrailleuse.*"[26] Standing on a height near Givonne, Prince Leopold recalled the spectacle of the bedraggled French army streaming back to Sedan, channeled by nonstop fire from Givonne, Illy, and Floing.[27] To stem the rout, General Ducrot reached for the only intact reserves he could find, General Jean Margueritte's light brigade of cavalry. In a breathless *tête-à-tête* at Cazal, Ducrot ordered Margueritte to push back the encircling Germans and punch a hole in their lines through which Ducrot could lead a breakout to the west. Unaware that

25 SHAT, Lc 2/3, Fays-les-Veneurs, 5 Sept. 1870, Gen. Wimpffen to Gen. Palikao.
26 SHAT, Lc 2/3, Sedan, 3 Sept. 1870, Gen. Douay, "Rapport sur la role du 7 Corps dans la bataille de Sedan."
27 BKA, HS 858, "Kriegstagebuch Prinz Leopold von Bayern."

General Wimpffen was pursuing an opposite plan on the opposite end of the battlefield, Margueritte agreed, leading his mounted *chasseurs* out from Illy in two massed lines toward Floing.

The Prussians stared in disbelief; they had two entire infantry corps with 144 guns deployed along this face of the triangle, all within range of the French attack and with perfect visibility. An officer in the Prussian 87th recalled the excitement of the corps artillery; the gunners limbered up and moved closer to the approaching French to improve their fire; "*sie kommen, sie kommen*" – "they're coming, they're coming," the men murmured as they worked. Fusiliers ran back to the shelter of their rifle companies and formed lines. While the Prussian artillery gunned shrapnel and canister into the French horse, the Prussian infantry delivered three aimed salvos, each bringing down a wave of cavalry, and then shifted to *Schnellfeuer*, individual rapid fire.[28] Colonel Gaston de Gallifet led his 3rd Chasseurs and the remains of the brigade in a second and third attack, these too were shattered, the last at 3 P.M. By the end, the French horses did not so much charge as pick their way gingerly over the piles of fallen mounts and men.[29] Watching from Frénois, King Wilhelm sighed: "*Ah, les braves gens.*"[30] Closer to the slaughter, Sergeant Oskar Becher of the Prussian 94th saw only senseless butchery: "There were heaped up bodies everywhere, yet one looked in vain for a single intact, undamaged corpse; the men had been mutilated [by the fire]. I spotted a beautiful pair of cavalry boots lying on the ground and picked them up; there were legs and feet still inside."[31]

Without reserves, lacerated by the Prussian artillery, Félix Douay's VII Corps fell apart. Flanked and overrun, Gustave Conseil-Dumesnil's 1st Division lost 50 percent of its strength in the battle.[32] Watching the French from a distance, a Prussian officer could not help but feel pity for them: "They were backed up against the Bois de la Garenne, so densely crowded in the narrow space behind their guns that there were no intervals between them. Each time they made as if to move forward for a counter-attack, our battery commanders would shout: "*Auf die Infanterie, vom rechten Flügel Schnellfeuer!*" – "Open fire on the infantry, from the right wing!"[33] Shell after shell burst in the French ranks. Abandoning all pretense at discipline, the French troops ran for the rear, dissolving the entire defensive front from Illy and Fleigneux down to Floing. The Prussians exploited the collapse, rushing forward to occupy the French positions and pour fire into the retreating units. Watching the

28 G. von Bismarck, pp. 135–6.
29 BKA, HS 849, Capt. Girl, vol. 3, pp. 37, 90.
30 Michael Howard, *The Franco-Prussian War*, orig. 1961, London, 1981, pp. 215–16.
31 Becher, p. 23.
32 SHAT, Lc 2/3, Sedan, 3 Sept. 1870, Gen. Douay, "Rapport sur la role du 7 Corps dans la bataille de Sedan."
33 G. von Bismarck, p. 137.

battle through his telescope from the height of Donchéry, Crown Prince Friedrich Wilhelm, nursing a sour stomach, found the "scene painful and repugnant; French infantrymen were running around unarmed, restless and bewildered."[34] The awkwardness of Marshal MacMahon's triangular position behind the Meuse now became fully apparent: "With French troops moving in and out of the center and along the periphery, there was constant confusion, no energy, no direction, and no support for threatened points. The tactical chaos on the French side was beyond description; the corps fought as isolated detachments, not concentrated units."[35]

More scenes of confusion ensued on the eastern angle of the French position, where General Ducrot's I Corps, punched backward by the Saxons and the Prussian Guard Corps, went to pieces once the Germans had reestablished their gun line on the ridge west of Daigny. Most of the I Corps fell back; the rest made a break for the Belgian border. Marching with the 3rd Zouaves, Captain Charles Warnet slipped into the ravines between the German troops at Illy and Givonne and escaped to the north.[36] Colonel Valentin Weissenburger of the French 17th attempted to march his regiment into the path of the Saxons only to watch it disintegrate before his eyes: "The shells exploding in our columns came from completely opposite directions, which confirmed that we were surrounded." Weissenburger's regiment, part of the depleted French V Corps, Wimpffen's only reserve, united briefly with the rest of its brigade before dissolving completely at 2:00: "The Prussians were firing into our backs; we were 3,500 men with no artillery against 60,000 Saxons with forty-eight guns." Though Weissenburger overstated Saxon numbers at Floing, his was certainly the hysterical impression created by the biting, overlapping German attacks. Some men ran in the direction of Sedan, others simply piled their arms on the ground and put their hands up. As he retreated, Weissenburger saw French units shouting: "*Ne tirez pas! On pose les armes!*" – "don't shoot! We're laying down our arms."[37]

In the closing circle around Sedan, German guns in mobile masses were cooperating so effectively that their fire often converged at ninety-degree angles on the same target, literally enfolding the terrified French in shellfire.[38] At noon, 200 Prussian and Saxon guns raked the Bois de la Garenne from end to end, killing hundreds of French fugitives and driving the rest into the green downs south of the wood. As the French emerged in the open, the German batteries followed them. German battery commanders had maneuvered their

34 Frederick III, *The War Diary of the Emperor Frederick III 1870–71*, New York, 1927, p. 89.
35 Maj. Johann Nosinich, "Der Krieg 1870–71," ÖMZ 4 (1872), pp. 155–6.
36 SHAT, Lc 2/3, Paris, 6 Sept. 1870, Capt. Warnet.
37 SHAT, Lc 2/3, 7 Sept. 1870, Col. Valentin Weissenburger, "Rapport."
38 SHAT, Lc 2/3, Sedan, 1 Sept. 1870, Col. Louis Chagrin, "Aprés la bataille."

guns into positions of textbook effectiveness, gaining a tactical advantage far more likely to be illustrated on a blackboard than ever actually achieved in the chaos of battle. On this sector alone, the Germans had brought 200 guns into action – as many as Confederate gunners had massed at Fredericksburg eight years earlier – and they ranged them across the front and the flanks of the French bunched densely in the woods. Once the Germans began firing, the French could find no cover anywhere. They were hit with a storm of shells whistling in from an arc of ninety degrees. A hill might shield French soldiers from shells fired from one direction, but they lay naked to projectiles smashing in from other angles. Worse, shellfire burst among the trees, adding jagged splinters to the shrapnel and shell fragments tearing into French units. The one-sided bombardment exhilarated the German gunners, who drove in for the kill against no resistance. For their helpless French targets, who watched the German gun flashes draw closer and closer, the sights, sounds, and shocks of this artillery massacre became a horror beyond description.

With six-pound shells bursting in their midst, the French troops dissolved in a great *sauve qui peut* headed for Sedan. There men tumbled into the ditches and frantically tried to climb the walls of the fortress. The crisis was eerily reminiscent of 1866, when the fortress commandant of Königgrätz had refused to admit the panic-stricken remains of Benedek's North Army. Small seventeeth-century fortresses like Sedan were not configured to harbor large field armies, a fact of modern war completely lost on the shell-shocked desperadoes milling around the gate, ditch, and causeway. Inside the fortress, the French garrison – a division-sized mob of stragglers – ran riot, looting, drinking, and destroying as the battle closed in.[39]

The Bois de la Garenne itself fell to the Saxons and troops of the Third Army in the late afternoon. Inside they found the demoralized wreckage of three entire French divisions. Further south, on the upland behind Bazeilles and La Moncelle, Lieutenant Josef Krumper was horrified by the tableau of war: rows of French backpacks – piled up as breastworks – only partially hid exploded, mashed corpses. Dozens of French cannon and *mitrailleuses* had simply been left behind by their fleeing (or dead) gun crews. The wounded were "mutilated, dying men, mostly artillery casualties, without arms, feet, legs, many with open skulls, their brains oozing out. The screams were horrible, from the awful wounds or the razor pain of the Chassepot bullet."[40] Here a Bavarian captain paused and vomited at the sight of a French gunner dismembered by a direct hit: "He had only a head, chest and one arm.... Most of the rest had been blown away by a shell that struck him directly." Nearby was a pile of butchered horseflesh, the remains of a general and his

39 SHAT, Lc 2/3, Sedan, 1 Sept. 1870, Col. Louis Chagrin, "Aprés la bataille."
40 BKA, HS 856, Landwehr-Lt. Josef Krumper.

staff literally blown to smithereens. Ordered to identify the dead general, a Saxon lieutenant found only a scrap of his underwear, labeled "*Géneral T.*"[41]

By the end of the battle, the Germans had almost 700 guns in action. Having neutralized MacMahon's 550 cannon early in the day, they had turned their fire on the French infantry and cavalry for most of the battle. The disparity in casualties testified to the awful effectiveness of the Prussian guns: 3,000 French dead, 14,000 French wounded, and 21,000 French prisoners against a total of 9,000 German dead, wounded, and missing. Sedan was an altogether different battle from Gravelotte, where German and French casualties had been equal; here the French lost at the rate of four-to-one, an unsustainable ratio. Watching the slaughter with Bismarck and Moltke on the height of Frénois, the American observer Phil Sheridan wondered how Napoleon III would survive it: "Oh no," Bismarck chortled. "The old fox is too cunning to be caught in such a trap; he has doubtless slipped off to Paris."[42]

Far from it: having slipped the prince imperial over the border into Belgium in the last days of August, the "old fox" was now conferring individually with his generals in Sedan, first Douay, then Ducrot, and finally Lebrun. Ducrot and Lebrun stood around on the battlements outside the *Quartier Impérial*, pretending to study the fortress guns while they waited. Wimpffen, alone and determined to renew his breakout at Balan, wondered where his generals were. No one answered his orders. "That was wrong," Wimpffen later wrote. "I was the general-in-chief, yet the emperor annulled my authority."[43] By this time, 3:00 in the afternoon, it hardly mattered. Reading an urgent summons from Wimpffen to "cover the rear of the army" while waiting to see the emperor, General Douay wearily dictated his reply: "I have only three intact brigades, little ammunition, and no artillery." There would be no holding the Prussians in the rear, or anywhere.[44]

At the tip of the spear, General Lebrun's divisions were no better off. General Jules Grandchamp noted that the men of his 1st Division had passed the entire battle without ammunition: "We had fired off most of it on the 30th, soaked the rest when we crossed the Meuse on the 31st, and spent the 1st with empty pouches. The formalities required for replacements were too great, more proof of our military deficiencies."[45] Napoleon III simply ignored Wimpffen's request that he ride out and place himself at the head of the

41 Dresden, Sächsisches Kriegsarchiv (SKA), ZGS 158, Lt. Hinüber, "Tagebuch." BKA, HS 849, Capt. Girl, vol. 3, p. 68.
42 Philip H. Sheridan, *Personal Memoirs of P. H. Sheridan*, 2 vols., New York, 1888, vol. 2, pp. 402–3.
43 SHAT, Lc 2/3, 1871, "Bataille de Sedan: Documents historiques concernant le Gen. de Wimpffen."
44 SHAT, Lc 2/3, Sedan, 3 Sept. 1870, Gen. Douay, "Rapport sur la role du 7 Corps dans la bataille de Sedan."
45 SHAT, Lc 2/3, Sedan, 2 Sept. 1870, Gen. Grandchamp, "Rapport Sommaire."

Fig. 11. Bazeilles after the battle

last breakout attempt; he raised the white flag instead. Though it ground forward, scores of excited but misinformed French troops crying "the Emperor is leaving Sedan; he will lead us," Wimpffen's last thrust broke down on the outskirts of Bazeilles, which by now was a wasteland of burnt and smashed houses and dead bodies. Wimpffen looked east and saw "a wide open plain, completely devoid of enemy troops." He was either fibbing or hallucinating; the Prussian 8th Division had arrived to reinforce the Bavarians at precisely this spot.[46] A witness who toured the entire battlefield later testified that the thickest concentration of French dead was in the gardens between Sedan and Balan, where the artillery casualties lay in columns, whole companies killed by shellfire as they attacked toward Bazeilles and then retreated.[47] (One can visit the ossuary at Bazeilles today and see the bones and perforated skulls of these poor men, exposed in the French style for posterity.)

As Wimpffen rode back to Sedan among 2,000 broken stragglers – all that remained of his "breakout to Carignan" – Louis-Napoleon dispatched an

46 SKA, KA-Abg. Potsdam, Nr. P 967, Villers-Cernay, 2 Sept. 1870, Gen. Hzg. Georg von Sachsen to King. SHAT, Lc 2/3, 1871, "Bataille de Sedan: Documents historiques concernant le Gen. de Wimpffen."
47 BKA, HS 858, "Kriegstagebuch Prinz Leopold von Bayern."

adjutant under a white flag with a letter for the Prussian king. Flanked by Moltke and Bismarck, who only now learned that the Emperor of the French was with his troops, Wilhelm I directed his son, Crown Prince Friedrich Wilhelm, to read the letter aloud: "Having failed to die amongst my troops, there is nothing left for me to do but place my sword in the hands of Your Majesty." For a moment there was "a church-like silence" on the height, and then everyone crowded around the Prussian king, shouting congratulations.[48] In his usual businesslike way, Moltke ignored the hubbub, advised the king to grant the cease fire, then sidled away with Blumenthal to compose the next day's orders. Bismarck dictated the reply to the French emperor: "Regretting the circumstances you find yourself in, I accept the sword of Your Majesty and appoint General Moltke... to negotiate the capitulation of the army that has fought so bravely under your orders." Offered a flask of brandy by his nephew, Bismarck toasted all present in English– "here's to the unification of Germany" – and drained the entire bottle.[49]

Sedan was another victory for Moltke's operational art and Prussian tactics. It was, as an Austro-Hungarian officer later wrote, "an artillery battle *par excellence*." Departing conclusively from the Napoleonic tradition of "grand batteries" – gun lines laying down frontal fire – the Prussians had operated with devastating effectiveness in "artillery masses," mobile batteries formed by enterprising officers who converged on key points, annihilated them with cross fires, and then moved on with other masses. It was this speed, initiative, and efficiency of the Prussian artillery that explained its stunning success; 230 reserve guns came forward to join the *Zirkel-Schlacht* and crush the French under the fire of 700 overlapping cannon.[50] No less impressive than the battle's result was the way that it was cobbled together against all the fog and friction of war. Moltke had set his armies in motion, but exerted little control over the actual "*Einschliessung*" or "encirclement" of the French army. This had been achieved by German combat units that had pressed ahead, studying the progress and meaning of the battle at every step. Here there was need for judgment and discernment as the following account makes plain. The battle was not won on a plot table with pins and markers; it was wrested by one lethally armed group of exhausted men from another amid chaos and confusion:

> "I was with the commander of the the the left-wing battery at Illy in the afternoon; he was looking at the French through his telescope and kept shaking his head and muttering; finally he yelled to the nearest lieutenant: 'What the hell is that over there? Shells are exploding *behind* the French guns and they're not ours!'

48 BKA, HS 849, Capt. Girl, vol. 3, p. 72. Sheridan, vol. 2, pp. 404–5.
49 Howard, pp. 218–19.
50 Capt. Hugo von Molnár, "Über Artillerie Massenverwendung im Feldkriege," ÖMZ 1 (1880), pp. 296–308.

The lieutenant raised his telescope, looked for a while and then shouted back: 'And their right wing and center batteries are limbering up and retreating.' – 'What do you think that signifies?' – 'Fire from behind!' – 'But from whom?' Slowly it dawned on us: the Prussian Guard artillery, the right wing of the Meuse Army, was now firing from the east, creating a total encirclement of the French. Until this moment, we infantry officers and battery commanders on the front line had been unaware that we were part of an enveloping attack by two entire armies."[51]

Having named himself army commandant over MacMahon's wishes and Ducrot's objections, General Wimpffen now inherited the unpleasant job of negotiating an armistice with Moltke and Bismarck, two of the most un-sentimental operators in Europe.[52] To Wimpffen's demands for "honorable capitulation" – the men allowed to march away with arms, baggage, and full military honors – Moltke refused. With the French emperor among the pris-oners of war, Moltke considered that the French government "offered no prospect of stability" and would have to be disarmed until a final peace could be negotiated.[53] Bismarck agreed: "The fortune of battle has delivered to us the best soldiers, the best officers of the French army; voluntarily to set them free, to risk seeing them march against us again would be madness."[54] To Wimpffen's plea that "generous terms" would win the "gratitude" and good behavior of the French nation, Bismark shot back: "It is a mistake to count upon 'gratitude,' especially the 'gratitude' of a nation.... Over the past 200 years France has declared war on Prussia thirty times and ... you will do so again; for that we must be prepared, with ... a territorial *glacis* between you and us."[55] Bismarck was already formulating the Prussian demand for Alsace and Lorraine; Wimpffen had the distinct impression that "the Germans would not quit French soil without obtaining a cession of territory."[56] Were Wimpffen to renew the fight, Moltke warned, his bedraggled force of 80,000 would be pulverized by the concentrated fire of 250,000 troops and 700 guns. The Prussian *chef* produced a sketch of the Prussian battery positions and matter-of-factly advised Wimpffen that the bombardment would commence at 9:00 the next morning. While Wimpffen stared at the sketch – unaware that the German batteries had fired off all of their ammunition in the course of the day – his shoulders slumped and all the fight seemed to run out of him.

51 G. von Bismarck, p. 138.
52 SHAT, Lc 2/3, 1871, "Documents historiques concernant le Gen. de Wimpffen."
53 SHAT, Lc 2/3, Fays-les-Veneurs, 5 Sept. 1870, Gen. Wimpffen.
54 Howard, p. 221.
55 H. Sutherland Edwards, *The Germans in France*, London, 1873, pp. 129–32.
56 Gen. Julius Verdy du Vernois, *With the Royal Headquarters in 1870–71*, 2 vols., London, 1897, vol. 1, pp. 136–8. SHAT, Lc 2/3, Fays-les-Veneurs, 5 Sept. 1870, Gen. Wimpffen to Gen. Palikao.

"We French generals accept the Prussian terms unanimously," was his only comment.[57]

To shield himself from the entire odium of the harsh Prussian terms, Wimpffen insisted that all of his generals – Lebrun, Ducrot, Douay, Pierre Dejean, and Jules Forgeot – sign a note agreeing to Moltke's terms. This they did. Louis-Napoleon did not. He still had hopes for his dynasty; if he could only extricate the army from Moltke's grip and march on Paris to douse any revolutionary flames, he might yet wring acceptable terms from the Prussians and secure the throne for his son.[58] Rising early on 2 September, he rode out to Donchéry to appeal personally to King Wilhelm I for leniency. Bismarck intercepted the French emperor, steered him into the courtyard of an inn, sat him on a bench and berated him for a full hour. The Prussians would show no mercy aside from the usual surrender formalities. Witnesses who watched them from a respectful distance noted that Bismarck gesticulated passionately while the emperor slumped deeper into his seat. Moltke appeared and reiterated that the Army of Châlons must give itself up unconditionally. Napoleon III had been under the impression that Moltke had lifted the siege of Metz to reinforce his numbers at Sedan. He was now disabused of that notion, as well as another: that Bazaine had used the respite to free his army and deliver it to Empress Eugénie. "*Ja, dann ist alles verloren,*" the emperor mumbled in the German that he had learned in his boyhood exile. "Yes, quite right, all *is* really lost." Permitted finally to see the Prussian king, Napoleon III entered the room in his general's uniform, with tears streaming down his cheeks.[59] Behind him came his *maison militaire*: Princes Achille Murat and Edgar Ney and Generals Henri Castelnau and Charles Pajol. According to Waldersee, the Prussian king could scarcely contain his delight with Louis-Napoleon's predicament; Wilhelm I had a long memory, and regarded Sedan as "our Tilsit," a reference to the vindictive French-imposed treaty of 1807 that had annexed half of Prussia's territory and population.[60]

Two hours later, General Wimpffen signed the Prussian-dictated armistice in the Chateau de Bellevue, a hilltop industrialist's mansion halfway between Sedan and Donchéry. Only the French officers were paroled, the 20,000 French troops captured during the battle and the 80,000 fugitives around Sedan were transported to prison camps. It is difficult to convey just how shocking this was for contemporaries. An Austrian witness described the "sensation," calling Sedan "one of the most stunning events in history...."

57 Maj. Johann Nosinich, "Der Krieg 1870–71," ÖMZ 4 (1872), pp. 155–6. SHAT, Lc 2/3, Fays-les-Veneurs, 5 Sept. 1870, Gen. Wimpffen.
58 SHAT, Lc 2/3, 1871, "Bataille de Sedan: Documents historiques concernant le Gen. de Wimpffen."
59 Frederick III, p. 99.
60 Alfred von Waldersee, *Denkwürdigkeiten*, 3 vols., Berlin, 1922, vol. 1, pp. 93–4.

Fig. 12. Napoleon III and Bismarck meet at Donchéry

An army of 100,000 that had fought twenty victorious campaigns in every part of the world laid down its arms...costing France the premier world power position that it had gained over the years at the cost of thousands of its sons killed in battle."[61] In Paris, Prince Richard Metternich went to Empress Eugénie to offer his condolences and found her "crushed, sleepless, weeping with desperation."[62]

61 "Die Schlacht bei Sedan," ÖMZ3 (1872), p. 49.
62 Vienna, Haus-Hof-und Staatsarchiv (HHSA), PA IX, 96, Paris, 2 Sept. 1870, Metternich to Beust.

10

France on the Brink

Germany exulted at the news of Sedan. Berliners illuminated the Prussian capital and sang a *Te Deum* in the cathedral. The phrase "German Empire" reverberated in declarations from every German state to King Wilhelm I demanding Alsace-Lorraine, financial reparations, and "that which was denied us in 1815: an independent, united German Empire with secure frontiers." Newspapers and mayoral offices from the Black Forest to the Baltic bombarded Bismarck and the Prussian king with congratulatory reminders that Alsace and Lorraine were prerequisites for "security against French ambition and as a just reward for our *national* victory." No one in Germany wished to waste the splendid opportunity presented by MacMahon's defeat and Napoleon III's capture. A popular assembly in Stuttgart affirmed that Alsace and Lorraine – German until 1582 – had to be taken back to assure the land connection between north and south Germany.[1] Few dared speak against annexation, because any who condemned the planned seizure of Alsace-Lorraine were arrested, their newspapers seized at the printer. Bismarck's liberal gadfly, Johann Jacoby, was dragged kicking off a podium while speaking the following words: "How would the [Germans] of Posen and West Prussia approve of a victorious Poland were it to demand their annexation at the point of a bayonet?" Still, as Britain's ambassador in Berlin wryly noted, "Jacoby stands against the 40 million Germans who *want* Alsace-Lorraine. Bismarck has made a martyr needlessly."[2]

For thousands of French troops, the lacerating Prussian barrages of Sedan were just the start of their miseries. Moltke had taken 83,000 French prisoners on 1 September, which were far too many to be comfortably accommodated in

1   London, Public Record Office (PRO), FO 64, 691, Berlin, 3 and 10 Sept. 1870, Loftus to Granville.
2   PRO, FO 64, 692, Berlin, 1 Oct. 1870, Loftus to Granville.

a poor region already picked clean by the opposing armies. Instead of building a prison camp, the Germans simply herded the Army of Châlons POWs on to the "Iges peninsula," the spit of land west of Sedan that is bounded on three sides by the Meuse. Here the French were interned until transports to Germany could be arranged: 83,000 men and 10,000 horses on six square miles of grass and dirt. Even heavily armed German guards were reluctant to traverse the peninsula. A Prussian officer strolling past an Algerian unit was beaten to the ground and robbed. When not accosted by the prisoners, the Germans were as likely to be attacked by the famished French horses. Sleeping in the open near Iges, a German officer was awakened and nearly crushed by hungry horses trying to eat the bread in his pockets.

It was a picture of misery: the dispirited French troops reduced to "scum, rabble and vagabonds" by their predicament. The stench rising from tens of thousands of dirty, tired men was nothing beside that of the dying horses. Many horses perished of hunger or wounds; 3,000 were dispatched by a Bavarian battalion ordered to kill any that looked sickly. Instead of burying the carcasses, the Bavarians rolled them into the Meuse. The carrion washed up all along the peninsula, bloated and stinking in the summer heat.[3] Working day and night, it took the Germans six days to return the putrefying battlefield to a habitable condition. All the while, thousands of men from the Bavarian I Corps and the Prussian XI Corps were put to work retrieving the captured cannon and caissons, clearing away unexploded shells, and collecting the Chassepot rifles thrown down by the French in their panicky retreat. The Chassepots were stacked like firewood in piles of 1,000. Dozens of Germans and their French prisoners were killed accidentally, when loaded rifles thrown on to the stacks discharged.[4] As the hard work proceeded, even French officers who had vowed to share the hardships of their men slipped away to more salubrious climes. Though not free to return home, high-ranking French officers were permitted on their word of honor – "*parole*" – to make their own way to Colmar for internment. Fifty-two used the opportunity to escape, General Auguste Ducrot the most famous of the group. After giving his word to the Prussians, he rode to Pont-à-Mousson in a carriage before doubling back to Paris in the night.

News of Sedan reached Paris on 3 September. Indignant mobs formed as reports trickled in that Marshal MacMahon and Louis-Napoleon had surrendered their army. Doubting Palikao's improbable "Proclamation to the French People" – that the emperor with just 40,000 men had been ambushed by 300,000 Prussians – the crowds became bolder in the afternoon, looting shops, smashing Napoleonic emblems, and closing menacingly on government

3 G. von Bismarck, *Kriegserlebnisse 1866 und 1870–71*, Dessau, 1907, pp. 142–5.
4 Munich, Bayerisches Kriegsarchiv (BKA), HS 839, "Erinnerungen 1870–71 des Soldaten Josef Denk," pp. 3–5.

buildings. In an emergency session of the legislative body convened at 1 A.M. on the 4th, Jules Favre proposed the dethronement of the dynasty, the creation of a "provisional government," and General Louis Trochu's promotion to "governor of Paris." Few dissented, for most of the right-wing *mamelukes* had already begun to flee Paris. Bereft at the news of his son's death at Sedan, Count Palikao moved that the vote be postponed until midday. Returning to the Palais Bourbon at noon on the 4th, the deputies met with vast crowds along both banks of the Seine. The Place de la Concorde teemed with 60,000 men, women, and children, "a motley crowd in blouses and coarse woolen shirts," who shouted and shook their fists: "*Déchéance* – downfall! – Death to the Bonapartes! Long live the nation!" Though national guards ringed the legislative body and held the bridge across from the Place de la Concorde, the guards sympathized with the demonstrators and brazenly reversed their arms or placed their kepis over the muzzles of their rifles to signal fraternization before pushing into the legislative chamber with the excited mob. Inside the chamber, Léon Gambetta, the republican leader, tried to shoo away the invaders; they gruffly pushed past him and neared Favre, who shouted and gesticulated in vain: "Let there be no scenes of violence...union is essential...it is not yet time to proclaim the republic!" Stamping past Favre, the demonstrators streamed through the half-empty chamber. Some gaped at the rich furnishings, others seated themselves at the desks, doodled on the official stationery, or simply rested their rifles on the floor and chanted for the republic.[5]

Gambetta and Favre, reasonable men who understood that the radicalism of Paris and the industrial centers had somehow to be squared with the conservatism of France's peasant villages and middle-class towns, were appalled. The special session of the legislative body had been convened to form a broad-based "provisional government" that would serve "until a constituent assembly" could be summoned from the provinces. Moderation was required, but the plan shattered when the revolutionary mob stamped through the Palais Bourbon, driving what moderates and conservatives remained inside to the exits. Gambetta and Favre now had little choice but to join the revolutionary procession back across the Seine to the Hôtel de Ville, where French republics were traditionally proclaimed from the balcony.

Not the broad-based movement desired by the republican leaders, the provisional government was little more than the pre-war republican delegation from Paris, a small political faction atop a vast country that was not very republican at all. Gambetta became minister of the interior, Favre minister of foreign affairs, Ernest Picard minister of finance, Jules Simon minister of education, Emile Kératry prefect of police. The navy and war portfolios

---

5   Washington, DC, National Archives (NA), CIS, U.S. Serial Set, 1780, Paris, 5 Sept. 1870, Washburne to Fish.

were given to the least imposing military men: Admiral Martin Fourichon and General Adolphe Leflô. Sixty-one year-old Fourichon, commander of the Mediterranean Fleet at the start of the war, had operated in a reassuringly passive way and would cause Paris no problems. Leflô, a sixty-six-year-old pensioner, had not seen action since the 1840s. Loyal to the republic in 1852, he had been arrested along with the other "republican generals" – Changarnier, Cavaignac, and Lamoricière – briefly imprisoned at Ham, and then exiled to the island of Jersey by Napoleon III. His reinstatement after Sedan hardly inspired confidence: "For eighteen years he has not been employed, which is bad preparation for office at such a moment," was the British military attaché's understatement. "But I suppose it was difficult to get anyone else."[6] General Louis Trochu, the pre-war Cassandra admired by parliamentary liberals, sat uneasily atop this new government as president and military governor.

While the Parisian workers surged around the Hôtel de Ville applauding their new republic, a delegation of deputies visited Empress Eugénie in the Tuileries and urged her to abdicate at once. All of the other Bonapartes had already fled abroad: Napoleon III taken by force to the *Schloss* at Wilhelmshöhe in Kassel, the prince imperial to Hastings, Princess Mathilde to Brussels, and Prince Jerôme to Florence. At first Eugénie refused to step down, but agreed when the violence outside mounted and mutinous national guards closed on the imperial palace. Entrusting her jewels to Princess Pauline Metternich, she fled through the Louvre picture galleries with a single lady-in-waiting. Veiled and sunk in the backseat of a hackney coach, she drove fearfully around Paris until she found temporary refuge at her dentist's house in the Avenue de l'Impératrice. She then slipped out of Paris early on 5 September. Her traveling companions later recorded that she passed much of the jolting thirty-six-hour carriage ride to Deauville just like the madwoman she was pretending to be, railing for the most part against General Trochu, who had deftly switched sides and joined the opposition the instant the republic was proclaimed.[7]

The new, post-Napoleonic "Government of National Defense" immediately split into moderate and radical factions, a condition that would complicate French military operations and armistice negotiations in the months ahead. Whereas moderates were for a prompt peace with the Prussians and a return to normalcy, radicals – impelled by the poor quarters of Paris, which viewed the war as a struggle between proletarian virtue and thieving monarchy – were for a "maximum war" (*"guerre à outrance"*) that would bleed the Germans and eject them from France at *any* cost. Favre tried to balance the factions with cumbersome rhetoric. "The dilemma of a republic," he wrote on 8 September, is that "its actions cannot be truly free unless they are devoted, fearless, and moderate, taking as their watchword the love of labor and

6 PRO, FO 27, 1814, Paris, 6 Sept. 1870, Claremont to Lyons.
7 Rupert Christiansen, *Paris Babylon*, New York, 1994, pp. 155–61.

respect for the right of all."[8] Harmless in America perhaps, such words were anathema in Red Paris, which saw the collapse of the Second Empire as the moment to abolish "moderation" and "the rights of all" in order to collectivize property and found a totalitarian state devoted to the interests of the proletariat. Having initially planned to abolish the hated Prefecture of Police, which had persecuted republicans under the empire, Trochu and Gambetta found that they needed it more than ever to curb the most incorrigible "reds," men like Auguste Blanqui, Félix Pyat, Gustave Flourens, and Théodore Sappia, who commanded the proletarian districts and called for "insurrection" and "terror" against the moderate Trochu-Gambetta regime. The "reds" rejected multiparty democracy and capitalism and demanded "*la Commune*": A new order of shared wealth and property in which the oppressive state would gradually wither away, replaced by local "communal" governments.

General Trochu quailed in his boots. In an unguarded conversation with the British military attaché in September 1870, he allowed that Paris was demoralized, his army all but useless, and the "lower classes only bent on pillage."[9] Parisian units were dangerously split between adherents of the commune and the republic; some battalions shouted "*vive la Commune*," others "*vive la République, pas de Commune!*"[10] In early October, Trochu was forced to depose Jacques Mottu, mayor of the eleventh arrondisement, who had not only removed crucifixes from schools and hospitals but actually forbidden church-going in his district. (Mottu was notorious for having evicted nuns from a convent, lewdly enjoining them to "stop loving Christ and start loving men, to produce sons for the republic.") On 8 October, Gustave Flourens attempted a communist coup, marching to the Hôtel de Ville with several hundred armed *communards*. Although Flourens's so-called *révolutionette* was crushed by troops loyal to Trochu, it drove a bloody wedge between Paris and the heartland, and more than ever convinced peasants of the truth of Marshal Bugeaud's folksy aphorism: "*Les majorités sont tenues à plus de modération que les minoritiés*" – "majorities are more inclined to moderation than minorities."[11]

In the Prussian camp, King Wilhelm I meanwhile sought to tamp down the exhilaration felt by his victorious officers. Addressing them after Sedan, he pointed out that "there is much bloody work ahead of us."[12] There would indeed be bloody work if the two sides could not agree upon peace terms. Having expected that Napoleon III would conclude a quick armistice after

8   NA, CIS, U.S. Serial Set 1780, Paris, 8 Sept. 1870, Favre to Washburne.
9   PRO, FO 27, 1814, Paris, 7 Sept. 1870, Claremont to Lyons.
10 PRO, FO 27, 1818, Paris, 9 Oct. 1870, Wodehouse to Granville.
11 Vienna, Haus-Hof-und Staatsarchiv (HHSA), PA IX, 96, Paris, 9 and 20 Oct. 1870, Hübner to Metternich. Louis Trochu, *L'Armée Française en 1867*, Paris, 1870, p. viii. F. Maurice, *The Franco-German War 1870–71*, orig. 1899, London, 1914, p. 290.
12 Alfred von Waldersee, *Denkwürdigkeiten*, 3 vols., Berlin, 1922, vol. 1, p. 93.

Fig. 13. French *gardes mobiles* in Paris

Sedan, Bismarck's hopes had been dashed by the revolution in Paris and the French emperor's own listlessness. In the days after Sedan, Prussian envoys met with the French and demanded a large cash indemnity as well as the cession of Alsace and Lorraine. All parties in France rejected the terms, insisting that any armistice be forged "on the basis of territorial integrity." France, in other words, would pay reparations for starting the war, but would, in Jules Favre's famous phrase, "cede neither a clod of our earth nor a stone of our fortresses."[13]

This intransigent attitude explained the frank disappointment expressed by Moltke and Bismarck at the capture of Napoleon III. A week before Sedan, Moltke and the chancellor had characterized such an eventuality as merely "embarrassing." They now saw that it was much worse than that. The emperor's capture and the ensuing revolt in Paris meant that there was no credible government to negotiate with. Major Gustav Fleschuez, a Bavarian staff officer who slept in the palace at Sedan occupied by Bismarck after the battle, was unexpectedly treated to an impromptu interview on the progress of the war with the most famous statesman in Europe. "Should we consider the war at

13 PRO, FO 425, 97, 120A, Paris, 6 Sept. 1870, Lyons to Granville.

an end with the capture of the French emperor?" Fleschuez asked Bismarck as he packed his things on 2 September. Bismarck, who was moving into Fleschuez's rooms, puffed thoughtfully on a cheroot before answering that the war would not end until "there is a government in Paris capable of conducting negotiations. Until such a government arises, we must continue our march on the capital." To American General Phil Sheridan, Bismarck confided that he would like to locate the fourteen-year-year-old prince imperial – by now safely ensconced in England – and place him on the French throne "under German influences."[14]

To end the war, the victors of Sedan closed relentlessly on Paris. Moltke moved his headquarters to Château Thierry on 15 September, to Ferrières four days later. General Sheridan marveled at the unquenchable thirst of the German troops for French wine: "Almost every foot of the way was strewn with fragments of glass from the wine bottles, emptied and then broken by the troops... The road was literally paved with glass and the amount of wine consumed (none was wasted) must have been enormous.... All the way down from Sedan there were two almost continuous lines of broken bottles along the roadsides."[15] To remove at least part of the new republican government from the German pincers that were weaving happily toward Paris, Gambetta dispatched Jules Favre and a "government delegation" to Tours on 13 September. Were Paris to be completely cut off, Favre and his ministers could organize the *guerre à outrance* from behind the Loire. The precaution justified itself several days later, when the Meuse Army, spreading along the right bank of the Seine, and the Third Army, arriving on the left, joined hands at St. Germain-en-Laye to cut Paris off from its hinterland.

German infantry struggling up the wet roads from the east never forgot their first glimpses of, as one put it, "the great world metropolis, its towers and domes, Notre Dame, the Arc de Triomphe!"[16] Paris would be a tough nut to crack, even for seasoned, confident German troops. The city of 2 million harbored a garrison of 400,000 troops and was ringed by powerful suburban forts sited on the limestone bluffs around the capital. Every approach to the city was barred by fortresses that bristled with 1,300 guns and commanded a sixty-mile circle around the city. The circle itself was four miles deep, every house, village, and road placed in a state of defense with clear fields of fire, stockades, entanglements, and loopholed walls and buildings. Though French discipline was lamentable – less than one-fifth of the French garrison were regulars or reservists, the rest *mobiles* and national guards – the well-placed

14 BKA, HS 846, Maj. Gustav Fleschuez. BKA, HS 858, "Kriegstagebuch, Leopold Prinz von Bayern." Philip H. Sheridan, *Personal Memoirs of P. H. Sheridan*, 2 vols., New York, 1888, vol. 2, p. 414.
15 Sheridan, vol. 2, pp. 421–2.
16 Dresden, Sächsisches Kriegsarchiv (SKA), ZGS 158, Lt. Hinüber, 19 Sept. 1870.

French guns, each supplied with 450 shells, initially balanced these defects. In September and October, French gunners had so much ammunition that whole batteries would open fire on single German sentries, sending them sprawling into their trenches under gouts of exploding earth.[17]

In theory, Moltke's position was untenable; he had little more than half the troops available to Trochu and had somehow to feed and clothe 240,000 men at the end of long, vulnerable supply lines. Operational art dictated that his besieging army be at least two or three times larger than Trochu's defending force, but in this case the ratio was reversed, augmenting Trochu's already considerable advantage of interior lines.[18] Using the element of surprise, Trochu could mass in the night opposite isolated points on the thin German line and strike them at dawn with overwhelming strength. To cause the German besiegers maximum difficulty, Trochu had ordered the destruction of all roads, canals, bridges, and railways out to a distance of fifty miles. Closer in, he had devastated the land by burning farms, razing villages, and slaughtering livestock to deny the Germans food and shelter. He even ordered the great forests of Paris burnt down, including the Bois de Boulogne, St. Cloud, and Versailles.[19] "You cannot imagine the waste and destruction of the villages around Paris," a Saxon officer wrote home in late September. "Everything demolished, cabinets smashed, beds carried away, the most gorgeous mirrors and furniture destroyed. Who has done this? Not the Prussians or the Saxons, but the French themselves. Here the inhabitants fear their own [troops] far more than us."[20] But the French had done their work well. Without ready supplies of food, forage, or fuel, the Germans would now have to dedicate precious rolling stock to rations and building materials, giving Trochu's ragtag army more time to improve the defenses of Paris.

Even if Bazaine surrendered at Metz, the Germans would never amass enough men and supplies for a complete and close investment of Paris. They would have to content themselves with cutting the flow of men and supplies to Paris, no mean feat in the rolling, partially forested ground around the capital, which was a perfect sanctuary for smugglers and a new class of soldier called the *franc-tireur*, a French deserter or civilian who took up arms to obstruct the German advance or plunder the same crops and homes needed to sustain the German army. By mid-September the *francs-tireurs* were buzzing around Paris, ambushing German patrols in the woods and sniping from

17 PRO, FO 425, 98, 188, Paris, 31 Oct. 1870, Claremont to Lyons. FO 64, 703, Versailles, 26 Oct. 1870, Capt. Henry Hozier.
18 Gen. H. A. Leer, "Über den Krieg 1870–71," *Österreichische Militärische Zeitschrift* (ÖMZ) 4 (1874), p. 45.
19 NA, CIS, U.S. Ser. Set 1789, Bismarck to Washburne, Versailles, 29 Oct. 1870. SKA, Abg. Potsdam, Nr. P967, Tremblay, 22 Sept. 1870, Prince Albert to King Johann. PRO, FO 27, 1815, Paris, 9 Sept. 1870, Claremont to Lyons.
20 SKA, KA, ZGS 72, Livry, 21 Sept. 1870, " Briefe Adolf Flies."

villages. Worried German mothers demanded that their conscript sons be shielded against "evil people wielding knives, bombs and poison."[21] Deeming the *francs-tireurs* criminals not soldiers, the Germans dealt harshly with every incident. When a Saxon officer was killed on the road near Beauvais, his headquarters forced the town to pay 400,000 francs reparations, about $40,000 today. When a Prussian patrol took fire from Héricourt, an uhlan squadron charged into the village and burned it to the ground.[22]

While engaged in this dirty war with the *francs-tireurs*, the overextended Germans also had to defend against breakouts by Trochu's garrison or break-ins by the reserve armies forming on the Loire.[23] An unintended consequence of France's slow mobilization was that *Garde Mobile* units called by the emperor on 31 August were only beginning to assemble in late September. Though largely untrained – troops of the 85th *Mobile* Regiment took only three practice shots before marching into battle – these thousands of men arrived late enough to avoid the envelopments at Metz and Sedan.[24] General Joseph La Motterouge found himself with 60,000 new recruits at Bourges; General Gabriel had 60,000 more at Belfort. If these "armies of the south" ever pulled themselves together, they could strike into Moltke's rear and cut his principal line of supply: the railway from Nancy to Paris via Toul, Châlons, and Meaux.[25] It was in this rather desperate climate, forgotten in hindsight, that Bismarck vowed to bombard the French capital if it did not submit. Krupp had invented a short, fifteen-centimeter rifled howitzer, whose indirect breeching fire had smashed down the walls of Strasbourg and forced its surrender in late September. It would do far worse to densely populated Paris, if it came to that.

The closer he came to Paris, the more Bismarck worried about the looming investment, for time was running out. Every day conceded to the French improved their defenses and eroded Prussia's international standing. Neutral powers that had predicted a long and inconclusive Franco-Prussian war now gaped at the speed and depth of Moltke's advance. In Florence, Italy's foreign minister treated the British ambassador to a rare emotional outburst: "Germany must be stopped! A united Germany with 60 million people and France annihilated? What will become of the balance of power?"[26] Although Bismarck had bought Tsar Alexander II's complicity by promising to help restore his naval access to the Black Sea and Mediterranean (cut off by the

21 SKA, ZGS 158, Lt. Hinüber, "Tagebuch," 12 Oct. 1870.
22 Paul Bauriedel, *Meine Erlebnisse während des Feldzuges im Jahre 1870-71*, Nuremberg, 1895, p. 63. SKA, KA, P 967, Vert galant, 23 Oct. 1870, Duke Georg to King Johann.
23 PRO, FO 64, 694, Berlin, 12 Nov. 1870, Loftus to Granville.
24 Vincennes, Service Historique de l'Armée de Terre (SHAT), Le 19, Auch, 18 Aug. 1871, Lt. Col. P. Taberne, "Rapport historique sur les opérations du 85e Regt. de Mobiles."
25 PRO, FO 27, 1817, Tours, 6 Oct. 1870, Lyons to Granville.
26 PRO, FO 425, 97, Florence, 2 Sept. 1870, A. Paget to Granville.

treaties ending the Crimean War), other powers were less biddable. King Vittorio Emanuele II of Italy was clearly tempted by French offers of Papal Rome – withheld from Italy by a French garrison – as well as Nice and Corsica in return for military assistance against Prussia.[27] Shrewd French politicians also concocted a "red scare" to entice a friendly intervention. Adolphe Thiers warned foreign ambassadors on 8 September that if the "moderate provisional government" collapsed because of further defeats or a harsh peace, "a violent red republic would install itself in France, with revolutionary propaganda and principles subversive of society." France, in other words, might fall like a domino in a revolutionary chain reaction emanating from the gritty *faubourgs* of Paris. (Europe took the warning seriously, only the U.S. and Spain according diplomatic recognition to the new republic in its early days.) Four days later, Thiers departed to put France's case directly to the European capitals; his first stop was London, then St. Petersburg, and finally Vienna. "A weak and irritable France," Thiers warned the powers, "unable to assist... but ready for every occasion to recover her lost prestige," would undermine the peace of Europe. In Paris, Victor Hugo threw his literary reputation behind Thiers's diplomatic offensive, informing "humanity (*le genre humain*) and the civilized states" of their "duty to save the French republic."[28]

Apprised of Bismarck's diplomatic plight and his reputation as a realist inclined to end wars with a minimum of fuss, Favre dug in his heels. "Bismarck will not take a province," he confided to an Austrian diplomat in early September, "for that would make a durable peace impossible." In meetings at Ferrières, a sumptuous Rothschild *château* where Prussian great headquarters had moved after Sedan, Favre offered instead "an indemnity of several billions and a fraction of the French fleet," but "not a piece of territory." Bismarck coldly rejected the offer, Favre discovering something unexpected: the usually level-headed Bismarck lost his composure when the subject was France, a country that the German chancellor held responsible for all of Germany's miseries since the seventeenth century. Bismarck angrily reminded Favre of the successive pillage and annexations of Richelieu, Louis XIV, and Napoleon Bonaparte. France would now be forced to pay for its past arrogance and depredations. "Bismarck is as crazed as the king and his entourage," Favre stammered after a conference at Ferrières. "All I get from him is hardness and inflexibility."[29]

Determined to wring a final settlement from the French before a "league of neutrals" coalesced against him, Bismarck moved to create a more cooperative

27 PRO, FO 27, 1815, Paris, 10 Sept. 1870, Lyons to Granville. FO 27, 1817, Tours, 6 Oct. 1870, Lyons to Granville. FO 425, 98, 259, Therapia, 15 Dec. 1870, Elliot to Granville.
28 SHAT, Le 19, Paris, 22 Sept. 1870, "Proclamation de Victor Hugo." PRO, FO 425, 142, Paris, 8 Sept. 1870, Lyons to Granville. FO 425, 183, London, 13 Sept. 1870, Granville to Lyons.
29 HHSA, PA IX, 96, Paris, "Briefe des Raphael Hübner aus Paris an Fürsten Metternich," Sept. 1870, Hübner to Metternich.

French government. When Favre refused to cede Metz and Strasbourg despite the advance of two Prussian armies on Paris, Bismarck threatened to unleash Marshal Bazaine and Napoleon III against the Provisional Government. The gambit had been painstakingly prepared, Napoleon III held not as a prisoner of war after Sedan, but as a "visiting monarch" in the days after his arrival at Schloss Wilhelmshöhe in Kassel, a little north German state annexed by the Prussians in 1866. Wilhelmshöhe had been thoughtfully stocked with the best wines and food and entrusted not to Prussian troops but to six-foot French guardsmen captured at Sedan and transported to the Schloss as a face-saving imperial guard. Bismarck, in short, was dangling the bloated, worn-out emperor over the republic's head, calling Napoleon III "the legitimate ruler of France" and dismissing Gambetta's new republic as no more than "*un coup de parti*" – "a partisan coup."[30] Returning from meetings with Bismarck at Ferrières on 13–14 September, a British embassy official reported that Bismarck had announced his decision to treat Napoleon III as the legal ruler of French provinces under Prussian occupation and had threatened to wield Bazaine and the navy against Favre's republic: "Does Marshal Bazaine recognize the present government? Does the fleet?" To Favre's efforts to speak for the army, Bismarck interrupted: "Will the troops at Metz recognize arrangements which might be entered into by you?"[31] Bismarck was plainly up to something, a plot detected by the British embassy:

> "Prussia has another string to her bow. Marshal Bazaine might find that it suits his purpose to stand fast by the Emperor. Then, if the Emperor were willing to make peace on the Prussian terms, Prussia would assist him to regain his throne with the aid of Bazaine and the 140,000 French troops now prisoners in Germany."[32]

News of Sedan reached Metz in a curious way. Lookouts around the fortress reported long lines of troops marching eastward across the Moselle on 6 September, from the left bank to the right. Bazaine exulted; the Prussians were on the run! But then the troops were observed to be unarmed, and French. Indeed they were prisoners of the Army of Châlons marching to Germany. Some were set free to accompany Prussian *parlamentaires* into Metz with the demoralizing news. At first, none of Bazaine's troopers believed the reports: that the emperor was a prisoner, that their "relief army" was no more. As night fell, however, they heard the raucous celebrations in the Prussian camps on both banks of the Moselle: music, hymns, hurrahs, and crackling bonfires. For the Prussians, the fires took the edge off of a cold, driving rain. For the French, who were now rationing everything including wood, there

30 PRO, FO 64, 691, Berlin, 3 and 16 Sept. 1870, Loftus to Granville. Eberhard Kolb, *Der Weg aus dem Krieg*, Munich, 1989, pp. 222–3, 308–12.
31 PRO, FO 425, 97, 181, London, 13 Sept. 1870, Granville to Lyons.
32 PRO, FO 27, 1816, Paris, 16 Sept. 1870, Lyons to Granville.

Fig. 14. Inside Fort St.-Julien, Metz

were no fires. Instead, the men huddled under canvas, or in the open, listening to the growling of their stomachs.

Famine now haunted everyone in Metz, where rations had been severely cut since 4 September. When oats and hay for the horses ran out, Bazaine gave the stupefying order to feed wheat to the animals, consuming the army's entire bread supply in a single day of ravenous munching.[33] Men now had to subsist on just 350 grams of unsalted horsemeat and a quarter-liter of wine daily. At first, only work horses were requisitioned, then, on 9 September, Bazaine began eating up the cavalry too. After canceling a planned breakout on the right bank by Leboeuf, Canrobert, and Frossard – the excuse this time was the "preponderance" of the numerically weaker Prussian force – Bazaine ordered each cavalry and artillery regiment and every engineering company to cull forty horses for slaughter. By 20 September, half of the army's horses had been butchered.[34] On 23 September, 200 famished French soldiers were

33 SHAT, Lt 12, Metz, 31 Oct. 1870, Maj. F.A. Léveillé.
34 SHAT, Lb 14, Gen. Manèque, "Projets d'opérations de détail ajournées ou executés." Charles Fay, *Journal d'un Officier de l'Armée du Rhin*, Paris, 1889, pp. 171–3. Joseph Andlau, *Metz*, Paris, 1872, p. 190.

killed when they attempted to push back Prussian outposts on the right bank to gather potatoes.

Hungry and immobilized, Bazaine dispatched two 40,000-man foraging parties along both banks of the Moselle on 7 October. Firing down measured, marked ranges, the Prussian guns blew the French wagons off the road and the Prussian infantry, standing in their trenches with Chassepots captured at Sedan, opened a rapid, biting fire at distances unimaginable with the needle rifle. Two thousand French troops fell dead or wounded in this *"opération de fourrage."* Others were observed scouring villages for food and forage, eating whatever they could find and stuffing their tunics and filling their arms with hay and straw before retiring.[35] The Prussians made no effort to pursue. They were not besieging Metz, merely investing it and waiting for French supplies to run out. French skirmishers who had ventured too far forward were swept up by Prussian *uhlans* and taken to headquarters for questioning. "Thin and feeble," the French prisoners spoke of a starved, vitiated garrison sickened by a steady diet of horsemeat and foul Moselle water.[36]

His freedom of action slipping away, Bazaine, who had let an entire week pass after Sedan before convoking his first council of war, summoned his generals a second time on 10 October "to decide what to do with the army." Bazaine opened the meeting "in somber tones," explaining that he was not in contact with Paris, had no hope of a relief army, and had rations for no more than ten days, when the last horses would be slaughtered. The Metz commandant, General Grégoire Coffinières, always as pessimistic as Bazaine, nodded eagerly throughout what amounted to a funeral oration. There were now 19,000 sick and wounded in the city's hospitals; typhus and smallpox were spreading; *"Metz l'invincible"* was dying. It would be best to do nothing more. Bazaine's generals, by now "habituated to submission" as an onlooker put it, nodded their assent. On the fortress's periphery, French infantrymen were not even bothering to fire at the Prussians lest they draw return fire. Convoys of Prussian food and drink were rolling unharmed through French fields of fire to feed the investing troops.[37] Stretching to make a virtue of this "regrettable indifference," Bazaine concluded that the army was actually performing a vital service: immobilizing 200,000 Prussian troops while "new forces organized in the interior" of France.[38]

After his failed breakout on 31 August, Bazaine's military situation had lurched from bad to hopeless. Reinforced with fresh drafts of manpower from Germany, Prince Friedrich Karl now deployed four corps with 300 guns on the left bank of the Moselle and three corps with 288 guns on the right. All

35 Adolf Matthias, *Meine Kriegserinnerungen*, Munich, 1912, pp. 52–4.
36 PRO, FO 64, 703, near Metz, 9 Oct. 1870, Capt. Henry Hozier to Granville.
37 SHAT, Lt12, Ban. St. Martin, 22 Sept. 1870, Marshal Bazaine to Gen. Frossard.
38 SHAT, Lt12, 28 Feb. 1872, "Déposition de Gen. Bourbaki." Andlau, pp. 277–80, 290, 295.

of the German troops were posted in trenches just beyond the range of the French fortress guns, ready to turn back any French escape attempt.[39] Bazaine now had little room for maneuver, even had he wanted it. He apparently did not. Chairing the first post-Sedan council of war on 12 September, he had announced that there would be no more "grand sorties," only "little operations" to harass the enemy and gather food. "You will all understand that I am driven to this course by the need to avoid the fate that has befallen Marshal MacMahon."[40]

Others suspected more nefarious motives: Bazaine's natural hesitancy augmented by political ambitions. Had Napoleon III survived Sedan, Bazaine would have held the emperor's last army and a winning hand in his rivalry with MacMahon. The emperor's capture and Gambetta's proclamation of the republic had ruined everything. Whereas Bazaine, with Bismarck's blessing, might have emerged from Metz to head a French reconstruction under the emperor or his son, he had no future with the republicans, who had attacked him bitterly during the "Mexican adventure." Moreoever, Bazaine was offended by Gambetta's selection of Trochu to head the Government of National Defense. Trochu had written stinging critiques of Bazaine's military operations in Mexico, widening the rift between Bazaine and the Bonapartes. Colonel Joseph Andlau, one of Bazaine's colleagues, recalled that "everyone at Metz knew of Bazaine's loathing for Trochu; he spoke openly of this, saying that he was personally insulted by the new government." In Andlau's judgment, Bazaine "was motivated by a mixture of rivalry in the present and frustration with the past, by hostility for the republic, but also by the pain of his own shattered hopes and thwarted ambitions."[41]

Andlau, no friend of Bazaine, may have been laying it on thick, but the marshal was unquestionably up to something. Throughout September and October, he pointedly withheld recognition of the Government of National Defense and continued to issue orders and administer military justice "in the name of the Imperial Government."[42] By early October, Gambetta, who had escaped Paris in a balloon on 8 October to infuse new energy into the Government Delegation at Tours, was anxious. Bazaine was treating separately with Bismarck, and the ancient strongholds of the Legitimist and Orleanist parties in Perigord, Saintonge, and Limousin were bubbling with intrigue. Comte de Chambord, the Bourbon pretender known as "Henri V," had moved to the Swiss border and enjoined his countrymen to abandon their "shattered political institutions and return to the way traced by Providence," a Bourbon restoration. The less hidebound Orleanists were even stronger; stunned by

39 PRO, FO 64, 703, near Metz, 9 Oct. 1870, Capt. Henry Hozier to Granville.
40 Andlau, p. 205.
41 Andlau, p. 196.
42 PRO, FO 425, 14, Tours, 18 Oct. 1870, Lyons to Granville.

the unexpected proclamation of the republic after Sedan, Orleanist politicians like Adolphe Thiers extended their reach in the officer corps and the provincial towns and villages and waited expectantly for the "popular backlash to the failure of the Defense Government and the excesses of the Red Party."[43] Although the republic had been proclaimed in Metz as elsewhere in France, Bazaine was stubbornly withholding his endorsement.[44] By mid-October, word came that the marshal was about to sign a separate peace with the Prussians, not for a Bonapartist restoration, "but for his own dictatorship." Queried by London, Britain's ambassador in Berlin fleshed out the rumor: "It would appear that Bazaine does not recognize the authority of the Provisional Government, and that he considers himself equally entitled with them to treat in the name of France."[45]

Indeed Bazaine did: In September and October 1870, Bazaine involved himself in two Bismarckian plots to restore an authoritarian government to France that would accept and enforce Prussia's hard peace terms. Bismarck sent "Regnier," a Prussian agent, into Metz on 23 September to strike a deal with Bazaine. Though Regnier and Bazaine met privately – refusing to admit any other generals to their talks and expelling Marshal Leboeuf when he barged into the room – French officers in Metz later reconstructed the gist of their meeting from Bazaine's offhand remarks and Regnier's revelations. The deal Bismarck offered was this: the Army of the Rhine would be allowed to leave Metz with its arms and baggage and repair to a "neutralized zone," where the deputies of the pre-revolutionary French senate and legislative body would convoke to reconstitute a conservative French government and ratify the peace terms agreed between Bismarck and Bazaine, who would then "reestablish order in France and force acceptance of the new government," whether a restored empire of the prince imperial or an authoritarian regency headed by Bazaine himself. Bismarck called this latter option the "*Dictature Bazaine.*" It would serve as a rubber stamp for Prussian war aims.

André Tachard, who spied on Metz for Gambetta, reported from "a sure source" that Bismarck had declared himself willing to forgo Alsace-Lorraine and content himself with five billion francs and the demolition of France's eastern forts if only France would restore the Bonapartes or some other royal house: "If France persists in wanting the republic, which would be a bad neighbor for Germany, we will persist with our territorial demands."[46] For a

---

43 PRO, FO 27, 1818, Tours, 14 Oct. 1870, Lyons to Granville. FO 425, 98, 59, Tours, 20 Oct. 1870, "Report by Mr. West on the prospects of the Orleanist and Legitimist parties in France."
44 SHAT, Lt12, Brussels, 30 Sept. 1870, Tachard to Favre.
45 PRO, FO 425, 383 and 284 and 74, Tours, 20 Oct. 1870, Lyons to Granville. Berlin, 25 Oct. 1870, Loftus to Granville.
46 SHAT, Lt12, Brussels, 30 Sept. and 3, 7, and 8 Oct. 1870, Tachard to Favre. Andlau, pp. 224–31, 236–7. Edmond Ruby and Jean Regnault, *Bazaine: Coupable ou victime?*, Paris, 1960, pp. 227–8.

few taut days in late September, Bazaine seemed to hold the future of France in his hands. Not quite committing himself to Bismarck, he was not rebuffing him either. "Bazaine is impenetrable," Tachard noted. "He promises nothing, but he *listens*" – "*il n'ait rien promis. Il écoute.*"[47]

But time was slipping away for the marshal, whose hungry army was a wasting asset. After his meeting with Regnier, Bazaine rode to the headquarters of General Charles Bourbaki, commander of the Guard Corps, who agreed to carry Bismarck's proposal of a Bazaine regency on behalf of the prince imperial to Empress Eugénie in exile at Hastings with Prince Louis. Disguised as a provincial doctor and escorted by Regnier, Bourbaki slipped through the Prussian lines around Metz, later admitting that "the facility with which he passed the German lines gave him reason to suspect connivance on the part of the German military authorities." Once clear of Metz, Bourbaki found seats, carriages, and even a special train reserved to speed him to Ostend. Before embarking for England, Regnier gave Bourbaki a false passport to conceal the affair from the British press. Tucked inside was "a report of a conversation with Bismarck on the importance of re-establishing the Imperial Government and the mode of doing so."[48]

Bourbaki's mission fizzled. Rubbed raw by her narrow escape from Paris and unwilling to serve the ambitions of Bazaine, Eugénie consented only to name Bazaine "*Lieutenant-Général de l'Empire.*"[49] The two were playing a waiting game. She might need him, and he might need her. Although each despised the other, neither was ready for a definitive break. Determined to make some use of his army before it starved, Bazaine opened the second round of negotiations with Bismarck on 12 October, dispatching his aide-de-camp to negotiate directly with the Prussians. General Napoléon Boyer arrived at Versailles – where Prussian great headquarters had moved from Ferrières – on the 14th, affirming that "the army in Metz remained faithful to the emperor and would have nothing to do with the republic of Parisian lawyers."[50] What Boyer proposed was this: If released from Metz, the Army of the Rhine would withdraw deep into southern France or even Algeria, permitting the Prussians to focus their attacks on Paris and win the war quickly. Once the republic was beaten, the Prussians would hand France over to Bazaine's army, which, reinforced by 140,000 French prisoners of war from German camps, would return to finish off the "demagogic anarchy" unleashed by Gambetta and restore conservative government.

47 SHAT, Lt12, Brussels, 30 Sept. and 3 Oct. 1870, Tachard to Favre.
48 PRO, FO 425, 97, 312, Brussels, 9 Oct. 1870, Lumley to Granville. 375, London, 19 Oct. 1870, Granville to Lyons. SHAT, Lt12, 28 Feb. 1872, "Déposition de Gen. Bourbaki."
49 Frederick III, *The War Diary of the Emperor Frederick III 1870–71*, New York, 1927, p. 171.
50 Moritz Busch, *Bismarck: Some secret pages of his history*, 2 vols, New York, 1898, vol. 1, pp. 188–9.

Boyer's proposals were stamped all over with Marshal Bazaine's diffident, rather devious personality. Holding himself aloof in Toulouse or Algiers, the marshal would let the Germans do his dirty work, and then arrive as a "savior," claiming that he had been forced by the "red revolution" to step aside with his army in the country's hour of need.[51] For the republicans in Paris and Tours, Bazaine's "military pronunciamento" – reported in the German press throughout October but suppressed in the French papers – was a supreme crisis.[52] Why were Bazaine's troops negotiating with the Germans instead of breaking out? Bazaine was brazenly going over the new government's head, plotting to destroy the republic and implant a monarchy or a military dictatorship. (French officers interviewed after the fall of Metz confirmed that a "Bazaine dictatorship" had been widely discussed in the French barracks.)[53] Internationally, Bazaine's timing was propitious, for many of the neutral powers had begun to resent the French provisional government's intransigence and its unwillingness to hold the national elections that, according to Italy's foreign minister, "would return an assembly with a strong pacific current."[54] The armistice terms that Bismarck had offered the French, though severe, were not excessive given France's instigation of the war. The Prussians would end the siege of Paris and declare the war at an end if the French would cede Alsace and half Lorraine, pay the Prussian war costs, and yield the Parisian forts of Valérien and St. Denis until the indemnity was paid.

American General Ambrose Burnside, sent by President Ulysses S. Grant to shuttle between Bismarck at Versailles and Favre in Paris and help arrange a peace, discovered that Favre would not even consider the Prussian terms. Instead, he repeated the French position that there "would be no armistice until the last German has been driven from French soil."[55] "The obstacle to peace is Paris," Emilio Visconti-Venosta, Italy's foreign minister, wrote in October. French politicians will not "accept certain conditions that the French *nation* might be disposed to accept," namely the cession of Alsace-Lorraine.[56] Rumors that the desperate French republican regime was offering to support Russian expansion in the Black Sea and Balkans and give Prussia a "free hand" in Holland, Belgium, and Luxembourg in exchange for withdrawal of the demand for Alsace-Lorraine only increased the impatience of the neutrals.[57] Yet,

51 SHAT, Lt12, Brussels, 5, 6, 22 and 30 Oct. 1870, Tachard to Favre. London, 12 and 27 Oct. 1870, Tissot to Favre. Fay, pp. 258–9.
52 SHAT, Lt12, Tours, Oct. 1870, Gambetta to Favre. Brussels, 1 Nov. 1870, Tachard to Favre.
53 SHAT, Lt12, Brussels, 31 Oct. 1870, Tachard to Favre.
54 PRO, FO 425, 98, 89, Florence, 22 Oct. 1870, Paget to Granville.
55 PRO, FO 425, 112, Tours, 31 Oct. 1870, Lyons to Granville. NA, CIS, U.S. Serial Set 1780, Paris, 3 and 4 Oct. 1870, Washburne to Fish. HHSA, PA IX, 96, Paris, 12 Oct. 1870, Hübner to Metternich.
56 PRO, FO 425, 98, Tours, 9 Oct. 1870, Lyons to Granville. 98, Florence, 22 Oct. 1870, Paget to Granville. 98, St. Petersburg, 21 Oct. 1870, Buchanan to Granville. FO 64, 703, Versailles, 25 Oct. 1870.
57 PRO, FO 425, 190, Brussels, 19 Nov. 1870, Lumley to Granville.

General Boyer's meeting with the Prussian leadership went badly. Informed by spies, deserters, and the notoriously indiscreet French newspapers of the true state of Bazaine's disintegrating army, Bismarck and Moltke answered Bazaine's offer of "cooperation" against the "republican menace" with an indifferent shrug. The question, Moltke insisted, was now purely military. With France beaten, Prussia had less need of "political cooperation." What use are your troops, Moltke asked rhetorically, when the French government is split between Paris and Tours, the cities are in revolt, and the north, south, and west of France are threatening to break away? Because Boyer, secluded in Metz for a month, had no reliable information with which to dispute these exaggerated claims, his negotiations foundered.[58] Under orders from Bazaine to obtain good terms from the Prussians, Boyer returned to Metz empty-handed on 17 October.

If the imperial government would not restore itself, Bismarck planned an appeal to the French nation. Recognizing that the French provinces were more conservative than the politicians at Paris and Tours and far less inclined to defend every "clod of earth" on the eastern frontier, Bismarck offered to help reconvene the French legislative body (which had never been legally dissolved) or facilitate elections for a new French legislature in October. When French elections for a constituent assembly were scheduled for 2 October, Bismarck promised to "provide every facility in the whole of France occupied by German troops." Fearing a pacifist landslide (a fear that gave insight into the true state of French opinion), Paris postponed the elections for two weeks. On 16 October, Gambetta and Trochu postponed them again, this time indefinitely. The reason given for the postponement was Bismarck's exclusion of Alsace-Lorraine from the pending elections ("they are regarded as already annexed to Germany"), but the greater worry was that France's war-weary peasant voters would return pragmatic conservatives, or even monarchists, to make peace at any price.[59] Bismarck had maneuvered brilliantly, exposing the hypocrisy and self-interest of the urban republicans and effectively turning the tables on a "provisional government" that was made to appear more interested in clinging to power than ending the war when it conclusively rejected Bismarck's offer of free electoral access to German-occupied France in early November.[60]

While the Prussians marched and plotted, the Parisians dug. Venturing out to see the spreading trenchworks in the Bois de Boulogne on 28 September, Raphael Hübner, an Austrian embassy official, passed barred shops and closed restaurants. Food was already running short or being hoarded by

58 Michael Howard, *The Franco-Prussian War*, orig. 1961, London, 1981, pp. 278–80. Otto Pflanze, *Bismarck and the Development of Germany*, 3 vols., Princeton, 1990, vol. 1, p. 476. Andlau, pp. 333–4.
59 PRO, FO 425, 98, Versailles, 28 Oct. 1870, Bismarck to Bernstorff.
60 PRO, FO 425, 98, Tours, 22 Oct. 1870, Lyons to Granville. Tours, 9 Nov. 1870, Lyons to Granville.

black-marketers. Cafés and restaurants had closed; vegetables, butter, cheese, eggs, and milk had all but disappeared. Having slaughtered everything edible in the *jardin des plantes*, Parisians increasingly subsisted on red wine, scraps of bread and horsemeat. Hübner was shot at and briefly arrested as he rambled through the *bois*. "I was caught and held by a hideous woman and a zealous imbecile, who shouted that I must be a German spy." Eventually released, Hübner returned to his embassy convinced that Paris was "a volcano" seething with paranoia and pent-up radicalism.[61] Though Trochu and Favre did their best to soothe the capital, they came under increasing pressure from the "red republicans," who were exasperated with Trochu's choice of war minister.

Under the circumstances it would have been difficult to conceive a less imposing figure than General Adolphe Leflô. Sent into exile in 1852 as one of the youngest French generals, he returned as one of the oldest, and dissipated his waning energy in bureaucratic hair-splitting. "To avoid confusion," Leflô admonished Trochu on 29 September, "we must change the title of the 'senior commander of the artillery' to the 'senior commander of the artillery of the army of Paris,' so as not to attribute to the said commander the administrative functions that belong properly to the war minister." On 7 October, Leflô "nationalized" all hunting rifles in France, a measure that even he, its author, admitted was all but useless given the difficulty of collecting the guns and supplying them with ammunition.[62] In the provinces, new draftees came forward reluctantly. Roger de Mauni, a twenty-three-year-old volunteer after Sedan, recalled the attitude of his *mobile* unit in Caen in October: "We strive in vain to set the example of cheerfulness and gaiety; the men droop their heads in the cold rain... they feel that the good times are over, and that misery is beginning."[63] Patriots like Mauni – whose troops received no bread, straw or even cartridges – burned with frustration, one writing Trochu in mid-October: "You must cut through the bureaucratic routines, formalities and jealousies and the invincible spirit of inertia that crushes us." He was addressing the wrong man; by October, Parisians, weary of Trochu's proclamations and regulations, had began calling him "*Géneral Trop-lu*" – "General Reads-too-much."[64] Indeed the archives steadily filled with Trochu's injunctions, some quite ludicrous: "To procure cartridges for their rifles, troops must henceforth present a voucher signed not only by their battalion commandant, but by the mayor of Paris as well."[65]

61 HHSA, PA IX, 96, Paris, 29 September 1870, Hübner to Metternich.
62 SHAT, Li6, 29 Sept. 1870 and 6 Oct. 1870, Gen. Leflô to Trochu and Gambetta.
63 David Clarke, ed. *Military Memoirs: Roger de Mauni, the Franco-Prussian War*, London, 1970, p. 35.
64 SHAT, Li2, Oct. 1870, "les habitants de la troisième circonscription de Paris au Gen. Trochu." Li3/4, Paris, 15 Sept 1870, Gen. Trochu to all Garde Mobile commandants. Maurice, p. 272.
65 SHAT, Li 3/4, Paris, 15 Sept. 1870, Trochu to Garde Mobile commandants.

For the successful defense of Paris, Metz was still the key. It contained 135,000 professional troops with 600 guns, three marshals of France, fifty generals, and 6,000 officers. Bazaine had somehow to extricate this force and maneuver to relieve Paris either with his own army or with new armies that could be formed and trained by his professional cadres. Yet he did nothing, canceling or "postponing" planned breakouts three times in September and again on 6 October.[66] Moltke, whose troops and communications ought to have been continuously attacked by Bazaine, could not believe his luck in drawing such a passive adversary. Indeed he considered the marshal's conduct so mysterious that he too concluded that "Bazaine was influenced, not only by military, but by political considerations.... At the head of the only unimpaired army in France he might find himself in a position of greater power than any other man in the country."[67] Still, the power was dissolving daily under the autumn rains. At a lugubrious "council of war" on 10 October, one of Bazaine's corps commandants despaired:

> "What cavalry is left to us is incapable of service. Our artillery has no more horses. The men are starved, and would not be able to march eight hours. Moreover, the Prussian rifles and cannon would inflict heavy casualties, and this would be the end of us, because four or five unwounded troops would fall out of the ranks to help every wounded man; the pretext would be 'first aid,' but they would really be trying to return safely to Metz, and we would be unable to hold them."

As the council adjourned, all of Bazaine's generals agreed that a breakout at this date, without horses or even a glimmer of offensive spirit among the broken men, would be "a fantasy" – "*c'est vraiment un rêve.*"[68] Only the Imperial Guards were reliable; the rest of the troops did not even bother to clean their rifles or keep their cartridges dry. Bourbaki's unexplained departure in September had sparked wild, unnerving rumors: the general had been killed in a duel with Bazaine; he had left in disgust at Bazaine's timidity; he was plotting to restore the Bonapartes; he was serving the new republic in Paris.[69] Whipped by confusion like this, French deserters assured the Prussians that "no one would fight anymore."[70] Bazaine may have welcomed the news. He was free to hunker some more and listen to the "*bruits de camp,*" the continuous grumbling and rumor-mongering of the men, who could not credit the ease with which they had been bottled up and neutralized after two stalemated battles: "Why were no precautions taken for our retreat? It

66 SHAT, Lb14, Gen. Manèque, "Projets d'opérations de détail ajournées ou executés." J. B. Montaudon, *Souvenirs Militaires*, 2 vols, Paris, 1898–1900, vol. 2, pp. 161–3.
67 Helmuth von Moltke, *The Franco-German War of 1870–71*, New York, 1892, pp. 104–5.
68 Fay, p. 251.
69 Andlau, pp. 236–7.
70 Matthias, p. 65.

must be a conspiracy!"[71] A few good men retained their fighting spirit. An anonymous letter from "a soldier of the Army of the Rhine" slipped under Bazaine's door on 25 September attested to the rage and frustration many felt at Bazaine's passivity.

> "You are aware of the rumors coursing through the army with regard to your inaction in the face of the enemy over the past twenty-two days.... This inaction has ruined our cavalry and will soon ruin our artillery, which will reduce the army to impotence. The tragedy at Sedan and the army's continued ignorance as to the plans of its generals makes it susceptible to the rumor that it is being prepared for delivery, *pieds et poings*, to the enemy. And yet the enemy outside is inferior to us in every way; you must be aware of that fact. Surrender the army to the enemy when you have 130,000 elite troops in hand? It is unthinkable."[72]

Lorraine's beastly weather would shortly rinse away even these last flickers of defiance. October was cold and wet, with a steady rain. In the Prussian trenches, the men slopped through knee-deep mud, crouching to avoid a howling north wind that blew tiles off the roofs of houses and stirred an epidemic of tuberculosis that killed hundreds of besieging troops. In the French camp, straw rotted and stank as thousands succumbed to dysentery. The long walls of the Metz fortress and its outlying forts were by now smeared with anti-Bazaine graffiti, some daubed in the night, others in broad daylight.[73] Bazaine further depressed morale by publishing daily bulletins describing the "*redoutes imprenables*" – "invincible redoubts" – of the Prussians. In the view of one officer at Metz, he was "deliberately demoralizing the officers and frightening the men," to make a capitulation more palatable.[74] By the third week of October, Prussian outposts were ordered to permit only two French desertions per day; the rest would be fired on and driven back to eat up more of Bazaine's dwindling supplies. The French who made it across tucked eagerly into Prussian rations and danced with joy to be out of Metz.[75]

On 28 October Bazaine ordered his regiments to deposit their flags and eagles at the Metz arsenal for surrender to the Prussians. This hugely controversial step was but one of many Bazaine controversies in the final days, because every unit preferred to burn its colors rather than give them to the enemy for boastful display in his palaces and garrison churches. Offered full military honors by Prince Friedrich Karl, Bazaine actually refused them. Instead of parading his troops over to the Prussian lines with shouldered arms, mounted officers and bands playing, he ordered the men to stack their rifles in Metz and await transport to German soil. Instead of spiking his 600 guns,

71 Montaudon, vol. 2, p. 163.
72 SHAT, Lt12, Metz, 23 Sept. 1870, "un membre de l'armée" to Marshal Bazaine.
73 SHAT, Lt12, Lille, 1 Nov. 1870, Préfet de Nord to Gambetta.
74 Montaudon, vol. 2, pp. 189–90.
75 Matthias, p. 65.

he handed the cannon over to the Prussians in working order. Many French troops revolted at this semi-treasonous conduct, sparking riots in Metz, an attack on General Coffinières's house, and a fire in the cathedral. The three conflagrations were successively doused by local national guards frantic that their city might be destroyed at its long-awaited hour of deliverance by Bazaine's furious *grognards*.

The next day, Metz and its army of 133,000 men with their 600 guns surrendered under a cold rain. The notorious *séparation* – the division of the enlisted men from their officers – occurred on 29 October, when the French officers delivered their troops into Prussian captivity and then returned alone and unguarded to Metz. This was a gross violation of a French army motto, *"tel vaut le chef, tel vaut le corps"* – "the officer counts no more than the soldier," which merely deepened the men's resentment and their conviction that they had been "sold out" by Bazaine and the officers.

For his part, Bazaine would not even face his men. He smuggled his wife across to the Prussian lines on the 27th, met covertly with the Metz paymaster on the 28th to collect the September and October salaries of a Senator and Marshal of France, and then slipped across to the German lines in the pre-dawn darkness of the 29th.[76] Unlucky to the end, Bazaine reached the German lines at Ars only to be turned back. Prince Friedrich Karl, still asleep in the chateau at Corny, could not receive the marshal at such an early hour. Pelted with stones and garbage, booed and hissed by his own troops, Bazaine withdrew for the day to a little cottage beneath the guns of Fort St. Quentin. There he remarked to one of his entourage: "This sad affair will have at least one good result: it will force Paris to cease its resistance and restore peace to our afflicted country."[77]

Unfortunately the surrender of Metz had the opposite effect. From Tours, Gambetta screamed defiance in the paranoid style that characterized the French republic in its early months: "The marshal has cost France 130,000 men and yielded virgin Metz without a fight. He has made himself an agent of the Man of Sedan, who was himself an accomplice of the invaders!" The republicans, Gambetta vowed, would fight harder, to drive out the Germans, avenge Bazaine's "treason," and restore the "national character" of a "corrupted" French army whose defeats at Sedan and Metz were not military failures but "sinister epilogues to the military coup of December 1852."[78]

Gambetta – the *"fou furieux"* – faced an uphill fight, because the new French republic's military situation had taken a disastrous turn. With Bazaine's army beaten, the Prussians now had virtually the entire pre-war French army

76 SHAT, Lt12, Brussels, 3 Nov. 1870, Tachard to Favre. SHAT, Lb9, Ban St. Martin, 28 Oct. 1870, "Ordre gl. No. 12." Howard, pp. 281–3.
77 Andlau, pp. 403–10. Léonce Patry, *The Reality of War*, London, 2001, pp. 159–60.
78 SHAT, Ld 3, 1 Nov. 1870, "Extrait du journal du Capitaine de Longalerie." SKA, ZGS 158, Paris, 1 Nov. 1870, Lt. Hinüber, "Tagebuch." PRO, FO 425, 98, 110, Tours, 31 Oct. 1870, Lyons to Granville.

in captivity, 250,000 men, four marshals, 140 generals, and 10,000 officers. ("At last Bazaine and MacMahon have joined forces," Parisians joked darkly.)[79] New infantry divisions forming in Paris and on the Loire would have to be commanded by retired colonels, navy captains, and admirals. Only two of the army's 100 regiments remained at large, the 35th and the 42nd. They had been garrisoned in Rome before the war and had only just returned to France. "Such a military disaster as this was never heard of," was the British military attaché's amazed comment on the surrender. Offered command of the surviving "French forces outside Paris" by Gambetta, General Charles Bourbaki recoiled in disgust and declined. He later explained himself to the British ambassador, an old friend: "All military affairs [of the republic] were in a state of utmost confusion, no records of men or amounts of material, no means of ascertaining where men and material were, no organization, no discipline." France, Bourbaki concluded, would need at least six months to build an army fit to range itself against an equal number of Germans, and this only if Tours ceded "unrestricted military authority" to the generals, which it would never do.[80]

While General Trochu and his Government of National Defense discussed Bazaine's capitulation at a meeting in the Hôtel de Ville on 31 October, they were attacked by a howling mob of workers and *mobiles* and imprisoned as "traitors" for fifteen hours. Though loyal troops rallied to free Trochu, the commander of the Seine national guard flagrantly went over to the *communards*, leaving the Hôtel de Ville arm-in-arm with Auguste Blanqui. "The enemy outside our walls was not the only one we had to contend with," General Ducrot later wrote. "Inside the walls was the revolution." Paris smoldered.[81]

For three entire days after the fall of Metz, the Prussian victors marveled at the unrestrained appetites of the fallen defenders. Adolf Matthias, detailed to guard a mass of French prisoners, wrote that "all the French did from 29–31 October was eat and talk about food. For miles around Metz the cook fires burned day and night, boiling, grilling, frying, and roasting."[82] Poking around in the captured forts above Metz, the Prussians found evidence of extreme French demoralization. The rooms and galleries were "filthy and shabby," the guns fouled with soot, rifles scattered everywhere. Magazine doors had been left wide open with shells and cartridges strewn on the floor. If someone had lighted a match, scraped a hobnailed boot on the floor or knocked out a pipe, the whole place would have gone up. Two miles down the road in the city of Metz there were far worse scenes of squalor and indolence. Lieutenant

---

79 Maurice, p. 290.
80 PRO, FO 425, Tours, 18 Oct. 1870, Lyons to Granville. Paris, 31 Oct. 1870, Col. Claremont to Lyons.
81 PRO, FO 425, 189, Paris, 7 Nov. 1870, Col. Claremont to Lyons. NA, CIS, U.S. Ser. Set 1780, Paris, 31 Oct. and 7 Nov. 1870, Washburne to Fish. Maurice, p. 289.
82 Matthias, pp. 69–71.

Richard Berendt, who entered the cavalry camp on the little island formed by the branching Moselle, found unburied corpses and carcasses and "tents crammed with sick and wounded." In the city, the wineshops were filled with men and officers drinking themselves silly.[83]

Despite its inglorious end, observers were struck by the indomitableness of Metz. Though Bazaine had wasted the asset, the place seemed to prove the validity of the late nineteenth-century principle of detached forts. For seventy days, the Prussians had tried and failed to engage Bazaine's army. Several times they had pushed field guns far enough forward to bombard Bazaine's encamped troops only to be smashed or driven back by well-aimed fire from the detached forts at St. Quentin, Plappeville, Woippy, St. Julien, Queleu and St. Privat. Had MacMahon ever arrived with his relief army, the Prussians would have been most unpleasantly gripped between two fires. Even without MacMahon, Metz sheltered 140,000 French troops for two months and pinned down 200,000 Prussians, who did not even attempt proper siege operations across such a vast space. Every army in Europe would heed the lesson, and build their own fortress complexes like Metz in the years before World War I.

To Bismarck's astonishment, even the fall of Metz failed to shake the French republic's determination to hold Alsace-Lorraine. "We are the government of national defense," Jules Favre, France's new foreign minister, told Bismarck. "You know what our program is: "not a clod of our earth or a stone of our fortresses." This gamecock spirit – necessitated by the rough mobs from Belleville and La Vilette that gathered every day in the Place de la Concorde to demand a hard line with the Germans – drove the pragmatic Bismarck to distraction. The cold season and the first cases of flu had appeared in the German camps. Already in the first week of October, 15 percent of the Meuse Army was sick, most with complications from their wounds, the rest with flu, dysentery, and typhoid fever.[84] Doctors watched nervously as the proportion of sick to wounded men surged, the Bavarian II Corps alone losing 17,152 men – more than half its strength and six times its losses in battle – to illness in October.[85] The French forts around Paris were armed and stocked with provisions. General Bourbaki had finally agreed to organize a republican army at Lille, and there seemed no obvious path to an armistice, a feeling underscored by regular, bloody French sorties.

Every few weeks, General Auguste Ducrot would probe the German lines around Paris, sallying with a modest force, hitting the Germans hard, and then retiring on the capital. Ducrot was testing the depth of the German trench lines and planning larger sorties for the day when a relief army appeared from

83 Richard Berendt, *Erinnerungen aus meiner Dienstzeit*, Leipzig, 1894, pp. 95–8.
84 SKA, P 967, Vert galant, 23 Sept. 1870, Duke Georg to King Johann.
85 BKA, HS 849, Capt. Celsus Girl, vol. 7, p. 18.

the south. On 19 September, straining south toward Tours and the Loire, Ducrot attacked the Germans at Chatillon and Bagneux. The Germans stood their ground, but when they counter-attacked, they were ripped by accurate shellfire from the forts at Issy, Vanves, and Montrouge. The same dismal pattern recurred on 13 October, when seven French battalions struck south again, drawing the Bavarians into the bowl of fire they had traversed in September.[86] As the Bavarians started forward, the French fortress guns on Mont Valérien opened up, hammering the Germans through St. Cloud and smashing down Napoleon I's pretty little summer palace, the very place where Napoleon III had declared war in July.

German morale sagged as the battle for Paris settled into trench warfare. The troops rotated every five days from the rear areas to the front lines where they worked like convicts, clearing barricades, abatis, and barbed wire, digging bomb-proof shelters, and winterizing houses abandoned by the French. One night in October a Bavarian officer awoke to find a house across the street burning furiously. Pulling on his boots, he ran across to awaken his troops. When he burst in shouting "the house is on fire," he found them all awake but unmoved on their straw pallets. "We know, and we've sent someone upstairs to watch the fire and warn us when the flames are getting close."[87] This demoralizing, time-wasting standoff infuriated Bismarck, who considered the French beaten. "Think about it," Bismarck shrieked at Favre one day. "Find a basis for peace, *propose* something!"[88] Favre had earlier described Bismarck as "crazed" by German nationalism; Bismarck thought Favre no less crazed to have committed himself to the inflexible program of "maximum war."

To put pressure on the republicans, Bismarck agreed to support national elections in the fourteen French departments controlled by the Prussians as well as the seventy-five others. New elections seemed the only way to create a French government able to cede territory, pay reparations, and resolve differences between the radical Government of National Defense in Paris and the more moderate Government Delegation in Tours. Bismarck and Moltke proposed to occupy all of France until elections could be held for a truly *national* government that, they assumed, would accept Prussia's terms. Prince Friedrich Karl warned a British officer in October that the Prussians would exert unbearable pressure. Paris and Tours would be brought under attack and 200,000 German troops would occupy southern France from Mulhouse across

86 SHAT, Li2, Gouv. De Paris, "Projet d'occupation de la position d'Avron." BKA, B 1237, Malabry, 18 Oct. 1870, Gen. Walter, "Relation." BKA, HS 849, Capt. Celsus Girl, vol. 5, pp. 69–71.
87 BKA, HS 846, Maj. Gustav Fleschuez.
88 HHSA, PA IX, 96, Paris, 29 Sept. and 12 and 29 Oct. 1870, Hübner to Metternich.

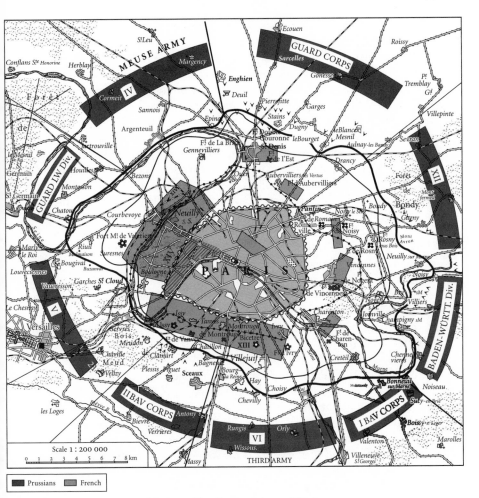

Map 12. The German siege of Paris

to Bordeaux the moment Bazaine surrendered at Metz. This last measure was in some ways the most menacing, because French peasants and townsmen would be expected to pay the daily costs of the occupying armies "until a settled government is returned with which peace can be concluded." Meanwhile, two entire German corps were readied for an assault on Normandy, to crush the army rumored to be forming under Bourbaki at Lille and carry off every pig, cow, and steer in the province to feed the German field armies. Bismarck also resolved to bombard Paris at the earliest possible date. He had no humanitarian scruples about shelling a civilian area. What he did worry about was the winter weather, which would make it difficult to move guns and shells from the siege works at Belfort, Strasbourg, Verdun, and Thionville to the battery positions around Paris.[89]

Those parts of France already occupied by the Prussians groaned at the burden. In October, the French paper *Pays* estimated the cost of the war to the French people at 12 billion francs, about $31 billion today. This monstrous sum included the costs of the mobilization and lost battles as well as property damage and business losses. Trade slumped, crops rotted on the vine, and investors suffered from the suspension of dividend payments at most French companies. In French towns and cities, silver coins vanished. Havre, Dieppe, Lille, and Evreux issued their own paper currencies. In Lyon, silversmiths coined plate, and English pounds and pence circulated in Bordeaux.[90] In a conversation with the British ambassador, Adolphe Thiers lamented the sudden removal of the Bonapartes and the creation of a republic, "which only irritates and alarms a great part of the population of the French provinces."[91] Outside Paris, there was deep hostility to the republic and the "balloon government" at Tours, which the peasants and provincial bourgeois increasingly identified with taxes, war-mongering, and "red revolution." Republican efforts to swing opinion behind the new government merely exacerbated the problem. Popular mayors once loyal to Napoleon III were dismissed and replaced with men more "republican" in spirit, who practiced a most unpleasant "absolutism in the provinces" throughout the fall and winter of 1870–71.[92]

Into this troubled landscape rode General Ludwig von der Tann in early October 1870. With Paris and its garrison strangely quiet ("Trochu, a soldier who dips his sword in ink and his pen in the scabbard," Parisians joked), Moltke felt confident enough to detach Tann with his Bavarian I Corps, a Prussian infantry division and two cavalry divisions to "scour the countryside down to the Loire." Having failed to compel a French surrender with the victories at Sedan and Metz, Moltke now sought to destroy the "relief armies" and insurgents forming around Orléans. A few more Prussian victories would persuade Tours and Paris of the futility of further struggle. The plan made perfect sense to Moltke. To his cold, footsore troops, it seemed just another step into a deepening quagmire.[93]

---

89 PRO, FO 64, near Metz, 10 Oct. 1870, Capt. Henry Hozier to Granville.
90 PRO, FO 64, Berlin, 25 Oct. 1870, Loftus to Granville.
91 PRO, FO 425, Paris, 8 Sept. 1870, Lyons to Granville.
92 PRO, FO 425, Tours, Nov. 1870, "Report by Mr. West on the state of France."
93 SKA, ZS 158, Lt. Hinüber, "Tagebuch," 12 Oct. 1870.

11

France Falls

The immediate objective of General Tann's new "Army Section" – a Bavarian corps, a Prussian infantry division and two Prussian cavalry divisions – was to find and destroy the French XV Corps under General Joseph La Motterouge. Ordered by War Minister Leflô to "do *something* for the sake of public opinion," La Motterouge had drawn in his brigades from Vierzon, Bourges, and Nevers and concentrated them at Orléans. Sent south by Moltke to preempt threats like this and "clear the country between Paris and the Loire," Tann left Etampes with five divisions in early October.

Marching and eating well in the flat, gold-stubbled Beauce, the Germans made good time. Each cross road that ought to have been held by the French was either deserted or lightly defended, allowing the Germans to punch through easily using their cavalry and guns to maximum advantage on plains so flat and featureless that, as one veteran put it, "the earth and sky swam together before your eyes." With most of France's regular army in captivity, the Germans collided with a strange soldatesca, including *francs-tireurs* (irregular "sharpshooters") and new formations of "partisans." Because the Germans were summarily executing *francs-tireurs* – depressing morale among would-be guerrillas – the government at Tours had created semi-official partisan companies that carried government pay books and wore uniforms, albeit outlandish ones. The *Partisans de Gers*, encountered by the Prussians at Etampes, wore long black coats, black trousers, red scarves, and broad-brimmed Calabrian hats. Most were either boys or men in their forties, which suggested to the Prussians that drafts for the regular army, reserves, and *gardes mobiles* had eaten up most of France's prime manpower.

If, as Victor Hugo claimed in September 1870, there were 10 million young Frenchmen "burning to join the fight," they were burning slowly. Their neighbors were not burning at all: Partisan prisoners complained that

Map 13. The war after Sedan, Sept. 1870–Feb. 1871

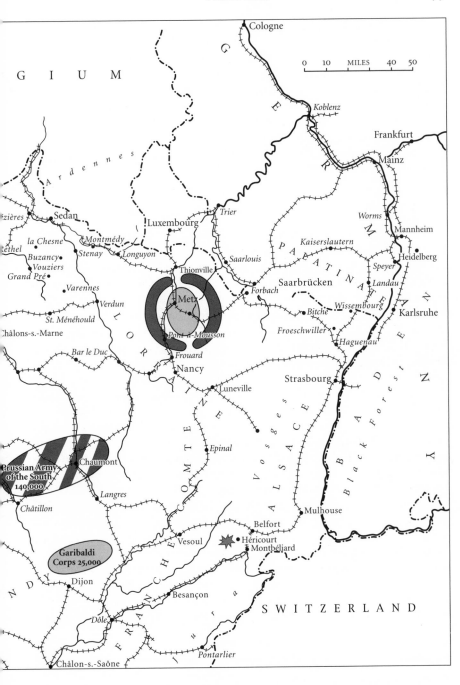

no French peasant would help them, guide them or fill their requisitions. They were shunned or shooed off everywhere they went lest they attract German reprisals.[1] For many military-aged Frenchmen, Bazaine's capitulation at Metz had banished all thought of fighting on: "If the troops at Metz dared not sally against the Prussians, how on earth would a new, badly armed, badly led army of green conscripts oppose a Prussian army that a Marshal of France with 160,000 men had considered invincible?"[2] Against fractured, demoralized opposition like this, the Germans rolled unmolested through Angerville and Pithiviers on 9 October before finally meeting real resistance just north of Orléans on a line between Artenay and Bucy-le-roi.

THE BATTLE OF ORLÉANS, 10–11 OCTOBER 1870

Anchored by his regulars, Turcos and chasseurs, La Motterouge held for an hour before his corps began to melt away, led by the undisciplined *mobiles*. Terrified by the thunder of the German guns and rifles which pinned their front while the German cavalry circumvented their flanks, the French ran into the Forest of Orléans, or straight south toward the city and its bridges. Along the way they met with carriages of elegantly dressed *Orléanais*, who had ridden out to watch the battle only to be swallowed up in the rout.[3] As night fell on 10 October, both sides rested, the Germans feasting and swilling in cottages that had been so hastily abandoned that they were still stocked with food and wine. After witnessing the panic-stricken rout of the French XV Corps, Tann assumed that La Motterouge would use the night to evacuate Orléans and escape to the south bank of the Loire. This was an acceptable outcome to Tann, who would then trumpet the capture of Orléans for propaganda purposes and use the city and its bridges to attack Tours from both banks of the Loire. For his part, La Motterouge felt constrained to cling to Orléans. To lose it would end his military career and force Gambetta's government delegation to flee further south.

While Tann distributed orders for the morning advance on 11 October, La Motterouge deployed the remains of his corps in defensive positions north of the city, from Saran south to the outskirts of Orléans, where the Orléans-Le Mans railway embankment offered excellent cover and fields of fire. In good hands, La Motterouge's position would have held indefinitely, for it was a natural fortress: stone houses and high-walled roads wending through vineyards and apple orchards. But France's reserve army contained a large number of bad hands: dispirited, reluctant reservists and *gardes mobiles*, who had no

1   London, Public Record Office (PRO), FO 64, 693, Berlin, 21 and 26 Oct. 1870, Capt. Hozier.
2   Vincennes, Archives Centrales de la Marine (ACM), BB4 906, Cherbourg, 16 Sept. 1870, Prefecture Maritime to Naval Delegate at Tours. Col. Andlau, *Metz*, Paris, 1872, p. 222.
3   F. Maurice, *The Franco-German War 1870–71*, London, 1914, pp. 381–3.

Fig. 15. The French defense of Orléans

intention of fighting to the death. Reviewing his troops before the battle, one of La Motterouge's colonels nearly choked with embarrassment: "They were shabbily dressed – dirty clothes and broken shoes – clutching cloth sacks without straps, and badly armed: old percussion rifles and tiny pouches that barely held a single packet of cartridges." Many of these new battalions had already lost 20–30 percent of their strength to "illness," which usually meant overweight, hastily conscribed civilians unable to march or work with their hands. Most of the *mobiles* were holding rifles for the first time, a dangerous development that explained their alarming "friendly fire" losses and somewhat mitigated the French loss of all but twenty-six *mitrailleuses* in the fighting at Sedan and Metz.[4]

On 11 October, Tann attacked the French positions before Orléans in three columns, which pushed in on the Chartres and Paris roads. Resistance was stoutest on the French right, where La Motterouge had deployed his regulars: the 39th Regiment and elements of the French Foreign Legion just

---

4 SHAT, Le19, Auch, 18 Aug. 1871, Col. P. Taberne, "Rapport historique." Ld 20, Lausanne, 22 Feb. 1871, Eduard Tallichet to Min. of War. Ld 4, Chanu, 15 Nov. 1870, 39 Regt., 3eme Bataillon, Garde Nationale Mobile, "Rapport." Ld 1, Tours, 26 Nov. 1870, Directeur d'Artillerie. Le 19, Auch, 18 Aug. 1871, "85e Regt. de Mobiles (Gers, Vienne): Rapport Historique."

arrived from Oran. Using the ground cleverly and fortifying Les Aides and the Faubourg Bannier, the French pinned down the Bavarian I Corps until two o'clock, when the Prussian 22nd Division smashed through La Borde on the French left, knocking La Motterouge's entire front backward. In truth, the French were already reeling. Withdrawing from Cercottes on the edge of the forest, Captain Edmond Duchesne of the 29th Regiment collided with leader-less bands of *mobiles* from the nearby Cher and Nièvre, who "had no cavalry, no artillery, and no sense of direction at all." Demoralized and hungry – they had not been fed for two days – the whole tangled ruck of French troops collapsed under the Prussian artillery, which fired from beyond the range of the French guns, sowing terror among the Duchesne's green infantry and their supports.

Whereas the Prussian guns fired nonstop, the poorly supplied French artillery ran through their shells in an hour.[5] A Bavarian who pushed through Les Aides and Bannier called both places "a second Bazeilles," a reference to the Meuse crossing at Sedan that had been reduced to smoking ruins by the end of the battle. In the Forest of Orléans, the Germans took prisoners in unfamiliar gray uniforms; they were French papal zouaves summoned in July but only just arrived from Rome.[6] Those lucky enough to escape the German pincers ran south or into the woods to the east, pursued by the sounds of German celebration behind them: thumping bands, lusty cheers, and joyful hymns. Many more were overrun, in most cases those troops La Motterouge could least afford to lose, namely 900 of 1,300 French Foreign Legionnaires and 3,000 other regulars.

By late afternoon, the advancing German troops, who suffered just 900 dead and wounded in the advance, streamed into Orléans itself. This amaz-ingly literate army, most of whom had read or heard about Schiller's "Maid of Orléans," crowded into the central square to gaze wonderingly at the statue of Jeanne d'Arc (*"Sauve la France!"*) and marvel at their easy victory. Gambetta's newest army had been thrashed and France conquered all the way down to the Loire. La Motterouge had retreated south to Gien, where he nervously straddled the Middle Loire and awaited a German pursuit.[7] Freshly arrived in Tours from Italy in the second week of October, Europe's greatest republican, Giuseppe Garibaldi, must have wondered why he had come. The French re-public was proving feckless both politically and militarily: Gambetta's army was stumbling from one bloody defeat to another and his government, in quite un-republican fashion, had again "postponed" already overdue national elections lest voters return conservative peace candidates to power.

5   SHAT, Ld 1, Argent, 20 Oct. 1870, Capt. Duchesne, "Rapport."
6   Munich, Bayerisches Kriegsarchiv (BKA), HS 856, Lt. Josef Krumper.
7   SHAT, Le 19, Paris, 25 June 1871, Col. d'Arguelle, "Résumé des Opérations de Guerre."

While Tours and Paris argued heatedly over Garibaldi – Jules Favre and General Trochu feared that the "red Italian" would irretrievably alienate France's conservative peasantry and bourgeoisie – Tann weighed his options.[8] Pursuit was quite out of the question for Tann's Army Section. Only 50,000 men, they were exceedingly vulnerable in hostile country several marches from the nearest friendly division. With large French reserves forming at Blois and Vendôme and the bulk of the French XV Corps intact at Gien, Tann, never the boldest of soldiers, felt marooned. Prince Leopold of Bavaria described the Army Section's anxiety: "We felt horribly exposed, surrounded by far more numerous troops, as if we were sitting at the bottom of a sack, whose opening the enemy had only to grasp and seal shut." Since Moltke would not sanction a retreat from the Loire, Tann improved his defenses. German work parties and French prisoners entrenched the southern bank of the Loire and built it into a redoubtable bridgehead, while most of Tann's infantry reequipped themselves with captured Chassepots to augment their defensive fire.[9]

With winter fast approaching, the Germans hauled in food like squirrels. "We found ourselves in the enemy's granary," a German officer noted. "Fruitful, cultivated lands reaching as far as the eye could see and all the way down to the Mediterranean."[10] Rules of war evolved since Frederick the Great entitled invaders to claim lodging, food, drink, fuel, clothing, and carriage from the invaded, and this the Germans did, with gusto. For payment, they devised a system that suited many French peasants and merchants. The Germans would give requisition papers to a mayor, who would then distribute them to the peasants and the shopkeepers, who would fill them, and then apply to the government delegation in Tours for reimbursement. Few avoided the temptation to inflate the charges. Thus, for example, an innkeeper would lodge and feed a Prussian staff officer for five francs, but submit expenses of ten francs, three of which would be skimmed off by the mayor as a commission.

Not everyone profited. Many Prussian troops simply took what they needed without paying, or scribbled a worthless chit: "*Requis par l'état-major, six oeufs*" – "requisitioned by the general staff, six eggs." After taking Orléans in October, Tann ordered the city to pay him 1.5 million francs, roughly $4.5 million in today's dollars. Officially, this common wartime practice was called a "*Contribution*" in lieu of plunder. Cities would pay ransom so as not to be sacked. In the Loire theater, it was standard practice for German units to deploy their cannon 1,500 yards from a village – beyond rifle range – and demand food, drink and quarters. If the peasants refused, their village would be bombarded. As the war progressed and the cold increased, the Germans would

8 PRO, FO 425, 98, Tours, 2 Nov. 1870, Lyons to Granville.
9 BKA, HS 858, "Kriegstagebuch Leopold Prinz von Bayern."
10 BKA, HS 856, Lt. Josef Krumper.

use any pretext to threaten an *"exemplarische Bestrafung"* – an "exemplary punishment." Fired on by a single *franc-tireur* near Chartres, a Saxon cavalry patrol unlimbered its battery and blasted the nearest village. Four shells were lobbed inside until the mayor appeared on the outskirts yelling and gesticulating. The Germans ceased firing, demanded food and money, and watched as the mayor scurried from house to house collecting whatever he could lay his hands on. "We took everything they gave us and left," a Saxon *Feldwebel* recalled. "The day was beastly, snow mixed with rain."[11] Entering the villages, sullen German troops met every French complaint with *"nix compra!"* – "I don't understand" – or *"Halts Maul, Pisang!"* – "shut up, you dagos." Nearly everyone in France felt oppressed by the war, and wanted an end to it.[12]

THE BATTLE OF CHÂTEAUDUN, 18 OCTOBER 1870

Ordered to suppress all organized resistance south of Paris, Tann rested his men for several days and then sent the Prussian 22nd Division against Châteaudun. It was by no means the obvious choice. "Where to?" Lieutenant Josef Krumper wondered. "No one knows; the army leadership is having a hard time making up its mind because the French positions are largely unknown." Krumper recalled ascending the cathedral of Orléans to gaze around the region and seeing nothing but "villages, vineyards and endless plains, the enemy's whereabouts are a big question mark."[13] At Châteaudun, a walled castle on good ground where the Loir, a tributary of the Sarthe, streamed through the hilly vineyards of Vouvray, the Prussians ejected a brigade of *francs-tireurs* and hastily drilled gendarmes on 18 October. Dressed in unfamiliar uniforms, the French defenders had at least as much to fear from their own comrades as from the Prussians. A French navy captain with a company of marines recalled arriving at Châteaudun and coming under volley fire from whole battalions of local *mobiles*, who mistook the blue-jacketed French naval infantry for Prussians. That unit alone lost thirty-eight men to "wild firing" by friendly units in the course of the day.[14] The citizens of Châteaudun fared worse; exasperated by the increase in *franc-tireur* attacks – snipers, ambushes, blown bridges, and even set-piece battles like this one – the Germans reacted furiously. Most German troops hewed to the maxim *"töte ich ihn nicht, so tötet er mich"* – "either I kill him, or he will kill me." Prisoners were mutilated, hostages taken to assure French collaboration, suspected guerrillas shot,

11 Oskar Becher, *Kriegstagebuch eines Vierundneunzigers aus dem Kriege 1870–71*, Weimar, 1904, p. 39.
12 H. Sutherland Edwards, *The Germans in France*, London, 1873, pp. 48–52. BKA, HS 858, "Kriegstagebuch Leopold Prinz von Bayern." Adolf Matthias, *Meine Kriegserinnerungen*, Munich, 1912, pp. 64–5.
13 BKA, HS 856, Lt. Josef Krumper.
14 SHAT, Ld 3, Capt. Jean-Marie du Temple, "Rapport sur le Campagne 1870-71."

and whole towns burned to the ground. Reflecting on this, a Bavarian captain explained that "in war, we must gauge human passions with a different measure than we use in our peacetime universities and churches."[15] Châteaudun, a market town of 7,000, subsided into smoking ashes after the battle, the inhabitants, in American observer Phil Sheridan's memorable phrase, "left with nothing but their eyes, to weep with over the war."[16]

Wheeling north, Tann surrounded Chartres on 20 October and compelled its surrender. That was the easy part, not least because the French had virtually no artillery in this early phase of the Loire campaign. Troops were ordered to fight "from the woods with great prudence and circumspection," a pathetic recommendation that must have rankled all concerned.[17] Determined to end the war before winter, Moltke ordered Tann westward along the Loire to Tours, where Gambetta, having fled Paris for Tours in a balloon on 9 October, had established the "government delegation" and assumed control of the war effort. One of Gambetta's first changes had been the removal of La Motterouge. In his place, Gambetta named General Louis Aurelle de Paladines, who took command of the XV Corps and new troops for a total strength of 60,000 men behind the Sauldre between Argent and Salbris. When combined with the large numbers of *francs-tireurs* that combed the countryside and provided Aurelle with thorough intelligence on German movements and the thousands of troops of the French XVI Corps mobilizing at Blois, Aurelle's *seemed* a formidable army capable of combining with the Paris garrison to squeeze Moltke hard. In reality, Aurelle's army was internally fractured, combining elements of the old army, scarcely trained march battalions, and big drafts of *gardes mobiles*, which were now euphemistically called "territorial divisions." Even by French standards, these territorials were breathtakingly undisciplined. They elected their own officers – having ousted their Bonapartist ones on 4 September – and frequently refused direct orders from the war ministry or the regular army headquarters.[18] To beat this runny pudding into something solid, Aurelle needed a defensible base and road junction closer to Paris where the French XVII and XVIII Corps could be formed, and the more advanced XV and XVI Corps gathered for a strike at Paris.

Orléans, of course, was the place. To plan its reconquest, Gambetta sent Charles Freycinet to a council of war at Salbris on 24 October. Although Gambetta considered civilian control of the military a key plank of the republic, his use of Freycinet as a roving troubleshooter grated on the generals, as did Gambetta's frequent memos "directing their attention to prescriptions of the army

15 BKA, HS 849, Capt. Girl, vol. 3, pp. 65–6.
16 Otto Pflanze, *Bismarck and the Development of Germany*, 3 vols., Princeton, 1990, vol. 1, pp. 482–3.
17 SHAT, Ld 1, Blois, 19 Oct. 1870, Gen. Pourcet to Gen. Duplanquer.
18 SHAT, Ld 1, Blois, 19 Oct. 1870, Garde Mobile de la Sarthe to XV Corps.

ordinances," most quite trivial or beyond his competence.[19] Gambetta brow-beat good officers and bad ones alike. To General Antoine Chanzy – one of the best – he wrote in mid-October: "Your men have already used more than 90 cartridges each; that exceeds the average of *all* battalions." Chanzy would have to content himself with 200,000 percussion cartridges, none for the Chassepot.[20] The last, incurable drop of poison in the civil-military rela-tionship may have been Gambetta's announcement of Bazaine's surrender on 31 October, which, to an army still largely officered by Bonapartists, spoke of the "corrupting power of Bonapartism" and the "treason of [France's] officers amid a national crisis."[21]

THE BATTLE OF COULMIERS, 9 NOVEMBER 1870

At Salbris – in the last relatively cordial days before Gambetta dropped that declamatory bomb – Freycinet and the French generals agreed to envelop Orléans from the west and south with 120,000 men. Tann's corps of 50,000 would be surrounded and destroyed, Orléans seized as a logistical and com-munications hub for the liberation of Paris. Aurelle's plan assumed that Tann would stand passively in Orléans until the French army closed around him on 11 November. However, warned of the French offensive, Tann marched out with 20,000 troops to meet the French late on 8 November. To secure his base on the Loire, Tann hoped to beat the French decisively in the open field. Elements of the two armies collided on the 9th – a cold, gray, windy day – around a village west of Orléans called Coulmiers. Confident that his weak corps would maneuver better than Aurelle's large but untrained French army, Tann risked the battle against steep odds. By late morning he was fully engaged against a large fraction of Aurelle's army; the rest stood massed in reserve at Saintry. With three times Tann's numbers – 60,000 French troops against 20,000 Bavarians – the French tried twice to smash through Coulmiers, once at 1:30, when waves of French infantry attacked in such numbers that the Bavarian infantry around Cheminiers fired off all of their cartridges and watched helplessly as their artillery moved closer to take up the slack and drive back the French attack columns.

Pausing to regroup, General Etienne Barry attacked a second time at 3:00, isolating a single regiment of Bavarians with seven regiments of his own. While Admiral Jean Jauréguibery's division pushed in from the French left at Gémigny and Cheminiers, the massively outnumbered Bavarians fought

---

19 Gambetta was minister of war, Freycinet his "*delegue au département de la guerre.*" SHAT, Ld 2, Tours, 31 Oct. 1870, Gambetta to all divisional and brigade generals." Ld 4, Tours, 17 Nov. 1870, Freycinet to Aurelle. In this, a typical note, Freycinet tells Aurelle to concentrate, not disperse, his *mitrailleuse* batteries.
20 SHAT, Ld 1, Tours, 18 Oct. 1870, Gambetta to Gen. Chanzy.
21 SHAT, Ld 3, 1 Nov. 1870, "Extrait du journal du Capitaine de Longalerie."

desperately, confirming the truth of at least half of Bismarck's assertion that Germans (in contrast to the French) "have that sense of duty which enables a man to allow himself to be shot dead alone in the dark."[22] But if the Bavarians were truly imbibing Prussian discipline and self-sacrifice, they were also aided by the poor coordination of the French units; Barry's division was typical of the Army of the Loire. It included a "march battalion" (draftees and rear-echelon personnel) of the 7th Chasseurs, the 31st "March Regiment" – the *real* 31st Regiment having been captured whole at Metz – and the 22nd Regiment of *gardes mobiles* from the Dordogne. For most of these men, it was all that they could do to stay on their feet, fire their rifles and cry *"vive la France!"* Small-unit tactics were quite beyond their reach. In this environment, the captious Bavarians were finally queens of the battlefield, proving adept at the Prussian tactics that they had adopted after 1866. One platoon leader judged Coulmiers a *Plänklergefecht* – a "skirmish battle" – in which Bavarian squads continually moved forward to reinforce a thickening skirmish line that scythed down the French attacks with rapid fire.[23]

French wounded at Coulmiers searched in vain for field hospitals or even a stretcher bearer. There were none, and many recalled crawling into abandoned houses like dogs to dress their own wounds and escape the cold.[24] Convinced that they would be "sent to Algeria to catch monkeys" if overrun and captured by the French, the Bavarians struggled bitterly with their backs to the wall. For many of them, this involved enduring monstrous enemy shelling. Aurelle's improvised army included a large number of twelve-centimeter naval guns, which, as one stunned German participant wrote, "flung shells like flour sacks at us." Crouched in the Montpipeau Wood, the Bavarians experienced the same terror that they had inflicted on the French in Sedan's Bois de la Garenne. "Too weak to attack, we were condemned to sit," a junior officer wrote. The creeping barrage drove many men to wit's end: "Shells plowed the field in front and then crashed into the wood, shattering trunks, tearing down branches and filling the air with fragments, splinters and shrapnel."[25]

In October, Gambetta had placed an order for fifty batteries of British field artillery and the first tubes were entering service now, as well as tens of thousands of Enfield and Springfield rifles from England and America.[26] Most German officers agreed that while the quality of the Army of the Republic's infantry was far worse than the Army of the Empire's, the republic made better use of its artillery, massing it nearer the fight and mixing in heavy caliber pieces

22 Moritz Busch, *Bismarck: Some secret pages of his history*, 2 vols., New York, 1898, vol. 1, p. 162.
23 BKA, B 1145, 11 June 1871, Lt. Johann Geiger. 12 June 1871, Unterlt. Theodor Schieber. SHAT, Ld 3, Gen. Aurelle, "Rapport sur la bataille de Coulmiers."
24 SHAT, Ld 4, Boulay, 15 Nov. 1870, Dr. Chapuy, XVI Corps.
25 Matthias, p. 95. In fact, most German POWs were interned on the islands off Brittany.
26 PRO, FO 425, 98, London, 19 Oct. 1870, "New York Tribune."

to outrange the Krupps.[27] Nevertheless, unable to breach the thin German line, the French cracked first at Coulmiers, General Barry's *mobiles* retreating in wild disorder even as the general himself waded into their midst to rally them. Restoring order with the help of his regulars, Barry attacked Coulmiers again as evening and a cold rain began to fall, only to discover that Tann had yielded it. Feeling pressure on his flank from Admiral Jauréguibery's thirteen battalions and with no reserves to hand, General Tann broke away to the east, marching to reunite with his 22nd Division and his cavalry brigades on the northern outskirts of Orléans. Leaving his position to join the retreat, a Bavarian officer was almost crushed by a twelve-centimeter shell that slammed down beside him. He stared horrified as the shell smoked and sputtered but did not explode.[28] Tann's corps retreated for two days through the winter's first blizzard, which dumped several inches of snow and then a deluge of cold rain on the hungry, frustrated troops.[29] While Tann regrouped and withdrew north to Angerville, Aurelle hurried to liberate Orléans on 10 November (and request a doubling of his salary.) In Tours, Gambetta savored the rare good news (and granted the request) and Trochu – informed of the victory by carrier pigeons – ordered drab Paris flagged with tricolors.[30]

There was more happy news: Three new French corps were finally afoot, the XVII at Vendôme, the XVIII at Gien, and the XX at Châteaudun. A rather dubious XXI Corps – 35,000 reservists and *mobiles* – under General Fiereck had taken up positions in Le Perche, the hilly southern border of Normandy around Le Mans. No French officer was under any illusions as to the fitness of these formations. Writing from Vendôme on 14 November, General Louis Durrieu described the XVIII Corps thus: "My 45th Regiment has Chassepots, the 70th carries the 1822 model musket, most of which have been rifled, some of which are still smoothbores.... Of my *franc-tireur* companies, some have Remington carbines, some have the Sharps or the Spicer rifle, some have.12 caliber revolvers." Without a standard rifle or caliber to simplify supply, few of Durrieu's men had more than ten or fifteen cartridges, nor did they have grease or brushes to clean their weapons. In Normandy, a *mobile* officer lashed out in frustration: "If they continue to equip us at this rate, we shall not be ready till the war is over." His troops were given percussion rifles and cardboard kepis that "dissolved into a soft pulp" under the first hard rain.[31] Medical support was appalling, regiments like Durrieu's 45th employing just one surgeon for 2,460 men.[32] If committed to battle, French

27 BKA, B982, Maj. Theodor Eppler, "Erfahrungen."
28 BKA, HS 856, Lt. Josef Krumper.
29 Dresden, Sächsisches Kriegsarchiv (SKA), ZS 158, Lt. Hinüber, "Tagebuch."
30 SHAT, Ld 4, Tours, 13 Nov. 1870, Freycinet to Gen. Aurelle.
31 David Clarke, ed. *Military Memoirs: Roger de Mauni, the Franco-Prussian War*, London, 1970, pp. 19, 40.
32 SHAT, Ld 4, Vendôme, 14 Nov. 1870, Gen. Durrieu.

battalions would fire off their ammunition in a few minutes and then litter the field with their untended wounded. Sometimes they would shoot down their own officers. Leading a skirmish with the Prussians on 18 November, a battalion commander in the French 36th March Regiment sent a captain and a lieutenant thirty yards forward to reconnoiter the Germans and watched in horror as his own troops – panicked by shots from the Prussian side – raised their rifles and shot the two French officers dead.[33] Nevertheless, Gambetta hoped that the new French units would make up in sheer numbers – more than 250,000 men augmented by swarms of *francs-tireurs* – what they lacked in experience.[34]

Moltke, of course, was furious at General Tann's loss of Orléans, all of the Bavarian wounded and 2,000 French POWs, who had been left behind in the retreat. The gains of October had been shattered by Aurelle's lumbering advance. Tann, held responsible for the setback in Prussian great headquarters, was returned to a corps command, his troops subordinated to a new Army Section reinforced with big detachments from Metz.[35] This beefed-up Army Section would be commanded by Grand Duke Friedrich of Mecklenburg-Schwerin: "an old bearded man with lively eyes, his eyes perpetually fixed on a map in his hand."[36] In addition to the Bavarian I Corps, the new Army Section included the Prussian III, IX, and X Corps and a cavalry division of the Second Army. After being vaccinated for smallpox, which was spreading amid the filth of war, these Prussian corps hastened west from Metz in early November and spread themselves protectively from Troyes to Chartres. Ordered to intercept and destroy any French attacks toward Paris from the southwest, they were also expected to suppress French resistance. Adolf Matthias, another of the Prussian army's university-trained privates (a rare species in the French military) recalled that there was hardly any resistance at all. Chaumont, a town of 7,000 halfway between Metz and Troyes, had been prepared for defense but then evacuated by its national guards, who had been pushed out, not by the Germans, but by their own mayor and neighbors, who had implored the men to leave "so that the city would not be shelled." Many French were relieved to see the Prussian march columns in the hope "that they would restore order and good government to the region."[37]

General Aurelle meanwhile had begun to convert Orléans into a heavily fortified base. Thousands of *mobiles* and reservists converged on the place and set to work building trenches, stockades, and warehouses. The northern bank of the river was built into a fortified bridgehead, its flanks anchored

---

33 SHAT, Ld 4, Dreux, 25 Jan. 1872, Cdt. De Coynart, "Combat de Torcay."
34 SHAT, Ld 4, St. Péravy, 15 Nov. 1870, Gen. Barry, "Ordre Géneral." Maurice, p. 399.
35 BKA, HS 849, Capt. Girl, vol. 1, p. 66.
36 BKA, HS 856, Lt. Josef Krumper.
37 Matthias, p. 81.

on the railway embankment and the Forest of Orléans. Twenty batteries of guns were dug in and trenches begun for an army of 100,000. The work proceeded slowly, Aurelle and his generals emitting a blizzard of admonishments to troops who would sneak away from their work details at the first opportunity. General La Motterouge had a soft touch, ordering his officers to "learn the names of their men and ask after their families, trades and education," because "a man who would willingly disobey an unfamiliar officer would have difficulty evading one who had spoken with him about his family, work and plans for the future."[38] Other generals were less kind. "Despite my orders forbidding soldiers to leave camp without permission," General Barry fulminated on 15 November, "I have learned that the village of Patay is overflowing with soldiers on unauthorized leave." Barry ordered "severe measures" to curtail the practice and began executing troops the next day to demonstrate his severity: two Arab tirailleurs, two French zouaves, and two friends from the 37th Regiment. In the weeks that followed, dozens of French soldiers were executed for a crime that echoed dully through the army records: "*refus de service à un supérieur avec menacer*" – "insubordination and threats to a superior."[39]

Unaware that the rot inside Aurelle's Army of the Loire was so advanced, Grand Duke Friedrich left the entire Prussian IX Corps at Fontainebleau to block a strike from Orléans before moving against Fiereck's Army of the West in mid-November. It was a chill, wretched campaign through deserted, hungry country. Worried that growing French forces in Le Perche might attack the Prussian line of investment around Paris from the west, Moltke ordered the destruction of Fiereck. As it chanced, Fiereck was easily disposed of. After retreating too precipitously before the Prussian Army Section, he was fired by Gambetta and replaced by a naval officer, Captain Pierre Jaurès. Jaurès too melted away, leaving the grand duke grasping at air. In Tours, the government delegation began to fret. With the Army Section roving freely through Le Perche, it was only a matter of time before the grand duke wheeled south to take France's second capital. Something had to be done to divert the Germans, and quickly.

In Orléans, Aurelle was in no hurry. He met every plea for action from Gambetta or Freycinet with the same reply: The men were not prepared; they would need months to become soldiers, and would huddle in the trenchworks around Orléans until they were ready for a mobile campaign. In Tours, Gambetta deplored Aurelle's caution. "Paris is starving," he reminded Aurelle in daily bulletins. "Make haste." The paradox of the post-Sedan French war effort was this: though pledged to a strategic offensive to recover lost ground and free Paris, the French army's only hope of survival against the better-trained, more mobile Germans was on the defensive. Whereas the French

---

38 SHAT, Ld 1, Bourges, 1 Oct. 1870, Gen. La Motterouge.
39 SHAT, Ld 4, Orléans, 15 Nov. 1870, "Rapport sur le terrain en avant d'Orléans."

generals took an appropriately cautious line – building an entrenched camp at Orléans "to secure the army against all enemy attacks" and encumbering every rifle company with a battalion-sized load of shovels, picks, and axes – the politicians, their very survival at risk, were unrestrained ultras.[40] "Redouble your efforts and ardor," Gambetta beseeched Aurelle in November, "recover your élan, your French fury. Never forget that Paris awaits us!"[41]

Freycinet shuttled between Tours and the army imploring the generals to attack. Aurelle refused: "It would be dangerous to trust to the deceptive mirage of sums on paper and take them for reality."[42] Quite right: Gambetta himself was only beginning a massive overhaul of the all but useless *garde mobile* in late November, more than doubling the number of NCOs per company and recommending that each regiment cull a battalion of its best men and reward them with superior wages and rations to yield a better combat soldier. In the meantime, more basic reforms were implemented. Unorganized *garde mobile* units – *les bataillons de Loiret*, for example – were formed into numbered divisions. New line regiments (those with numbers greater than 100) were formed into new corps (those with numbers greater than XII.) Those *garde nationale* units that could be located were assigned fortress defense. All of these reforms would take time, as would Tours's efforts to oust incompetent *mobile* officers who often ignored Gambetta's orders to relinquish their commands.[43] Despite these incapacitating flaws, Gambetta and Freycinet pressed Aurelle to attack the Germans in the last week of November. Detecting the arrival in theater of Prince Friedrich Karl with more reinforcements from the lines of Metz, the republican leaders felt constrained to strike an early blow. Under no illusions as to the promise of any blow, early or otherwise, Aurelle pushed much of his XX Corps to the northernmost edge of the Forest of Orléans, where they clashed with Prince Friedrich Karl's southernmost units – three brigades of the Prussian X Corps – who were posted at Beaune-la-Rolande under General Konstantin von Voigts-Rhetz to give early warning of any French thrust toward Paris.

THE BATTLE OF BEAUNE-LA-ROLANDE, 28 NOVEMBER 1870

Early on 28 November General Aurelle attacked. Although he had little faith in his troops, he enjoyed a massive numerical advantage at Beaune-la-Rolande:

40 SHAT, Ld 1, Tours, 21 Sept. 1870, Vice-Adm. Fourichon to all generals. Ld 4, Paris, 15 Nov. 1870, Capt. Emile Mareille.
41 SHAT, Ld 4, Tours, 12 Nov. 1870, Gambetta to Gen. Aurelle. Orléans, 15 Nov. 1870, "Rapport sur le terrain en avant d'Orléans."
42 Michael Howard, *The Franco-Prussian War*, orig. 1961, New York, 1981, p. 305.
43 SHAT, Ld 1, Blois, 19 Oct. 1870, Garde Mobile de Dept. de la Sarthe to Gen. Pourcet (XV Corps). Ld 5, Tours, 23 Nov. 1870, Gambetta to Divs. Territoriales. Ld 2, Tours, 29 Oct. 1870, Gambetta to Divs. Territoriales. SHAT, Li 2, Paris, Dec. 1870, Gen. Isidore Schmitz, "Rapport sur les opérations de la Defense de Paris du 26 Nov. au 3 Dec. 1870."

60,000 troops and 140 guns of the French XVIII and XX Corps against Voigts-Rhetz's 9,000 men and seventy guns. Marching fifteen miles a day in pursuit of the evanescent French, the Prussians were worn out, and their nearest reinforcements – General Konstantin von Alvensleben's 5th Division – were ten miles away at Pithiviers, a full day's march. Even with his greenhorns – *gardes mobiles* from the Auvergne, Dauphiné, and Pyrenéan departments – Aurelle liked his chances if the Germans at Beaune could be swiftly overrun. The initial French attack aimed to do just that: Advancing through the southern outskirts of Beaune, the entire French XVIII Corps – destined for Bourbaki, but still under the provisional command of General Billot – hit several companies of the Prussian 56th Regiment at Juranville while General Charles Crouzat's XX Corps rolled back the Prussian 57th Regiment. That left just thirteen Prussian companies walled inside Beaune-la-Rolande, a scarcely defensible place at the best of times. Ringed by rising ground, the town was vulnerable to encirclement and bombardment. Only its six-foot high south wall, fronted by the narrow stream of the Rolande, and its elevated, walled churchyard could be deemed strongpoints. These the 1,200 defenders culled from the Prussian 16th and 57th Regiments resolved to exploit.

Two entire brigades of the French XX Corps charged the Beaune churchyard at 11:30. The Prussian companies inside the churchyard recalled watching in frustration as the French splashed across the Rolande, which, though only 400 yards distant, was beyond the reach of the Dreyse rifle. If armed with Chassepots, the Prussians would have made the river run red, as it was, they endured more frustration while the French slid and wallowed through the gluey mud or picked their way through vineyards and fencing wire before finally tramping into effective range. After assuring that every infantryman had a Frenchman in his sights, the Prussian NCOs bellowed "*Los!*" – "fire!" – at 200 paces. Fire and smoke exploded into the French columns, which shivered, reformed, and came on again. Each of the repeated French attacks broke down completely on the edge of the village, where the corpses and wounded lay in heaps. General Crouzat later described the nightmarish scenes around Beaune, where French columns pushed into barricaded streets and loopholed walls, only to be thrown back by salvos of aimed fire. His only real attacking troops, the 3rd Zouaves, "covered the outskirts with their [700] dead and wounded." Every one of Crouzat's staff officers was killed or wounded trying to organize the attack. Less disciplined units like the *Mobiles des Vosges* disintegrated completely amid the chaos.[44]

For the Germans inside Beaune-la-Rolande, the experience was no easier on the nerves. Shells screamed in from the northwest and *mitrailleuse* fire peppered the walls, knocking out chunks of stone and goring or decapitating

---

44 SHAT, Ld 6, 3 Dec. 1870, Gen. Crouzat, "Rapport sur le combat de Beaune."

any man who exposed himself at the wrong moment. A Hanoverian private recalled the fear that spread among the men as more and more of their officers were struck down. He remembered the colonel of the 57th Regiment moving down the thinning lines of men to encourage them but also insist on fire discipline as there seemed no end to the French attacks and there were no German reserves. It was desperate, close-in fighting as eleven French battalions – supported by thirty guns – struggled against the determined defenders, who sometimes set their own barricades on fire to drive back Crouzat's attackers. The French sent a second attack at 1:30; this too was repulsed. With no more ammunition than what they had in their haversacks, the Prussians waited until the French bayonet charge was upon them before opening fire. After thirty minutes of butchery, the French broke off, some units retreating, others working their way round to the northwest to hit the Prussians in a less defended quarter.

General Wilhelm von Woyna, who had traveled far since his first fight at Spicheren, was ready for them. After retreating in the morning, he had reformed the Prussian 38th Brigade just north of Beaune. There at Romainville he beat back a French brigade and then detached several companies to Les Roches, a flat-topped hill that overlooked Beaune's east end. At Romainville, Woyna was shortly reinforced by the vanguard of Alvensleben's 5th Division, several infantry companies and gun batteries, which pitched in against a mass of several thousand French troops assaulting the western wall of Beaune-la-Rolande. On the opposite end of town, Woyna's men scrambled to the top of Les Roches, knelt and fired into masses of French *mobiles* of Billot's XVIII Corps, who were loping up the hillside or attacking the eastern edge of Beaune. This lopsided firefight, at ranges of less than 200 yards, lasted until nightfall: Ten Prussian companies holding off as many French battalions until Billot – hearing the thunder of German artillery for the first time – drew back to Orme, a little village south of Beaune. In Beaune, exhausted cheers went up, the beleaguered defenders thrilled to be alive and in the vicinity of reinforcements.

In total darkness, General Crouzat hazarded a last attack up the road from Orme. Thick columns of French infantry tramped along the road yelling "*en avant! en avant!*" – "forward!" The German defenders roused themselves a last time and shambled into line. "*Ruhigste Feuerdisziplin!*" – "calmest, strictest fire discipline!" – the NCOs reminded their squads, who were badly shaken by all they had been through and by the wild shouts coming from the approaching French battalions. Still, the men held their fire and let the French close to 100 paces before commencing rapid fire. The Germans could hear the bullets striking home and the raw screams of the French, some of whom pushed right up to the German lines before ebbing back. Others were not so bold; watching the XVIII Corps from a distance, General Crouzat recalled that most of the French troops ignored the order to attack, discharged their rifles from a great distance, and ran away.[45] Beaune-la-Rolande more than any other battle in this last phase of the war revealed the strength of Germany's professionals and the weakness of France's unseasoned reserves. "We were hardened steel," a German veteran recalled. "Every company had lost dozens of men, but what remained was the best quality. You could rely uncondition-ally on the men to your left and right."[46] Nine thousand German troops had successfully repulsed 60,000 French, and the disparity in casualties was even more striking, 850 German dead and wounded against 8,000 French. Com-menting on battles like Beaune-la-Rolande, Russia's leading military critic, General Heinrich Leer, scoffed at the French war effort: "After Metz and Sedan, we lost all interest, for the weakness of the French gave the Germans full liberty of movement. *Anything* was possible; there was no need even for boldness, for even the riskiest strokes were easy."[47] Touring the corpse-strewn battlefield on 30 November, Prince Friedrich Karl would undoubtedly have contested the last part of Leer's statement. "Only Gravelotte was this bloody," he muttered.[48]

A French sortie from Paris that should have coincided with the battle of Beaune-la-Rolande finally stumbled forward on 30 November. Trochu had sent word of the sortie to Tours by balloon on the 26th, but winds from the south had pushed the balloon all the way to Norway. Four entire days passed before the accident was discovered and a copy of the message routed to Tours. Late on the 30th, an excited Freycinet convened a council of war at Aurelle's headquarters on the road between Orléans and Châteaudun. The entire Army of the Loire – 90,000 infantry, 5,600 cavalry, and 260 guns – must wheel right and commence a march on Paris. Aurelle protested that they were too late. The battle around Paris would be decided before the Army of the Loire even moved. Tours was unyielding; there must be another offensive, some effort to concert with Paris.

THE BATTLE OF LOIGNY, 2 DECEMBER 1870

General Antoine Chanzy's XVI Corps moved forward to attack the nearest units of the Army Section at Loigny, just north of Orléans, on 2 December. Here the numbers on either side were roughly even – 35,000 apiece – and Chanzy was demolished in a three-day battle, losing 7,000 dead, wounded, and missing, 2,500 of whom arrived unscathed in the German camp. The fight-ing was fierce and primitive, both armies deployed in vast brigade-strength

---

45 SHAT, Ld 6, 3 Dec. 1870, Gen. Crouzat, "Rapport sur le combat de Beaune."
46 Matthias, p. 94.
47 "General Heinrich Antonowitsch Leer über den Krieg 1870-71," *Österreische Militärische Zeitschrift* (ÖMZ) 4 (1874), p. 42.
48 Matthias, pp. 86–8. Howard, pp. 306–7.

skirmish lines in open fields that offered no cover against the whizzing bullets and shrapnel. Many German units, caught in the open by *mitrailleuse* fire, suffered greater casualties than the French, and advanced only by swallowing their fear and sprinting at the enemy, piling up 4,000 German dead and wounded in the course of the day. "Because of the din of shells and musketry, it was impossible to hear or even shout commands," Lieutenant Joseph Krumper recalled. "Our only chance was to crouch down and close with the French as quickly as possible. All I remember of that day is a flash of lightning before my eyes, when I fell forward, blood everywhere, my lower jaw shot clean away."[49] Krumper somehow kept his men moving forward, but Aurelle's army, beaten back at Loigny and Poupry, broke and fled in disorder. Survivors recalled stumbling through the twilight pursued by German shells that cracked and burst all around them.[50] For Mecklenburg's 35,000 troops, who had driven back repeated French storm attacks from ranges as close as fifty yards, it had been a close call. The men were dog-tired and frozen. A Saxon infantryman remembered that "my shoes fell apart in the battle and I had to bind the soles back on with my coat sleeves."[51]

Loigny sounded the death knell of Aurelle's Army of the Loire. Beset by cold, hunger and snow, the French troops had no more stomach for the war and halted their push toward Paris. When Prince Friedrich Karl massed his entire strength above Orléans and attacked on 3 December, the French army fell apart. Employing the successful tactics used at Sedan, the Prussians first shelled the dense French fortifications along the edge of the Forest of Orléans and only attacked with infantry once all defensive fire had been suppressed. Stunned and panicked by the rain of shells, the French began to break. Once General Joseph Pourcet's XV Corps, Aurelle's best-trained and equipped formation, dissolved, the rest of the units followed, streaming through the woods, roads, and villages toward Orléans. Observing the wild flight, Aurelle abandoned all hope of holding Orléans. His army had split into two uncoordinated halves, the XVI and XVII Corps north of the Loire, the XV, XVIII and XX Corps south of the river. Angrily brushing off Freycinet's objections, Aurelle ordered a return to the Sologne, the forested region south of the Loire, a mission impossible for his troops north of the river.

Late on 4 December, the first German troops re-entered Orléans, marching past files of indifferent French prisoners and fugitives. Aurelle moved away to the south with just half of his army; he had lost 20,000 men in this last battle, only 2,000 of them combat casualties. The rest were unwounded or lightly wounded prisoners, an unmistakable sign of demoralization. German newspapers delighted in the lopsided victory: 28,000 Germans with 196 guns

49 BKA, HS 856, Lt. Joseph Krumper.
50 SHAT, Ld 7, Dec. 1870, XVI Corps to 1st Div.
51 Becher, pp. 44–9.

had routed 87,000 French troops with 264 guns.[52] Despondent, Gambetta abandoned Tours and moved the government delegation to Bordeaux, where it arrived on 10 December. In Paris, General Trochu affected indifference – "the loss [of Orléans] in no way diminishes our resolve" – but was deeply depressed. Before this second battle of Orléans the French had assumed that the division of their Army of the Loire into two ineffective halves would be temporary. They now recognized that it was permanent.[53]

THE SIEGE OF PARIS, WINTER 1870–71

In Paris, the quality of life was plummeting every day. The city of 2 million had eaten up most of its food stocks and now faced famine. Meat, even mule and horsemeat, had disappeared, and a chicken could not be had for less than $75, butter for $60/pound, a cord of firewood for $750. Only price-controlled bread was affordable, which explained the regular, violent "bread panics" that exploded whenever bakers ran out of loaves. Fed on little more than bread and wine, ordinary people were starving; the U.S. embassy, which maintained 4,300 destitute Parisians throughout the siege, submitted reports like this: "I sent a messenger [with money] to visit a family of seven; they live on dry bread in a sixty-three-square-foot attic with no fire, and have just burned their bed as a last resource. There was a seven-year-old boy on the floor, so weak that he could not lift his head."[54]

Under tremendous social pressure to act, Trochu ordered General Ducrot's sortie of 29 November, which triggered a vicious three-day battle on the eastern outskirts. Though intended to coincide with Aurelle's thrust north from Orléans, this sortie also aimed to derail German logistics. Using boat bridges that would be towed into place late on the 28th, Ducrot's troops would surge across the Marne at Joinville, Neuilly, and Brie, drive the Germans out of Champigny and Villiers, and place themselves on the direct line of communication between Prussian great headquarters at Versailles – west of Paris – and Lagny – east of the city – which was Moltke's principal railhead to Germany. If it took hold, Ducrot's sortie would set back Bismarck's bombardment plans and empty the kitchens and magazines of every Prussian unit south and west of Paris. It would also give Ducrot what he called an "*ouvrage*" or outwork beyond the Marne. With rested infantry, guns on the crests of St. Maur and Avron, and a base in the Bois de Vincennes, the Paris garrison would have an opening to the southeast and an eventual junction with the Loire Army.[55]

---

52 Maurice, p. 420.
53 SHAT, Li 2, "proclamations."
54 Washington, National Archives (NA), CIS, U.S. Serial Set 1780, 9 Jan. 1871, Washburne to Fish. The values given are approx. 2003 values: a chicken then cost $5, a pound of butter $4, a cord of wood $50.
55 SHAT, Li 2, Paris, Dec. 1870, Gen. Isidore Schmitz, "Rapport sur les opérations de la Defense de Paris du 26 Nov. au 3 Dec. 1870."

Fig. 16. German infantry drive back the French at Villiers

Sadly for the French, Ducrot's engineers miscalculated the speed and depth of the Marne and failed to tow the bridges into position on the 28th, leaving masses of French infantry – three entire corps – stranded on the wrong bank of the Marne with nothing to do on 29 November. Moltke meanwhile hustled thousands of German reserves into Villiers and Champigny, where they greeted the French attack on the 30th – when the bridges finally floated into place – with withering rifle and shellfire.

Alerted by the failed crossing the previous day that a breakout was imminent, the Prussians had been zeroed in on the French columns before they even touched the Marne. When Ducrot ordered a diversionary attack toward Malmaison on the western outskirts of Paris with his *gardes mobiles*, the Prussians ignored the feint and poured concentrated fire on the main effort at Champigny and Villiers. A Prussian veteran explained their sureness of touch: "The difference in the colors of the trousers of the French army, those of the Line always being red, never failed to inform us, by the position assigned to the men of the Line, where the enemy meant to deal his principal blow." Daybreak on the 29th had revealed thousands of *Rothosen* on the Marne, giving away the game entirely.[56] When the red-trousered French 35th, 42nd,

---

56 SKA, ZS 158, Lt. Hinüber, "Tagebuch." Maurice, p. 294.

and 114th Regiments charged through Champigny on 30 November, they were hit in both flanks by Saxon and Württemberg infantry and guns, which pressed them back across the Marne. Packed in battalion columns, the French suffered grievously; although they had 80,000 troops at the point of attack – far more than the Germans – the terrain was so narrow that they could not spread and exploit their numbers. The Germans just fired and fired till they were out of ammunition.

In the Parc de Villiers, the the Württemberger wheeled their captured *mitrailleuses* to within 300 yards of the French columns before opening fire, hacking France's 136th Regiment to bloody pieces before trampling it with a deftly executed counter-attack. A French officer captured at Villiers divulged his men's fear of the Germans: *"ils criaient toujours, ils venaient comme une avalanche, et tout était fini"* – "they bellow, they attack like an avalanche, and then, suddenly, it's all over."[57] In the furious three-day battle at Villiers and Champigny, the French lost 12,000 men. With losses like these, there would not be many more *Rothosen* to spearhead Ducrot's attacks. Having pledged on 29 November that he would emerge from battle "dead or victorious," Ducrot found himself the irresistible butt of jokes, and worse. Heavy German counter-attacks on 2 December nearly broke through the French defenses at Champigny, before ebbing back. Implored by Gambetta to resume his attack toward Fontainebleau and a junction with the 120,000 troops of the Army of the Loire, Ducrot instead left his dead unburied and retreated back across the Marne with 100,000 troops, reentering Paris on the 4th. He had clung to the left bank of the Marne and absorbed massive casualties until 3 December to unite with the promised relief army, but it had never come. Ducrot was losing faith in Gambetta's promises, Trochu too. In a conversation with the British military attaché after the Villiers defeat, Trochu admitted that "he had steeled himself against every misfortune.... Nothing good will happen, but I'll resist to the last to save my military honor."[58]

If morale was low in Paris, it was fading in Prussian great headquarters at Versailles as well, where the king's ministers and generals had begun to fight bitterly over the conduct of the war. Weak though the French military efforts were, they were sufficient to prolong the war, placing enormous strain on the Prussian army and the German economy. Like most professional military men, Moltke was proceeding deliberately, pushing his columns deep into France to surround and disarm the remaining French armies. To Bismarck, who annoyed the Prussian generals by appearing at meetings in his *Landwehr*

---

57 SKA, KM 968, Le Vert Galant, 9 Dec. 1870, Duke Georg to King Johann. SHAT, Li 2, Paris, Dec. 1870, Gen. Isidore Schmitz, "Rapport sur les opérations de la Defense de Paris du 26 Nov. au 3 Dec. 1870."
58 SHAT, Ld 1, Tours, 21 Sept. 1870, Vice-Admiral Fourichon to all generals. PRO, FO 425, London, 30 Dec. 1870, Gen. Claremont to Lyons. Howard, pp. 342–7. Maurice, pp. 304–6.

general's greatcoat, such precautions seemed time-consuming and unnecessary. The main thing was to force the French *government* to terms, and the way to do this was to ring Paris with heavy artillery and bombard its streets, murdering civilians until the republican regime came to its senses and agreed to terms.

Reports that French civilians and *francs-tireurs* were killing or torturing German prisoners merely confirmed Bismarck in his views. The German chancellor suspected that the French had killed 600 healthy Prussian POWs in Lille. When the Garibaldians, recently arrived from Italy, threatened to cut the ears off of fourteen Prussian prisoners if the Germans took reprisals against Vittel, Bismarck exploded, exhorting the army to hang or shoot all suspected *francs-tireurs* and burn the villages that sheltered them. Varice, Ourcelle and Ablis, near Orléans, were burned to the ground in November after villagers cut German telegraph wires or aided *franc-tireur* ambushes. Many more towns would be burned out – "*eingeäschert*" – before the war ended, a return to brutality last experienced when the Napoleonic Wars had blazed across Europe sixty years earlier. Though Bismarck never went so far as his wife – "shoot and stab all the French, down to the little babies" – he insisted that there be no "laziness in killing" so long as France continued its futile resistance. If a French village refused German exactions, Bismarck wanted every male inhabitant hanged. If French boys spat at German troops from bridges or windows, Bismarck wanted the troops to shoot them dead. When French women and children picked through trash or scavenged for potatoes on the fringes of Paris, Bismarck wanted the German gunners to fire into them. Troops who quailed would be executed. Bismarck only voiced the threat; his troops implemented it. When 400 crudely uniformed *francs-tireurs* overran a Prussian outpost near Toul in January, the Prussian 57th Regiment furiously counter-attacked and burned the nearest village, Fontenoy-sur-Moselle. Finding few "citizen soldiers" there, they went on a killing spree, spearing the inhabitants with their bayonets and heaving them into the flames.[59] Ironically, a Prussian army that had deplored the atrocities and mass casualties of the American Civil War was now grimly embarked on a wholesale Americanization of the Franco-Prussian War, Bismarck doing his utmost as General William T. Sherman might have said, "to make France howl."[60]

Moltke fought back, arguing more equably that bombardment of civilian areas would outrage international opinion and that the fifteen-centimeter Krupp cannon and twenty-one-centimeter mortars and ordnance needed for the bombardment would not be available until January 1871, by which time

59 John Horne and Alan Kramer, *German Atrocities, 1914*, New Haven, 2001, pp. 141–2.
60 Dresden, SKA, ZS 158, 13 Dec. 1870, Lt. Adolf Hinüber, "Tagebuch." Pflanze, vol. 1, pp. 483–4. Busch, vol. 1, pp. 295–6. Frederic Trautmann, ed. *A Prussian observes the American Civil War*, Columbia, 2001, pp. 197–9.

Paris would have starved anyway. "Let them die like mad dogs," General Albrecht von Blumenthal muttered in January. "They have brought it upon themselves."[61] Here was a textbook clash of civil-military decision-making. "The question," Moltke wrote the king on 30 November, "as to when the artillery attack on Paris should or can begin, can only be decided on the basis of *military* views. Political motives can only find consideration in so far as they do not demand anything militarily inadmissible or impossible." Moltke was most anxious about his lines of supply. Only three railways served the interior of France from Germany, and sabotage and the resistance of the French garrisons at Belfort, Langres and Mézières blocked two of the three lines for the entire war, and stopped the third well short of Paris (and the Loire) at Château-Thierry until November, when it was finally extended to Lagny (the object of Ducrot's 29 November sortie.)[62] Supplies, ammunition, and troops run in from the German states had to contend with long waits, traffic jams, and then a long march or wagon-ride from the Marne to the outskirts of Paris. Bismarck's demand that fresh troops, supplies, and shrapnel be sidetracked to make room for Krupp's heavy artillery and ammunition struck Moltke as impertinent and ill-advised.

Moltke's placement of logistics – what was "admissible and possible" – above larger *political* considerations infuriated Bismarck, who duly exploded: "The men freeze and fall ill, the war is dragging on, the neutrals waste time discussing it with us.... All this so that certain people may be praised for saving 'civilization,'" a reference to Moltke's qualms about shelling civilians. Bismarck, seeking a more integrated war effort, criticized Moltke's "departmental jealously" and his "optimistic conjectures" about operations on the Loire, where, Bismarck worried, Germany's numerically "inferior forces might be destroyed at any moment" by enemy action, "frost, snow, or a dearth of victuals and war material." From Bismarck's perspective, any amount of brutality was justified to end the war before Prussia's hand was further weakened by "unforeseen accidents in battle, sickness, or the intervention of neutrals."[63] He called this *"Politik im Krieg"* – the "wartime political effort" – in which military means had to be bent unquestioningly to the policy aim. Here traditional roles were reversed – the soldier stressing moderation, the statesman annihilation – but once Roon broke ranks and backed Bismarck, the king came round to his chancellor.

While the Prussians argued, General Ducrot launched another breakout, this time to the north toward Le Bourget on 21 December. With the Army of the Loire beaten and cut in half, Ducrot now sought to unite with France's

61　Lothar Gall, *Bismarck*, 2 vols, London, 1980, vol. 1, p. 365.
62　Howard, pp. 374–6, 380.
63　Otto Prince von Bismarck, *Bismarck: The man and the statesman*, 2 vols., London, 1898, vol. 2, pp. 108, 121. Gall, vol. 1, p. 365.

Fig. 17. A Bavarian siege gun on the outskirts of Paris

35,000-man Army of the North under General Louis Faidherbe. This improbable plan showed just how desperate Ducrot's predicament had become, for Faidherbe's army, characterized by the general himself as "a flock of men without arms, without leaders, without training," survived chiefly because there were scarcely any German troops around Faidherbe's bases at Lille and Amiens. For the Germans, it was enough to isolate those places – which, like Paris, communicated with Tours and Bordeaux by semaphore or pigeon – while hammering away at Paris and the last French units on the Loire. To enforce Faidherbe's isolation, the Prussian Guards threw back Ducrot's thrust at Le Bourget on 21 December, shooting down 983 more men and officers. Like it or not (probably not), the Paris garrison was beginning to substantiate Gambetta's boast that the republic would be sustained "even at the risk of self-immolation."[64]

For Moltke, it only remained to begin immolating the powerful French forts that ringed Paris and staved off every Prussian attack. With seventy-six heavy-caliber guns and plentiful ammunition finally in place, the Germans

---

64 PRO, FO 425, 98, Bordeaux, 2 Jan. 1871, Lyons to Granville. SKA, ZS 158, Lt. Hinüber, "Tagebuch." Maurice, pp. 307–9, 312–15. Howard, pp. 391–2.

smashed the French fort at Mont Avron on 27–28 December, then pushed forward to destroy Forts Vanves, Issy, and Montrouge on 5 January, the day that Count Harrach sketched his famous painting of Moltke contentedly observing the bombardment through a round attic window (the *oeil de boeuf*) near Versailles. By then, the first German shells were already whistling down the Left Bank to explode in the Jardin du Luxembourg and near the Panthéon. On 4 January, twenty-five Parisian noncombatants – including many women and children – were killed or wounded by Prussian artillery. Charles Swager, an American from Louisville, lost a leg when a Prussian shell burst in his hotel room in St. Sulpice. By mid-January, Trochu reported 189 civilian casualties, including forty-five women and twenty-one children. In three weeks of firing, the German gunners had hit hospitals, schools, churches, prisons, and apartment houses, but were still far behind the death toll wrought by cold and hunger, which were killing 3,000 to 4,000 Parisians every week in January.[65]

Suffering miserably, Parisians demanded a last effort to break out by their 400,000 garrison troops. Trochu refused, on the grounds that another sortie would only fail and kill more Frenchmen in what would be "a mere act of despair." There was more despair on 18 January, when the German princes gathered in the Palace of Versailles to proclaim "the unity of the German nation" under their newly fledged *Kaiser* or Emperor, King Wilhelm I of Prussia. The ceremony in the Hall of Mirrors was calculated to humiliate France, the Versailles palace and *salle des glaces* having been constructed 200 years earlier by Louis XIV, whose military campaigns had shattered Germany into the impotent statelets that were only now being unified by Bismarck. Perhaps the Germans tried too hard, or made the pageant more Prussian than German: "I cannot begin to describe to you," Prince Otto of Bavaria wrote to his brother, "How infinitely and agonizingly painful I found the scene.... It was all so cold, so proud, so glossy, so strutting and boastful and heartless and empty." In fact, that "proud, glossy, strutting" exercise memorialized in paintings was just the culmination of three months of patient haggling by Bismarck, who, while the war raged, entertained a parade of German princes in Versailles. Most had required a sweetener to assure their "free accession" to the new empire, none more than mad Ludwig II of Bavaria, who, needing funds for his pleasure palaces and travels with Richard Wagner, demanded cash in advance and 300,000 marks per annum from the notorious "Guelph Fund," which was the Hanoverian state treasure seized by the Prussians after Königgrätz. Masking his delight behind a suitably Wagnerian mien, it was King Ludwig II who signed the famous "Kaiser letter" of 2 December 1870, offering King Wilhelm I of Prussia the new German crown on behalf of the

---

65 Washington, DC, CIS, U.S. Serial Set 1780, 9 Jan. 1871, Washburne to Fish.

German princes. Wilhelm accepted, but grudgingly. "This is the end of the old Prussia," he grumbled to his chancellor.[66]

With the fall of Paris imminent, Bismarck girded for the end game, with the same ruthlessness that the Germans would mete out in 1940. If Paris fell but the Bordeaux government continued to resist, Bismarck vowed to dismember France and suck the economic life from it. He made the threat explicit on 14 January: "If Paris submits but France fights on, Germany will annex Alsace-Lorraine, occupy Paris and the territory between the Channel and the Loire and force those provinces to bear all the costs of the war until a peace party forms in unoccupied France strong enough to impose its will on the government of the moment." Bismarck's German-occupied France would be fitted with "defensible boundaries" and effectively annexed until every German demand was met. Odo Russell, Britain's envoy to Versailles, reported that Bismarck – fearing the toxic influence of a French republic on the European monarchies – was angling for a Napoleonic restoration, hence the belittling reference to "government of the moment." With all of France craving peace under *any* regime, Russell concluded that the Gambetta government was slowly committing "suicide."[67]

General and "Provisional President" Louis Trochu also gave every appearance of having a death wish, agreeing to unleash a third and final sortie on 19 January. Ninety thousand French troops funneled past the fortress at Mont Valerien into the German-held gap between Bougival and St. Cloud. On this four-mile front, the French converged on St. Cloud and Buzenval, where they were picked apart and hammered down by German artillery. Firing down from the high ground of Garches, the Prussians brought more and more batteries into action while Ducrot's, pulled over rough ground by emaciated wheel horses, fell further and further behind. If the French could have broken through at either place, they would have swarmed down to Versailles by nightfall, administering a rude shock to the ongoing celebration of the German Empire. But Ducrot's last thrust weakened and collapsed, many of the troops falling out to dig for potatoes or ransack German supply dumps. By late afternoon, panicked French infantry were being blown to pieces by a continuous storm of Prussian shells. With 8,000 men and officers dead, wounded or missing (sixteen times the Prussian losses), Ducrot retreated into Paris for the last time, where he resigned his command and gave it to General Joseph Vinoy.[68]

On the Loire front, France's last intact army had been smashed into two pieces by the fighting around Orléans in December. Rather than replace

---

66 Pflanze, vol. 1, pp. 499–501. Gall, vol. 1, p. 370–2.
67 PRO, FO 425, 98, Berlin, 14 Jan. 1871, Loftus to Granville. Versailles, 19 Jan. 1871, Russell to Granville.
68 NA, CIS, U.S. Serial Set, 1780, Paris, 25 Jan. 1871, Washburne to Fish. Maurice, pp. 317–23.

Aurelle as commander-in-chief, Gambetta had retired the general and agreed to the establishment of two small armies where previously there had been one large one. North of the Loire, General Antoine Chanzy commanded the XVI and XVII Corps, while General Charles Bourbaki (who had escaped from Metz after Gravelotte) replaced Aurelle south of the river, taking over the XV, XVIII, and XX Corps and pulling back to Bourges to regroup. Retreating through Vierzon on 7 December, Aurelle stopped for lunch with the mayor and did not bother to conceal his loathing of Freycinet – "*notre infatigable Carnot*" – and "*il signor Gambetta*," the low-born son of Italian grocers, who must have pricked certain social prejudices of Count Louis d'Aurelle de Paladines. According to Aurelle, Freycinet, that "indefatigable Carnot" – a sarcastic reference to Lazare Carnot, the "organizer of victory" in the French Revolution's most desperate hour – had tied the army in knots with "his constantly changing and often contradictory dispositions" and had demoralized the troops by blaming the generals for every reverse. While Aurelle lunched, he would have seen evidence of this demoralization as thousands of leaderless French troops surged through Vierzon demanding food, drink and shelter from the terrified inhabitants.[69] Convinced that the bickering French were on their last legs, Moltke urged Prince Friedrich Karl to finish them off before the start of armistice negotiations. If this last sword could be knocked from Gambetta's hand, the Germans would be able to impose the harshest possible terms.

THE BATTLE OF BEAUGENCY, 8–9 DECEMBER 1870

To corral Bourbaki, Friedrich Karl marched the III Corps upstream to Gien with orders to pivot there and turn south to cooperate with the IX Corps and a cavalry division, which crossed to the left bank at Orléans and plunged south toward Bourges. Mecklenburg, meanwhile, was ordered to march down the Loire to Tours, where Chanzy would probably make a last stand. With many of his troops streaming back to Blois in panic and confusion, Chanzy grouped three divisions in defensive positions at Beaugency and made a stand, his right wing resting on the Loire, his left in the Forest of Marchenoir, Chanzy himself in the middle of the line at Josnes. Although he would have been wiser to cross to the left bank of the Loire to escape the Prussian pincers and reunite with Bourbaki, Chanzy was deceived by erroneous reports from Aurelle and Gambetta that Ducrot had broken out of Paris on 2 December and reached Etampes. He later explained that he felt bound to remain on the right bank of the Loire to await Ducrot, but really he remained because of the "mass confusion" that gripped his little army. Disorganized by defeat

69 SHAT, Le 19, Cher, 9 Dec. 1870, "L'Occupation de Vierzon."

and continual rain and snow, the men could hardly be shifted.[70] Racked by bouts of malarial fever, Chanzy himself was not very mobile, and his rather unambitious aim became simply this: preserve France's last field forces for the peace. With 100,000 troops in hand, the French would be able credibly to threaten a resumption of hostilities if the Germans were too demanding. If those troops were ever enveloped and annihilated, the French would find themselves prostrate and defenseless.

On 8 December and again on the 9th, the French and Germans struggled all along the line at Beaugency. German veterans of this battle recalled that it was the fiercest many of them had ever experienced. With superior numbers, Chanzy hurled one bayonet charge after another at the central, walled villages of Cravant and Beaumont, which both sides considered keypoints of the otherwise featureless battlefield. Oskar Becher, an NCO in the Prussian 94th Regiment, recalled the maddened pace set by the repeated French attacks on Cravant, which differed little from the bayonet charges of 1793. With so many untrained conscripts, the French simply herded them into battalion columns and launched them at the Prussians, preceded by barrages of shrapnel and bursts of *mitrailleuse* fire. Pressed on all sides, Becher's men would fire off all of their rounds and then plunge their shaking hands into the ammunition wagons, which had been wheeled right up to the firing lines. Filling their pockets and haversacks with cartridges, they would resume shooting, trying to ignore the cracks of shrapnel. "Not a minute passed without a shell bursting within ten yards of me," Becher recalled. "Those of us who survived did so only because so many of the French projectiles failed to explode." Images of the close-in fighting remained burned in Becher's mind forever: the shell that decapitated his platoon leader and spattered brains on Becher's coat, the shell that ripped both legs off the drummer boy, the sight of his battalion commander running up and down the line holding out boxes of cartridges for the quick-firing troops. Although a German counter-attack pressed to within a half-mile of Chanzy's headquarters on 9 December (nearly capturing Gambetta, who had come up to observe the fighting), Mecklenburg reluctantly broke off the battle. With hundreds of irreplaceable officer casualties and no more than 24,000 German effectives, he hesitated to plunge deeper into the belly of Chanzy's 100,000 man army lest he, rather than Chanzy, be encircled and destroyed. "For me," Sergeant Becher reminisced, "there was only one bright spot in that horrid battle, the death of a soldier I will call Private P. He was the worst kind of malingerer, and I'd had to punish him so many times that I feared his revenge and was pleased when, calling to him to help me tear down a fence, I saw a shell rip his head off."[71]

70 SHAT, Le 19, Paris, 25 June 1871, Col. Charles d'Arguelle, "Résumé des operations de guerre."
71 Becher, pp. 50–8.

No less than the French, Mecklenburg's troops were famished, frozen, exhausted and, as Becher's last observation suggests, near the breaking point. Wherever they requisitioned in December 1870, the answer was the same: *"Nisk de pain, nisk de viande, nisk de vin, monsieur, nisk du tout, du tout, du tout"* – "no bread, no meat, no wine, good sir, no nothing, nothing, nothing..."[72] Few of these hungry Germans had rested more than a day or two since Coulmiers and their filthy uniforms were literally disintegrating. Lice were a constant torment, as was the fear of smallpox in dirty camps and villages. Boots fell apart or vanished in the mud, and locally procured shoes proved too small for the big-boned German troops. Even Prince Leopold of Bavaria could do nothing for the men of his artillery regiment, who, by early December, were shuffling along peasant-style in wooden clogs stuffed with straw, wrapped in requisitioned blankets of every stripe and color. Many Germans simply took to wearing French uniforms, which explained complaints from some French prisoners that they had been captured by Prussian troops whom they had mistaken for French comrades.

Just reaching and acclimating to this wintry theater proved too much for many German draftees. Of thirty-two replacements received by the 3rd Bavarian Regiment on 18 November, twenty went directly to the hospital suffering from colds and exhaustion.[73] German draftees strong enough to join their units were astonished by the appearance of the old comrades, few of whom bore any resemblance to a conventional soldier. With the temperature dropping, the whole German army focused increasingly on food, sex, and malice. A Hanoverian enlisted man recalled that "the humor got nastier and nastier;" troops would enter French towns yelling *"Mademoiselle, voulez-vouz baiser?"* – "Miss, would you like to fuck?" They would sing *Deutschland, Deutschland über alles"* at the top of their lungs to anger any Frenchmen within earshot. *"Rollen"* – slang for *requirien* or requisition – became the leading pastime, one German passing another would invariably ask, *"Hast du etwas gerollt?"* – "have you swiped anything today?" A Bavarian officer recalled the evaporation of discipline in his platoon whenever it passed a village: "If the men suspected that there was bread in those places, the march columns would dissolve in the hunt for it. The troops behaved like savages and had only one thought – bread – which they had been without for weeks."[74] Entering Tours in December, a Prussian private recalled the hatred displayed by the French townspeople, who glowered from their cafés and windows. "We returned their hatred," the private later wrote.[75] At a cottage near Blois, Private

72 Friedrich Leo, *Kriegserinnerungen am 1870–71*, Berlin, 1914, p. 43.
73 BKA, HS 856, Lt. Joseph Krumper.
74 BKA, HS 856, Lt. Joseph Krumper.
75 Matthias, pp. 148–9.

Friedrich Leo saw another Prussian soldier leading away the proprietor's cow and calf. The peasant ran after the Prussian with tears streaming down his face, crying *"c'est un malheur"* – "it's a catastrophe." Wanly smiling, the Prussian agreed; pointing to the cow he said, *"grand malheur,"* the calf, *"petit malheur."*[76] For the exhausted French peasantry, friendly troops were no less of a misfortune. Roger de Mauni, a twenty-three-year-old *mobile*, who stopped for the night with his unit at a farm near Le Mans, recalled that "the poor woman of the house did not dare, in spite of my entreaties, to come near the fire. She spends her days shivering and weeping in a dark corner.... Her husband has lost an arm and her sons are little children. The sight of this family fills one with sorrow."[77]

Frustrated at the slow progress of operations on the Loire, Moltke ordered Prince Friedrich Karl to reinforce Mecklenburg, resume overall command of the Loire campaign, and finish Chanzy off. Worried that Bourbaki might knife into his flank or rear if he turned to face Chanzy, Friedrich Karl reluctantly complied, stopping the III corps in its tracks at Gien and sending it by forced marches *back* toward Orléans, where it would follow the Prussian X Corps into action at Beaugency. For Chanzy, everything now hinged on Bourbaki's willingness to hasten into action with the bulk of the old Army of the Loire and disengage him. Time was critical, the IX Corps's Hessian division having stormed Chambord on 10 December and probed as far as Blois the next day, gaining a bridge and a foothold in Chanzy's rear. Still, Bourbaki's 150,000 troops at Bourges did not budge. Bourbaki tried, ordering his XV Corps to secure the routes to Orléans from Bourges and Vierzon, but the sullen troops ignored his orders. Ordered by Gambetta to redouble his efforts, Bourbaki replied by inviting Gambetta to visit his dispirited army. The experience stunned Gambetta, who cabled Freycinet that it "was the saddest sight he had ever seen," a French army "in veritable dissolution."[78]

By this late date the Germans were also flagging. No less than 50 percent of the Army Section's officers had been killed or wounded in the Loire campaign and the fighting units were gutted by wounds, flu, or typhus. Some German battalions had been reduced to 150 men commanded by lieutenants. Many Prussian infantry companies that had counted 250 men in August were down to fewer than fifty effectives.[79] Instructions distributed to French officers for the interrogation of German POWs make clear that France was staking everything on a war of attrition: French interrogators were instructed to obtain precise information on German company, squadron and officer strength and

76 BKA, HS 858, "Kriegstagebuch Leopold Prinz von Bayern." Leo, p. 74. Matthias, p. 84.
77 Clarke, pp. 120–1.
78 SHAT, Ld 20, Lyon, 4 March 1871, Gen. Bourbaki to Gambetta. Howard, p. 386.
79 BKA, HS 858, "Kriegstagebuch Leopold Prinz von Bayern."

the frequency and quality of "*Ersatz*" (replacements) from Germany to "proceed in this critical work of estimating German casualties, effectiveness and morale."[80] Still, the notion that the Germans might be more demoralized than his rabble must have seemed fantastic to Chanzy, a former governor of Senegal, who was ailing in the bitter cold. Unaided by Bourbaki, he lurched away from the Loire and retreated toward Le Mans. With its big rail junction and lines to Nantes, Brest and Paris, Le Mans was Chanzy's last hope. He could either fight the Germans to a standstill there, or use the railway to escape and fight another day.

Tactically, Chanzy's change of course made sense, but it failed to impress his despondent troops, who, like the surly peasants at every halt, failed to see the point of further fighting or retreat. Although Gambetta and Freycinet wished to prolong the war to moderate Germany's harsh terms, embody two new corps of *mobiles* at Bourges and Cherbourg, and take delivery of American and British war material, the soldiers at the front lacked conviction; they were the proverbial "unthanked doing the unnecessary for the ungrateful." For them, the war seemed futile, and they melted away in droves at every opportunity.[81] Shivering in the sleet and snow, with little to eat, hundreds of French troops remained hiding in the Forest of Marchenoir when the XXI Corps began its withdrawal to Vendôme, and the other French units lost dozens of stragglers at every bend and dip in the road.

After a rest at Vendôme on 16 December, Chanzy resumed his retreat toward Le Mans, which lay fifty miles west across hilly, barren country. Only the slow pursuit of Prince Friedrich Karl and Mecklenburg saved Chanzy's ragged army. The Germans staggered through the few hours of December daylight and then, hewing to the old army motto "*besser das schlechteste Quartier als das schönste Bivuak*" – "the most squalid room is better than the most beautiful campsite" – they scattered at every halt to find shelter and a fire.[82] Even the cavalry could not pursue, for the roads were so icy that the troopers had to dismount and lead their horses. Much time was lost reacting to attacks by *francs-tireurs*, who knew the roads and terrain much better than the Germans. Although no match for German combat units, the *francs-tireurs* put enormous pressure on the Prussian supply lines. After the war, the Germans estimated that there had been 37,000 of them, and they shrewdly focused their attacks on German rail stations, supply depots, and convoys. With one-third of France under German occupation and hundreds of miles of vulnerable supply lines behind his armies, Moltke was forced to detach 105,000 troops to guard

80 SHAT, La 36, Bordeaux, 31 Dec. 1870, Bureau de reconnaissances, "Instructions pour l'interrogatoire des prisonniers."
81 SHAT, Le 19, Paris, 25 June 1871, Col. Charles d'Arguelle. Wolfgang Schivelbusch, *The Culture of Defeat*, orig. 2001, New York, 2003, p. 173.
82 PRO, FO 425, 98, London, 19 Oct. 1870, "New York Tribune." BKA, HS 858, "Kriegstagebuch Leopold Prinz von Bayern."

the shipments of food, fodder, drink, and ammunition that kept his 500,000 front-line troops in action.[83] Many of the Landwehr units posted at fifteen-mile intervals behind the lines felt, as one put it, "like cowboys in Indian country." Barricaded inside station houses or supply dumps, they drove off repeated attacks by *francs-tireurs*, who had an unerring instinct for the soft targets on the Prussian line of march.[84] The Prussians refused to recognize the existence or legality of the "Armed Nation" invoked by Gambetta and Garibaldi in November, and insisted that every French combatant wear military uniform, on pain of death. Out of uniform, "citizen volunteers" were difficult to engage, for, as one Prussian officer put it, they invariably "threw away their rifles, stuck their hands in their pockets and strolled away like peace-loving peasants whenever things got hot."[85] The German response to most such incidents was to shoot the peace-loving peasant in the back of the head, regarding every *Blaukittel* – "blue smock," the traditional dress of the French workingman – as a potential guerrilla. "We caught a 'blue smock' with a rifle," a Badenese lieutenant wrote from Dijon in October. "He cried, blubbered and begged us to spare him. He swore that he was just a simple worker. Now, wasn't that just too childish? He, a civilian, who shot at our soldiers, and now asked for our forgiveness because he 'was just a worker.' That was too naïve of him. Two minutes later, he lay cold and pale on the grass by the edge of the wood."[86]

Whenever the *francs-tireurs* succeeded in blowing up a bridge or a section of railway track – a frequent occurrence – they imposed crippling shortages on the Prussians. When they cut telegraph wires, they queered their movements. "Naturally we killed a lot of innocents in reprisal," a German officer allowed. "But that was the fault of the *francs-tireurs*, who should have heeded the old saying: '*Schuster, bleib bei deinem Leisten*' – 'shoemaker, stick to your lasts.'" A less sanctimonious Prussian officer, with grim memories of the counter-insurgency, noted that the guerrilla war reminded him of a different saying: "*Jeder Mensch hat einen moralischen Schweinhund in der Tasche; es kommt nur darauf an, wie weit man ihn hervorsehen lässt*" – "Every man carries a devil in his pocket; it only varies how much of that devil is permitted to emerge."[87] With Germany's manpower fully committed, Prince Friedrich Karl's march columns, filled with a high percentage of new recruits (who tired and blistered easily), were proceeding almost as slowly as the French, and this last month of the war seemed to pass in slow motion as the two frozen, exhausted armies plucked at each other with numb fingers. "It's an open question," a Bavarian

83 Maurice, pp. 542–6.
84 A. B., *Kriegsgeschichtliche Betrachtungen über den kleinen Krieg*, ÖMZ 3 (1876), pp. 253–5.
85 Becher, p. 61. BKA, HS 858, "Kriegstagebuch Leopold Prinz von Bayern."
86 C. Betz, *Aus den Erlebnissen und Erinnerungen eines alten Offiziers*, Karlsruhe, 1894, pp. 163–6. Horne and Kramer, pp. 140–1.
87 G. von Bismarck, *Kriegserlebnisse 1866 und 1870–71*, Dessau, 1907, p. 122.

officer jotted in his diary, "what costs more men, these endless marches or a bloody battle. My platoon is down to ten men, with eight 'missing.' They'll come back, for where can they go in this blighted country?"[88]

Relations between Moltke and Bismarck were by now as frosty as the January weather. Both men were run-down by their massive responsibilities. Attempting to snuff out the last French resistance, Moltke became increasingly irate, telling Crown Prince Friedrich Wilhelm at a dinner in early January that "we must fight this nation of liars to the bitter end." If left to his own devices, he would have fought every French army in the provinces to extinction, then shelled Paris, occupied it, and sent its entire garrison back to Germany in chains. When the crown prince, a rare liberal in Prussian circles, worried about the political and diplomatic repercussions of such a campaign, Moltke grumbled that he was "only concerned with military matters." Bismarck was wiser, and understood that strategy and policy could not be separated: "We are poised on the tip of a lightning rod; if we lose the balance I have been at pains to create, we shall find ourselves on the ground."

Bismarck's balancing act involved reining in Moltke while staving off British and Russian attempts to include the Franco-Prussian War termination in a general European conference on outstanding diplomatic questions like Russia's recent re-militarization of the Black Sea. Seizing upon the distraction of the Franco-Prussian War, Russia in November 1870 had begun rebuilding its naval bases in the Black Sea, a clear violation of the treaty that had ended the Crimean War fourteen years earlier. To avoid a war with the Russians to reimpose the terms of the Treaty of Paris, the British hoped to revive France as an ally as quickly as possible, which clearly necessitated a quick end to the Prussian invasion and mild peace terms. To buy time, Bismarck summoned a preemptive conference of great powers on 3 January 1871. Now more than ever he needed to end the Franco-Prussian War, and reacted furiously when he learned that Moltke was negotiating with Trochu behind his back, to secure Trochu's surrender while Moltke's field armies ratcheted up their efforts against Chanzy and Bourbaki.

Bismarck and Moltke had disagreed on virtually every step since Sedan. The chancellor had desired an all-out assault on the French capital in the fall and rued the slow pace of Moltke's Loire campaign, which scattered scarce troops across a vast theater and made it difficult for the Prussians to make the entire French people "feel" the full, harsh impact of the war.[89] Now Bismarck grasped that Paris was the key to everything, and that it had to be squeezed until it capitulated, even if this required some relaxation of pressure in the provinces. Thus, the chancellor spent much of January fighting Moltke's

88 BKA, HS 856, Lt. Joseph Krumper."
89 Pflanze, vol. 1, p. 478.

Fig. 18. Well-shod *francs-tireurs* in action

influence in Versailles and, after threatening resignation, was rewarded with two sharply worded cabinet orders from Wilhelm I directing Moltke always to submit his communications with Trochu to Bismarck, and to brief Bismarck on all military matters "until he had no cause for complaint," clever wording that gave Bismarck unfettered access to Moltke's plans.[90] The "civilian in the cuirassier tunic," Moltke's sneering nickname for Bismarck, had vanquished his rival.

THE BATTLE OF LE MANS, 10–11 JANUARY 1871

On New Year's day 1871, Moltke ordered Prince Friedrich Karl to sweep westward with his entire army on the arc from Vendôme to Chartres and swallow up the three corps and twenty-odd battalions of Breton *gardes mobiles* that Chanzy had concentrated at Le Mans. Mecklenburg led with the army's right – his 22nd and 17th Divisions now renamed the XIII Corps – which marched down the Huisne from Chartres, while Friedrich Karl's X, IX, and III Corps ground forward on the left and center swatting aside isolated French divisions before arriving on the outskirts of Le Mans. Here Chanzy had constructed formidable positions, fortifying the wooded plateau that faced the German advance and using the waters of the Sarthe to cover his flank and rear above and below the town. The Germans struck this position on 10 January. Theirs was an uncoordinated attack, the troops and guns moving slowly into position along narrow, twisting lanes blocked with snow, and making no progress on the first day. The battle resumed on the 11th, when the Prussian Third Corps bore the brunt of the battle, hitting repeatedly at Chanzy's fortified plateau – the Chemin aux Boeufs – and taking heavy casualties. Long after dark, General Konstantin von Voigts-Rhetz arrived beneath the plateau with his X Corps, formed his brigades into company columns, and attacked the position. Tactically unsound, the gamble worked, surprising a regiment of *mobiles* and sparking panic all across the French position. As the Germans climbed briskly through the darkness, Chanzy could not hold his men. Sleepless, wet, cold, and hungry, they ran for their lives. Chanzy would lose most of his men that night – 25,000 dead and wounded and 50,000 deserters – and his army effectively ceased to exist. "When I wrote the story of our retreat to Le Mans, I thought I should never again see a greater misfortune," a young *garde mobile* officer wrote on 13 January. "I was mistaken.... France is sinking from one abyss into another." He never forgot the panicked "stragglers, their faces so ghastly and...all the dead and dying animals, turned into skeletons and embedded deep in the ice and snow, while they were still breathing."[91]

Touring the Le Mans battlefield the next day, a Prussian private noted that "it became clear to us that the French were not only beaten but demoralized. The roads were littered with their packs and rifles. Whole units came over to us to surrender. Thirty French infantrymen surrendered to one of

90 Eberhard Kolb, *Der Weg aus dem Krieg*, Munich, 1989, p. 307. Gall, vol. 1, pp. 373–4. Howard, pp. 433–9.
91 Clarke, pp. 110, 116.

my friends. We asked ourselves how this army could have kept us so busy, for they were utterly untrained, could not march or shoot, and were not equal to the physical and mental shocks of war."[92] This perceptive Prussian private had been a university student before the war, and against impossibly clever invaders like this, Chanzy led his demoralized remnants across the Sarthe toward Laval, where they were greeted by the unquenchably optimistic Gambetta. "What could... the invading armies do against 38 million resolute Frenchmen who had sworn to conquer or die," he bellowed out to general disbelief. For Chanzy's men – and the great mass of French citizens – the war was over, and everyone except Gambetta knew it.[93]

LAST GASP IN THE EAST

On the day that Chanzy's army dissolved, General Edwin von Manteuffel reached Châtillon to command a new German "Army of the South" formed by Moltke of the XIV, VII, and II Corps to find and destroy France's last field army: the 110,000 troops of Bourbaki's "Army of the East." Arriving from the quiet of Rouen, Mantueffel was thrust immediately into a fast-moving situation. The failure of Ducrot's breakouts in Paris and Chanzy's retreat from the Loire in late December had persuaded Gambetta and Freycinet to change Bourbaki's mission fundamentally. With no hope of rejoining Chanzy or reaching Paris, Bourbaki would instead annihilate the big German garrison at Dijon, relieve the fortress of Belfort, and then proceed to cut every road, bridge, and railway feeding and supplying the German armies in France. If the French could not actually defeat the Prussian armies in battle, they would make their lives so miserable that they might just pack up, offer reasonable terms, and leave.

For this latest strategy to work, everything turned on Bourbaki's energy and resourcefulness. Unfortunately, the general disappointed, losing far more time than was necessary in concentrating his three widespread corps at Dijon before advancing gingerly into battle in early January. With the roads blocked by snow or iced with *verglas*, Bourbaki relied more than usual on his railroad to Chalon-sur-Saône, but the rail service, deserted by its civilian personnel, proved dismally slow, deploying men and material in a trickle that served only to warn the Germans of the new plan and give them time to rush in reinforcements from Lorraine, Alsace, and Baden.[94] For weeks Freycinet had been urging Gambetta to fire Bourbaki – "it is this making of a fetish of our old military glories that has ruined us!" – but Gambetta saw no one better qualified in an officer corps that had already been thoroughly combed out,

92 SHAT, Le 19, Paris, 25 June 1871, Col. Charles d'Arguelle. Leo, pp. 64–5.
93 Howard, p. 403.
94 SHAT, Ld 20, Lyon, 4 March 1871, Gen. Bourbaki to Gambetta.

and consented only to the addition of a "ministerial aide" to Bourbaki's staff, a useless half-measure.[95]

In the week needed to shift the Prussian VII and II Corps from Lorraine to Burgundy, the 40,000 men of General August von Werder's largely Badenese XIV Corps were the German "Army of the South." Having driven Werder from Dijon without battle in late December, General Bourbaki pursued him to Vesoul on 5 January with 110,000 troops. With hordes of French troops closing from the west, Werder, heavily encumbered with industrial machinery and rolling stock stolen from Dijon and Bourges, braced for the worst.[96] Yet no attack came. Famished in a winter landscape, the French spent most of early January scrounging for food. What few supplies Bordeaux succeeded in delivering were gobbled up in a single day. Because the pay of the troops was in arrears and the government delegation had instituted no Prussian-style system to pay mayors and peasants for quarters and food, the entire French army was reduced to begging at doors and gates, which were invariably barred. Most of Bourbaki's horses perished in January; never fed, combed or shod, the horses shriveled up or collapsed by the side of the road, where hungry *troupiers* butchered them with their knives. Marches were ludicrously slow because of the large proportion of unfit *mobiles*, who needed frequent rests. At every halt, French officers, from the generals down to the lieutenants, would hurry off to find the warmest quarters, leaving their units in the hands of the NCOs and enlisted men, a practice that the troops answered with "profound loathing and defiance."[97]

Besides some skirmishing along Werder's narrow front, Bourbaki refused to close with the isolated German corps, informing Gambetta that he would conserve his troops by "maneuvering" Werder out of France. He proposed the same improbable solution for Belfort, which was under siege by just eleven German reserve battalions. Although Bourbaki's caution had more to do with the chaos of his arrangements and the poor quality of his troops, he could not possibly have believed that the battle-hardened Germans would relinquish their east-west lifelines without a fight. Nevertheless, Bourbaki sat idly on the road between Vesoul and Belfort from 10–13 January. It was as if he *wanted* to give the Prussian VII and II Corps time to finish their deployment and find his exposed flanks and rear. Only then would Bourbaki be justified in ordering a retreat. Bourbaki made his last effort on 15 January, pushing all four of his corps up to the Lizaine, a stream west of Belfort, where Werder, now in contact with the besieging forces behind him, was girding for a last stand.

95 Howard, p. 413.
96 PRO, FO 64, Versailles, 1 Nov. 1870, Capt. Hozier.
97 SHAT, Ld 20, Lausanne, 22 Feb. 1871, Eduard Tallichet to Gambetta.

THE BATTLE OF HÉRICOURT, 15–17 JANUARY 1871

In freezing temperatures and cutting winds, the battle sputtered and flared for three entire days. Once again, the French guns fired an alarming number of dud shells, which, by now, the gunners assumed was sabotage.[98] The French fought across the frozen Lizaine on the 16th, made a breakthrough near Héricourt, and opened the road to Belfort, but Bourbaki refused to exploit the victory. Instead he fell back to guard his section of the Besançon to Belfort railway. "How would we feed the army without it," were his less than immortal words on the occasion. To a young officer's plea that he make one last stab at relieving Belfort on 17 January, Bourbaki – perceived as rather young and glamorous the previous summer – replied: "I'm twenty years too old. Generals should be your age."[99] Six thousand more French troops had been killed or wounded in the operation, for naught. An agent sent into the French camp by Gambetta to interview dozens of enlisted men and officers reported that Bourbaki's defeatism had knocked the wind out of an already winded army: "Héricourt made an evil impression; neither the men nor the officers could make sense of [Bourbaki's] incomprehensible hesitation." The troops also deplored the caution of their officers, who, in pointed contrast to their Prussian counterparts, "were slow to expose themselves to fire and were always hanging back behind their men." Self-doubt only exacerbated existing tensions within the Army of the East, "pitting the officers against the men, zouaves against the line, and everyone against the *mobiles.*" Many of the French officers admitted that they were Bonapartists, who, if they had not exactly impeded operations at Héricourt, had not exactly expedited them either.[100]

Meanwhile, Paris and its 2 million inhabitants shook under an intensifying Prussian bombardment. With twenty-four-pound siege guns installed at St. Denis and Aubervilliers, the Prussians could fire into the heart of the French capital and hit both banks of the Seine.[101] German shells and incendiaries now added to the misery of hunger. In January 1871 most Parisians were subsisting on a daily ration of nine ounces of "bread" – a concoction of flour, oatmeal, rice, peas, and beans – and whatever horsemeat or herring they could scrounge. The repulse of Trochu's last sortie and Chanzy's defeat at Le Mans had triggered riots in the third week of January. All of the working-class quarters like Belleville, La Villette, and Montmartre seethed with rumors and paranoia. It was easy to see why: Paris in the industrial age was a young

98 SHAT, Ld 20, Lausanne, 22 Feb. 1871, Eduard Tallichet to Gambetta.
99 Howard, p. 426.
100 SHAT, Ld 20, Lausanne, 22 Feb. 1871, Eduard Tallichet to Gambetta.
101 Gen. Julius Verdy du Vernois, *With the Royal Headquarters in 1870–71*, 2 vols., London, 1897, vol. 1, pp. 250–2.

man's city filled with transplanted peasants. Wifeless, childless, poor, un-
educated, and now, because of the war, unemployed, they loitered in cafés,
where they read or were read to from *Réveil* and *Combat*, the two papers most critical of Trochu and the republican war effort. With most factories and workshops closed for the duration of the war, workers passed
their time listening to orators, who enunciated the anarchist and communist
ideologies that united poor migrants from every corner of France in what
the British embassy called a "virulent hatred" of their employers and ruling
class.[102] Always a threat to the stability of the Second Empire, these men
would shortly become the revolutionary *Communards*. They tended to take
Gambetta's slogans literally – "the Republic is immortal" – and firmly believed that Trochu, Chanzy and Bourbaki were but tools in a vast right-wing
conspiracy: "the priests, prefects and [imperial] officers conspired with feline
skill to lose the war, for a lost war would incline the nation to a monarchy
again. Hence the reactionaries say *'mieux les Prussiens que la République'* –
'better the Prussians than the Republic.'"[103] This comment, uttered by one of
Gambetta's appointees, perfectly expressed the view of working-class Paris.
On 20 January, a Paris mob battered down the door of Mazas prison and
freed all of the "insurrectionists" – including Gustave Flourens – who had
been arrested after the *révolutionette* of 31 October. Although there were
nearly 500,000 troops in Paris, none lifted a finger against the rioters. Violent
revolution was at the door, crowds assembling daily to demand bread,
Trochu's removal, and *"la Commune."*[104]

Under explosive pressure like this, Jules Favre wisely came round to
Trochu's view that the war had to end, and quickly. French units in the front
line were deserting en masse, some officers crossing to the Germans and asking permission to bring their entire companies or battalions into captivity.[105]
Favre passed through the Prussian lines a last time to meet with Bismarck
at Versailles on 23 January. After three days of negotiations, they signed an
armistice ending the war late on the 26th. The three weeks' armistice would
take effect on 28 January 1871, when the forts and walls of Paris would surrender, delivering 2,000 cannon, 177,000 rifles, and mountains of ammunition
to the Prussians. The French would then have until 19 February to hold elections and seat a national assembly that would ratify or reject the armistice. In
the unlikely event that the peace-craving nation rejected the terms, the Prussians would resume the war from greatly improved positions against a largely
disarmed adversary.

102 PRO, FO 27, 1786, Paris, 20 Dec. 1869, Edw. Malet to Lord Lyons, "Report on the industrial
    and artisan classes of France."
103 SHAT, Le 19, Cher, 9 Dec. 1870, "L'Occupation de Vierzon."
104 NA, CIS, U.S. Serial Set, 1780, Paris, 25 Jan. 1871, Washburne to Fish.
105 SKA, ZS 158, Lt. Hinüber, "Tagebuch."

Word that Manteuffel's corps had pushed down the Saône and engaged Garibaldi's 25,000 troops at Dijon gave Bourbaki all the excuse he needed to begin his retreat away from Belfort, but, again, he was too late. After surging across the Langres plateau in the third week of January, Manteuffel had steered his two corps southwest of Bourbaki, to Dijon and Dole, where they turned to surround France's last army on 21 January. Sent east with his army in December to cut Moltke's vital communications, Bourbaki now found himself in the exact predicament prepared for the Germans. He was marooned in the barren Swiss border region without any sustaining railways or roads, trapped in the cul-de-sac formed by the Saône, Doubs, and Ognon rivers by 140,000 German troops. When Manteuffel's troops seized the Lyon railway a few days later, Bourbaki took the only route left to him, the road east to Pontarlier and neutral Switzerland.

Gambetta, still hopeful that Bourbaki and Garibaldi would combine and break out to the west to continue the struggle, was dumbstruck: "Are you truly marching to Pontarlier? Pontarlier near Switzerland? Is this not an error? I am stupefied! If the enemy attacks you, you will be forced into Switzerland to capitulate." Like MacMahon at Sedan, Bourbaki felt himself being crushed against a neutral, inviolable frontier. The moment French troops touched the Swiss border they would have to surrender their weapons to the Swiss and permit themselves to be interned for the duration of the war. Such a step would effectively end the conflict, hence Gambetta's frantic telegrams from Bordeaux: "Leave your impediments, take your best troops and march valiantly back toward Dole, Dijon and Auxonne. Only *there* will you be able to save France!"[106]

Of course Marshal MacMahon had chosen to fight on French ground at Sedan rather than cross into Belgium and be disarmed, but by now Bourbaki and his men had no such qualms. "You continue to believe that you have a well-constituted army here," Bourbaki cabled Gambetta on 24 January. "I have frequently advised you that the opposite is the case." Indeed France's Army of the East was a shambles and clung together only to wring supplies from the cold, desolate uplands. (Until the 1960s, the phrase *"l'armée de Bourbaki"* would survive as French slang for mass disorganization.) The men staggered shoeless and shivering through the Jura and simply refused to fight the Germans who nipped at their heels along the way. Their officers had no maps of the region and, as a veteran put it, "knew not where they were going or where they had come from."[107]

After ordering the retreat to Pontarlier on 26 January, Bourbaki – stung by the accusing dispatches from Gambetta and Freycinet – placed his service

106 SHAT, Ld 20, Lyon, 4 March 1871, Gen. Bourbaki to Gambetta. Howard, pp. 428–9.
107 SHAT, Ld 20, Lausanne, 22 Feb. 1871, Eduard Tallichet to Gambetta.

revolver against his right temple and pulled the trigger. The blast threw him backward, opened a nasty wound in his forehead, but did no other damage, the bullet rather miraculously flattening against his skull and plowing under the skin to the other side of his head, where a surgeon later extracted it.[108] It was a sad denouement for this son of Greek immigrants, who had clambered to the very summit of the French Second Empire. With Bourbaki confined to the garrison hospital in Besançon, General Justin Clinchant, a corps commandant, took over the army, but found little left to command. The army had dissolved long before the Germans trapped its columns in the mountains, where fighting flared all day on the 29th before word was carried to both sides that an armistice, signed in Versailles late on 26 January, had been in effect since the previous day. Peace descended for a moment, but then Manteuffel and, the next day, Clinchant, learned that, in an excess of optimism, Favre had exempted the departments of Doubs, Jura, and Côte d'Or from the armistice. Though Bourbaki had shot himself three days earlier, Favre still counted on a great French victory in the east that would roll back the German demands. Better informed of reality, Clinchant hurried to push his ragtag army into Switzerland. Better the Swiss than the Prussians was his judgment, and so 80,000 French troops – all that remained of France's Army of the East – filed across the border at Les Verrières and Les Hopitaux on 1 February 1871. The Franco-Prussian War was over.

108 SHAT, Ld 20, Lyon, 4 March 1871, Gen. Bourbaki to Gambetta.

12

The Peace

Two men had made the Franco-Prussian War, and now only one remained to conclude it. The other, released from his post-Sedan captivity in Kassel, made his doleful way to England in March 1871, to begin his exile with the empress and prince imperial at Camden Place, a twenty-room mansion in Chislehurst, Kent. French republicans watched this gathering of Bonapartes nervously, for recent history suggested that they were, in Emile Zola's words, "a strange family that never dies, which goes on, with its pale and moribund children... with their pockets empty one day, then safes full of money the next. They live in palaces, they die on rocks. They mint coins with our blood. And they are still there, at our throats, or at the bottom of some ditch, watching us and ready to jump on our shoulders."[1] And yet here was one Bonaparte who would not clamber back; Louis-Napoleon would die of anguish and kidney stones in 1873. *Lou-Lou* the prince imperial – a Woolwich graduate in the meantime – would follow his father to the grave six years later, killed by Zulus at the age of twenty-three while riding in South Africa with the Natal Horse and attempting to burnish his military credentials for the role of Napoleon IV. Undisputed master of France and Central Europe, Bismarck – "the genius of the actual," the European statesman most able to divine and interpret current trends – began to fumble in a most uncharacteristic and ultimately tragic way.

If one analyzes Bismarck's life and career, his entire success was owed to his energy and insight. Where others were blinded by sentiment, tradition, politics, or theory, Bismarck went to the heart of every question: what was its impact on Prussia? If political capital were expended, would there be a profit for the Hohenzollern kings? Whether in the Crimean War, the Austro-Prussian War, or the Luxembourg Crisis, Bismarck had always expended just

1   Cited in David Baguley, *Napoleon III and his regime*, Baton Rouge, 2001, pp. 282–3.

the effort required to strengthen Prussia – the weakest of the great powers – and position Berlin for its next test. Where moderation had been required – neutrality in the Crimea, mild terms for the Austrians in 1866, compromise with Napoleon III over Luxembourg – Bismarck had been unimpeachably moderate, even at the cost of violent scenes with his king and generals: "We do not live alone in Europe," he always reminded them, "but with three other powers who hate and envy us."[2] He was a born diplomat. He had no real friends and was never elected to any public office, but he inspired confidence like no other statesman. He spoke frankly, usually kept his word, and displayed remarkable concentration. In his *Personal Memoirs*, General Phil Sheridan recalled driving in a carriage to the front with Bismarck at Gravelotte. Although the two generals were passing through excited columns of troops and hearing the first explosions of the pivotal battle of the Franco-Prussian War, Bismarck spoke of nothing but his great affection for America and his concern that President Ulysses S. Grant recognize France, not Prussia, as the aggressor in the war.[3]

Yet for all of his tact and perspicacity, Prussia's swift victory in 1870–71 came as something of a shock to Bismarck, who had not anticipated the blundering of the experienced French marshals and the collapse of the French army. Having grown up in a society that scrimped and saved and looked admiringly at the riches and world power of France, Bismarck recognized that luck – in the form of a blundering Bazaine – had been with the Prussians in this war, but that it might not hold. He must have shared some of the skepticism of an English visitor to Königsberg in 1862 who had read Virgil's phrase over the main gate – *To rule the nations* – and laughed: "I remember reading those words and wondering at the time how a second-rate power could venture to entertain such ideas."[4] Thus perhaps, the need for a hard line in 1871: The French "have not forgiven us for Königgrätz and will not forgive us our victories now," Bismarck wrote after Sedan, "no matter how generous our peace terms."

Bismarck's terms would not be generous at all. All of Bismarck's insight, his "genius of the actual," seemed to desert him when he dealt with Favre and Gambetta. Lothar Gall attributes this to Bismarck's memory of a weak, small Prussia that as recently as the 1850s had been ignored or bullied by the other powers: "He was very far from projecting this present success [in 1870–71] into the future and assuming a permanent condition of power-political superiority on the part of Prussia-Germany."[5] Bismarck also had a fear of

2   Robert I. Giesberg, *The Treaty of Frankfort*, Philadelphia, 1966, p. 20.
3   Philip H. Sheridan, *Personal Memoirs of P. H. Sheridan*, 2 vols., New York, 1888, vol. 2, pp. 364–6.
4   H. Sutherland Edwards, *The Germans in France*, London, 1873, p. 40.
5   Lothar Gall, *Bismarck*, 2 vols., London, 1986, vol. 1, pp. 362–3.

republics, which he considered bound to clash with monarchies. In this, he was driven more by *Idealpolitik* than his more characteristic *Realpolitik*: That is, Bismarck should have been able to see that bourgeois republicans like Thiers, Favre and Freycinet were quite conservative when compared with their "red" adversaries. Indeed even as the peace process ground forward, they were busily repressing the really radical republicans in Paris. On the date that the treaty was officially signed in Frankfurt-am-Main – 10 May 1871 – they were moving troops up to the walls of Paris, preparing the military repression of the Paris Commune that would kill 30,000 *Communards* in the last week of May. But Bismarck never credited his French republican rivals with much strength or pragmatism. The German chancellor's post-war vision of France was cynical and negative: "The band of thieves will remain, even if their captain changes." Such loose talk was unworthy of a great statesman. Instead of cultivating Thiers as a like-minded conservative, Bismarck deliberately set out to humiliate him with an unpopular treaty. With no domestic support and no fellow republics in Europe, the French leadership would find itself alone, and quite powerless to wage a war of revenge.[6] The Prussian military joined eagerly in this Bismarckian sport: General Albrecht von Blumenthal, perhaps responding to demands by German Social Democrats for a peace based on the right of "national self-determination" in Alsace-Lorraine and elsewhere, burst out: "We have more to fear from this Republicanism than from France.... Under France's poisonous influence, our government would be gradually transformed into a republic."[7] So the Prussians demanded annexations and a crippling indemnity to keep the French republic down and give the Hohenzollern kings time establish themselves solidly in the non-Prussian half of Germany.

There were also domestic-political factors at work. "Let's put Germany in the saddle," Bismarck had announced in 1867. "It will know how to ride."[8] In fact, it did not. Though the Austro-Prussian War had effectively reduced the number of sovereign German states from thirty-nine to six, those that remained beyond the reach of Berlin – Baden, Hessia-Darmstadt, Württemberg, Bavaria and Saxony – were hard to integrate. Bismarck had deliberately fanned war fever in July 1870 to generate popular support for national unification. The Ems telegram had been a brilliant piece of theater that had converted a dynastic insult into a national one, and Bismarck (and his loyal newspaper editors) had billed the looming conflict as "a great national war" against "foreign aggression and presence" on sacred German soil. The German victories in

6   Allan Mitchell, *Bismarck and the French Nation 1848–1890*, New York, 1971, pp. 57, 77–9.
7   Field Marshal Albrecht von Blumenthal, *Journals of Field Marshal Count von Blumenthal for 1866 and 1870–71*, London, 1903, p. 278. Eberhard Kolb, *Der Weg aus dem Krieg*, Munich, 1989, pp. 172–3.
8   Gall, vol. 1, p. 368.

August and September 1870 created a patriotic stir in Germany, but did not remove the anxieties of still independent states that had reluctantly voted war credits in July 1870 and still hoped for a loose German Confederation with purely diplomatic rather than organic constitutional bonds. Indeed such was Bavaria's reluctance to commit to Prussia that Munich never formally declared war on France, which must have seemed odd to the thousands of Bavarians cut down at Froeschwiller, Sedan, Orléans, and Coulmiers.[9] Having constructed a war for "German unity and power," Bismarck had no time for talk of a "loose Confederation," and he, therefore, welcomed some prolongation of the war after Sedan to buy time for the negotiations in October and November 1870 needed to pull Saxony, Baden, Hessia, Bavaria, and Württemberg into a Prussian state.[10] The outcome of those parleys, carried on amid all the distractions of war and Bismarck's struggle with Moltke, was anything but satisfactory. *Einheit* – unity – was achieved at the expense of *Freiheit* – freedom. The German Empire became, in Karl Marx's words, "a military despotism cloaked in parliamentary forms with a feudal ingredient, influenced by the bourgeoisie, festooned with bureaucrats and guarded by police."[11] Indeed many historians would see Germany's "escape into war" in 1914 as a flight from all of the internal-political contradictions forged by Bismarck at Versailles in the fall of 1870.[12]

Culturally, Bismarck had forced the Catholic states very much against their will into a "federal union." The representatives of Bavaria and Württemberg had agreed to join Bismarck's *Deutsches Reich* only after a grueling month of negotiations in Versailles, where they had repeatedly been threatened. Prussia would either take them over, cut them loose economically, or subvert them with jingoistic appeals to the masses.[13] Politically, Bismarck had hedged his own personal power as Reich chancellor by placing obstacles in the path of democratic reform. The Reichstag itself – symbol of the united German state – was not nearly as democratic as it seemed; indeed Bismarck had conceived it in the 1860s as a means to mobilize tractable peasant voters and use their conservative votes to drown the reform program of the liberal middle-class at elections.[14] As this ploy unraveled in the industrializing, urbanizing *Gründerzeit* after 1870, it merely increased the instability in Berlin. When the massive new Reichstag chamber was finished in 1889, Kaiser Wilhelm II refused

9 Otto Pflanze, *Bismarck and the Development of Germany*, 3 vols., Princeton, 1990, vol. 1, pp. 490–1.
10 Frederick III, *The War Diary of the Emperor Frederick III 1870–71*, New York, 1927, pp. 166–7.
11 Cited in Hans-Ulrich Wehler, *The German Empire, 1871–1918*, orig. 1973, New York, 1991, p. 30.
12 Volker Berghahn, *Germany and the Approach of War in 1914*, 2nd edition, New York, 1993, pp. 19–23.
13 Pflanze, vol. 1, pp. 501–4.
14 Wehler, p. 53.

to place the words over the main door that had originally been planned: *"Dem deutsche Volk"* – "For the German people." The chamber was *his*, not theirs. It is easy to understand his pique; by 1912, anti-monarchical Social Democrats would be the biggest party in the Reichstag.

Bismarck had anticipated much of this, and to further weaken the power of parties and parliament, he had given the German *Kaiser* wide emergency powers, the exclusive right to initiate legislation, and had placed a conservative *Bundesrat* or "federal council," with a Prussian blocking minority, over the popularly elected Reichstag. The existence of the Bundesrat underlined the fact that sovereignty, in Bismarck's empire, was never held by the German people, but by the twenty-two princes and three free cities who had convened in the camp of the Prussian army at Versailles in January 1871. Bismarck had also made the German chancellor responsible not to parliament – whose resolutions were always nonbinding – but to the emperor, an insuperable conflict of interest. Barely satisfactory in 1871 – "the girl is ugly," one Prussian politician commented at the time, "but must be married somehow" – these constitutional arrangements would be generating enormous tension in Germany by 1914. Looking at all of the concessions and dodges needed to unify Germany in 1870–71, one of Bismarck's best biographers rightly concludes that the *Reichskanzler* had "melted together ingredients that could not form an alloy.... The creative element [was] actually the destructive one."[15]

Part of Bismarck's plan to end the Franco-Prussian War in 1871 required prompt French elections, to return the expected majority for *peace* that everyone in France but Gambetta fervently desired. Under Bismarck's protection, elections for a national assembly were held in French and German-occupied France on 8 February. To no one's surprise, anti-war conservatives running on platforms like "peace and liberty" distanced themselves from Gambetta's "war to the knife" rhetoric and took 500 of 676 seats in the new assembly. The delegates convened at Bordeaux on 12 February and chose Adolphe Thiers as president a week later. Leaving the same ministers who had run France since 4 September in place, Thiers went to Versailles and haggled with Bismarck for five bitter days before exhaustedly – he was seventy-four-years-old – signing the provisional peace treaty on 26 February. For Thiers, who had fought tyranny his entire life, penning diatribes against Charles X in the 1820s and suffering arrest and exile after Louis-Napoleon's *coup* in 1851, there was nothing quite like the tyranny of Bismarck. The chancellor never let up, and when Thiers refused to cede Belfort in addition to Strasbourg and Metz, Bismarck threatened a resumption of the war. After consulting with the king and Moltke, Bismarck relented on Belfort in exchange for a gloating victory parade through Paris in March by 30,000 German troops and additional Prussian annexations

15 Scott W. Murray, *Liberal Diplomacy and German Unification*, Westport, 2000, pp. 119–20. Gall, vol. 1, p. 377. Pflanze, vol. 1, p. 502.

in Lorraine: the blood-soaked villages between Mars-la-Tours and St. Privat with their vast German war cemeteries.[16]

Whenever Thiers dug in his heels at the negotiations in Versailles, Bismarck simply refused to speak or understand French until the Frenchman came round to the Prussian's way of thinking.[17] When Thiers, who had toured the European capitals in the fall to build an anti-Prussian coalition, threatened another appeal to Europe "if Prussia did not moderate its demands," Bismarck waved the bloody shirt of Bonapartism for the last time: "If you speak to me of Europe I shall speak to you of Napoleon.... Remember the plebiscite and the peasantry, the officers and the soldiers ... with just a little cleverness it could not be difficult for Louis-Napoleon to win over 100,000 soldiers among the prisoners in Germany." Uttering a faint "excuse me," Thiers desisted. Although Bismarck himself had been willing to forgo Belfort and Nancy (a late demand by General Roon), and even return Metz to the French – "I don't like so many Frenchmen in our house who don't want to be there" – he had been blocked by Wilhelm I and Moltke, who judged Metz and its frontier fortifications "the keys to the German house."

There was also the matter of public opinion. Dispatched into Germany to gauge the mood of Austria and the south German states in the fall of 1870, Jules Favre's deputy reported that "the whole of Germany had become drunk with the unheard-of, unhoped-for success of its arms.... I spoke with many individuals between the Rhine and the Danube, but I never met anyone who would have consented to a peace without territorial gains."[18] Heinrich von Treitschke's famous September 1870 essay – "What do we demand from France?" – evinced man-in-the-street sentiment in Germany: Alsace and Lorraine "are ours by the right of the sword.... At all times the subjection of a German race to France has been an unhealthy thing; today it is an offense against the reason of History – a vassalship of free men to half-educated barbarians."[19] With the German emperor, generals, politicians, and public thus aroused – "we must have guarantees!" – Bismarck probably never stood a chance of securing the sort of mild peace he had dictated to the Austrians in 1866: no annexations (the king had wanted Bohemia and Troppau) and an indemnity just one-sixtieth the size of this one. Cheated in 1866, Roon and Moltke bore down at Versailles and secured 5 billion francs ($15 billion today), Lorraine up to Metz and Thionville, all of Alsace, and a victory parade through the streets of Paris. Bismarck, who had led the "anti-Metz faction" at

16 Washington, DC, National Archives (NA), CIS, U.S. Serial Set 1780, Paris, 1 March 1871, Washburne to Fish. Giesberg, pp. 108–13. Alistair Horne, *The Fall of Paris*, London, 1965, pp. 309–14.
17 Frederick III, pp. 314–15. Kolb, *Der Weg aus dem Krieg*, pp. 360–2.
18 Frederic Reitlinger, *A Diplomat's Memoir of 1870*, London, 1915, pp. 81–2.
19 Murray, p. 122.

Versailles, quite uncharacteristically wilted under the pressure: "The soldiers will not hear of giving up Metz, and perhaps they are right."[20]

For a France bankrupted by war, the indemnity stung. Adolphe Thiers, who offered 1.5 billion francs, protested that the French government would be unable to raise 5 billion. Then Prussia will occupy France, Bismarck interrupted, "and we will see if *we* can get 5 billion from it."[21] Detached observers were alarmed by this departure from the tradition of reparations for war expenses alone, the *Economist* observing in March 1871 that "to exact huge sums of money as the consequence of victory suggests a belief that money may next time be the object as well as the actual reward of battle. A flavor of huckstering is introduced into the relations between States." Nevertheless, Bismarck insisted: "France being the richest country in Europe, nothing could keep her quiet but effectually to empty her pockets."[22] Overall, the German chancellor felt that he had been mild: "So moderate a victor as the Christian German does not exist in the world anymore." He had agreed to reduce the indemnity from six to five billion francs, and had not taken Belfort or Nancy.[23] Out of cards to play, the Bordeaux assembly ratified the Prussian terms overwhelmingly – 546 to 107, with twenty-three abstentions – and commenced its move back to Paris in early March. Léon Gambetta, who had campaigned against ratification – warning of the "German barbarian hordes" – resigned his seat and offices and left for Spain, where he read about the signature of the formal peace treaty at Frankfurt-am-Main on 10 May 1871.[24]

Diplomatically, the war sent shock waves through a world long accustomed to a balance of power in Europe. In Britain on 9 February, Benjamin Disraeli stood in the House of Commons and bitterly regretted that "this war represents the German Revolution, a greater political event than the French Revolution of the last century." Considering Bismarck's harsh treatment of the French negotiators, Disraeli observed that "there is not a diplomatic tradition which has not been swept away. You have a new world, new influences at work . . . . The balance of power has been entirely destroyed."[25] From Austria-Hungary, Foreign Minister Friedrich von Beust complained to Thiers that "I don't see *Europe* anymore." The familiar landscape of five balanced great powers and a dozen biddable "middle states" had been shredded by the Prussian victories in 1866 and 1870–71. The opposition between Berlin's

20 Moritz Busch, *Bismarck: Some secret pages of his history*, 2 vols., New York, 1898, vol. 1, pp. 417–18. A. J. P. Taylor, *Bismarck*, orig. 1955, New York, 1967, p. 133.
21 Giesberg, p. 110.
22 Sheridan, vol. 2, p. 409.
23 Fritz Stern, *Gold and Iron*, New York, 1977, pp. 153–4.
24 Kolb, *Der Weg aus dem Krieg*, p. 353.
25 Cited in John Lowe, *The Great Powers, Imperialism, and the German Problem 1865–1925*, London, 1994, p. 41.

anxiety – that France would rise again and a "revenge coalition" would unite against Germany – and the rest of Europe's conviction that Germany had become colossal and threatening would generate burning friction in the decades ahead, and be a principal cause of World War I.

Some took comfort from this instability. Accused by Napoleon III of "Machiavellian perfidy" before the war, Austrian Emperor Franz Joseph I revealed a glint of just that at a crown council after Gravelotte, when he wondered aloud whether it might not be a *good* thing for the Prussians to annex Alsace, Lorraine, and any other part of France they might like: "The occupation of those places would not exactly be peaceful and serene," he chuckled.[26] Was Prussia losing by winning? For the Austrians, of course, this was cold comfort at best, for Germany would drag them too into the abyss in the next war.

Militarily the war's lessons were clear organizationally and less so tactically. Armies that had begun to adopt Prussian methods after 1866 accelerated the process after 1870. Universal conscription was introduced to swell the ranks, enable Moltkean "pocket battles," and replace casualties that the Franco-Prussian War had generated in shocking quantities. General staffs were established or expanded. Professional military education, war games, and staff rides were introduced from Washington to Tokyo. Railways, telegraphs, medical arrangements, and logistics were given a very business-like emphasis in every war ministry.[27] Although the cumulative result of these changes would be *mutual* slaughter, far worse than that inflicted by the rather devil-may-care French on the rigorous Prussians in 1870–71, that probability was not allowed to obstruct the march of progress. Gung-ho soldiers just looked the other way. "There was a measure of infantilism in Europe's enthusiastic espousal of militarizing tendencies," wrote John Keegan, "but "clever men and responsible governments found wordy arguments to justify themselves."[28] Not so clever men too: In 1887, the Prussian war minister – General Walther Bronsart von Schellendorff – chose not to procure new artillery so that he could focus resources on morale, leadership and the infantry fight. Like many of his generation, Bronsart prized "*Schneid*" – "pluck" – over technology. "One can also have *too much* artillery," Bronsart rather illogically declared at a time when battlefields were expanding in size, and more and more batteries were needed to buttress one's own infantry, and catch the enemy's in what soldiers were calling a "fire sack."[29]

26 Kolb, *Der Weg aus dem Krieg*, pp. 182–3.
27 Wilhelm Deist, "Preconditions to waging war in Prussia-Germany, 1866–71," in Stig Förster and Jörg Nagler, eds. *On the Road to Total War*, Cambridge, 1997, pp. 316–18.
28 John Keegan, *A History of Warfare*, New York, 1993, p. 357.
29 Eric Dorn Brose, *The Kaiser's Army*, Oxford, 2001, pp. 62–3. Antulio J. Echevarria II, *After Clausewitz*, Lawrence, 2000, pp. 218–20.

As Bronsart's confusion demonstrates, the tactical lessons of 1870–71 were less clear than the organizational ones. The Prussian recipe in 1866 had been simple: They had waited for Austrian infantry attacks, cut them down with rapid fire, and then briskly counter-attacked in company columns led in by swarms of skirmishers. As the Prussians closed in, their company columns subdivided into platoons and pushed into the skirmish line to envelop the enemy. Whether attacking or defending, the Prussians had made optimal use of their breech-loading Dreyse rifle, which could be loaded and fired five times more rapidly than the muzzle-loading Austrian Lorenz. After Königgrätz, the French had rearmed with their own breech-loader, the Chassepot, and adopted defensive tactics aimed at shattering infantry attacks far downrange. In theory, the Prussians should have been stymied in 1870–71, but had won through despite the excellent French rifle and tactical discipline. How? With artillery: Cumbered with a rifle that was already obsolete in 1870, the Prussians relied almost entirely in the war on their breech-loading, steel-tubed Krupp guns, which hit farther, faster, and more accurately than France's bronze muzzle-loaders. Indeed the major battles of 1870–71 were decided by the Prussian artillery; the Prussian infantry attacks into the lines of Chassepots proved ineffective or even suicidal. General Julius Verdy du Vernois, a Prussian veteran of 1866 and 1870–71, said as much after Gravelotte: "The improvements in firearms and the greater explosive force of the powder of the present day make it certain that the effect of firearms will be correspondingly greater [in our future wars] than it is today, when it is already sufficient...to repel any attack."[30]

Despite the avoidable carnage in 1870–71 – Moltke's armies lost 117,000 killed and wounded in the war – most post-war analysis credited the Prussians with dash and movement. Colonel Charles Ardant du Picq, killed at Mars-la-Tour, etched this hypothesis in military professional circles in his posthumous *Battle Studies*. Based on Ardant's interviews with French troops and officers in 1868 and his brief experience of the Franco-Prussian War, *Battle Studies* praised the psychological benefits of the Prussian tactics. It was wrong to sit on the defensive and trust in a superiority of armament or material. Better to attack, or risk being swept away by an enemy's essentially psychological "determination to get to close quarters." In sum, the "moral action" of attacking troops would defeat the "destructive action" of defending ones. This was nonsense on stilts, but nonsense that was eagerly subscribed by most European armies *despite* actual experience during and after 1870–71. In his analysis of Gravelotte, General Ferdinand Foch – a leading apostle of the new French "offensive spirit" after 1871 – wrote that the Prussians had won because

30 Gen. Julius Verdy du Vernois, *With the Royal Headquarters in 1870–71*, 2 vols., London, 1897, vol. 1, p. 98.

of their "pure morale and unswerving doctrine," because of their "single-minded devotion to the capital idea: Hit, and hit hard."[31] Foch's certainty – which he maintained steadfastly until 1915 – makes an interesting contrast with King Wilhelm I's doubts, loudly expressed on the field at Gravelotte: "He complained bitterly that the officers of the higher grades seemed to have forgotten all that had been taught them so carefully at maneuvers, and had apparently all lost their heads."[32] No matter: To modern thrusters like Foch and Louis Grandmaison (and Kaiser Wilhelm II, who scaled back fortress plans in 1903 so as not to stand accused of "creeping into hiding"), the very circumstances surrounding Ardant's death near Mars-la-Tour seemed to confirm the colonel's theories.[33] Outgunned and outnumbered on 16 August 1870, the Germans had marched boldly into a storm of Chassepot and cannon fire and broken through. Ardant, condemned to play a waiting game, had been killed behind the lines by a shellburst. But that German breakthrough – and most others in the war – had far less to do with "psychological" factors (French *élan*, German *Schneid*) than with Bazaine's refusal to send any of his ample reserves (like Ardant du Picq's 10th Regiment) to the threatened point. With or without "moral action," it seemed increasingly hazardous to employ the tactics of 1866 and 1870 in an age of breech-loaders and repeaters, as a Russian general, engaged against the Turks in 1878, despondently noted:

> "We tried hard to imitate the German *Schwarm* tactics of 1870, but failed because the high-quality Turkish rifles made it impossible to attack like the Germans in France. Then, the Germans had crept into range, shielding their main units behind a long chain of skirmishers. That practice no longer works, for the Turkish rifles can hit out to 2,500 paces, cutting down as many of our reserve troops as skirmishers.... Inevitably, our reserve units begin to panic and push forward into the skirmish line, not because they feel safer there, but because they need to *do something*. The result is chaos and mass casualties."

Across Bulgaria, Russian attacks foundered on their own dead, piles of corpses so thick that the Russians could not go forward. "It was madness," the general concluded.[34] Yet were the Prussians not nearly as mad in 1870? Faced with a stringently defensive enemy determined not to repeat the errors of the Austrians in 1866, the Prussians had fought like Russians at Spicheren, Froeschwiller, Mars-la-Tour and Gravelotte. They had absorbed tremendous casualties attacking into fire, more than twice as many at Gravelotte as in the entire Austro-Prussian War. Only their Krupp guns and superior numbers had saved them. The cannon had blasted holes in the French lines and the

31 Gen. Ferdinand Foch, *De la Conduite de la Guerre*, 3rd ed., Paris, 1915, pp. 481–2.
32 Blumenthal, p. 98.
33 Brose, pp. 128–9.
34 Gen. Zeddeler, "Das Gefecht der russischen Infanterie im letzten Krieg," *Österreichische Militärische Zeitschrift* (ÖMZ) 3 (1878), p. 219.

numerous German reserves had replaced the heavy casualties and facilitated broad flanking maneuvers. Still, it was a bloody, inelegant way to win; German losses had been thirteen times higher than in 1866, and had the French generals only counter-attacked each time the Prussians stumbled, the war may well have ended differently. The Prussians might have been repulsed, Bismarck toppled, the French Second Empire "re-founded" for the teenaged prince imperial's long reign. No, the post-Sedan tendency to credit the Prussians with superior tactics was wrong. The Prussians had merely used their artillery to rescue their own faltering infantry attacks and smash the hesitating enemy or put him to flight. Had every European army heeded this essential lesson, millions of lives might have been spared the holocaust of 1914–18, when hordes of attacking infantry and dismounted cavalry were routinely ripped to pieces and reduced, as one observer put it, "to the task of offering targets to the artillery."[35]

Sleepy French villages had also offered targets to the Prussian artillery in the war, yet few Germans shed tears over this afterward. "Where the people's war breaks out," Julius von Hartmann explained in 1878, "terrorism becomes a principle of military necessity." For all of the study and analysis that the Germans expended on their wars of unification, they spent comparatively little effort on the problem of civilians, volunteer levies and what Hartmann – a leading military theorist – called terrorism. This did not bode well for the future. As the years passed, old German veterans simply forgot that the *francs-tireurs* had inflicted fewer than 1,000 casualties on German forces, and fought badly. Lapsing into old age, German analysts – led by Moltke, who passed his opinions down to his nephew – propounded the view that the *Franktireurkrieg* had been a waking nightmare of murder, mutilation and mayhem, and would have to be pitilessly dealt with in future wars. Most of the German army commanders in 1914 had served as junior officers in 1870–71, and they too were only too ready to deal harshly with any civilian interference in their plans. In 1914, as in 1870–71, French, Belgian and Russian civilians would put themselves beyond the protection of international law simply by aiding, abetting or even living in the vicinity of irregular troops. The Germans killed hundreds of innocent civilians in Belgium in 1914 – often in mass executions – and burned the cathedral city of Louvain in five days of panic and murder. One can perhaps sympathize with both sides; the innocent civilians caught in the jaws of war, but also the fearful German conscripts who, as a Prussian colonel put it in 1899, were "also men, with a right to be treated with humanity. Exhausted after a long march or battle, soldiers who come to rest in a village have a right to be sure that the peaceful inhabitants shall not change suddenly into furious enemies."[36] This argument is as old as war itself; unresolved by

35 Holger H. Herwig, *The First World War*, London, 1997, pp. 59–60.
36 John Horne and Alan Kramer, *German Atrocities, 1914*, New Haven, 2001, pp. 142–6.

the Franco-Prussian War, it was nevertheless brought into the modern age and focused. Monstrous atrocities meted out by Russian, Turkish, Austro-Hungarian, and German troops in the First World War would focus it still more sharply.

Conventional wisdom in 1871 purported that with his harsh indemnity and annexations, Bismarck had "crippled France for thirty to fifty years." The war alone had cost the French 12 billion francs ($36 billion today), to which had to be added Bismarck's 5 billion francs indemnity, the spoliation of fourteen French departments, and the costs of a wartime inflation that had quadrupled the French money supply while drawing down the metal reserves.[37] Yet France roared back, impelled in large part by its own modernization. The Third Republic, proclaimed three days after Sedan, spread banks, schools, roads, and railways into the provinces, reduced illiteracy, improved public health, spurred industry, inculcated a sense of being "French" (as opposed to Gascon or Breton), and reformed an army that, for all its pre-war grittiness and legends, had been an unhealthy, dim-witted institution. Substitution was abolished in January 1873 and universal conscription and a one to three-year military service requirement introduced in 1889. The effect was stimulating, flushing fresh-faced, educated youth into ranks formerly occupied by middle-aged, illiterate sots.

The French reforms also paved the way for the *Union sacrée* of 1914–18, when French of all classes and outlooks rallied behind national aims. This was new and, in Eugen Weber's view, occasioned in part by the Franco-Prussian War, which mobilized far more men (and women) than had fought in any French conflict since the Revolutionary Wars, making "the connection between local and national interests" and yanking France from its deep-rooted provincialism. Even the bloody repression of the Paris Commune had its benefits; reassured by the conservatism and ruthlessness of Thiers – "King Adolphe I" to the *Communards* – wary French peasants finally accepted that republican governments could "maintain order," and began voting for them, rooting republicanism in France. Like the figure of Marshal Bazaine, the *Communards* also provided a useful "stab-in-the-back" legend: France fell not because it was weak, but because it had been betrayed by a duplicitous marshal and by unpatriotic "reds," who "rebelled at the very moment the French nation was lying...defenseless at the feet of the victorious enemy." When Gambetta returned to French politics from his brief Spanish exile, he proved reassuringly moderate, joining with Thiers to condemn red republican agitation.[38] The younger generations were brought up by regiments of "black

---

37 Vienna, Haus-Hof-und Staatsarchiv (HHSA), IB 27, (1871), Vienna, 28 June 1871, Agent to Prince Metternich, "Ansichten über die Situation in Frankreich." Public Record Office (PRO), FO 64, 693, Berlin, 25 Oct. 1870.
38 Wolfgang Schivelbusch, *The Culture of Defeat*, orig. 2001, New York, 2003, pp. 134–8. Gordon Wright, *France in Modern Times*, 5th edition, New York, 1995, pp. 210–14. Mitchell, pp. 81–2.

hussars," the rigorously republican, black-robed schoolteachers sent into the provinces from Paris. Even the imperious Charles de Gaulle, born in 1890 to royalist parents, never considered himself anything but a republican. The shift of loyalties was jarring but complete, best characterized – in clear contrast to the German experience – by a French journalist in 1914: "This country lets itself be gently run by men who have no pretensions to provide it with an arrogant doctrine, a superior government.... It does not seek to borrow its prosperity from its institutions; it simply prospers."[39] There was also a new respect for the army in France. After 1871, French citizens decreasingly viewed their soldiers as "*voleurs*" (thieves) and "*pillards*" (pillagers) and increasingly accepted them as "our troops." Indeed village society came to value military service as a way to "*dégrossir*" or civilize their young men.[40]

Was collision inevitable between this reformed, newly confident French nation and the nervous German Empire? Were the seeds of World War I planted with Bismarck's decision to take Alsace-Lorraine? Had the Germans, as Tsar Alexander II declared in 1870, "created an inexpugnable hatred between the peoples?"[41] It certainly looked that way in 1871, when the Bordeaux Convention that ratified Thiers's controversial armistice rang with pugnacious, wounded rhetoric. One deputy called the treaty "a sentence of death," another expressed his shock that "universal manhood suffrage should give approval to the dismemberment of France." Victor Hugo concluded an impassioned speech with the vow that France would "exact a terrible revenge... and rise up to retake Lorraine, then Alsace, then.... Trier, Mainz, Cologne and Koblenz."[42] But tempers had cooled considerably by 1914 when most French had reconciled themselves to the loss of Alsace and Lorraine. "As for me," the celebrated French thinker Rémy de Gourmont wrote on the eve of World War I, "I wouldn't give the little finger of my right hand for those forgotten provinces. My hand needs it to rest on as I write. Nor would I give the little finger of my left hand. I need it to flick the ash from my cigarette."[43] French statesmen were hardly more aggressive: René Viviani, the notoriously provincial French premier in July 1914, was just sophisticated enough to know that he must not repeat Gramont's error of July 1870, namely "falling into the trap laid by Bismarck in the form of the 'Ems telegram'... declaring war on Prussia [and] thereby forfeiting international support."[44] In fact, it would take another round of German aggression – the Kaiser's "blank check" to Austria and the Younger Moltke's invasion of Belgium and France – to trigger the

39 Maurice Agulhon, *The French Republic 1879–1992*, orig. 1990, New York, 1995, pp. 113, 140–1.
40 Eugen Weber, *Peasants into Frenchmen*, Stanford, 1976, pp. 296–8.
41 Kolb, *Der Weg aus dem Krieg*, pp. 182–3.
42 Giesberg, pp. 119–20. Schivelbusch, pp. 146–7.
43 Schivelbusch, p. 183.
44 John F. V. Keiger, "France," in Keith Wilson, ed., *Decisions for War 1914*, New York, 1995, p. 124.

Great War with its 38 million dead, wounded and missing. We must look then at Germany to see the real scar left by 1870–71.

Riven internally, the new German Empire was not well-equipped to manage what would become sharp rivalries with a defeated France, a leery England, and an ever more confident and assertive Russia. Besides the suffocating power of Bismarck, who stifled new men and opinions, the war of 1870–71 had given a "fresh baptism of moral legitimacy" to a Prussian court and establishment that had seemed backward before the war.[45] By forging a German nation and realizing the idealistic hopes of 1848 – when German liberals had tried and failed to create a German nation-state – the Prussian king and *Junkers* had grafted themselves tightly on to the German state. The war thus empowered a whole class of militarists who linked Germany's health to war and expansion. Clear-headed Germans recognized this even in 1870 when one commentator deplored Wilhelm I's creation of a "warrior state . . . based on the permanent use of war" to achieve political objectives.[46] To his credit, Bismarck restrained the soldiers after the war, famously declaring the Reich a "satiated power" and constructing a complex alliance system that kept the peace for a time. Nevertheless, the constitution that he had devised for the North German Confederation in 1867 and for the German Empire in 1871 facilitated the triumph of militarists once Bismarck passed from the scene in 1890. Determined to buttress his own power and preserve ancient prerogatives of the Prussian king, Bismarck created a system that was likely to fail in the twentieth century, and *bound* to fail once the German crown passed to twenty-nine-year-old Kaiser Wilhelm II in 1888.

The most cherished prerogative of the Prussian monarchs was their ability to command and organize armed forces and wage war without parliamentary oversight. This prerogative was the one most strongly reinforced by the Franco-Prussian War, which slid the keystone into a national mythology of struggle and conquest, whose first plastic manifestation was the victory column or *Siegessäule* erected after the war in Berlin. Its murals depict the heroic come-from-behind victory of a German nation enslaved by Napoleon and freed by Bismarck, Moltke, Roon, and, most importantly, King Wilhelm I. One of the crowning panels, which depicts the king bravely enduring a French fusillade, encapsulated the German belief that strong armed forces wielded by a despotic monarch were a forgivable sin. The German liberals, who had unanimously deplored the illegal financing of the Prussian army by Bismarck, Roon, and Moltke in the 1860s, quickly forgave the "militarists" after Sedan; indeed they applauded Wilhelm I's promotion of Bismarck from Count to Prince and his gifts to the chancellor from the public purse: 1 million *taler* ($15 million today) and the vast estate of Friedrichsruh near Hamburg, which

45 Pflanze, vol. 1, p. 506.
46 Cited in Wehler, p. 30.

comprised 17,000 acres and the largest forests of uncut timber in Germany.[47] Against faint opposition like this, Kaiser Wilhelm II had far less difficulty than might otherwise have been expected driving Germany toward a catastrophic war in the years 1890–1914.

When Moltke – worried by growing French and Russian armies – began to echo Bismarck's caution about Germany's place in Europe, Wilhelm II brushed him aside and elevated his less cautious *sous-chef*, General Alfred von Waldersee. That man, who had posed as an artist to sketch Austria's Prague fortifications in 1866 and infiltrated the Parisian *boudoir* of General Barthélemy Lebrun's mistress to gather intelligence in 1869–70, spent the twilight of his career no less adventurously, trying to persuade the Kaiser to invade Russia preemptively and destroy it too as a threat.[48] Resentful of Britain's overseas empire and America's writ in the western hemisphere, Wilhelm II embarked on a battleship-building program in the 1890s that shattered Germany's finances and alienated Great Britain, an otherwise natural ally. In 1891, Wilhelm II replaced General Waldersee with an even more aggressive strategist, Field Marshal Alfred von Schlieffen, who has justly gone down in history as the embodiment of all that was wrong with German strategy and war planning. The Schlieffen Plan, a titanic Sedan or Königgrätz, aimed to envelop the entire French army without regard for the political and *larger* military consequences. Though Schlieffen died in 1905, his plan was implemented in 1914 with disastrous consequences. Germany's mad decision to bid for war in 1914 and throw away decades of economic expansion was but the culmination of a school of thought launched in the wars of 1866 and 1870–71. Its dangerously insouciant slogan would have been that of Friedrich von Bernhardi, who, recalling Sedan in his *Germany and the Next War* (1912), concluded that "the appropriate and conscious employment of war as a political means has always led to happy results."[49]

Who won the Franco-Prussian War? The answer to that question was never as obvious as it seemed. Just hours after Sedan – the greatest victory of the modern age – Vienna's *Neue Freie Presse* reminded Bismarck that "nations tend to slip on the blood that they have shed. Victory is a poor advisor."[50] And indeed it is strange and disorienting to alight these days at the Metz railway station – built of heavy turrets and rusticated stone in Wilhelm II's "German historicist" style – or to walk the battlefields from Froeschwiller to Gravelotte. One is struck by the number of triumphal monuments installed by the Germans in the years after the Treaty of Frankfurt to glorify the deaths of 28,000 young Germans in the struggle to reclaim *Elsass* and *Lothringen*.

47 Taylor, p. 134. Stern, pp. 280–2, 290.
48 Martin Kitchen, *The German Officer Corps 1890–1914*, Oxford, 1968, pp. 64–71.
49 Friedrich Bernhardi, *Germany and the Next War*, New York, 1912, pp. 42–3.
50 Schivelbusch, pp. 144–5.

Most of the monuments – great granite slabs and cenotaphs sprouting iron crosses or *Pickelhauben* – reflected the prevailing view that Germany had won a great, irreversible war of survival, and secured its place in the world, to say nothing of Alsace-Lorraine. Today those German monuments suffocate under haystacks, wheat, vines, and orchards. French farmers rattle past them in tractors or knock their farm tools impatiently against them before turning onto east-west roads that still bear reminders – *"Route de 3ème Armée"* – of Patton's bloody march across Lorraine to Germany in 1944.

In the fields around Mars-la-Tour, I looked for the farmhouse where Bismarck had sought his wounded son Herbert in August 1870. The circumstances of that visit – comprehensible only to a German perhaps – capture the essential tension and fatuity of the Prussian state better than any amount of academic analysis. Finding his injured son and every other man in the makeshift hospital hungry, Bismarck asked the Prussian surgeon why he did not make a meal of the turkeys and chickens scratching around in the farmyard. The surgeon replied that he could not slaughter the birds because they were not government property. With all of the paternal indignation that he could muster, Bismarck drew a revolver and threatened to slaughter the animals himself before finally drawing his wallet instead and agreeing to pay twenty francs for fifteen chickens, a sum that would presumably find its way to the owner of the farm. Had the story ended there, there may yet have been hope for the democratic evolution of Germany in the nineteenth century. But Bismarck, whom the king had made a major general in the euphoria after Königgrätz four years earlier, stopped himself and slid the wallet back into his pocket. "At last I remembered that I was a Prussian general, and I ordered [the surgeon] to do as I told him, whereupon he obeyed me."[51] Bismarck and Moltke were not clairvoyants, but did they ever imagine the reckless lengths to which other Prussian generals would run once blessed by the great victories at Gravelotte and Sedan?

51 Busch, p. 67.

Bibliography

UNPUBLISHED DOCUMENTS

Austria Haus-Hof-und Staatsarchiv (HHSA), Vienna. Consulted Politisches Archiv (PA) for France, Prussia, Italy, and the German states. Police archives – BM-Akten to 1867 and Informationsbüro (IB) from 1868–71. Kriegsarchiv (KA) Militärkanzlei seiner Majestät (MKSM) and Kriegsministerium-Präsidium (KM-Präs.)

France Service Historique de l'Armée de Terre (SHAT). Consulted all records of the Armée du Rhin, Armée de Châlons, Armées de Paris, Armées de la Loire, Armée de Vosges, and Armée de l'Est. Also Archives Centrales de la Marine (ACM.)

Germany Bayerisches Kriegsarchiv (BKA), Munich. Consulted Generalstab (GS), Handschriften-Sammlung (HS), B-Akten (field reports) and many unpublished manuscripts. Sächsisches Kriegsarchiv (SKA), Dresden. Consulted Zeitgeschichtliche Sammlung (ZS), Geheimes Kabinett, Sächsischer Militärbevollmächtiger in Berlin, various KA-Akten pertaining to military operations and reports.

Great Britain Public Record Office (PRO), London. Consulted Foreign Office (FO) records for France, Prussia, and the German states as well as Confidential Print "Respecting the War Between France and Germany."

United States National Archives (NA), Washington, DC. Consulted all Congressional Information Service (CIS) records pertaining to the Franco-Prussian War and Ambassador Elihu Washburne's reports from Paris and Tours.

SECONDARY SOURCES

Agulhon, Maurice. *The French Republic 1879–1992*. Orig. 1990; New York, 1995.

[Andlau, Col. Joseph d'], *Metz: Campagne et Négociations*. Paris, 1872.

Anon. *Deutschland um Neujahr 1870*. Berlin, 1870.

Arnold, Hugo. *Unter General von der Tann: Feldzugserinnerungen 1870–71*. Munich, 1896.

Ascoli, David. *A Day of Battle: Mars-la-Tour, 16 August 1870*. London, 1987.

Audoin-Rouzeau, Stéphane. *1870: La France dans la Guerre.* Paris, 1989.
Baguley, David. *Napoleon III and his regime.* Baton Rouge, 2001.
Bauer, Max. *Von der Maas-Armee.* Halle, 1871.
Bauriedel, Paul. *Meine Erlebnisse während des Feldzuges im Jahre 1870–71.* Nuremberg, 1895.
Bazaine, F. A. *L'Armée du Rhin depuis le 12 Août jusqu'au 29 Octobre 1870.* Paris, 1872.
Episodes de la Guerre de 1870 et le Blocus de Metz. Madrid, 1883.
Mémoire et Rapport sur les Opérations de l'Armée du Rhin et sur la Capitulation de Metz. Paris, 1873.
Becher, Oskar. *Kriegstagebuch eines Vierundneunzigers aus dem Kriege 1870–71.* Weimar, 1904.
Bell, Harry (ed.) *St. Privat: German Sources.* Fort Leavenworth, 1914.
Berendt, Richard. *Erinnerungen aus meiner Dienstzeit.* Leipzig, 1894.
Berghahn, Volker. *Germany and the Approach of War in 1914,* 2nd edition. New York, 1993.
Bernhardi, Friedrich. *Germany and the Next War.* New York, 1912.
Betz, C. *Aus den Erlebnissen und Erinnerungen eines alten Offiziers.* Karlsruhe, 1894.
Billroth, Theodor. *Chirurgische Briefe aus den Kriegs-Lazarethen in Weissenburg und Mannheim.* Berlin, 1872.
Bismarck, G. von. *Kriegserlebnisse 1866 und 1870–71.* Dessau, 1907.
Bismarck, Otto Prince von. *Bismarck: The man and the statesman,* 2 vols. London, 1898.
Blumenthal, Field Marshal Albrecht von. *Journals of Field Marshal Count von Blumenthal for 1866 and 1870–71.* London, 1903.
Bremen, Walter von (ed.) *Denkwürdigkeiten des preussischen Generals der Infanterie Eduard von Fransecky.* Leipzig, 1901.
Brogan, D. W. *The French Nation.* London, 1957.
Brose, Eric Dorn. *The Kaiser's Army.* Oxford, 2001.
Bucholz, Arden, *Moltke and the German Wars, 1864–1871.* New York, 2001.
Moltke, Schlieffen and Prussian War Planning. Providence, 1991.
Bury, J. P. T. and R. P. Tombs. *Thiers 1797–1877.* London, 1986.
Busch, Moritz. *Bismarck: Some secret pages of his history,* 2 vols. New York, 1898.
Clarke, David. *Military Memoirs: Roger de Mauni, the Franco-Prussian War.* London, 1970.
Corbin, Alain. *The Village of Cannibals.* Cambridge, MA, 1992.
Cox, Gary P. *The Halt in the Mud: French Strategic Planning from Waterloo to Sedan.* Boulder, 1994.
Crane, Edward A. (ed.) *The Memoirs of Dr. Thomas W. Evans: Recollections of the French Second Empire.* 2 vols. London, 1905.
Dorsch, Paul, ed. *Kriegszuge der Württemberger im 19. Jahrhundert.* Stuttgart, 1913.
Noch ein Schwabenbuch: Württembergs Söhne in Frankreich 1870–71. Stuttgart, 1911.
Ducrot, General. *La Journée de Sedan.* Orig. 1871; Lyon, 1989.
Eberstein, Alfred von. *Erlebtes aus den Kriegen 1864, 1866, 1870–71 und mit FM Helmut Graf Moltke.* Leipzig, 1899.

Echevarria, Antulio J. *After Clausewitz*, Lawrence, 2000.

Edwards, H. Sutherland. *The Germans in France: Notes on the method and conduct of the invasion*. London, 1873.

"Ex-Trooper." *The French Army from Within*. New York, 1914.

Fay, General. *Journal d'un Officier de l'Armée du Rhin*. Paris, 1889.

Förster, Stig and Jörg Nagler (eds.) *On the Road to Total War*. Cambridge, UK, 1997.

Foerster, Wolfgang. *Prinz Friedrich Karl von Preussen: Denkwürdigkeiten aus seinem Leben*, 2 vols. Stuttgart, 1910.

Fontane, Theodor. *Der Krieg gegen Frankreich, 1870–71*, 4 vols. Orig. 1873–76; Zurich, 1985.

Wanderungen durch die Mark Brandenburg, 4 vols. Orig. 1859–82. Berlin, 1998.

Forbes, Archibald. *My Experiences of the War between France and Germany*, 2 vols. Leipzig, 1871.

Frederick III. *The War Diary of the Emperor Frederick III 1870–71*. New York, 1927.

Freudenthal, Friedrich. *Von Stade bis Gravelotte: Erinnerungen eines Artilleristen*. Bremen, 1898.

Friedjung, Heinrich. *The Struggle for Supremacy in Germany 1859–1866*. Orig. 1897; London, 1935.

Fulbrook, Mary (ed.) *German History since 1800*. London, 1997.

Gall, Lothar. *Bismarck: The White Revolutionary*, 2 vols. London, 1986.

Giesberg, Robert I. *The Treaty of Frankfort*. Philadelphia, 1966.

Goerlitz, Walter. *History of the German General Staff, 1657–1945*. Orig. 1952; New York, 1995.

Gooch, Brison. *The New Bonapartist Generals of the Crimean War: Distrust and Decision Making in the Anglo-French Alliance*. The Hague, 1959.

Gouvernement de la Défense Nationale, *Procés-Verbaux des Séances du Conseil 1870–71*. Paris, 1905.

Groote, Wolfgang and Ursula Gersdorff (eds). *Entscheidung 1870: Der deutsch-französsische Krieg*. Stuttgart, 1970.

Herwig, Holger H. *The First World War*. London, 1997.

Hindenburg, General-Feldmarschall von. *Aus meinem Leben*. Leipzig, 1934.

Holmes, Richard. *The Road to Sedan: The French Army 1866–70*. London, 1984.

Horne, Alistair. *The Fall of Paris*. London, 1965.

Horne, John and Alan Kramer. *German Atrocities, 1914*. New Haven, 2001.

Howard, Michael. *The Franco-Prussian War: The German Invasion of France, 1870–71*. Orig. 1961; London, 1981.

Jarras, General Louis. *Souvenirs*. Paris, 1892.

Keegan, John. *A History of Warfare*. New York, 1993.

Kitchen, Martin. *The German Officer Corps 1890–1914*. Oxford, 1968.

A Military History of Germany: From the Eighteenth Century to the Present Day. Bloomington, 1975.

Koch, H. W. *A History of Prussia*. New York, 1978.

Kolb, Eberhard. *Europa vor dem Krieg von 1870*. Munich, 1987.

Der Weg aus dem Krieg: Bismarcks Politik im Krieg und die Friedensanbahnung 1870–71. Munich, 1989.

Kühlich, Frank. *Die deutschen Soldaten im Krieg von 1870–71: Eine Darstellung der Situation und der Erfahrungen der deutschen Soldaten im Deutsch-Französischen Krieg.* Frankfurt, 1995.

Le Goff, Jean Yves. *Le Général Adolphe Le Flô.* Lesneven, 1993.

Leo, Friedrich. *Kriegserinnerungen an 1870–71.* Berlin, 1914.

Lindner, Theodor. *Der Krieg gegen Frankreich und die Einigung Deutschlands.* Berlin, 1895.

Litzmann, Karl. *Ernstes und heiteres aus den Kriegsjahren 1870–71.* Berlin, 1911.

Lonlay, Dick de. (Hardoln, N.) *Français et Allemands: Histoire Anecdotique, Guerre de 1870–71,* 6 vols. Paris, 1888.

Lowe, John. *The Great Powers, Imperialism, and the German Problem 1865–1925.* London, 1994.

McMillan, James F. *Napoleon III.* London, 1991.

Massow, Anton von. *Erlebnisse und Eindrücke im Kriege 1870–71.* Berlin, 1912.

Matthias, Adolf. *Meine Kriegserinnerungen.* Munich, 1912.

Maurice, Major General Sir F. *The Franco-German War 1870–71.* Orig. 1899; London, 1914.

Mitchell, Allan. *Bismarck and the French Nation, 1848–1890.* New York, 1971.

Moltke, Helmuth von. *The Franco-German War of 1870–71.* New York, 1892.

Extracts from Moltke's Military Correspondence. Fort Leavenworth, 1911.

Moltke's Military Correspondence, 1870–71. Orig. 1923; London, 1991.

Montaudon, General Jean-Baptiste. *Souvenirs Militaires,* 2 vols. Paris, 1898–1900.

Mosse, W. E. *The European Powers and the German Question, 1848–71.* Cambridge, UK, 1958.

Murray, Scott W. *Liberal Diplomacy and German Unification.* Westport, 2000.

Ollivier, E. *L'Empire Libéral.* Paris, 1904.

The Franco-Prussian War and Its Hidden Causes. Boston, 1914.

Palat, Barthélemy Edmond. *Bibliographie générale de la guerre de 1870–1871.* Paris, 1896.

Papiers et Correspondance de la Famille Impériale: Pièces trouvées aux Tuileries. Paris, 1870.

Patry, Léonce. *The Reality of War.* London, 2001.

Pflanze, Otto, *Bismarck and the Development of Germany,* 3 vols. Princeton, 1990.

Plessis, A. *The Rise and Fall of the Second Empire 1852–71.* Orig. 1979; Cambridge, UK, 1985.

Price, Roger. *Napoleon III and the Second Empire.* London, 1997.

Priese, Johannes. *Als Totenkopfhusar 1870–71.* Berlin, 1936.

Rauch, Fedor von. *Briefe aus dem grossen Hauptquartier 1866 und 1870.* Berlin, 1911.

Reitlinger, Frederic. *A Diplomat's Memoir of 1870.* London, 1915.

Ris, Richard. *Kriegserlebnisse.* Auerbach, 1911.

Roth, François. *La Guerre de 1870.* Paris, 1990.

Ruby, Edmond and Jean Regnault, *Bazaine: Coupable ou victime?* Paris, 1960.

Schivelbusch, Wolfgang. *The Culture of Defeat.* Orig. 2001; New York, 2003.

Shand, Alexander Innes. *On the Trail of the War.* New York, 1871.

Sheehan, James J. *German History 1770–1866.* Oxford, 1989.

Sheridan, Philip H. *Personal Memoirs of P. H. Sheridan,* 2 vols. New York, 1888.

Showalter, Dennis E. *Railroads and Rifles*. Hamden, 1975.

Simpson, F. A. *Louis-Napoleon and the Recovery of France*. London, 1965.

Stern, Fritz. *Gold and Iron*. New York, 1977.

Strachan, Hew. *European Armies and the Conduct of War*. London, 1983.

Taylor, A. J. P. *Bismarck*. Orig. 1955; New York, 1967.

Trautmann, Frederic (ed.) *A Prussian Observes the American Civil War*. Columbia, 2001.

Trochu, Gl Louis Jules, *La Politique et le siége de Paris*. Paris, 1873.

L'Armee Francaise en 1867. Paris, 1870.

Truesdell, Martin. *Spectacular Politics*. New York, 1997.

Verdy du Vernois, General Julius von. *With the Royal Headquarters in 1870–71*. London, 1897.

Vizetelly, Ernest Alfred. *My Days of Adventure: The Fall of France 1870–71*. London, 1914.

The Court of the Tuileries, 1852–70.

Waldersee, Graf Alfred von. *Denkwürdigkeiten*, 3 vols. Berlin, 1922.

Washburne, Elihu Benjamin. *Recollections of a Minister to France 1869–77*, 2 vols. New York, 1887.

Wawro, Geoffrey. *The Austro-Prussian War*. Cambridge, UK, 1996.

Warfare and Society in Europe, 1792–1914. London, 2000.

Weber, Eugen. *Peasants into Frenchmen*. Stanford, 1976.

Wehler, Hans-Ulrich. *The German Empire, 1871–1918*. Orig. 1973; New York, 1991.

Wetzel, David. *A Duel of Giants*. Madison, 2001.

Williams, Roger L. *The French Revolution of 1870–71*. New York, 1969.

Napoleon III and the Stoeffel Affair. Wortland, 1993.

Wilson, Keith (ed.) *Decisions for War, 1914*. New York, 1995.

Winning, Leopold von. *Erinnerungen eines preussischen Leutnants aus den Kriegsjahren 1866 und 1870–71*. Heidelberg, 1911.

Wright, Gordon. *France in Modern Times*, 5th edition. New York, 1995.

Zeldin, Theodore. *Emile Ollivier*. Oxford, 1963.

Zins, Ronald. *Les Maréchaux del Napoléon III*. Lyon, 1996.

Index